good stats.

Substance Abuse

and Employee Rehabilitation

Substance Abuse

and Employee Rehabilitation

Robert Thompson, Jr.

The Bureau of National Affairs, Inc., Washington, D.C.

Library of Congress Cataloging-in-Publication Data

Thompson, Robert, Jr.
  Substance abuse and employee rehabilitation / Robert Thompson, Jr.
    p. cm.
  ISBN 0-87179-649-X
  1. Employee assistance programs—United States. 2. Substance
abuse—Treatment—United States. I. Title.
HF5549.5.E42T46 1990
658.3′82—dc20   90-2629
                                      CIP

Published by BNA Books, 1231 25th St., N.W.
Washington, D.C. 20037
Printed in the United States of America
International Standard Book Number 0-87179-649-X

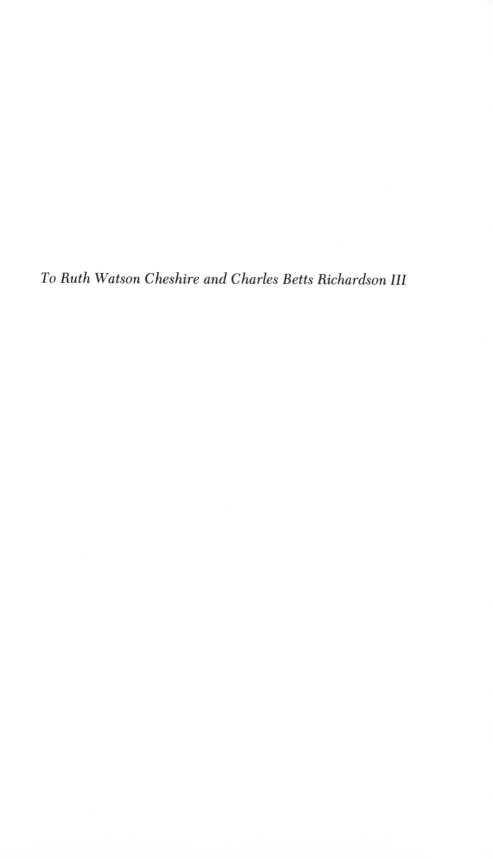

To Ruth Watson Cheshire and Charles Betts Richardson III

Acknowledgments

No book on this subject could or perhaps even should be written solo. This one certainly was not. Many special people participated in the research, compilation, and review of this material, but to several I am particularly grateful. Steve Giles and Dannie Fogleman were instrumental in assisting with the legal, referral, and EAP materials. Bill Steinhaus also assisted on these issues and became the best in-house editor anyone could hope to have. Kelli Smith and Rob Coggins were invaluable in their assistance at compiling and reproducing what seemed like millions of pages over the months it took to produce this work. Likewise, Ruth Peek and Joyce Keel were wonderful at finding recovery items that people said could not be found. Libba McKinney saved the day with assistance on the inpatient and outpatient materials and Jeannie Howard and Carol Saunders helped us finish it off. I am particularly grateful to Nuala Browne and Peter Browne for their incomparable support, thoughts, and vision that helped promote the ideas contained in this work all along. I am very much indebted to one person, for without that special person, Marsha Ferguson, who typed, proofed, read, and encouraged, this work never would have been finished. Finally, there are two groups to which I am particularly grateful. The first consists of Roger Milliken, Tom Malone, Bruce Corbett, Larry West, Tommy Hodge, Erskine Kirksey, Jack Burch, and Ken Carter of Milliken & Company. Without their determination and steadfastness in developing a substance abuse prevention process before such ideas became popular, I doubt I would have had the opportunity to immerse myself in this subject and develop with them many of the programs and processes discussed in this book. To them I am deeply appreciative. The second group is very special to me for completely different reasons. I will be eternally grateful to my family, Deidre Thompson and Bobby Thompson, whose tolerance and constant support through the evenings and weekends gave me the time, strength, and perseverance to accomplish what needed to be done. To my family and to all of these wonderful people, I thank you.

Robert Thompson, Jr.
July 1990

Introduction

The "war on drugs" in the streets, at the borders, and in the workplace has become one of the most talked about developments in recent times. Rarely can we open a newspaper or watch the evening news without seeing a story about substance abuse. Where substance abuse was once considered a problem only of the ghetto or the bowery, we now are recognizing its existence in all walks of life. In the business setting, workplace drug testing and rehabilitation programs are currently operating or under consideration in almost all large corporations and are increasing in small business operations. Substance abuse affects every conceivable job or occupation in our society and it is being seen from the warehouse to the production floor all the way to the boardroom. As former U.S. Secretary of Labor Ann D. McLaughlin stated recently, "Truly, substance abuse is an equal opportunity destroyer."

Around the country many business executives, government officials, and other employers are becoming increasingly alarmed by the growing problems of alcohol and drug abuse and generally want to do something to help stem the tide before substance abuse impairs significant portions of the working population. While a few commentators have suggested the ill-conceived idea of legalization of drugs, in contrast, more and more private and government employers are working increasingly toward a "Drug Free American Workplace." While many employers have determined that drug testing is a useful weapon in the war on drugs, it should not be considered an end in itself. Many employers are recognizing that drug testing is only one component of a comprehensive substance abuse prevention program. They realize that identifying the problem of substance abuse naturally leads to concerns of how to deal with the people who are substance abusers. Increasingly, there is a tendency to offer some form of rehabilitation as part of an overall substance abuse program. Regardless of the scope of an employer's substance abuse program, it should be thoughtfully considered and debated among the various departments and operations of the employer's business organization. The substance abuse program that is developed should be an individualistic program that fits the business organization and personality of the particular employer.

Many reasons exist to establish substance abuse programs. The most commonly stated are basic: safety, productivity, quality, cost savings, and health. Studies indicate that on any given day, approximately 25 percent of the average daily work force is impaired due to substance abuse or psychiatric problems. Further, the cost to business due to substance abuse has been approximated at over $100 billion a year. Many employers determine that substance abuse is a greater problem than originally was assumed only after an accident occurs where a worker is impaired because of substance abuse. Other employers find that workers' compensation premiums are skyrocketing because of accidents caused by substance abuse. Still other employers have found their employees making complaints regarding their safety when they work with others who are impaired because of substance abuse. Other evidence of substance abuse problems in the workplace include decreased productivity, problems of quality, and poor workmanship. Other businesses will find their goods rejected by customers because of problems in quality due to substance abusing workers. And, many employers will discover escalating costs that when investigated include low productivity due to substance abuse.

Studies now indicate that well-administered substance abuse programs offer tremendous cost savings to business in terms of increased safety, increased productivity and quality, decreased use of health insurance premiums, decreased turnover, and many other factors. Many employers have found that by establishing substance abuse programs, all employees benefit from reduced insurance costs. This occurs because the minority of the employees who are substance abusers and their families have been found to utilize the vast majority of health and insurance benefits. Thus when their usage decreases, other employees no longer have to subsidize those health care costs. Of the numerous reasons for establishing substance abuse programs, the bottom line seems to be that a good substance abuse program that includes a rehabilitation mechanism will significantly improve the health of employees and decrease costs of any business.

With both these goals in mind—the employees' health and the business costs—this book discusses the spectrum of substance abuse from addiction to recovery in the workplace. The underlying thesis of this book is that by establishing an effective policy, articulating definitive procedures, and by instituting an effective rehabilitation program, the vast majority of substance abusing employees in the workplace may be identified, rehabilitated, and returned to work to operate at a much higher level of productivity, quality, efficiency, safety, and health. Furthermore, this book is organized along the precepts of substance abuse programs in theory and in practice. The textual portion of the book conveys information on what is involved in establishing substance abuse policies, procedures, and rehabilitation programs. The detailed appendices of this book are working tools for any substance abuse or human resource professional or any attorney who needs to have original source materials available to develop comprehensive substance abuse programs.

The book presents the problems of substance abuse in the workplace and then discusses the dynamics of how these problems can be approached and solved. Part I discusses the significance of substance abuse and considers the legal issues involved in the substance abuse area. The impact of the problem of substance abuse in the workplace is discussed at length (Chapter 1), and the all-important legal framework and battleground of issues concerning substance abuse, including recent Supreme Court decisions, are discussed (Chapter 2). Part II discusses the guidelines for establishing substance abuse policies, procedures, and training. Establishing substance abuse policies is critically important for any substance abuse program and allows the employer to outline a philosophy on how substance abuse will be treated (Chapter 3). The importance of substance abuse procedures cannot be overstated, because, particularly from a legal standpoint, it will determine whether the overall substance abuse program will succeed or fail. In this context, drug testing is discussed from both a procedural and a legal standpoint (Chapter 4). The education and training of both managers and employees is crucial if the employer expects all of its employees to understand, live by, and support its substance abuse program (Chapter 5).

Once the problem has been introduced, the legal issues discussed, and the substance abuse policies and procedures developed, Part III reviews the guidelines for establishing comprehensive substance abuse programs. After a summary introduction (Chapter 6), the different types of substance abuse programs are discussed in detail including employee assistance programs (Chapter 7), rehabilitation referral programs (Chapter 8), inpatient rehabilitation programs (Chapter 9), outpatient rehabilitation programs (Chapter 10), and aftercare and long-term rehabilitation programs (Chapter 11). The employer connection for all of these substance abuse rehabilitation programs is usually the employee assistance program or EAP. EAPs may be one of the most constructive and useful developments in modern substance abuse history, particularly for combatting substance abuse in the workplace. Instead of simply firing employees who are found to be abusing alcohol or drugs, many employers have made the decision to encourage their employees to recognize the problem of substance abuse and attempt rehabilitation. An employee assistance program, whether it operates internally, or by using external EAP contractors, is an excellent method for detecting substance abuse at its early stages, directing rehabilitation of the employee, usually in conjunction with groups such as Alcoholics Anonymous or Narcotics Anonymous on a long-term basis, and returning that employee to a useful working relationship contingent upon his or her maintenance of a drug free condition. How that employee is rehabilitated, whether in an inpatient or outpatient setting, the latter being potentially more cost effective, will depend upon the employer's program and basic treatment philosophy, as well as the particular medical and psychiatric circumstances involving the individual. Furthermore, once the employee successfully completes rehabilitation and begins aftercare and long-term rehabilitation recovery, more employers begin to continue their interest in the entire process, and thus are involved with the employee from addiction to recovery.

The appendices of this book provide a reference guide on substance abuse and substance abuse rehabilitation and programs. The appendix is a working tool for practitioners in the field of substance abuse, whether they be human resource or substance abuse professionals, attorneys, or others in the private or public sector. Appendices D, E, and F give detailed examples of substance abuse policies, procedures, and programs that have been used by other employers in this area. Appendix C contains a suggested model policy, procedure, and program that can be adapted for the vast majority of employers. Appendix A contains a quick reference to the drugs of abuse and Appendix B presents a glossary of substance abuse terminology. Appendix G lists the schedules of controlled substances under the Federal Controlled Substances Act. Appendix H presents the most common materials from Alcoholics Anonymous to which substance abuse practitioners may be frequently referred. Finally, Appendix I gives the Code of Professional Conduct for Certified Employee Assistance Professionals that was developed by the Employee Assistance Certification Commission

(EACC) of the Employee Assistance Professionals Association, Inc. (EAPA, formerly ALMACA, Inc.) and the Code of Ethics developed by the Employee Assistance Society of North America (EASNA).

It is hoped that this book will prove useful in both theory and practice for readers and practitioners in the substance abuse field in terms of discussing the issues, developing substance abuse programs, and handling the various substance abuse related problems that appear on a daily basis. While a substance abuse prevention program cannot solve all of the employer's problems, significant cost savings and other more intangible benefits can be derived from such programs. The bottom line is simply this—a comprehensive program of substance abuse prevention (including both detection and rehabilitation) is the most effective means available to employers in solving the problems of workplace substance abuse and in working toward a drug free American workplace.

Contents

Part Two. Guidelines for Establishing Substance Abuse Policies, Procedures, and Training

Part One

Significance of Substance Abuse and Legal Framework

Chapter 1

Significance of Substance Abuse in the Workplace

The problem of substance abuse in the workplace is not new. Every form of civilized society has had some form of mind-altering substances. As a result, every form of civilized society has also had some form of substance abuse, which has *always* led to restrictions on the use of the substances. Restrictions have ranged from outright bans, to qualified prohibitions, to sanctions arising from religious rituals, to severe physical punishments and incarceration, to age limitations, to control by certain groups of professionals. And perhaps it is human nature that through the centuries people have been determined to violate these restrictions, even when they faced harsh consequences for doing so. For instance, in China, men who were found with coffee beans were tortured and killed, and men who drank too much alcohol had their tongues cut out. The ancient Aztec and Mayan priests would disappear for days while they worshiped their gods in rituals using psilocybin mushrooms or peyote, but if the tribesmen did the same, they were summarily executed. Today, in Saudi Arabia, alcohol and other mind-altering substances are banned, and violators, including visiting Americans, are punished severely. Currently, in Iran heroin and opium addicts are placed in labor camps instead of hospitals. In the United States, the prohibition era and our current drug control laws have not been able to legislate substance abuse out of existence. We must deal with it—particularly in our workplaces.

Today, in everyday America, substance abuse runs rampant throughout the workplace and costs employers big money. A few examples are instructive. In Chicago, a tool manufacturing company almost went bankrupt because its bookkeeper, who was regularly taking Quaaludes, lost checks, failed to allocate funds, and was not keeping up with inventory. In a Los Angeles chemical plant, an employee secretly shot heroin twice a day in the bathroom until he caused a sulfur explosion that badly burned him. He sued his employer and won $5,000 through Workers' Compensation. In 1983, the District of Columbia Police Department fired 35 recruits and suspended 10 veterans for using marijuana, cocaine, and PCP. In Silicon Valley, California, a high-tech company intentionally overproduces because it knows much of its output will be spoiled by employees who snort their lines of cocaine from a microscope slide. Some Silicon Valley companies don't let their executives make any decisions after lunch. In Georgia, an electronic equipment manufacturer found his sales force was providing cocaine to customers rather than taking them out for drinks. In Florida, a drunken employee drove a forklift backwards off the loading dock, killing himself. In Texas, a plant worker who was sent home early because he was drunk killed three motorists. The company has been sued for wrongful death for its failure to restrain the visibly intoxicated employee.

Statistics of Substance Abuse

A study of the statistics and facts concerning substance abuse in the workplace leads to some terrifying observations. Researchers have found the following information on substance abuse in the workplace:

- Between 10 percent and 23 percent of all U.S. workers use dangerous drugs *on the job.*[1]
- As many as one in five workers in the United States has a drug and alcohol problem.[2]
- 65 percent of young workers entering the work force have used illegal drugs.[3]
- Some 14.7 million adults and adolescents suffer from alcoholism or problem drinking, an estimated 7 percent of the adult population and 19 percent of young people between 14 and 17 years of age.[4]
- One out of three Americans 12 years of age or older has used marijuana, hallucinogens, cocaine, heroin, or psychotherapeutic drugs and one in five has done so within the past year.[5]
- In recent years, alcohol and drug abuse have cost the U.S. economy more than $100 billion annually.[6]

- A recent study shows that lost profits as a result of alcohol and drug abuse amount to $10 billion a year in the construction industry alone.[7]
- Alcoholism by itself causes about 500,000,000 lost workdays per year.[8]
- At least seven companies responding to a survey said they estimated the cost of substance abuse to them to be more than $50,000,000 a year each.[9]
- The majority of employers who responded to a recent survey said that between 6 percent and 16 percent of their employees have a drinking problem.[10]
- Lost productivity, absenteeism, and medical expenses related to drug and alcohol abuse cost employers an average of 3 percent of their total payroll.[11]
- A typical drug-abusing employee:
  - is late for work 3 times more often than nonabuser;
  - requests early dismissal or time off during work 2.2 times more often than nonabusing workers;
  - has 2.5 times as many absences of 8 days or more;
  - uses 3 times the normal level of sick benefits;
  - is 5 times more likely to file workers' compensation claims;
  - is involved in accidents 3.6 times more often than other employees.[12]
- A poll by the National Drug Abuse Treatment Referral and Information Service, which is run by Fair Oaks Hospital in New Jersey, showed that 75 percent of 227 drug users admitted to using illegal drugs on the job. The poll also found that:
  - 64 percent said that drugs hindered their job performance;
  - 18 percent admitted to a drug-related accident;
  - 25 percent said they had been fired for previous drug use; and
  - 38 percent said they feared a salary increase would increase their drug consumption.[13]
- A 1988 survey conducted as required by the Anti-Drug Abuse Act of 1986 found that 9 percent of the 950,000 employees tested by surveyed business establishments in the preceding year had tested positive for drugs classified under Schedules I or II of the Controlled Substances Act.[14]
- The same survey showed that of 3.9 million job applicants tested, 12 percent had positive results.[15]

- Industry by industry, the Bureau of Labor Statistics found the following rates of positive drug test results for current employees and applicants:[16]

Industry	Employees	Applicants
Mining	6.1	12.7
Construction	12.0	11.9
Durable goods manufacturing	12.2	11.2
Nondurable goods manufacturing	8.9	12.7
Transportation	5.6	9.9
Communications and public utilities	7.8	5.5
Wholesale trade	20.2	17.4
Retail trade	18.8	24.4
Services	3.1	9.9

Studies on the treatment and perception of alcohol and drug abuse in the country indicate the following:

- Only 15 percent of those suffering from alcoholism receive any formal treatment for their potentially fatal disease;
- There were more than 127,000 alcohol-related deaths annually, including more than 27,000 automobile fatalities in 1988;
- Up to half of all hospitalized patients suffer from alcohol-related illnesses, including cirrhosis of the liver, pancreatitis, esophageal cancer, peptic ulcers, and tuberculosis;
- Four out of five Americans see alcohol abuse as a major national health problem and one out of three admitted that drinking has caused trouble in the family;
- Any treatment of alcoholism is better than no treatment, according to research studies, and about two-thirds of all treated individuals improve or recover;
- Barriers to adequate treatment include myths about alcoholism and drug dependencies, lack of insurance coverage, and regulations that impede the development of treatment facilities.[17]
- Forty-three percent of a CEO group recently surveyed by Mercer-Meidinger-Hansen, Inc., estimated that substance abuse cost them 1 percent to 10 percent of payroll. 135 respondents estimated that the dollar costs range from $1 million to $200 million a year—amounts that exceeded some companies' after-tax profits.[18]

- Substance abuse among General Motors' 472,000 workers and their dependents cost the company $600 million in 1987 alone.[19]
- One 1985 survey of callers by the 800-COCAINE National Hot Line found the average caller to be 30 years old with more than 14 years of schooling. Of those surveyed, 33 percent earned over $25,000.[20]
- Other research has indicated that a serious cocaine user is typically:
  - Well educated (14 years of education)
  - Employed (77%)
  - Well-paid (37% earn over $25,000 annually)
  - Engaged in illegal activities to support the drug habit (56%)[21]
- The National Institute on Drug Abuse (NIDA) estimates that one in every five workers ages 18–25 and one in every eight workers ages 26–34 uses drugs on the job.[22]

Identifying the Problem—Drugs, Alcohol, and Addiction

In a recent publication, the National Institute on Drug Abuse made the following statement: "The human cost to society and the social, economic, and legal cost to business have created a new awareness of the multifaceted problems resulting from alcohol and drug abuse, and there is consensus among government and business that action must be taken to lessen these costs."[23] The enlightened approach that has been advocated by a number of experts is essentially to recognize the alcohol or drug problem; identify the individual's problem with substance abuse or addiction; and identify the treatment alternatives that are available.

Alcohol and Drugs

Although much of the controversy involved with substance abuse in the workplace deals with illicit drugs such as cocaine, marijuana, and PCP, the extent of alcohol abuse in the workplace far exceeds the abuse of all illegal drugs combined. The term substance abuse in this work will always refer to the abuse of alcohol as well as the other drugs in the workplace because alcohol is also a drug. The illegal drugs including cocaine, marijuana, heroin, mescaline, LSD, peyote, PCP, amphetamines, barbiturates, codeine, and benzodiazepines (Valium, Xanax, etc.) are itemized and explained in Appendix A, "Drugs of Abuse." Employers should have a working knowledge of these drugs, including the street names or slang terms, as well as the paraphernalia associated with each of these drugs. Appendix B, "Glossary of Substance Abuse Terminology," presents this information in detail.

Addiction

It has been estimated that of all the individuals who abuse alcohol or drugs, only about 10 percent will become alcoholics or drug addicts. Recent studies, however, indicate that this figure may actually be anywhere from 10 percent to 20 percent of substance abusers.[24] Regardless of the percentage, the impact on the workplace is not unnoticed. It is becoming increasingly important for employers to recognize addictive disease and understand its nature. The beneficiary of this recognition and understanding is not only the suffering, addicted employee but also the employer who will thereby become much more enlightened in dealing with the problem of substance abuse in the workplace and will consequently become more effective in eliminating the costs associated with it.

Numerous studies have indicated significant differences between individuals who abuse alcohol or drugs and those who become addicted.[25] A substance-abusing employee is one who chooses to abuse alcohol and drugs either in or outside the workplace and whose abuse may adversely affect job performance. This individual consciously desires to use alcohol or drugs. On the other hand, the addicted person, whether an alcoholic or a drug addict, uses the alcohol or the drugs on the job or off the job because he or she *has to*. One quick way of identifying an alcoholic or addicted person as opposed to an individual who simply abuses substances for recreation may be to use the Johns Hopkins 20 Questions Survey. The Johns Hopkins 20 Questions refer specifically to alcohol use but can be modified to apply to the use of other mind-altering substances as well:

	Question	Yes	No
1.	Do you lose time from work due to drinking?		
2.	Do you drink because you are shy with other people?		
3.	Do you drink to build up your self-confidence?		

4. Do you drink alone?
5. Is drinking affecting your reputation—or do you care?
6. Do you drink to escape from study or home worries?
7. Do you feel guilty after drinking?
8. Does it bother you if someone says that maybe you drink too much?
9. Do you have to take a drink when you go on a date?
10. Do you make-out better when you drink?
11. Do you get into financial troubles over buying liquor?
12. Do you feel a sense of power when you drink?
13. Have you lost friends since you started drinking?
14. Have you started hanging out with a crowd where stuff is easy to get?
15. Do your friends drink *less* than you do?
16. Do you drink until the bottle is done?
17. Have you ever had a complete loss of memory from drinking?
18. Have you ever been to a hospital or been busted due to drunk driving?
19. Do you turn off to any studies or lectures about drinking?
20. Do you *think* you have a problem with liquor?

Scoring the responses to these questions is as follows: One *Yes* to any of the questions means you may be an alcoholic. *Yes* to any two questions means that you *probably* are an alcoholic. If you answer *Yes* to *three or more*, you are definitely an alcoholic.

As is indicated by the focus of these questions, the nature of alcohol or drug addiction is such that it begins to take over the individual's life. As a result, alcoholics and addicts do not leave their alcohol or drug problems at the door when they walk into work. The National Council on Alcoholism and Drug Dependence has developed a chart about "How an Alcoholic Employee Behaves" through the various stages of progressive alcoholism. (See Exhibit 1.) The chart indicates that as an individual progresses through the early, middle, and late phases of his or her disease, detectable signs of steadily deteriorating attendance, behavior, and job performance begin to appear. Although this chart indicates the progressive nature of addictive

Exhibit 1   How an Alcoholic Employee Behaves

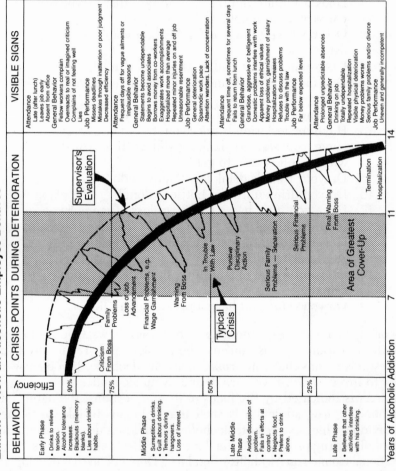

Source: Reprinted with permission from National Council on Alcoholism and Drug Dependence.

disease, it must be understood that not every individual who suffers from alcoholism or drug addiction goes through the entire progression from early substance abuse to termination or death. Exhibit 2 presents the recovery side of alcoholism, indicating that death is not the inevitable end of addiction, but that rehabilitation and recovery from addiction are possible.

Although an addicted person may be constitutionally different from a casual substance user, no form of substance abuse should be tolerated in the workplace. Helping employers to understand the patterns of substance abuse and how to handle the problem is one of the basic purposes of this work. This book will attempt to present the reader with methods for the identification and rehabilitation of substance abusers through the proper functioning of an employer substance abuse program and the various rehabilitation treatments that are available.

Substance Abuse Programs

Since the significance of substance abuse throughout the country has been recognized only recently, the response of employers, and thus the programs for dealing with the substance abuse problem, are a relatively recent phenomenon. The key initiative for any employer is to recognize that the problem exists in every workplace, and then implement a substance abuse program that is appropriate for that particular workplace. Although initially the extent of the employer response may be directly related to the extent of the problem, eventually the employer must devise a program that is responsive to the needs of the employees and yet makes economic and practical sense for the employer. Later chapters in this book will discuss extensively the development of substance abuse policies, procedures, and programs. However, as a prelude, the employee assistance program must be mentioned.

One of the most creative innovations in the workplace in the last few decades is the employee assistance program or EAP. Such a program is a mechanism for identifying substance abuse problems and referring individuals to treatment ranging from initial counseling to comprehensive rehabilitation. As will be discussed, EAPs are one of the most adaptive mechanisms for dealing with any workplace substance abuse problem, regardless of the extent of abuse. Less costly but probably less effective alternatives to EAPs do exist and

Exhibit 2   Disease of Alcoholism

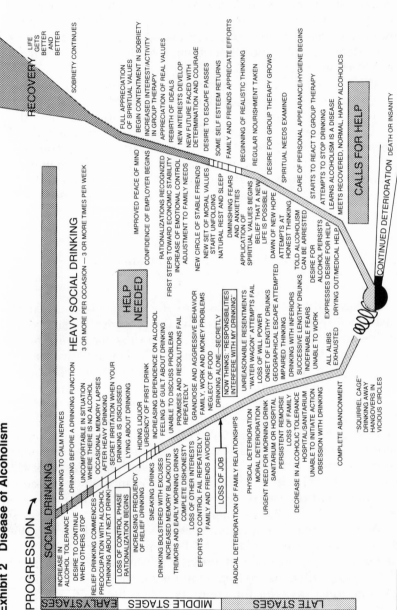

Source: Reprinted with permission from Southeast Council on Alcoholism & Drug Problems.

will be discussed. Employers can operate rehabilitation referral programs that focus solely on identification and referral of troubled employees. However, because of the increasingly significant negative impact that substance abuse is having in the workplace, an increasing number of employers are utilizing EAPs complemented by various rehabilitation programs that generally can be categorized as inpatient, outpatient, and aftercare rehabilitation programs.

Government Initiatives

Based on the fundamental assumptions that substance abuse in America in general and in the workplace in particular is at crisis proportions and that substance abuse in the workplace can be dealt with effectively, on September 15, 1986, President Reagan signed Executive Order 12564, establishing the goal of a drug free federal workplace. The order made it a condition of employment for all federal employees to refrain from using illegal drugs on or off duty.[26] In a letter to all executive branch employees dated October 4, 1986, the president reiterated his goal of ensuring a safe and drug free workplace for all federal workers.[27]

On July 11, 1987, Congress passed legislation that implemented the executive order under Section 5 of the Supplemental Appropriations Act of 1987[28] in an attempt to establish uniformity among federal agency drug testing plans, reliable and accurate drug testing, employee access to drug testing records, confidentiality of drug test results, and centralized oversight of the Federal Government's Drug Testing Program.[29] The executive order and the subsequent Federal Personnel Manual Letters[30] serve as guidelines for establishing employee assistance programs for dealing with substance abuse in the federal government.

Subsequently, there was an explosion of drug testing of employees, development of substance abuse programs, and a great deal of media coverage on the subject. Additionally, the Department of Health and Human Services published guidelines for drug testing facilities in the federal workplace.[31] Furthermore, in 1988, prior to the election, Congress passed the Drug Free Workplace Act, which is a portion of the Anti-Drug Abuse Act of 1988.[32] In the larger piece of legislation (the Anti-Drug Abuse Act of 1988), Congress established a cabinet-level position entitled Director of the Office of National Drug Control Policy, commonly known as the "drug czar," for the purpose of coordinating the nation's efforts at fighting drugs. The influence and effect of the drug czar's activities should be felt in the workplace as well as at the United States' geographic borders in the future.

Finally, President Bush in September 1989 submitted the administration's 1989 National Drug Control Strategy "for congressional consideration and action."[33] Concerning the workplace the President stated the following:

> The federal government has a responsibility to do all that it can to promote comprehensive drug-free workplace policies in the private sector and in state and local government. Employers will be encouraged to (1) develop and communicate to all employees a clear drug policy, setting out expectations of behavior, employee rights and responsibilities, and actions to be taken in response to an employee found to use illegal drugs; (2) establish an employee assistance program or other appropriate mechanism; (3) train supervisors in how to identify and deal with employees who are using drugs; (4) educate employees about the established plan; and (5) provide careful means to identify employees who use drugs, including drug testing where appropriate. The federal government will also move quickly to implement and strengthen regulations for the Drug-Free Workplace Act of 1988, which requires federal contractors and grantees to have drug-free workplace plans in effect.[34]

Pursuant to the president's executive order and other authorizing legislation or directives, various federal agencies have begun establishing regulations dealing with private employers that they regulate, or with which they contract. These regulations establish various requirements for drug testing, EAPs, education and training, and so forth.

In many cases these executive, regulatory, and legislative efforts to attack the substance abuse problem in the workplace have been challenged through the legal system. To date, however, the U.S. Supreme Court has denied every challenge to drug testing in substance abuse programs and in effect has cleared the way for the further implementation of carefully prescribed substance abuse programs. (See Chapter 2, "Legal Framework for Substance Abuse in the Workplace.")

Following suit, private enterprise also has been quick to respond to the problem of substance abuse in the workplace. The number of large and small companies throughout the country that have established drug testing and EAPs has skyrocketed in the last five years. Many employers who previously did not even realize they had a problem now are beginning to deal effectively with substance abuse identification and rehabilitation.

Conclusion

The economic and human cost of substance abuse in the workplace is staggering. With billions of dollars and millions of lives at stake, it makes good economic as well as humanitarian sense for both government and industry to develop practical, legal, and realistic substance abuse programs in order to deal with the problem in the workplace. The remainder of the materials in this book should help employers to achieve that end.

Notes

1. National Institute on Drug Abuse (NIDA), *Strategic Planning for Workplace Drug Abuse Programs* (Washington, D.C.: Department of Health & Human Services, 1987), 4.
2. Businesses for a Drug Free America/American Council for Drug Education (BDFA/ACDE), "Drug Abuse in the Workplace," 3 *National Report on Substance Abuse*, (Apr. 12, 1989), 2.
3. NIDA, *supra* note 1.
4. CompCare, *Facts About Alcohol and Drug Problems* (Newport Beach, Cal.: Comprehensive Care Corp., 1984), ii.
5. *Id.*
6. Harwood, et al., *Economic Costs to Society of Alcohol and Drug Abuse and Mental Illness: 1980.* (Research Triangle Park, N.C.: Research Triangle Inst., 1984), 3. (This report was prepared for the Alcohol, Drug Abuse and Mental Health Administration.)
7. BDFA/ACDE, *supra* note 2, at 2.
8. *Id.*
9. *Id.*
10. *Id.*
11. *Id.*
12. NIDA, *supra* note 1.
13. Payson & Rosen, "Substance Abuse: A Crisis in the Workplace," *Trial*, July 1987, 25–32, at 25, citing a poll conducted by the National Drug Abuse Treatment Referral and Information Service.
14. U.S. Department of Labor, Bureau of Labor Statistics, *Survey of Employer Anti-Drug Programs*, Report 760, January 1989, 9.
15. *Id.*
16. *Id.*
17. CompCare, *supra* note 4.
18. Mercer-Meidinger-Hansen, Inc., *Substance Abuse in the Workplace* (New York: Author, 1988).
19. Freudenheim, "Worker Substance Abuse Is Increasing, Survey Says," *N.Y. Times*, Dec. 12, 1988, 8, 42.
20. Mithers, "High on the Job," *Glamour*, Aug. 1986, 252.
21. U.S. Department of Labor, *What Works: Workplaces Without Drugs* (undated), 5.

22. *Id.*
23. National Institute on Drug Abuse, *Consensus Summary: Interdisciplinary Approaches to the Problem of Drug Abuse in the Workplace* (Washington, D.C.: Department of Health & Human Services, 1986) DHHS Pub. No. (ADM) 86-1477, 1.
24. Kamerow, et al., "Alcohol Abuse, Other Drug Abuse, and Mental Disorders in Medical Practice," *Journal of the American Medical Association*, Vol. 225, 1986, 2054-57, at 2054. Salner, "Cocaine Addiction Still Puzzles Experts," *Greenville, S.C. News*, July 6, 1989, 7A.
25. Vaillant, *The Natural History of Alcoholism: Causes, Patterns and Paths to Recovery* (Cambridge: Harvard Univ. Press, 1983).
26. Executive Order No. 12,564, Drug Free Federal Workplace, 51 Fed. Reg. 32,889 (1986).
27. National Drug Policy Board (NDPB), "Outline of Model Plan Prepared by Interagency Coordinating Group," Dec. 1, 1987, 1.
28. Pub. L. No. 100-71, 101 Stat. 391, 468–471, codified at 5 U.S.C. §7301 (1987).
29. NDPB, *supra* note 27.
30. Federal Personnel Manual (FPM) Letters 792-16 and 792-17.
31. 53 Fed. Reg. 11,970 (1988).
32. Pub. L. No. 100-690, 102 Stat. 4181 (Nov. 1988).
33. National Drug Control Strategy Report (Sept. 1989); see President Bush's accompanying letter.
34. *Id.* at 57.

Chapter 2

Legal Framework of Substance Abuse in the Workplace

There are many kinds of potential legal challenges an employer must consider when developing a substance abuse program designed to achieve a drug free workplace. The following discussion will identify the most common potential challenges and discuss ways for employers to avoid them. When implemented properly, a substance abuse prevention program will benefit employers and employees and allow both to deal better with drug and alcohol problems.

More important, when a properly designed program is fully implemented and utilized, the chances of a successful legal challenge are greatly decreased.

The discussion of the legal issues is divided into three sections. The first covers federal issues including the United States Constitution and federal laws such as Title VII of the Civil Rights Act of 1964, the federal Vocational Rehabilitation Act of 1973, the National Labor Relations Act, the Railway Labor Act, and the Drug Free Workplace Act, as well as federal regulations that impact substance abuse programs. The second examines general legal implications, including negligence law, contract law, and tort law, in addition to state common law and other statutory restrictions on an employer's right to screen individuals for the use of psychoactive substances. Finally, this chapter addresses the legal implications unique to employee assistance programs.

Federal Law

Constitutional Implications

Before beginning a review of the constitutional implications of an employer's substance abuse program, certain foundations must be established first. It must be understood from the outset that the

United States Constitution reaches only actions undertaken by the government, that is, public employers.[1] Private employers are subject to constitutional restrictions on workplace substance abuse programs only in certain highly regulated industries such as nuclear power, railroads, and horse racing,[2] or when acting in concert with a law enforcement agency. Therefore, the following review of constitutional rights involves principles that regulate the testing of employees in the public sector only. However, an understanding of the principles involved in the public sector will prove instructive to private employers so that they may understand the legal issues involved as well as the misconceptions of many people, particularly employees, in this area concerning what their constitutional rights are. Further, while the federal principles may not apply to private employers, an understanding of the limits on public employers often proves useful in formulating private employer substance abuse programs.

Right of Privacy

While most Americans have personal notions of the "right of privacy" concerning certain aspects of their lives that should not be subject to involuntary intrusion by others, the constitutional "right of privacy" encompasses far fewer personal activities than might be expected. Surprisingly, there is no specific constitutional provision guaranteeing a right to privacy. Instead, certain Supreme Court decisions have held that personal decisions on matters such as marriage, family, and childbearing are protected privacy rights.[3] Since the Constitution does not specifically mention the right to personal privacy, the Supreme Court found these personal rights as part of the "liberty" protected by the Fourteenth Amendment, defining this liberty as "a right of personal privacy, or a guarantee of certain areas or zones of privacy."[4] For the most part, employers need not be particularly concerned about legal aspects of the right to privacy. However, if the employer's substance abuse program offends the employee's notions of privacy, then the employer may have morale problems that may undermine the functioning of the substance abuse program or lead to legal challenges on other topics.

Search and Seizure

More often than not, claimed violations of the right of privacy lead to a discussion of the U.S. Constitution's Fourth Amendment ban on unreasonable searches and seizures.[5] As was previously mentioned, while this claim has been brought against both public and private employers, it has only been successfully raised against public employers.

Courts uniformly now appear to have determined that the taking of bodily fluids, particularly for the purpose of subjecting the fluid to drug screening, constitutes a search and seizure within the meaning of the Fourth Amendment.[6] Even though the taking of a bodily fluid for purposes of a drug screen may be a search as defined by the courts, it is not necessarily improper or impermissible. The Fourth Amendment's protections only ban *unreasonable* searches and seizures. Therefore, it must first be determined whether the public employer's actions were "unreasonable."

Typically, whether a search was reasonable hinges upon whether the public employer had either a showing of cause or, as is typically the case in public employer actions, a "reasonable suspicion" that the employee was using drugs.[7] While a search and seizure typically requires reasonable suspicion to avoid violating the Fourth Amendment, recent Supreme Court decisions support the argument that certain occupations are so important to public safety and national security that a warrant or individualized suspicion is not necessary to make testing reasonable under the Fourth Amendment.[8]

While many legal issues involving the detection, prevention, and treatment of substance abuse remain unresolved, two Supreme Court decisions have resolved several issues. In *Skinner v. Railway Labor Executives' Ass'n*,[9] the secretary of transportation had issued regulations requiring blood and urine tests of employees who were involved in train accidents. Other regulations authorized breath and urine tests for employees who violate safety rules. Under these regulations, the railroads conducted the tests. The issue in *Skinner* was whether these practices violated the Fourth Amendment's prohibition on unreasonable searches and seizures.

The Court first decided that the tests involved sufficient government action to invoke the protections of the Fourth Amendment, which protects a person against government action but not against purely private action. These regulations, issued by the secretary of transportation, preempted "state laws, rules, or regulations covering the same subject matter."[10] They also superseded " 'any provision of a collective bargaining agreement, or arbitration award construing such an agreement.' "[11] The paramount purpose of these regulations was to promote public safety. The tests were mandatory, both on the part of the employee and the employer. Based upon the broad authority and extensive coverage of these regulations, the Court found the test to be government action.

The Court next determined that a urinalysis must be deemed a search within the meaning of the Fourth Amendment. But was the mandatory urinalysis in this case unreasonable? The Court found that railroad safety involves a special need for governmental action like the "supervision of probationers or regulated industries, or its operation of a government office, school, or prison."[12] The railroads are an industry already heavily regulated in the interests of safety. The Court found that the required testing, as a part of the safety program, was reasonable, even without a warrant.

The Court then decided that there need not be individualized suspicion before drug testing. The intrusion was limited in light of the extensive regulation already present in the railroad industry. The regulations were designed to minimize the intrusion into the private passing of urine. There was no requirement that the passing of urine be observed by an independent official; the sample was collected in a medical environment; it was collected by persons unaffiliated with the railroad; and therefore, it was no more intrusive than a physical examination.

The Court likened the railroad industry to the nuclear power industry and indicated that a similar analysis should be used for testing persons in that industry. Because of the difficulty of detecting signs of substance abuse, the Court found that testing without individualized suspicion is an important part of the prevention of drug abuse, and that the possibility of being tested without notice and without individualized suspicion enhanced the deterrent effect of the rule. The Court emphasized the fact that these tests were administered to employees in safety-sensitive positions where drug and alcohol abuse is especially hazardous to society.

A companion case to *Skinner* is *Treasury Employees v. Von Raab*,[13] wherein Treasury Department regulations required drug screening for three categories of employees: those involved in the interdiction of drugs and the enforcement of narcotics laws, those required to carry firearms, and those who handle classified material. Test results would not be turned over to any other government agency or prosecutors without the employee's written consent. The Supreme Court upheld the regulations that required drug testing of employees involved in drug interdiction and those who are required to carry firearms. The Court also approved testing of employees who handle sensitive information. However, because the regulations used the term classified, the Court needed to know who would be covered before it decided this question.

The Supreme Court's decisions are already having an impact on drug testing cases pending before the many federal courts. While these decisions do not settle the entire subject, they do provide guidance for both the courts and employers dealing with these issues.[14]

Random or unscheduled drug tests of public employees have been the most closely scrutinized of the drug testing procedures. Random testing procedures have been upheld in certain employment contexts, both public and private, where public safety is paramount or in specific highly regulated industries.[15] Courts that have upheld random testing in the public sector have done so after finding a diminished expectation of privacy because of the type of work involved, and after finding that the government's interests were either substantial or the action necessary because of the circumstances.[16]

Due Process

Another issue of constitutional importance involves the Fifth Amendment requirement that the government provide a person with due process before depriving him of "life, liberty or property."[17] This Amendment essentially mandates a fair decision-making process before an individual's basic rights are affected. Within the area of drug testing, the Fifth Amendment may also be implicated by claims that an employee's privilege against self-incrimination is violated by providing a sample for a drug screening procedure. However, the Supreme Court determined that a criminal defendant who was receiving treatment at a local hospital after an automobile accident did not have his privilege against self-incrimination violated after a blood sample was drawn at the direction of police. The Supreme Court determined that, although he was compelled to provide the sample, Fifth Amendment privileges were not violated because the blood sample was not testimonial in nature.[18] In a similar vein, the argument against self-incrimination has been unsuccessful in the drug testing arena as well.[19]

Some courts have determined that the Fifth Amendment's due process safeguards require an employer to have a fair decision-making process before an individual's basic rights are affected or before deprivation of property.[20] As with other constitutional areas, the due process requirements apply only to government action.

Accuracy and Reliability. Due process as applied to the area of drug testing requires that a drug screening test be done in an accurate and reliable fashion. Courts have held that the use of the enzyme multiplied immunoassay technique (EMIT), when confirmed by gas chromatography/mass spectrometry (GC/MS), has such a high degree of reliability that an employee's due process rights are not violated when they are used in an employment determination.[21] Where an employee's termination was based upon an unconfirmed drug screen such as an EMIT alone, some courts have determined that the decision was arbitrary and capricious and thus a violation of due process.[22]

Notice and Hearing. Since public employees have a property interest in their employment, courts have held that prior to terminating the employment relationship the public employer must protect the employee's procedural due process rights by providing the employee with notice and opportunity for a hearing. This notice, while preferably in writing, may be accomplished orally when the circumstances indicate the employee has been sufficiently apprised of the evidence against him prior to the hearing.[23]

Due process rights may also be implicated when the drug testing process provides no right to rebut test results or when employees are not given notice of the reason for disciplinary action. In the case of *Capua v. City of Plainfield,*[24] the district court stated that the city's testing program violated constitutionally protected liberty and property interests without due process of law, since the testing program lacked notice requirements or standards and since procedural and confidential safeguards were inadequate. The court also noted that the termination of employees who tested positive for drugs violated due process since the city refused to afford firefighters the full opportunity to evaluate and review their personal test or to have their own specimens confirmed or retested.

Laws and Regulations

There are several federal laws of which an employer must be aware when instituting a policy to combat substance abuse in the workplace. The federal laws addressed herein include: Title VII of the Civil Rights Act of 1964, the federal Vocational Rehabilitation Act of 1973, the National Labor Relations Act, the Railway Labor Act, the Drug Free Workplace Act, and regulations issued by the

Department of Transportation and those issued by the Department of Defense. Executive Order 12564 as well as Federal Personnel Manual Letters 792–16 and 792–17 also will be discussed.

Title VII of the Civil Rights Act of 1964

Title VII of the Civil Rights Act of 1964 generally provides that it is an unlawful employment practice for an employer to discriminate against any individual or to deprive any individual employment opportunities because of such individual's race, color, religion, sex, or national origin.[25] This prohibition applies to employers engaged in an industry affecting commerce who have 15 or more employees for each working day in each of 20 or more calendar weeks in the current or preceding calendar year. Liability under Title VII may be predicated on either a disparate impact theory or disparate treatment theory. As defined by the Supreme Court, the disparate impact theory involves employment practices that are facially neutral in their treatment of different groups, but that in fact fall more harshly on one group than another and cannot be justified by business necessity. Proof of an employer's discriminatory motive is not required under this theory. Under the disparate treatment theory, liability is premised upon the conduct of an employer in treating some people less favorably than others because of one of the factors listed above. In order to recover under this theory, the plaintiff is required to establish that the challenged employment decision was made based upon a discriminatory motive.[26]

With regard to the implementation or operation of a substance abuse policy, an employer is most likely to be presented with a claim that the policy has a disparate impact on a protected class as opposed to claims that the policy is being enforced so as to give rise to disparate treatment. This is because an employer may avoid disparate treatment liability simply by enforcing its policy in a uniform manner. For example, a black plaintiff may not prevail under the disparate treatment theory if the discipline imposed upon him for a violation of the policy is the same as that imposed upon a white employee for a similar violation.

As was previously mentioned, under the disparate impact theory, it is the consequences of an employment policy or practice rather than the employer's motivation that are of principal concern. Under this theory, the plaintiff has the initial burden of identifying the challenged practice and showing, normally through statistics, that it has a significant adverse impact. The burden of production then shifts to the employer to demonstrate a business justification for the challenged practice, which may consist of showing the job relatedness of the requirement. Once the employer satisfies its burden, the plaintiff then must prove that the challenged practice is not justified by business necessity, or must prove the existence of equally effective alternative practices that would accomplish the employer's goal with a reduced impact on the members of the protected group.[27]

In *New York City Transit Authority v. Beazer*,[28] the Supreme Court concluded that the Transit Authority's blanket exclusion from employment of job applicants and employees on methadone or those participating in methadone maintenance programs did not violate Title VII. The black plaintiff had sued alleging that the screening had an illegal disparate impact since it eliminated a disproportionate number of blacks and Hispanics. Even though the Court noted that for purposes of argument there was a disparate impact, nevertheless the blanket exclusion was justified due to the difficulty and cost of separating "employable" methadone users from "unemployable" ones, the task of monitoring continuously their progress in the rehabilitation program, and the problems of assuring they did not pose an obstacle to the safe operation of the transit system. The Court reasoned that the Transit Authority had successfully demonstrated the job relatedness of its narcotics rule, which was designed to promote legitimate goals of safety and efficiency.

In one of the few cases involving disparate treatment in the substance abuse arena, a federal district court in Florida held that a city-maintained policy that prohibited hiring applicants who had used marijuana at any time during the six-month period immediately preceding the application did not violate Title VII. The court found that the policy had been applied uniformly and also that there was no gross disparity in the racial composition of individuals in the position for which the applicants were applying so as to raise an inference of discrimination.[29]

This is not to say, however, that every objective criterion utilized by an employer to screen out applicants for employment on the basis of possible substance abuse would withstand scrutiny under Title VII. For instance, 17 states have adopted restrictions on employer use of information concerning employee arrests that did not result in conviction. In addition to being based on the reasoning that arrest without conviction is not valid evidence of the employee's commission of a crime, the statutes were enacted due to the fact that minorities are arrested with greater frequency than whites. Thus, an employer policy rejecting applicants on the basis of arrest records has been found to have a disparate impact on minorities in violation of Title VII. This reasoning has been articulated almost uniformly among the states that have such legislation.

In general, an employer's utilization of objective or subjective criteria as a basis for refusing to hire an applicant or discharging an employee will be upheld if the employer is able to show the job relatedness/business necessity of the policy, even if the policy has an adverse impact upon a protected class.

Vocational Rehabilitation Act of 1973

The Vocational Rehabilitation Act of 1973 (the Rehabilitation Act) is the primary federal law prohibiting federal contractors having contracts in excess of $2,500 and recipients of federal financial assistance from discriminating against individuals on the basis of their handicap. The Act defines the term "handicapped individual" as a person who has a physical or mental impairment which substantially limits one or more of such person's major life activities, has a record of such impairment, or is regarded as having such an impairment.[30] Moreover, the definition of physical or mental impairment expressly includes the diseases of drug addiction and alcoholism. The 1978 amendments to the Act explicitly recognize that the denial of employment opportunities on the basis of alcohol or drug abuse may be justified only under limited circumstances:

> [The term handicapped individual] does not include any individual who is an alcoholic or drug abuser whose current use of alcohol or drugs prevents such individual from performing the duties of the job in question or whose employment, by reason of such current alcohol or drug abuse, would constitute a direct threat to property or the safety of others.[31]

This interpretation has been accepted by several courts considering alcoholism or drug abuse a handicap.[32]

Generally, an employer has an obligation to accommodate an individual's handicap, including drug or alcohol dependence, unless the accommodation would impose an undue hardship on the operation of the employer's business. Reasonable accommodation varies with the circumstances, but accommodation that requires a substantial or fundamental alteration of the business is unreasonable.[33] Therefore, the United States Postal Service had no duty to accommodate an alcoholic who was discharged for an off-duty attempt to kill himself and his wife, even though the attempt was related to alcoholism.[34] Likewise, since the Rehabilitation Act requires only that an "otherwise qualified handicapped individual" not be discriminated against "solely by reason of his handicap," it was held that a discharged compliance officer employed by the mayor of Macon, Georgia, who was convicted three times for driving under the influence, was not a violation of the Act since his discharge was not due to his alcoholism but was instead due to his convictions which illustrated his inability to function effectively in his position.[35]

National Labor Relations Act

For employers of unionized employees, there are basically three different approaches that may be taken when implementing or operating a substance abuse policy: to bargain over a policy with the union, to advise the union of a policy but not bargain, or to implement a program unilaterally without any advance notice to the union. Which approach any specific employer chooses will depend, in large part, upon its particular relationship with the union and the language of their collective bargaining agreement.

A subset of this section of the National Labor Relations Act (NLRA) on implementation of a policy in a unionized setting deals with whether the employer and union should submit the dispute to arbitration and whether a refusal to do so by the employer is grounds for the union bringing suit under Section 301 of the Labor Management Relations Act for breach of the labor agreement's arbitration provision. This chapter will not attempt to cover this subset of the law in the unionized setting as it has been covered extensively in other publications.[36]

One key issue in the area of unions and drug policies centers around whether the institution of a testing program is a mandatory subject of bargaining. A mandatory subject of bargaining may be generally defined as those statutory topics such as wages, hours, and other terms and conditions of employment. The Supreme Court has long held that "the duty is limited to those subjects, and within that area neither party is legally obligated to yield. . . . As to other matters, however, each party is free to bargain or not to bargain, and to agree or not to agree."[37] Therefore, it is not a violation of the Act for the union to insist, to the point of deadlock, upon bargaining over a mandatory subject. Conversely, a party has no right to insist on bargaining on a nonmandatory or permissive subject. An employer may unilaterally put into effect a policy that is a permissive subject of bargaining without violating the Act, but may only change a mandatory subject after bargaining in good faith to impasse or deadlock.[38] Moreover, this topic must be divided into two categories: current employees and applicants.

Current Employees. The employer in *Lockheed Shipbuilding & Construction Co.*[39] initiated pulmonary function and audiometric tests for new employees. The employees had to pass the tests as a condition of employment. The union filed a charge alleging a violation of Section 8(a)(5) of the NLRA since the employer had failed to bargain with the union over the tests. The National Labor Relations Board (the Board) agreed, holding the unilateral implementation of the medical screening test, the results of which were used "for the purpose of terminating new employees or refusing to hire applicants for employment," did violate Section 8(a)(5).

On June 15, 1989, the Board decided two cases under the NLRA which involved the unilateral implementation of drug testing programs by employers. The unions in each case charged that the new drug testing program was a change in the terms and conditions of employment and was therefore a mandatory subject of bargaining, prior to implementation.

In *Johnson-Bateman Co.*,[40] the Board ruled that the implementation of a post-accident drug and alcohol testing program was a mandatory subject of bargaining. The employer had a drug and alcohol policy that prohibited employees from possessing or being under the influence of drugs or alcohol while working. The company also had a management-rights clause that allowed the company to discipline and discharge its employees, and to issue, enforce, and change company rules. Nevertheless, the Board ruled that implementation of a drug testing program was a change in the character and method of accident investigation, which affected job security. Therefore, the program was a term or condition of employment.

The Board relied on earlier cases that held that a new requirement of a physical examination and the implementation of polygraph testing were mandatory subjects of bargaining. The Board found drug testing to be similar. The Board found that there had been no prior discussion of drug testing during negotiations and therefore could not infer a "clear and unmistakable waiver" by the union. The Board also rejected the company's contention that the implementation of a drug testing program was an entrepreneurial decision. It did not "involve the commitment of investment capital" and it was not "taken with a view toward changing the scope and nature" of the business. For those reasons the implementation of the program was a mandatory subject of bargaining.

A possible argument for management attempting to have the *Johnson-Bateman* decision either overturned or not enforced is that the Board relied, in part, on the case of *Locomotive Engineers v. Burlington Northern Railroad*, [41] that was effectively overruled by the Supreme Court's decision in *Consolidated Rail Corp. (Conrail) v. Railway Labor Executives Ass'n.* [42] (See the discussion of the Railway Labor Act on the following pages.) Since *Conrail* and *Locomotive Engineers* were decided under the Railway Labor Act, which has different standards and conditions for mandatory bargaining than the NLRA, this argument may not carry the day for management seeking to implement a drug testing program, even though the Supreme Court has been sympathetic to testing employees for drug use. Regardless, these issues under the NLRA will certainly continue to be litigated in the coming years.

Applicants. In the other case decided by the Board, *Minneapolis Star Tribune*, [43] the Board ruled that the implementation of a drug testing program for applicants was *not* a mandatory subject of bargaining. The Board ruled that applicants are not employees within the meaning of the NLRA, nor are they members of the same bargaining unit with employees. The Board also found that the testing of applicants does not affect the terms and conditions of employment of the current employees.

On the other hand, the Board ruled that the union was entitled to information on the applicant drug testing for two reasons. First, the union serves as a check on employer discrimination in hiring and employment. The union was concerned that the testing was being used in a discriminatory manner. Second, the union has a duty, on its own, to eliminate discriminatory hiring practices for which it may be held responsible.

These two cases clarify for now the Board's position on an employer's unilateral implementation of a drug screening program. The decisions are not in keeping with the NLRB General Counsel's memorandum instructing the regional offices to handle charges alleging that an employer failed to bargain over drug testing as though drug testing was a mandatory subject of bargaining. [44] The General Counsel's memorandum specified that this duty covered applicant testing as well. Because of the Board decisions, the issue for now appears to be clearer, but litigation undoubtedly will continue.

Railway Labor Act

The Railway Labor Act[45] (RLA) controls labor disputes occurring in the transportation industry involving common carriers. Under the RLA, disputes are classified as major or minor disputes. Major disputes involve new rates of pay, rules, or working conditions. Parties may not resort to economic self-help, such as the union striking on the carrier unilaterally implementing a major program, in a major dispute until they exhaust the RLA's mediation procedures. The mediation procedures include negotiation, mediation, and possible presidential intervention with a Presidential Emergency Board. In contrast, minor disputes involve the interpretation of existing agreements. These must be resolved by arbitration, and a union may not strike over a minor dispute. The company may implement the changes during arbitration. Courts may decide whether the dispute is major or minor and, if it is a major dispute, issue an injunction to maintain the status quo during settlement proceedings.

The Supreme Court ruled in *Consolidated Rail Corp. (Conrail) v. Railway Labor Executives' Ass'n*[46] that "disputes concerning the addition of a drug-testing component to a routine physical examination are minor disputes." The Court held that this issue could be resolved by an interpretation of an existing agreement between the railroad and the unions, and the railroad's position was arguably justified by the agreement. The Court made no suggestion as to who should prevail at arbitration, only that the dispute was arbitrable.

The factual background supporting the Court's determination was that the railroad had been using drug testing as a part of its required physical examinations for many years. Testing occurred if the physician thought the employee may have been using drugs, or during a physical after an extended absence if the employee had a prior drug-related problem. Conrail argued that based on the past practice of using drug testing as part of its screening for fitness for duty it was entitled to continue the practice on an expanded scale. The union argued that the new policy was materially different because it allowed suspicionless testing and increased focus on the disciplinary effects of the drug testing.

The Court found the company's position—that it had discretion in the area of a drug policy—was not frivolous or insubstantial: "Conrail's interpretation of the range of its discretion as extending to drug testing is supported by the general breadth of its freedom of action in the past, and by its practice of including drug testing within routine medical examinations in some circumstances."[47] Because Conrail had discretion and the expanded scope of the testing was arguably within its discretion, the dispute was a minor dispute and required arbitration.

The Supreme Court in *Conrail* cited two circuit court cases agreeing with its holdings on similar facts.[48] On the other hand, the Ninth Circuit had previously ruled to the contrary.[49] That Ninth Circuit decision is, in effect, overruled by the Supreme Court's decision in *Conrail*.

One case finding the dispute over the implementation of a drug testing program to be a major dispute was *Teamsters v. Southwest Airlines*,[50] wherein the full Fifth Circuit reversed the panel decision. The court of appeals' decision was handed down one day after the Supreme Court's *Conrail* decision, and although it makes no reference to *Conrail*, it arrives at the same result. The court of appeals found the dispute over the drug policy to be a minor dispute.

Therefore, there is no longer a split in the circuits on this issue. If companies who are subject to the RLA have been using drug testing in the past or if they are arguably allowed to test for drugs by a management-rights clause in the collective bargaining agreement, any dispute over the implementation of a drug testing program is a minor one, which must be arbitrated and over which the union may not strike. The company may implement the program during arbitration. These rulings do not mean, however, that the company will prevail at arbitration.

Drug Free Workplace Act of 1988

The Drug Free Workplace Act of 1988, passed by Congress on October 21, 1988, as part of the larger legislation entitled the Anti-Drug Abuse Act of 1988,[51] requires most federal contractors and all federal grant recipients to implement a comprehensive substance abuse policy. Under the provisions of the Act, contractors and grantees must certify to the granting or contracting agency that it will provide a drug free workplace. To make this certification, the employer must fulfill the following requirements: (1) publish a policy statement notifying employees that the unlawful manufacture, distribution, dispensation, possession, or use of a controlled substance is prohibited in the workplace, and specifying what actions will be taken against employees for violation of such prohibitions; (2) establish a program to inform employees of—among other things—the dangers of drug abuse in the workplace and the availability of drug counseling, rehabilitation, and employee assistance programs; (3) provide all employees with a copy of the policy statement and notify the employees that, as a condition of continued employment, the employee must abide by this statement and notify the employer if he or she is convicted of a criminal drug offense occurring in the workplace within 5 days of the conviction; (4) notify the contracting officer of an employee conviction within 10 days of the contractor learning of the conviction, and within 30 days of receiving notice of the conviction, impose a sanction on the convicted employee, up to and including discharge, or require the employee to satisfactorily complete a drug rehabilitation program; and (5) make a good-faith effort to continue to maintain a drug free workplace. (See Appendix C, "Model Policy, Procedures, and Program" for a model policy that takes into account the provisions and requirements of the Drug Free Workplace Act.)

If the contractor is an individual, he or she must agree not to engage in the unlawful manufacture, distribution, dispensation, possession, or use of a controlled substance while performing the contract. The Drug Free Workplace Act, however, does not cover all employees of federal grantees or contractors; it covers only those employees "directly engaged" in the performance of work on the federal contract or grant. The Act does not, however, require certification by subcontractors. The Act also does not require a contractor or grantee to establish any kind of substance abuse or drug testing program. On the other hand, it does not prohibit drug testing programs.

Additionally, the Drug Free Workplace Act does not require an employer to adopt a comprehensive employee assistance program; it instead requires only that employers inform employees of "any available" counseling, rehabilitation, and EAP services. Provision of a list of community substance abuse treatment centers may satisfy the Act's requirements although the tendency of many employers is to implement or expand existing EAPs.

The Drug Free Workplace Act contains very detailed enforcement provisions. Under the Act, the government may suspend a grant or contract payment and/or terminate the grant or contract. The government may also suspend or debar (for a period not to exceed five years) the contractor if the head of the granting or contracting agency determines that: (1) the contractor or grant recipient has made a false drug free certification; (2) the contractor or grantee has violated the certification by failing to carry out the requirements of the Act; or (3) such a number of the grantee's or contractor's employees have been convicted of criminal drug statute violations occurring in the workplace as to "indicate that the contractor has failed to make a good faith effort to provide a drug-free workplace."[52]

If the contracting officer determines that cause for suspension or debarment exists, he or she will initiate an "appropriate action" in accordance with the Act, and other applicable agency procedures. The head of an agency may waive a termination, suspension of payment, or debarment with respect to a particular contract or grant if the agency head determines that such action would "severely disrupt" the operation of the agency to the detriment of the federal government or the general public.

Department of Transportation Regulations

On November 21, 1988, the Department of Transportation (DOT) issued a final rule as an amendment to regulations of the DOT and its operating divisions—the Federal Aviation Administration, the Coast Guard, the Federal Railroad Administration, the Federal Highway Administration, the Urban Mass Transportation Administration, and the Research and Special Programs Administration. In general, the rule provides that employers in various transportation industries must begin drug testing programs affecting approximately four million employees.[53] Each of the operating divisions issued amendments to their operating regulations. This discussion will focus upon the Federal Highway Administration's regulations, since it impacts upon the greatest number of employers and employees.

Federal Highway Administration (FHWA).[54] Effective December 21, 1988, motor carriers with 50 or more drivers were required to have a drug testing program in place by December 21, 1989. Motor carriers with fewer than 50 drivers are required to have a program in place by December 21, 1990.[55] The term "motor carrier" is defined by the FHWA, for purposes of the drug testing law, as a for-hire motor carrier or a private motor carrier of property. The regulations require testing drivers of "commercial motor vehicles" with a gross weight of 26,001 or more pounds.[56]

The FHWA regulations require that, at a minimum, a motor carrier's program include: (1) a drug testing program that prohibits a driver from using controlled substances; (2) a rule that no driver shall be on duty if the driver tests positive for use of a controlled substance; and (3) a policy that a driver who tests positive for the use of a controlled substance is medically unqualified to operate a commercial motor vehicle.[57]

There are currently five types of drug tests that are required by the regulations: pre-employment, reasonable cause, biennial examinations, post-accident, and random testing:

(1) *pre-employment*—all driver applicants are to be tested prior to hiring by the motor carrier;

(2) *reasonable cause*—behavior indicating reasonable cause must be observed by two supervisors, or one supervisor, if trained in the detection of drug use;

(3) *biennial physical examinations*—currently required physical examination program must be expanded to include detection of controlled substances;

(4) *post-accident*—where there is reasonable suspicion that the driver was using drug(s), the driver shall be tested within 32 hours of any reportable accident;[58]

(5) *random*—Although currently enjoined by the U.S. District Court for Northern California, this provision would require that the tests be reasonably spread through a 12-month period and the program test 50 percent of eligible drivers on an annualized rate.[59]

Moreover, motor carriers are required to institute an employee assistance program. At a minimum, the program must:

(1) educate drivers of the hazards of using controlled substances;

(2) educate supervisors on the hazards of controlled substances and the manifestations of use or abuse; and

(3) include at least 60 minutes of training on these subjects.[60]

As with the regulations of other DOT operating administrations, the FHWA regulations include the actual Procedures for Transportation Workplace Drug Testing Programs issued by DOT. These regulations set forth the mandatory collection and chain of custody procedures, the types of drugs to be tested for, as well as the quality control and laboratory certification requirements.[61] As a result of these regulations the five drugs that are tested for have become known as the "Federal Five," and include: marijuana, cocaine, opiates, amphetamines, and PCP.

Department of Defense Regulations

On September 28, 1988, the Department of Defense (DOD) published an interim rule containing the department's drug free work force policy, a drug free work force clause to be inserted in certain DOD solicitations and contracts, and a request for comments on the interim rule.[62] Effective October 31, 1988, the Department of Defense began including the drug free work force requirements in all acquisitions, solicitations, and contracts.

The interim rule specifies that the drug free work force clause must be included in all solicitations and contracts involving access to classified information or where the contracting officer determines that such clause is necessary in the interest of national security, health, or safety. The contractor must agree to institute and maintain a program for achieving the objectives of a drug free work force.

Although nowhere in the rule or contract clause is there any mention of random testing, the department, in February 1989, issued a series of questions and answers on the rule that specifies that DOD contractors will be required to add random drug testing to their personnel procedures, going so far as to say that "the requirements of the clause cannot be satisfied without some provision for random testing." In addition, a contractor "may," but need not, establish a drug testing program (1) when there is a reasonable suspicion that an employee uses illegal drugs; (2) when an employee has been involved in an accident or unsafe practice; (3) as part of or as a follow-up to counseling or rehabilitation for illegal drug use; or (4) as part of a voluntary employee drug testing program. The rule also states that a contractor "may" establish a drug testing program for job applicants.[63] Finally, the contractor must agree to include as part of the program an EAP that "emphasizes high level direction, education, counseling, rehabilitation, and coordination with available community resources; supervisory training to assist in identifying and addressing illegal drug use by contractor employees; provisions for self-referral as well as supervisory referrals to treatment with maximum respect for individual confidentiality consistent with safety and security issues." The program must also establish provisions for identifying drug users, including mandatory testing for positions that have an effect on public health, safety, and national security.

Finally, the DOD's questions and answers provide the following four guidelines: (1) the interim rule applies, in general, only to private contracts involving access to classified information; (2) the interim rule applies only to employees working on a covered contract; (3) the rule does not preempt contrary collective bargaining agreements or state and local laws; (4) the interim rule is not contrary to the Drug Free Workplace Act of 1988 and, therefore, a contractor may be required to satisfy the requirements of both.

Executive Order 12564[64]

In September 1986, President Reagan issued an executive order designed to make the federal government a drug free workplace, stating "[p]ersons who use illegal drugs are not suitable for Federal employment." The executive order required the head of each government agency to establish both a voluntary testing program and a mandatory program for determining the use of illegal substances by employees in sensitive positions. Sensitive position employees are defined to include employees granted access to classified information, individuals serving under presidential appointment, law enforcement officers, and other positions that the agency head determines involve law enforcement, national security, the protection of life and property, public health or safety, or other functions requiring a high degree of trust and confidence.[65]

Executive Order 12564 allowed testing of federal employees when: there is reasonable suspicion of an employee using drugs; there is an examination authorized by the agency regarding an accident or unsafe practice; or part of or as a follow-up to counseling or rehabilitation for illegal drug use through an EAP.[66]

Federal Personnel Manual (FPM) Letters 792–16 and 792–17

Two months after the issuance of Executive Order 12564, Federal Personnel Manual (FPM) Letter 792–16 was released by the Office of Personnel Management, with later revisions incorporated in FPM Letter 792–17. The FPM letter spelled out the requirements for random testing of employees in sensitive positions. After incorporating the definition of sensitive as set forth in Executive Order 12564, the FPM letter mandates that each agency head designate the employees to be tested based upon "the nature of the agency's mission, its employees' duties, the efficient use of agency resources, and the danger that could result from the failure of an employee to discharge his or her duties adequately."[67]

Additionally, the letter specifies that reasonable suspicion testing can take place when there is "an articulable belief that an employee uses drugs from specific and particularized facts and reasonable inferences from those facts."[68] The reasonable suspicion may be based upon the following circumstances:

(a) observable phenomena, such as direct observation of drug use and/or the physical symptoms of being under the influence of a drug;
(b) a pattern of abnormal conduct or erratic behavior;
(c) arrest or conviction for a drug related offense; or the identification of an employee as the focus of a criminal investigation into illegal drug possession, use, or trafficking;
(d) information provided either by reliable and credible sources or independently corroborated;
(e) newly discovered evidence that the employee has tampered with a previous drug test.[69]

The FPM Letters 792-16 and 792-17 and Executive Order 12564 have been the basis of a majority of the federal drug testing cases.[70]

State Law and General Legal Implications

State Constitutional and Statutory Implications

In contrast to the United States Constitution discussed earlier in this chapter, many states have constitutional provisions that protect individuals and prevent infringement by both the state and other individuals, including employers. The constitutions of at least eight states have specific provisions protecting rights of privacy: Alaska, Arizona, California, Florida, Hawaii, Illinois, Louisiana, and Montana. In addition, several states have enacted laws regulating the disclosure of medical information.

State "Rights of Privacy" Provisions

Alaska. "Right of Privacy. The right of the people to privacy is recognized and shall not be infringed. The legislature shall implement this section."[71]

Arizona. "Right to Privacy. No person shall be disturbed in his private affairs, or his home invaded, without authority of law."[72]

California. "All people are by nature free and independent, and have certain inalienable rights, among which are those of enjoying and defending life and liberty; acquiring, possessing, and protecting property; and pursuing and obtaining safety, happiness, and privacy."[73] This right of privacy applies to actions of private as well as public employers.[74]

California is one of the only states in which a court has interpreted a state constitutional right of privacy as it applies to private employer drug testing. In *Wilkinson v. Times-Mirror Corp.*,[75] a subsidiary company, Matthew Bender & Co., instituted a pre-employment testing program. Matthew Bender required job applicants to consent to the procedure after a conditional offer of employment was made. The California Court of Appeals in upholding this program noted that the drug testing was done as part of a pre-employment physical examination; applicants were specifically notified that any job offer would be conditioned upon the applicant consenting to the drug test; and the collection procedures presented minimum intrusion into individual rights of privacy. The court, however, specifically refused to address the constitutionality of testing current employees and stated that their holding did not address the constitutionality of all pre-employment testing programs.

Florida. "Every natural person has a right to be let alone and free from governmental intrusion into his private life except as otherwise provided herein. This section shall not be construed to limit the public's rights of access to public records and meetings as provided by law."[76] Also, "Searches and Seizures. The right of the people to be secure in their persons, houses, papers, and effects against unreasonable searches and seizures, and against the unreasonable interception of private communications by any means, shall not be violated."[77]

Hawaii. "Searches, seizures and invasion of privacy. The right of the people to be secure in their person, houses, papers and effects against unreasonable searches, seizures, and invasions of privacy shall not be violated; and no warrants shall issue but upon probable cause, supported by oath or affirmation, and particularly describing the place to be searched and the persons or things to be seized or the communications to be intercepted."[78]

Illinois. "Searches, seizures, privacy and interceptions." This provision is similar to Florida's. Art. 1, sec. 6. "Right to remedy and justice. Every person shall find a certain remedy in the laws for all injuries and wrongs which he receives to his person, privacy, property or reputation. He shall obtain justice of law, freely, completely, and promptly."[79] In Illinois, privacy proscriptions in the state constitution apply only to government action.[80]

Louisiana. "Right to Privacy. Every person shall be secure in his person, property, communications, houses, papers, and effects against unreasonable searches, seizures, or invasions of privacy. No warrant shall issue without probable cause supported by oath or affirmation, and particularly describing the place to searched, the persons or things to be seized, and the lawful purpose or reason for the search. Any person adversely affected by a search or seizure conducted in violation of this Section shall have standing to raise its illegality in the appropriate court."[81]

Montana. "Right of Privacy. The right of individual privacy is essential to the well-being of a free society and shall not be infringed without the showing of a compelling state interest."[82]

Medical Information

Additionally, an employer's disclosure of medical information about an employee to a third party, including other employees, may infringe upon the employee's right of privacy. Such privacy rights may be protected by state common law, by general state privacy statutes, or by specific state medical privacy laws. The following is a discussion of the states with statutory restrictions on employer disclosures of employee medical information.

California. The California constitution protects an employee's right of privacy in his or her medical records.[83] "Identity of methadone drug patients or former patients is not be be disclosed" by health care providers except with consent, or between professionals involved in treatment, or upon a court order, or for protection of state elected officials. Disclosures must be logged in the patient's file.[84]

> No requester shall acquire medical information regarding a patient without first obtaining [written] authorization from that patient. Nor may a user of medical information further disclose it unless specific permission is included on the patient's authorization form. By law, the authorization must be in at least eight-point type, clearly separate from other language on an application form, and signed by the patient or a relative. It must state the types of medical information authorized to be disclosed, who may disclose and who may acquire

the information, and the purposes of the disclosure. The authorization must include an expiration date. The patient is entitled to a copy. . . . Also, medical information may not be disclosed to an employer unless the individual authorizes the disclosure or is part of a medical plan that authorizes such release.[85]

Colorado. The state criminal theft statute has been amended to make clear that "confidential information, medical records information" is considered a "thing of value" under the statute.[86] The criminal code also states, "Any person who, without proper authorization, knowingly obtains a medical record or medical information with the intent to appropriate [it] to his own use or to the use of another, who steals or discloses to an unauthorized person a medical record or medical information, or who, without authority, makes or causes to be made a copy of medical record or medical information commits theft."[87]

Florida. "A licensed health-care provider must furnish copies of patient records to the patient or his or her legal representative, upon request, and may not disclose them to others without consent of the patient, except by subpoena."[88]

Massachusetts. A person "shall have a right against unreasonable, substantial or serious interference with his privacy."[89] In *Bratt v. IBM Corp.*,[90] the Massachusetts Supreme Court held that disclosure of private medical facts about an employee through an intracorporate communication "is sufficient publication to impair an employee's right to privacy." The court said that, in evaluating whether an employer's disclosure of medical information concerning an employee constitutes an unreasonable interference with the employee's privacy right, a court should "balance the employer's legitimate business interest in disseminating the information against the nature and substantiality of the intrusion."[91]

Minnesota. "A physician may not disclose confidential information acquired in his professional capacity."[92]

Nevada. "A patient may refuse to disclose or forbid any other person from disclosing medical information."[93]

Rhode Island. "Organizations that keep medical information must adopt policies to assure confidentiality."[94]

Texas. "Medical information identifiable as to individuals is to be kept confidential in state files."[95]

Virginia. "Individual medical data in state files is exempt from public disclosure."[96]

Wisconsin. Patient records must be kept confidential except for use in health care, for processing payments and claims, and research.[97]

State Legislation on Drug Testing

The following is a brief discussion of the states that have enacted legislation impacting employment-related drug testing in the private sector.

Connecticut. The Connecticut law[98] regulating urinalysis drug testing covers both job applicants and employees. An employer may not require a job applicant to be tested unless the applicant is informed in writing at the time of the application that the employer intends to test, the initial test is confirmed by two confirmation tests, the second of which is as reliable as Gas Chromatography/ Mass Spectrometry, and the applicant is provided a copy of the test results.

An employee may not be required to submit to urinalysis unless the employer has reasonable suspicion that the employee is "under the influence of drugs or alcohol which adversely affects or could adversely affect such employee's job performance."

Random testing is not permitted unless authorized by federal law, the employee is in a position designated safety-sensitive by the Commissioner of Labor, or random testing is part of an employer-approved or sponsored EAP.

The statute provides for civil action against employers violating this law with injunctive relief specifically available.

Iowa. Iowa's statute[99] applies to chemical drug tests conducted for the purpose of detecting the presence of a chemical substance in an individual. The statute applies to both job applicants and employees.

A job applicant may only be tested as part of a pre-employment physical and then only after notice to the applicant before the application stage. Applicants must also be personally informed of the requirement at the first interview.

Before an employee may be tested, the employer must have probable cause, the employee must be in a safety-sensitive position, the lab must be approved by the Department of Health, and the test confirmed by an alternative method. Moreover, the employee must be given a chance to rebut a positive test and the first time an employee tests positive, the employer must provide a substance abuse evaluation and, if recommended, treatment in an approved program.

Maine. On July 7, 1989, Maine adopted a law restricting the right of employers to conduct drug testing. The law[100] allows testing of applicants, and probable cause testing of employees, but restricts random testing to employees at a nuclear generating facility and on jobs where an employee would "create a substantial risk of direct and immediate serious physical injury to the public or co-workers. . . ."

Probable cause is defined as "a reasonable ground for belief in the existence of facts that induce a person to believe that an employee may be under the influence of a substance of abuse." The law specifically prohibits evidence of probable cause to be based on an anonymous informant, information about off-duty use, or a single work-related incident.

The law also requires as a prerequisite to drug testing that an employer establish an EAP and give employees 60 days' written notice of the testing policy including the jobs subject to random testing and an explanation of the random testing procedure. All testing is to be conducted in a medical facility by medical personnel and no employee can be required to remove clothing or submit to observation while producing the urine sample.

All positive tests must be confirmed by gas chromatography/ mass spectrometry (GC/MS) and employees must be allowed to retain a portion of the sample for retesting if they desire. Applicants who test positive may be rejected; however, employees must be offered rehabilitation. Employees may be discharged or disciplined only after two positive tests or one positive test if rehabilitation was completed during the preceding 12 months. Employers who violate the law may be assessed triple damages for back wages, attorney's fees, and court costs.

Minnesota. The Minnesota statute[101] only prevents drug or alcohol testing done by an employer on an arbitrary and capricious basis.

The testing must be done pursuant to a written drug and alcohol testing policy. The minimum standards of the policy are not set out by statute but, whatever its content, written notice must be given to all those subject to testing.

A job applicant may not be tested unless a job offer has been made to the applicant.

An employee may be requested to undergo a test as part of a routine physical examination as long as testing is done no more than once annually and at least two weeks' advance notice of the testing is given. Random testing is available only for employees in safety-sensitive positions. Additionally, testing may be required if there is a reasonable suspicion. Reasonable suspicion may be based upon the employee violating written work rules.

An employee may not be disciplined or discharged unless the initial positive test has been confirmed. Moreover, even after confirmation, an employee may not be discharged unless he or she was first given the opportunity to participate in a treatment program and has refused to do so or has failed to successfully complete the program.

Montana. The Montana statute[102] regulates testing in two types of employment situations. First, drug testing may not be required as a condition of employment except for employment in hazardous work environments or in safety-sensitive positions.

Second, a drug test may not be a condition of employment unless the employer has reason to believe that the employee is drug- or alcohol-impaired on the job. The law only prohibits the requirement of a test; it does not preclude the test from being requested by either party.

A person must be given a copy of any test results and the opportunity, at his or her own expense, to obtain an independent confirmatory test of the same sample.

An employer violating this statute is guilty of a misdemeanor. The statute does not specifically allow for a private right of action, nor does it prohibit such an action for damages.

Rhode Island. The Rhode Island statute[103] does not apply to job applicants. Employers are free, therefore, to require any type of testing as a condition of hiring. An employer may not require or subject any employee to a body fluid or tissue test as a condition of continued employment.

An employee may be tested if the employer has reasonable grounds to believe, based upon objective facts, that the employee's use of controlled substances is impairing his ability to perform his job. The sample collection may be done in private only and the testing must be done in conjunction with a legitimate treatment program.

Positive tests must be confirmed by GC/MS or other equally accurate methodology and an employee must be given the opportunity to have the confirmed test reviewed at an independent laboratory.

Employers who violate this statute are guilty of a misdemeanor and may be sued civilly. The relief available in a civil action includes compensatory and punitive damages as well as attorney's fees, costs, and injunctive relief. Rhode Island is currently the only state that specifically provides for punitive damages.

Utah. The Utah statute[104] states at the outset that it is based upon a legislative finding that fair and equitable drug and alcohol testing in the workplace is in the best interests of employers, employees, and society.

The statute permits testing of job applicants as a condition of hiring and testing of employees as a condition of continued employment. There is no requirement that there be any indication of job impairment as a condition of testing. The cost of the testing must be borne by the employer.

The statute is the only one currently that requires that, at companies instituting a testing program, management must also submit to testing on a periodic basis.

Only confirmed positive tests or refusal to be tested may provide the basis for disciplinary or rehabilitative action with respect to an employee. Employers must, prior to implementation of a program, develop a written testing policy, distribute it to employees, and make the policy available to prospective employees.

Employers are protected in many ways against possible legal action related to testing. An employer is not liable for any action taken against an employee unless the action was based on a false test result. Even then the employer is not liable for money damages as long as its reliance on the test results was reasonable and in good faith. Similarly, no action for defamation will lie unless the employer discloses a false test result with malice.

Vermont. The Vermont law,[105] one of the most restrictive (to employers) of statutes to date, generally prohibits drug testing of job applicants and employees with only limited exceptions. Random or companywide testing may only be done when required by federal law or regulation.

An applicant may only be tested if the offer of employment is conditional on a negative drug test, the test is part of a comprehensive physical examination, notice of the drug(s) to be tested is provided at least 10 days prior to the test, and the testing program is in accordance with the provision of the act.

An employee may be tested only if there is probable cause to believe that the employee is using or is under the influence of a drug on the job, a bona fide rehabilitation program is available, the test is administered in accordance with the requirements of the act, and the employee is protected from termination unless he or she tests positive in a test administered after completion of a rehabilitation program.

The statute mandates that an applicant or employee who has a positive test be given the opportunity to explain and have the sample retested.

The act creates a private right of action in which the employer has the burden of proving that it has met the requirements of the statute with respect to administration of the test and confidentiality. The state may seek a civil penalty or institute criminal action.

General Legal Implications

Whereas U.S. constitutional issues implicate government employers almost exclusively, the general legal areas such as negligence law and contract law outlined below can and do apply to private employers as well.

Negligence Law

Negligent Hiring. The first area of employer negligence involves the negligent hiring or retention of a substance abusing employee who injures a fellow employee or other third party, such as a customer. These cases illustrate the importance of controlling substance abuse in the workplace. An employer has a duty to foresee the potential dangers an impaired employee presents and, if a court determines that it was foreseeable that the employee's condition would result in the injury, the employer may be held liable for damages.

In 1984, the owners of a New Mexico motor inn were found liable for the actions of an intoxicated employee. The employee sexually molested a guest who later sued the hotel claiming the hotel was negligent in hiring and retaining the employee. The employee had previously been discharged from his job at the motor inn because of drinking. The hotel later rehired him, even though other employees knew he drank regularly on the job. The New Mexico Court of Appeals found that there was enough evidence for a jury to decide whether the hotel should have foreseen the employee's behavior.[106]

Additionally, an employer has the duty to provide and maintain a safe workplace for employees. An employer fails this obligation when he hires an individual who injures co-workers as a result of substance abuse that the employer carelessly fails to detect. A breach of this duty may not only constitute negligence, but may also violate statutory law. For example, the Occupational Safety and Health Act requires that an employer "furnish to each of his employees employment and a place of employment which are free from recognized hazards that are causing or likely to cause death or serious physical harm to his employees."[107] Potential hazards of a substance-impaired co-worker clearly are extensive.

Negligent Testing. It is also possible for an employer and its chosen drug testing laboratory to be found liable for negligent testing. The employer's duty to test with care is, however, broader than acting prudently in selecting their drug testing laboratory. It may also include properly training employees who will administer the test, assuring that the test will be performed correctly, taking adequate care to protect the chain of custody over the urine samples, and ensuring confidential treatment of test results.

In 1976 an employee lost his job and benefits with a company as a result of an employer-hired physician's report of the employee's poor physical condition. The Texas Court of Appeals determined that the doctor, as an agent of the employer, owed a duty to the employee not to injure him physically or otherwise, and allowed the employee to recover damages if the doctor's negligence in giving inaccurate health reports was the probable cause of plaintiff's termination.[108] In 1982, two applicants were refused employment after positive urine tests. The applicants proved negligence in showing the laboratory failed to use an alternative chemistry confirmation test as suggested by the instructions of the screening device manufacturer. Because of the failure to follow the manufacturer's instructions, the laboratory agreed to settle out of court with the two job applicants.[109]

In a similar case, a plaintiff was rejected as a pilot because of a pre-employment physical examination. The applicant sued the airline alleging that the diagnosis was inaccurate. The airline had employed the doctor to give the pre-employment physical examinations and, as a result, the appeals court in California found that it was an issue for trial to determine whether the employer could be held vicariously liable for the doctor's alleged negligence.[110]

Finally, in another case, the Oregon Court of Appeals ruled that there was a triable issue of fact presented as to whether the employer was vicariously liable since a jury could infer that an employee's drug use was within the scope of employment. The employee had ingested the drugs to combat depression and remain alert while staying up late to finish a job bid. After ingesting the hallucinogenic drug at work, the employee later raped a woman in her home. Even though the woman had no connection with the employer or the job, the court denied the employer's efforts to have the case dismissed.[111]

Defamation (Libel and Slander). A properly implemented substance abuse program should ensure that test results will remain confidential. An employer has a limited privilege to use the information obtained from urinalysis. Because of the limitation, however, employers should both require that the laboratory confirm test results and ensure that neither the laboratory nor employer publicize test results beyond those people who absolutely need to know. The common law tort of defamation prohibits an employer from communicating false information about an employee to a third person if the information injures the business or reputation of the employee. However, as in non-employment-related circumstances, truth is an absolute defense to a defamation action. Similarly, an employee's consent to a disclosure protects an employer from a defamation suit and points out that it is important for a program to include a consent and release form authorizing the employer to receive and the laboratory to release the urinalysis results.[112]

State common law defamation actions have been successful in at least two instances where medical reports or test results were used to spread false information about the individual, or were released to persons without a "need to know." In *Houston Belt & Terminal Railway Co. v. Wherry*,[113] a former employee was awarded $200,000 in damages because his employer falsely reported he was a drug addict based upon a trace amount of methadone detected in a urinalysis. The test results were later proved inaccurate but only after the company's director of labor relations wrote a letter to the Department of Labor stating that the trace amounts of methadone constituted grounds for the plaintiff's termination.

Another court upheld a jury verdict of defamation where an employer's statement that the plaintiff was fired for drug abuse failed to include other reasons for termination. The court found that the employer's statement was false because it was not the "whole truth" but was only a secondary aspect of the retaliation against the plaintiff for failing to promote a superior's son. The court also found that the employer's limited privilege to communicate internally was waived because the employer acted with malice.[114]

Contract Law/Employment-at-Will

This area of law predominantly deals with employers who have union contracts or employment contracts with individuals. In this area, the employer should look to the collective bargaining agreement or employment contract before implementing a substance abuse program and adjust the program accordingly. (See the discussion of the National Labor Relations Act, earlier in this chapter.)

Moreover, a breach of contract or wrongful discharge claim can be made in the absence of an employment contract as exceptions to the basic rule of employment-at-will. The employment-at-will rule generally states that the employment relationship can be terminated at any time for any reason by either of the parties. Although the majority of states still adhere to the concept of employment-at-will, there is an increasing trend to find an exception to the employment-at-will doctrine when an employee is discharged for an impermissible reason or without regard to the rules and policies governing the workplace. Current exceptions to the at-will doctrine take three forms: public policy exceptions, employee handbooks, and an implied covenant of good faith and fair dealing.

Public Policy Exceptions. Several states have judicially recognized a public policy exception to the employment-at-will doctrine. The definition of public policy utilized by various courts differs in some respects from state to state. It is generally agreed, however, that a public policy violation is determined by whether an employer's conduct contravenes the letter or purpose of a constitutional, statutory, or regulatory provision or scheme.[115] These cases often arise when an employee is terminated for refusing to commit an unlawful act or for participating in an act protected by public policy.[116]

Since the public policy exception to the employment-at-will doctrine is normally based on an employer's contravention or violation of a statutory or regulatory provision, as more states enact legislation regulating an employer's use of substance abuse screening, the greater the potential becomes for claims by employees of violation of the public policy against drug testing. An example of the challenge to an employer's drug testing as a violation of public policy occurred in Wyoming wherein the federal court deciding the case determined that an employee's termination for refusing to submit to a drug screen did not violate Wyoming's public policy.[117]

Employee Handbooks. A growing number of state courts have ruled that an employee handbook disseminated to prospective or current employees may become part of the contract of employment between the employer and employee so as to limit the employer's right to discharge an at-will employee.[118] The circumstances under which the provisions of an employee handbook will become part of the contract of employment vary greatly from state to state. Some states differentiate between dissemination of the handbook at the beginning of the employment and distribution during the course of an employee's employment. Other states view the handbook as an offer for a unilateral contract that is binding when validly accepted by the employee.[119] Some states require the handbook to provide a definite term of the employee's employment in order to be binding,[120] while other states will give contractual status to simple oral assurances by an employer that an employee's job is secure.[121]

In states that incorporate the provisions of an employee handbook into the employee's contract of employment, both the employer and the employee are required to act in accordance with the terms contained in the handbook. With regard to a substance abuse policy, therefore, if the policy and disciplinary procedures are contained in an employee handbook and the handbook is given to employees, the provisions of the policy will be binding on both parties. Thus, an employee may use the handbook as the basis for a wrongful discharge action if the employer fails to follow the terms and conditions contained therein. At the same time, however, an employer may rely on a handbook as a basis for upholding disciplinary action if the employee's conduct is in violation of the substance abuse policy.

It is also possible for an employer to prevent its employee handbook from becoming part of the employment contract. It is generally held that the placement of a permanent disclaimer in the handbook stating that the employer will not be bound by any of the provisions and that the employer has the right to change the provisions of the handbook effectively prevents the handbook from becoming binding on the parties.[122]

Covenant of Good Faith and Fair Dealing. An implied covenant of good faith and fair dealing may be held to limit an employer's right to discharge an employee at will. So far, this theory has been applied in only a few states. In California, the covenant was interpreted to protect a long serving employee from discharge without good cause.[123] In Massachusetts, the covenant has been used to impose liability when an employer terminates an at-will employee for the purpose of depriving the employee of previously earned commissions;[124] while in Montana, the covenant was used to bind an employer to the dismissal policies contained in its employees' handbook so as to preserve the peace of mind of employees and prevent an injustice.[125] The ony reported case challenging a drug testing program and asserting a violation of a company's implied covenant of good faith and fair dealing was rejected by the same U.S. District Court in Wyoming that refused to find a violation of state public policy discussed previously.[126]

Since the doctrine of good faith and fair dealing generally imposes a requirement of good faith on an employer in all of its dealings with employees, an employer would have no liability under this theory if it enforces its substance abuse policy in a fair and reasonable manner and in accordance with the provisions of the employee handbook. On the other hand, as the public policy exceptions to the employment-at-will doctrine continue to grow, more employers may find themselves defending discharges for violation of company policy or breaches of implied employment contracts.

Employee Assistance Programs

As with other aspects of the substance abuse prevention program, an employee assistance program may have separate legal implications that should be considered by an employer. Several of the issues, including state constitutional privacy rights and medical information statutes, have been discussed previously and may apply to EAPs. The two most commonly implicated issues include confidentiality and malpractice.

Confidentiality

The concepts of confidentiality and privilege both apply to information obtained by a medical professional. The concepts are, however, separate and distinct. Confidentiality is a legal duty imposed upon a professional to keep medical records private and secure. From the perspective of an EAP professional, confidentiality requires that the client's EAP records be kept private, secure, and separate from other corporate and departmental records. As was previously discussed in this chapter (see "State Constitutional and Statutory Implications") many states have statutes governing confidentiality. Additionally, other laws require a medical professional to maintain the confidentiality of a client. Under certain circumstances, federal regulations apply to EAPs. Generally, federal regulations require confidentiality only when the program is related to alcohol abuse or drug abuse education, training, treatment, rehabilitation, or research and is conducted either in whole or in part, directly or by grant, contract or otherwise, by a U.S. department or agency; required under a license, registration, or other authorization from a U.S. department or agency; assisted by federal funds directly through grants or contracts, or indirectly by funds supplied to a state or local government unit; or assisted by the Internal Revenue Service through a tax-exempt status or income tax deduction for contributions.[127]

The regulations require that prior to a medical professional releasing confidential information, there must be a written consent by the patient or his authorized legal representative. The regulations specify that the following items must be included on the consent forms: name of the program that is to make the disclosure; name or title of the person or organization to which disclosure is to be made; name of the patient; purpose or need of the disclosure; extent or nature of the information to be disclosed; statement that the consent can be revoked and a specific date, event, or condition upon which consent will expire; and dated signature of the patient.[128]

In limited circumstances, a medical professional may disclose information without prior written consent. Such circumstances would include a court order or when a patient commits or threatens to commit certain crimes. Similarly, while all 50 states require certain medical professionals to report child abuse, until 1986 there remained some controversy regarding whether federal regulations allowed the reporting of child abuse when the medical or social service program is operated with federal funds. On August 27, 1986, the federal regulations were amended to exempt the reporting under state law of incidents of suspected child abuse and neglect to appropriate state or local officials.[129]

A person who wrongfully discloses confidential information subject to federal regulations may be subject to a fine of up to $500 for the first offense and up to $5,000 for each subsequent offense.[130]

As was previously discussed (see "State Law and General Legal Implications"), certain provisions of an employer's substance abuse prevention program may create an implied contract. In the area of EAPs, an implied promise of confidentiality may arise from policy statements made in an employee handbook; a court may find that the policy of confidentiality spelled out in an employee handbook is sufficient to allow an action for breach of that promise.[131] An employee's expectation that the information he discloses to an EAP counselor will remain confidential is the key to the potential creation of an implied contract of confidentiality. For this reason, employees using or consulting the EAP should be made to understand that there are circumstances under which there will be a disclosure without the employee's consent.

As was previously mentioned, most state statutes and the federal regulations provide for exceptions to the duty of confidentiality when the patient commits, or threatens to commit, a crime. Failure of a counselor to disclose this information may result in damages being awarded against the professional or his or her employer. The duty to disclose dangerous behavior by an EAP participant first developed in California in the case of *Tarasoff v. Regents of the University of California*,[132] wherein a graduate student at the University of California confided in his psychologist at the university-sponsored counseling service about his intentions to kill a female student who did not return his affection. The psychologist considered the threats to be serious and called the campus police who detained this student. The student was later released when he appeared rational. The psychologist reported these events to the director of the counseling service, a psychiatrist, who determined that no further action need be taken. Neither the woman nor her family were warned of the threats and, after her murder by the student, a lawsuit was filed by her parents against the university, the psychologist, the director of the counseling service, and the police.

The Supreme Court of California found that, based upon the special knowledge generated by the therapist/client relationship, a therapist who determines, or pursuant to the standards of his profession should determine, that his patient presents a serious danger of violence to another, incurs an obligation to use reasonable care to protect the intended victim against such danger. This reasonable care may require that the therapist takes steps to warn the intended victim, to notify the police, or to take whatever steps are reasonably necessary under the circumstances.[133]

The court based its decision upon the special knowledge that the therapist obtained, and it felt the therapist may have been the only person who could control the patient. The duty to warn under the *Tarasoff* theory has been upheld in several state courts, including Alaska, Georgia, Kentucky, New Jersey, and Vermont.[134] Furthermore, as a result of *Tarasoff*, California and other states have passed laws that specify when a therapist's obligation to warn arises. California's statute specifies that a psychotherapist's duty arises only when the patient has communicated to the therapist a serious threat of physical violence against a "reasonably identifiable victim or victims."[135] Similarly, the American Psychological Association considered a model bill which required that there be an actual threat of physical violence versus the serious threat under California law.

Malpractice

The area of malpractice by EAP professionals or other therapists is a subset of negligence law discussed previously in this chapter. (See "General Legal Implications.") Because of the special relationship between an EAP professional and a participating employee and its similarity to the relationship between a psychotherapist and patient, it is reasonable to assume that a case alleging negligence or malpractice by an EAP professional would be considered under the same standards as one involving social workers or psychotherapists. In order to prove liability by an EAP professional, an individual must be able to show the following elements: an EAP practitioner had a duty to an employee; there was a breach of this duty; the practitioner was negligent; the individual suffered damages; and there was no intervening event between the behavior of the therapist and the resulting injury.[136] Moreover, in order to prove negligence, the patient must be able to show that the therapist failed to follow acceptable standards of care in the profession.

Misdiagnosis

The first area of potential malpractice for an EAP practitioner is in the area of misdiagnosis. Misdiagnosis results from a negligent failure by the professional to assess any problem, or failing to assess the correct problem. In one Michigan case, an out-of-court settlement in the amount of $2.8 million was paid to four children whose mother was murdered by their father. The lawsuit claimed negligence by the licensed family and marriage counselor, alleging that the therapist should have referred the client to a staff psychiatrist once the counselor learned of threats by the patient to kill his wife and then commit suicide. The lawsuit alleged that the counselor committed malpractice by failing to properly refer the patient once the counselor determined that the case was clearly beyond the counselor's qualifications. [137]

Negligent Referral

The above case also touches upon the second potential area of malpractice by an EAP practitioner: failing to refer employees to a proper source. This negligent referral reasoning may be stretched to include a requirement that an EAP professional refer employees only to referral sources who have proven track records.

An example of negligent referral liability may be inferred from a case out of Pennsylvania wherein the court found liability on the part of an employer failing to exercise due care in choosing a competent doctor to whom the employer sent employees for treatment. [138]

Defamation

There are defamation considerations unique to EAPs. As was previously mentioned, defamation is a written communication (libel) or an oral communication (slander) by one person that harms the reputation of another. There have been cases wherein an employer's disclosure of the results of drug screening tests were actionable as defamation. [139] From the perspective of an EAP professional, it is possible that a wrong diagnosis may well constitute defamation. An EAP professional should document what clients were doing, what they said, and what they looked like, rather than making a diagnosis which may prove to be incorrect. Additionally, EAP professionals should make no claims that all information will remain strictly confidential; however, they should likewise ensure that the information is disclosed only to the individuals within the company on a "need-to-know" basis.

Conclusion

The body of federal and state statutory and case law regulating the issues raised by substance abuse in the workplace continues to grow. As employers develop substance abuse policies to deal with the problems associated with workplace substance abuse, it is advisable that they consider the variety of legal theories, statutes, and regulations discussed in this chapter. Although this discussion has attempted to outline the many issues faced by an employer when implementing and enforcing a substance abuse policy, it is virtually impossible to undertake an exhaustive discussion covering every possible situation since the legality of any policy is largely dependent on the facts and circumstances surrounding each employer's business. Because of this, an employer should obtain legal counsel in the development of, and prior to the implementation of, such a policy.

As will be discussed in subsequent chapters, as a practical matter, an employer who decides to implement a substance abuse policy would do well to give notice to employees and educate the employees on the importance of the policy as well as the procedures that will be used. Effective communication and education often will reduce the number of potential legal challenges. Similarly, if an employer follows the method of implementation set forth in the remainder of this work, most, if not all, of the possible legal challenges will be eliminated. The policy, procedures, and program are designed to help employers avoid the appearance of invading employee privacy, providing procedures that are fair and consistent, preventing discrimination as well as limiting as much as possible any possible legal exposure to the employer, its company, or anyone else involved in the process. Additionally, these materials are designed to comply with current federal laws and regulations that impact an employer's policy. With these considerations in mind and with competent legal counsel, employers can establish comprehensive employee substance abuse programs avoiding many of the legal pitfalls that now exist.[140]

Notes

1. *Rendell & Baker v. Kohn*, 457 U.S. 830 (1982); *Greco v. Halliburton Co.*, 674 F. Supp. 1447, 2 IER Cases 1281 (D. Wyo. 1987).
2. *Rushton v. Nebraska Pub. Power Dist.*, 844 F.2d 562, 3 IER Cases 257 (8th Cir. 1988) (nuclear power); *Skinner v. Railway Labor Executives' Ass'n*, 489 U.S. ___, 4 IER Cases 224 (1989) (railroads); *Shoemaker v. Handel*, 795 F.2d 1136, 1 IER Cases 814 (3d Cir.), *cert. denied*, 479 U.S. 986, 1 IER Cases 1136 (1986) (horseracing); *see also Thomson v. Marsh*, 884 F.2d 113, 4 IER Cases 1445 (4th Cir. 1989).

3. *Whalen v. Roe*, 429 U.S. 589 (1977) (marriage); *Prince v. Massachusetts*, 321 U.S. 158 (1944) (family relationships); *Roe v. Wade*, 410 U.S. 113 (1973) (abortion); *Griswald v. Connecticut*, 381 U.S. 479 (1965) (procreation and contraception).
4. *Roe v. Wade, supra* note 3.
5. U.S. Const. amend. IV: "The right of the people to be secure in their persons, houses, papers, and effects, against unreasonable searches and seizures, shall not be violated, and no Warrants shall issue, but upon probable cause, supported by Oath or affirmation, and particularly describing the place to be searched, and the persons or things to be seized."
6. *See, e.g., Skinner v. Railway Labor Executives' Ass'n*, 489 U.S. ___, 4 IER Cases 224 (1989), *rev'g on other grounds sub nom. Railway Labor Executives' Ass'n v. Burnley*, 839 F.2d 575, 580, 2 IER Cases 1601 (9th Cir. 1988) (citing cases); *Caruso v. Ward*, 133 Misc.2d 544, 506 N.Y.S.2d 789, 2 IER Cases 238 (N.Y. Sup. Ct. 1986), *rev'd on other grounds*, 534 N.Y.2d 142, 530 N.E.2d 850, 3 IER Cases 1537 (1988).
7. *O'Connor v. Ortega*, 480 U.S. 709, 725–726, 1 IER Cases 1617 (1987) (noninvestigatory, work-related purposes, as well as for investigations of work-related misconduct, should be judged by the standard of reasonableness under all the circumstances ["as to] both the inception and the scope of the intrusion"); *Federal Employees v. Weinberger*, 818 F.2d 935, 2 IER Cases 145 (D.C. Cir. 1987); *Lovvorn v. City of Chattanooga*, 846 F.2d 1539, 3 IER Cases 673 (6th Cir. 1988); *Patchogue-Medford Congress of Teachers v. Patchogue-Medford Union Free School Dist. Bd. of Educ.*, 510 N.E.2d 325, 2 IER Cases 198 (N.Y. Ct. App. 1987); *Jones v. McKenzie*, 628 F. Supp. 1500, 1 IER Cases 1076 (D.D.C. 1986), *rev'd and vacated in part*, 833 F.2d 335, 2 IER Cases 1121 (D.C. Cir. 1987).
8. *Skinner v. Railway Labor Executives' Ass'n, supra* note 2; *Treasury Employees v. Von Raab*, 489 U.S. ___, 4 IER Cases 246 (1989); *Air Traffic Specialists v. Dole*, 2 IER Cases 68 (D. Alaska 1987).
9. 489 U.S. ___, 4 IER Cases 224 (1989).
10. *Id.*, 4 IER Cases at 230.
11. *Id.*, quoting 50 Fed. Reg. 31,552 (1985).
12. *Id.*, 4 IER Cases at 232.
13. *Supra* note 8.
14. *Harmon v. Thornburgh*, 878 F.2d 484, 4 IER Cases 1000 (D.C. Cir. 1989), *cert. denied sub nom. Bell v. Thornburgh*, 493 U.S. ___ (1990) (circuit court allowed random testing of Justice Department lawyers with top secret clearances); *Federal Employees v. Cheney*, 884 F.2d 603, 4 IER Cases 1164 (D.C. Cir. 1989), *cert. denied*, 493 U.S. ___, 4 IER Cases 1888 (1990) (circuit court sanctioned random testing of civilian drug counselors in the Army's Alcohol & Drug Abuse Prevention and Control Program).
15. *See, e.g., Caruso v. Ward, supra* note 6; *City of Palm Bay v. Bauman*, 475 So.2d 1322 (Fla. Dist. Ct. App. 1985); *Lovvorn v. City of Chattanooga, supra* note 7; *Rushton v. Nebraska Pub. Power Dist.*, 844 F.2d 562, 3 IER Cases 257 (8th Cir. 1988); *Shoemaker v. Handel*, 795 F.2d 1136, 1 IER Cases 814 (3d Cir.), *cert. denied*, 479 U.S. 986, 1 IER Cases 1136 (1986); *Transport Workers Local 234 (Philadelphia) v. Southeastern Pa. Transp. Auth.*, 863 F.2d 1110, 4 IER Cases 1, 130 LRRM 2553 (3d Cir. 1988), *remanded*, 492 U.S. ___, 131 LRRM 2760 (1989); *Thomson v. Marsh*, 884 F.2d 113, 4 IER Cases 1445 (4th Cir. 1989).

16. *Skinner v. Railway Labor Executives' Ass'n*, 489 U.S. ___, 4 IER Cases 224 (1989); *McDonnell v. Hunter*, 809 F.2d 1302, 1 IER Cases 1297 (8th Cir. 1987); *Harmon v. Thornburgh, supra* note 14.

17. U.S. Const. amend. V: "No person shall be held to answer for a capital, or otherwise infamous crime, unless on a presentment or indictment of a Grand Jury, except in cases arising in the land or naval forces, or in the Militia, when in actual service in time of War or public danger; nor shall any person be subject for the same offense to be twice put in jeopardy of life or limb; nor shall be compelled in any criminal case to be a witness against himself, nor be deprived of life, liberty, or property, without due process of law; nor shall private property be taken for public use without just compensation."

18. *Schmerber v. California*, 384 U.S. 757 (1966).

19. *Shoemaker v. Handel, supra* note 15; *Treasury Employees v. Von Raab*, 816 F.2d 170, 2 IER Cases 15 (5th Cir. 1987), *aff'd in part, vacated in part and remanded*, 489 U.S. ___, 4 IER Cases 246 (1989); *Hester v. City of Milledgeville*, 598 F. Supp. 1456 (M.D. Ga. 1984), *aff'd in part on other grounds, rev'd in part on other grounds and remanded on other grounds*, 777 F.2d 1492 (11th Cir. 1985).

20. *Board of Regents v. Roth*, 408 U.S. 564 (1972).

21. *Treasury Employees v. Von Raab*, 489 U.S. ___, 4 IER Cases 246 (1989); *Air Traffic Specialists v. Dole*, 2 IER Cases 68 (D. Alaska 1987); *Rushton v. Nebraska Pub. Power Dist., supra* note 15.

22. *Jones v. McKenzie*, 628 F. Supp. 1500, 1 IER Cases 1076 (D.D.C. 1986), *rev'd on other grounds*, 833 F.2d 335, 2 IER Cases 1121 (D.C. Cir. 1987), *cert. denied sub nom. Jenkins v. Jones*, 490 U.S. ___, 4 IER Cases 352 (1989).

23. *Copeland v. Philadelphia Police Dep't*, 840 F.2d 1139, 2 IER Cases 1825 (3d Cir. 1988), *cert. denied*, 490 U.S. ___, 4 IER Cases 352 (1989).

24. 643 F. Supp. 1507, 1 IER Cases 625 (D.N.J. 1986).

25. 42 U.S.C. §2000e-2 (1978).

26. *Teamsters v. United States*, 431 U.S. 324, 14 FEP Cases 1514 (1977).

27. *Wards Cove Packing Co. v. Atonio*, 490 U.S. ___, 49 FEP Cases 1519 (1989).

28. 440 U.S. 568, 19 FEP Cases 149 (1977).

29. *Drayton v. City of St. Petersburg*, 477 F. Supp. 846 (M.D. Fla. 1979).

30. 29 U.S.C. §706(7) (1984).

31. *Id.*

32. *Railway Labor Executives' Ass'n v. Burnley*, 839 F.2d 575, 2 IER Cases 1601, 1613 (9th Cir. 1988), *rev'd on other grounds, sub nom. Skinner v. Railway Labor Executives' Ass'n*, 4 IER Cases 224 (1989) ("plain language of the [Act indicates] that only alcoholics or drug users whose problems are under control are protected from discriminatory treatment"); *Anthanas v. Board of Educ., School Dist. 111, Highwood-Highland Park*, 28 FEP Cases 569 (N.D. Ill. 1980) (rehabilitated alcoholic is handicapped within meaning of Rehabilitation Act).

33. *Southeastern Community College v. Davis*, 442 U.S. 397, 405 (1979).

34. *Richardson v. United States Postal Serv.*, 613 F.Supp. 1213, 40 FEP Cases 703 (D.D.C. 1985).

35. *Huff v. Israel*, 573 F. Supp. 107, 33 FEP Cases 253 (M.D. Ga. 1983), *vacated*, 732 F.2d 943, 37 FEP Cases 1816 (11th Cir. 1984); *see also Copeland v. Philadelphia Police Dep't*, 840 F.2d 1139, 2 IER Cases 1825 (3d Cir. 1988), *cert. denied*, 490 U.S. ___, 4 IER Cases 352 (1989) (accommodating a drug

user within the ranks of a police department would constitute substantial modification of essential functions of police department and cast doubt upon integrity of police).

36. DeCresce, et al., *Drug Testing in the Workplace* (Washington, D.C.: BNA Books, 1989); Denenberg & Denenberg, *Alcohol and Drugs: Issues in the Workplace* (Washington, D.C.: BNA Books, 1983).
37. *NLRB v. Wooster Div., Borg-Warner Corp.*, 356 U.S. 342, 42 LRRM 2034 (1958).
38. *Marine & Shipbuilding Workers v. NLRB*, 320 F.2d 615, 53 LRRM 2878 (3d Cir. 1963), *cert. denied*, 375 U.S. 984, 54 LRRM 2134 (1964).
39. 273 NLRB 171, 118 LRRM 1283 (1984) and 278 NLRB 18, 121 LRRM 1211 (1986).
40. 295 NLRB No. 26, 131 LRRM 1393 (1989).
41. 838 F.2d 1087, 127 LRRM 2812 (9th Cir. 1988), *vacated and remanded*, 492 U.S. ___, 131 LRRM 2759 (1989).
42. 491 U.S. ___, 131 LRRM 2601 (1989).
43. 295 NLRB No. 63, 131 LRRM 1404 (1989).
44. NLRB Office of the General Counsel, Guideline Memorandum GC 87-5 (Sept. 8, 1987).
45. 45 U.S.C. §151 et seq.
46. *Supra* note 42.
47. *Id.*
48. *Railway Labor Executives' Ass'n v. Norfolk & W. Ry.*, 833 F.2d 700, 705–6, 126 LRRM 3121 (7th Cir. 1987); *Maintenance of Way Employees Lodge 16 v. Burlington N.R.R.*, 802 F.2d 1016, 1024, 123 LRRM 2593 (8th Cir. 1986).
49. *Locomotive Eng'rs v. Burlington N.R.R.*, *supra* note 41.
50. 842 F.2d 794, 128 LRRM 2225 (5th Cir. 1988), *vacated*, 875 F.2d 1129, 131 LRRM 2761 (5th Cir. 1989).
51. Pub. L. No. 100-690, §§5151-5160, 102 Stat. 4307 (Nov. 1988).
52. Pub. L. No. 100-690, 102 Stat. 4181 (Nov. 1988).
53. Pub. L. No. 100-690, §5153(1)(C), 102 Stat. 4307 (Nov. 1988).
54. Department of Transportation, Final Rule, Controlled Substance Testing, 49 C.F.R. §§391 and 394 (1988).
55. Federal Highway Administration, 53 Fed. Reg. 47,151 (1988) (to be codified at 49 C.F.R. §§391).
56. *Id.* §391.93.
57. *Id.* §391.85.
58. *Id.* §391.95.
59. *Id.* §§391.99, 391.103, 391.105, 391.109, and 391.113. *See also Owner-Operators Indep. Drivers Ass'n v. Burnley*, 705 F. Supp. 481, 3 IER Cases 1835 (N.D. Cal. 1989).
60. *Id.* §391.119.
61. 49 C.F.R. §40 (1988).
62. 48 C.F.R. §223-7500 (1988).
63. *Id.* §252.233-7500(a)(ii–iii); *see also* 67 DAILY LAB. REP. G-1 (BNA) (Apr. 10, 1989).
64. 51 Fed. Reg. 32,889 (1986).
65. *Id.* at 32,890.
66. *Id.*
67. FPM Letter 792-16(3)(a)(2) (1986).

68. *Id.* §3(c).
69. *Id.* §3(c)(2)(a–e).
70. *See, e.g., Treasury Employees v. Von Raab,* 489 U.S. ___, 4 IER Cases 246 (1989); *Mulholland v. Department of the Army,* 660 F. Supp. 1565, 2 IER Cases 868 (E.D. Va. 1987); *Gov't Employees v. Dole,* 670 F. Supp. 445, 2 IER Cases 841 (D.D.C. 1987); *Air Traffic Specialists v. Dole,* 2 IER Cases 68 (D. Alaska 1987); *Federal Employees v. Weinberger,* 818 F.2d 935, 2 IER Cases 145 (D.C. Cir. 1987); *Agriculture Employees v. Lyng,* 706 F. Supp. 934, 3 IER Cases 1779 (D.D.C. 1988); *Hansen v. Turnage,* 3 IER Cases 1181 (N.D. Cal. 1988). It is still unclear at this point whether the Supreme Court's recent decisions, as discussed earlier in this chapter, will settle many of the cases arising from the Executive Order or FPM Letter or whether more litigation will be spawned over the definition of sensitive positions, among other things.
71. Alaska const. art. I, §22 (1972). *Ravin v. State,* 537 P.2d 494 (Alaska 1975) (Alaska constitution protects individuals' possession of small amount of marijuana in own home).
72. Ariz. const. art. II, §8 (1912, as amended).
73. Cal. const. art. I, §1 (1972).
74. *White v. Davis,* 13 Cal.3d 757, 775, 533 P.2d 222 (1975) (California constitution prohibits public and private employers from secretly gathering personal information, and prohibits the overly broad collection or retention of personal information regarding employees or applicants, unless the employer has a "compelling interest"); *People v. Davis,* 92 Cal. App.3d 250, 260–1, 154 Cal. Rptr. 817, 813 (1979) (individual has no constitutional rights to use or possess cocaine at home); *National Org. for Reform of Marijuana Laws v. Gain,* 100 Cal. App.3d 586, 161 Cal. Rptr. 181 (1979) (individual has no constitutional right to possess marijuana in one's own home).
75. 264 Cal. Rptr. 194, 4 IER Cases 1579 (1989).
76. Fla. const. art. I, §23 (1980).
77. Fla. const. art. I, §12 (1968).
78. Haw. const. art. I, §5 (1968).
79. Ill. const. art. I, §12 (1970).
80. *See Barr v. Kelso-Burnett Co.,* 106 Ill.2d 520, 478 N.E.2d 1354, 120 LRRM 3401 (1985).
81. La. const. art. I, §5 (1975).
82. Mont. const. art. II, §10 (1972).
83. *Division of Medical Quality v. Gherardini,* 93 Cal. App.2d 669, 156 Cal. Rptr. 55 (1979).
84. Cal. Welf. & Inst. Code §4353 (1981).
85. Cal. Civ. Code §56 (1981).
86. Colo. Rev. Stat. §18-1-901 (1981).
87. Colo. Rev. Stat. §18-4-412 (1981).
88. Sections 455.241 and 395.017 (amended, 1983).
89. Mass. Gen. Laws ch. 214, §1B (1974).
90. 392 Mass. 508, 467 N.E.2d 126 (1984).
91. *Id.,* 467 N.E. 2d at 129; *see also Bratt v. IBM Corp.,* 785 F.2d 352 (1st Cir. 1986) (company policy that assures confidentiality of medical information, when coupled with Massachusetts state statute guaranteeing employee's right of privacy, imposed a "heavy burden" on employer to justify disclosure of medical information without consent of employee).

92. Minn. Stat. Ann. §595-02(4) (1986 & Supp. 1987).
93. Nev. Rev. Stat. §49.215-245 (1971).
94. R.I. Gen. Laws §5-37.3.3 (1978).
95. Tex. Rev. Civ. Stat. Ann. art. 4447d (1987).
96. Va. Code Ann. §2.1-342(b) (1988).
97. Wis. Stat. Ann.§146.82 (1980).
98. 1987 Conn. Acts §87-551:1 (1987).
99. Iowa Code §730.5 (1987).
100. Me. Rev. Stat. Ann. tit. 26, §681 (1989).
101. Minn. Stat. §181.950 (1987).
102. Mont. Code Ann. §39-2-304 (1987).
103. R.I. Gen. Laws §28-6.5-1 (1987).
104. Utah Code Ann. §34-38-1 (1987).
105. Vt. Stat. Ann. tit. 21, §511 (1987).
106. *Pittard v. Four Seasons Motor Inn*, 688 P.2d 333 (N.M. Ct. App. 1984), *appeal denied*, 685 P.2d 963 (N.M. 1984).
107. Occupational Safety and Health Act, 29 U.S.C. §654 (1970).
108. *Armstrong v. Morgan*, 545 S.W.2d 45 (Tex. Ct. App. 1976).
109. *Triblo v. Quality Clinical Laboratories*, Docket No. 82-226166-C2 (Mich. App. July 15, 1982).
110. *Olson v. Western Airlines*, 191 Cal. Rptr. 502 (Cal. App. 1983).
111. *Chesterman v. Barmon*, 727 P.2d 130, 1 IER Cases 1385 (Or. Ct. App. 1986), *aff'd*, 753 P.2d 404 (Or. 1988) (plurality opinion).
112. *Merritt v. Detroit Memorial Hosp.*, 265 N.W.2d 124 (Mich. Ct. App. 1978).
113. 548 S.W.2d 743 (Tex. Ct. App. 1976), *cert. denied*, 434 U.S. 962 (1977).
114. *O'Brien v. Papa Gino's of Am.*, 780 F.2d 1067, 1 IER Cases 458, 121 LRRM 2321 (1st Cir. 1986).
115. *See, e.g., Parnar v. Americana Hotels*, 65 Haw. 370, 652 P.2d 625, 115 LRRM 4817 (1982).
116. *Kelsay v. Motorola*, 74 Ill.2d 172, 384 N.E.2d 353, 115 LRRM 4371 (1978) (filing a workers compensation claim); *Nees v. Hocks Laboratories*, 536 P.2d 512, 115 LRRM 4571 (Or. Sup. Ct. 1975) (filing safety complaint); *Garibaldi v. Lucky Food Stores*, 726 F.2d 1367, 1 IER Cases 354, 115 LRRM 3089 (9th Cir. 1984), *cert. denied*, 471 U.S. 1099, 1 IER Cases 848, 119 LRRM 2248 (1985).
117. *Greco v. Halliburton Co.*, 674 F. Supp. 1447, 2 IER Cases 1281 (D. Wyo. 1987).
118. *See, e.g., Toussaint v. Blue Cross & Blue Shield*, 408 Mich. 579, 292 N.W.2d 880, 115 LRRM 4708 (1980); *Small v. Springs Indus.*, 292 S.C. 492, 357 S.E.2d 452, 2 IER Cases 266 (1987).
119. *See, e.g., Pine River State Bank v. Mettille*, 333 N.W.2d 622, 115 LRRM 4493 (Minn. 1983).
120. *Mau v. Omaha Nat'l Bank*, 207 Neb. 308, 299 N.W.2d 147, 115 LRRM 4992 (1980).
121. *See, e.g., Eales v. Tanana Valley Medical Group*, 663 P.2d 958, 115 LRRM 4505 (Alaska 1983).
122. *Supra* note 118.
123. *Cleary v. American Airlines*, 11 Cal. App.3d 443, 168 Cal. Rptr. 722, 115 LRRM 3030 (1980).

124. *Maddaloni v. Western Mass. Bus Lines*, 368 Mass. 877, 438 N.E.2d 351 (1982).
125. *Gates v. Life of Mont. Ins. Co.*, 196 Mont. 178, 638 P.2d 1063, 118 LRRM 2071 (1982).
126. *Supra* note 117.
127. 42 C.F.R. Part II, ¶2.1 et seq.
128. *Id.* ¶2.31(a).
129. 42 U.S.C. §290dd-3 and ee-3 (as amended 1986).
130. 42 C.F.R. Part II, ¶2.14.
131. *Woolley v. Hoffmann-LaRoche*, 491 A.2d 1257, 119 LRRM 2380 (N.J. Sup. Ct. 1985).
132. 118 Cal. Rptr. 129, 529 P.2d 553 (1974), *vacated on other grounds*, 131 Cal. Rptr. 14, 551 P.2d 334 (1976).
133. *Id.*, 551 P.2d at 340.
134. *Division of Corrections, Dep't of Health & Social Servs. v. Neakok*, 721 P.2d 1121 (Alaska 1986); *Bradley Center v. Wessner*, 161 Ga. App. 576, 287 S.E.2d 716, *aff'd*, 250 Ga. 199, 296 S.E.2d 693 (1982); *Evans v. Morehead Clinic*, 749 S.W.2d 696 (Ky. Ct. App. 1988); *McIntosh v. Milano*, 168 N.J. Super. 466, 403 A.2d 500 (1979); *Peck v. Counselling Serv. of Addison County*, 146 Vt. 61, 499 A.2d 422 (1985); *see also Lipari v. Sears, Roebuck & Co.*, 497 F. Supp. 185 (D. Neb. 1980) (construing Nebraska law).
135. Cal. Civ. Code §43.92 (1985).
136. *Bradley Center v. Wessner*, 250 Ga. 199, 296 S.E.2d 693 (1982).
137. *Buwa v. Smith*, 84-1905 NMT (Cir. Ct., Berrieu County, Mich., Aug. 20, 1986).
138. *Allegheny v. American Car & Foundry Co.*, 198 F.447 (M.D. Pa. 1912), *cert. denied*, 231 U.S. 747 (1913).
139. *See Houston Belt & Terminal Ry. v. Wherry*, 548 S.W.2d 743 (Tex. Ct. App. 1976), *cert. denied*, 434 U.S. 962 (1977).
140. Finally, as an aid to employers and legal counsel, the Table of Cases immediately preceding the Index has been provided as a compilation of the major cases which have shaped the development of the law in the area of substance abuse. In addition, the current status of cases pending in the federal courts is contained in the Drug Prevention Litigation Report available from the U.S. Department of Justice, Civil Division.

Part Two

Guidelines for Establishing Substance Abuse Policies, Procedures, and Training

Chapter 3

Developing a Substance Abuse
Policy Statement

A comprehensive program for dealing with substance abuse in the workplace should always include the three principles (or three P's) of good human relations—policy, procedure, and program. Where these three principles were a luxury in the past, they are now a necessity if an employer wants its substance abuse program to work. Education and training of management and employees on substance abuse in general and the employer's program in particular are critical for proper understanding and acceptance of and cooperation with the substance abuse program by all the parties involved.

In general, an employer first should establish a clearly articulated *policy* on the subject of substance abuse and communicate the policy to all applicants and employees. Second, definitive *procedures* should be developed, communicated, implemented, and consistently administered to all employees, including management. Third, where employees with substance abuse problems are identified, the employer's *program* dealing with substance abuse should be developed and explained to all employees.

Having a clearly defined, written, and well-communicated substance abuse policy, procedure, and program is absolutely critical to accomplishing the employer's objective of preventing substance abuse in the workplace. It is also, however, only half of the battle. The other half consists of implementing the process consistently. Any wavering or inconsistency in the administration of the program can be devastating to the employee's perception of the fairness of the program. This is not to say there can be no flexibility. As a matter of fact, there is a significant amount of interpretation and flexibility necessary in dealing with substance abuse problems, but, if the employer wants the program to work, the employee perception of consistency is critical.

Part One of this book introduced the problem of substance abuse and discussed why employers should establish policies and procedures for dealing with the problem. Additionally, that section discussed the current status of the law related to workplace substance abuse issues and practical considerations that help employers to minimize legal exposure. Part Two begins by examining the technical aspects of substance abuse policies and procedures and moves on to discuss education and training programs that are necessary for the proper communication and implementation of the employer's substance abuse program.

Need for a Firm Foundation

A clear and comprehensive policy statement is the foundation of a successful substance abuse program. Its importance cannot be overemphasized because the policy explains management's position on substance abuse, establishes goals for the eradication of substance abuse in the workplace, and introduces a plan for the achievement of those goals. Thus, drafting a policy statement is the first step in implementing a substance abuse program.

Developing a Philosophy

An effective policy statement should be thoughtfully considered before being initiated. Management must adopt a philosophy that will provide continuity under the varying circumstances in which the substance abuse program will be applied. A basic philosophical decision, for example, is whether management's response to substance abuse will be punitive or rehabilitative. If management's response is punitive, to what extent will the employee be punished? Will punishment begin with a warning, suspension, or immediate discharge? If management's response is rehabilitative, how far will management go in its efforts to restore the employee to productivity? To what extent in terms of cost and administration is management committed to rehabilitation? Other philosophical decisions that must be made involve management's position on health, safety, quality control, security, and morale. These decisions, among others which will be suggested in this chapter, must be made early in the planning of a substance abuse program, and the policy statement must reflect management's underlying philosophy to provide a basis for future action.

Management Support

The policy statement must reflect the philosophy of top management and front-line management alike. Otherwise, the program will fail in practice because it will be enforced inconsistently, and employees will sense a lack of enthusiasm for it on the part of some managers.

At the philosophy development stage, top management should call a meeting that would involve all of the various interests within the company or agency. Those invited at a minimum would include executives, and representatives from operations, personnel or human resources, legal, medical, occupational safety, and other affected areas of the organization. To the extent that these departments exist, all should come prepared to discuss the problem and make suggestions on the basic approach the employer should take to the problem of substance abuse. In addition, it is not unusual for managers to ask other employers about their substance abuse programs.

Once this initial meeting or series of meetings has taken place, it is important that top management meet with front-line management so that the front-line managers will be able to share their experiences with and opinions about substance abuse problems in the workplace, as well as their own ideas about how the substance abuse problem can be stopped. A special meeting or meetings with front-line management or supervisors will underscore top management's commitment to pursue the goals of the policy statement aggressively. Requesting the participation of, and integrating the expertise of, front-line managers in development of the policy will give them a vested interest in the program and avoid the mistake of developing a substance abuse program in a vacuum based on top management's beliefs alone.

Union Support

Employers with a unionized work force should consider involving union representatives in the drafting of a policy statement to ensure their support for the substance abuse program. If properly approached, the union will accept the program for what it is—a benefit for their members. Once the union has embraced the goals of the policy statement, they will insist that the program procedures be followed. As a result, front-line management will be more willing to use the program procedures.

Because of the traditionally adversarial nature of labor-management relations, cooperation may not be likely at first. However, an informal labor-management committee may succeed where a formal collective bargaining format would fail. Genuine efforts by management to involve union officials fully, from policy sessions to supervisor training sessions, will increase the probability of union support. Increasingly, substance abuse programs are being required of employers, particularly under federal and state drug free workplace requirements. Therefore, unions that until now have opposed substance abuse programs will be required to cooperate. In such circumstances, many unions are becoming more responsive to substance abuse problems in the workplace and more cooperative in working with management to develop such programs.

Written Policy

The policy statement must be in writing if it is to produce positive results. The written policy statement should articulate management's expectations in specific terms and let employees know the seriousness of management's concern with substance abuse.

Experts agree that supervisors are much more willing to enforce the provisions of the substance abuse program when a written policy statement exists.[1] Without clear guidance, supervisors and managers may not know how to deal with employees' substance abuse problems constructively. As a result, management will become frustrated as the program goes unenforced or is enforced in a manner that causes more problems than it solves. The written statement will give supervisors the guidance they need to do their part in ensuring the success of the overall program. Additionally, federal law now requires that certain government contractors not only have written policies, but also provide copies of these written policies to employees covered by these federal contracts.[2] With the rapidly increasing number of federal and state laws and regulations on the subject of substance abuse, a written policy should be considered mandatory, not advisable.

Issues to be Addressed

When drafting the policy statement, management should focus on the effect substance abuse has on an employee's ability to perform work satisfactorily and safely. Although a successful statement must be carefully crafted to meet the needs of individual employers, certain issues should always be considered in drafting a comprehensive policy statement.

Employee Health and Safety

Management's concern for the health and safety of its employees should be pointed out in the policy statement. Employees are the employer's most valuable resource, and their safety and overall well-being are extremely important. In this section of the policy, an employer usually states its commitment to safeguarding the health of its employees and to providing a safe place for its employees to work. An employer may also link its commitment with its employees to its commitment to its customers or clients in order to provide the highest quality product or service possible.

Recognition of Substance Abuse

The policy statement should show management's recognition of the problem of substance abuse and the dangers caused by alcohol and drugs in general and in the workplace in particular. Also, management's commitment to a drug free workplace. Employers usually recognize in this section that because substance abuse, either at work or away from work, can seriously endanger the safety of employees and render it impossible to supply top-quality products and services, the company has established the substance abuse program to detect users and rehabilitate or remove abusers of alcohol, drugs, or other controlled substances.

Illegal Drug Possession

Management's position on illegal drug possession, use, or sale on or off the job and/or on or off the employer's premises should be stated. Employees should be instructed that the possession, use, or sale of illegal drugs on or off the job or on or off the employer's premises is prohibited. Employers usually state in no uncertain terms that they are committed to preventing the use and/or presence of these substances in the workplace. Typical statements used by government contractors state that the employer "prohibits the unlawful manufacture, distribution, dispensation, presence, or use of alcohol, drugs, or other controlled substances on its property or worksites."

Alcohol

Management's position on alcohol use on the job and/or on the employer's premises, and the use of alcohol off the job that adversely affects an employee's job performance should be addressed.

Illegal Drug-Related Activities

The employer's position on illegal drug-related activities, arrests, and convictions should be explained, particularly when the employer is required to report drug-related convictions to federal or state authorities. For example, some employers state that "on projects covered by the Drug-Free Workplace Act or other federal or state contracts, laws, or regulations, all employees will be required to notify the employer of any conviction of a violation of a criminal drug statute in the workplace within five days, and the employer will so notify the federal or state contracting agency within ten days."

Job Performance

The relationship between drug and alcohol abuse and satisfactory job performance should be shown. Employees should be instructed regarding what constitutes unacceptable job performance, as well as management's concern for its business reputation and its commitment to maintaining the confidence of the public and to providing its customers or the public with high quality products and services.

Drug Testing

The employer's utilization of drug testing as it pertains to applicants and employees, and the circumstances where drug testing will be implemented, as well as itemization of the different types of drug testing is important in the policy statement. The usual types of drug testing include testing applicants as well as testing employees for cause; testing as part of annual or biennial physical examinations; testing employees who occupy sensitive positions from a safety, health, or security standpoint; testing where required by a customer's programs or by a contract with federal or state agencies; testing following accidents; or testing in conjunction with the employer's rehabilitation program.

Rehabilitation

Employees should be instructed by management as to the availability of employee assistance programs or referrals to outside agencies. For example, many employers state in the policy that the employer's employee assistance program is available to all employees and their families for the purpose of dealing with alcohol or drug problems (or other problems) before these problems become serious enough to affect job performance or become life-threatening. Often employers state the name of the EAP or rehabilitation facility in the policy or give a phone number that employees and their families can use.

Penalties

The penalties for violating the policy should be listed. Employees should be instructed that violation of the policy may result in disciplinary action up to and including discharge.

Education

Since education programs are required by certain federal laws or regulations, many employers describe their program concerning management's commitment to educating employees and others concerning substance abuse in general and in the workplace in particular. For instance, many employers will state that they will present a Drug Free Awareness Education Program for all supervisors and employees on a periodic basis.

Federal or State Law

Certain federal laws and regulations including the Drug Free Workplace Act of 1988, and regulations under the Department of Defense and Department of Transportation and other agencies, outline specific requirements that should be mentioned in the employer's policy. For instance, the Drug Free Workplace Act requires that employers give the employees a copy of the mandatory substance abuse policy. As a result, many employers incorporate these requirements into the policy to make sure that they are covered from a legal standpoint. Other federal requirements include education programs, notification of criminal convictions, requirements for employee assistance programs, and mandatory drug testing.

Scope

An explanation of the scope of the policy, or individuals covered by the policy, including applicants, employees, supervisors, and outside vendors and contractors must be addressed. It is important for an employer to state precisely whom the policy is intended to cover so that an individual may not later claim ignorance or lack of notice. It is also helpful for employee morale if employees in non-management positions understand that their supervisors are expected to abide by the same rules.

Depending upon the employer's preference, some of these issues may be addressed in the procedure section of the substance abuse policy rather than in the policy statement.

Policy Communication to Employees

Complete communication of the substance abuse policy to all people affected by it is imperative. Management, supervisors, unions, and employees at all levels, as well as anyone doing business with the company, must clearly understand what is expected of them and the consequences that may result from failure to adhere to the policy. To reiterate: The policy should be presented in writing to all employees and supervisors.

The policy statement should be read at employee meetings and at orientation of new employees. It should be included in the employer's manual of rules and regulations, as well as in any employee handbook.

If the employer has a newsletter or some other publication, the policy statement should be described and elaborated upon in a positive way as it relates to health, safety, and quality control at the employer's facilities. Employees should be encouraged to make comments and suggestions as to how the policy might be improved. Other methods for effectively communicating the policy statement include letters to employees' homes and announcements on bulletin boards.

Employee Acknowledgement of Policy

Because of the increasing complexity of substance abuse programs, including increased federal, state, and contractor- or vendor-required participation, many employers have concluded that precise acknowledgement by an employee or any others covered by their substance abuse policy is essential. Acknowledgement may be accomplished by the employee signing a form acknowledging that he or she has read the employer's substance abuse policy, has had it explained to him or her, or has received a copy of the policy. In dealing with contractors and vendors, often the substance abuse program requirement is made a provision of the contract between the parties. Predictably, as substance abuse programs continue to proliferate, particularly with greater governmental involvement, acknowledgement becomes important from a legal standpoint in order to avoid claims of ignorance of the policy or lack of notice.

Conclusion

The policy statement is the first step in developing a comprehensive substance abuse program. It is a critical element because it allows the employer to explain to its employees its philosophy concerning substance abuse and how the employer intends to handle the problem. A policy statement should reflect a commitment to safeguarding the health of employees, to providing a safe work environment for employees, and to ensuring high quality products and services to customers. Appendix D provides four sample substance abuse policies. Appendix C, "Model Policy, Procedures, Programs," provides a complete example of a model policy, procedure, and program.

Notes

1. Beyer & Trice, "A Field Study of the Use and Perceived Effects of Discipline in Controlling Work Performance," 27 *Academy of Management Journal*, Vol. 27, 1984, 743–64. "A written, published drug testing policy that takes steps to conduct testing in the least offensive manner possible would also be helpful in obviating employees' privacy expectations and in preserving the dignity of the employee." DeCresce, et al., *Drug Testing in the Workplace* (Washington, D.C.: BNA Books, 1989), 31.

2. Under the Drug Free Workplace Act, employers must "publish[] a statement notifying employees that the unlawful manufacture, distribution, dispensation, possession, or use of a controlled substance is prohibited in the person's workplace and specifying the actions that will be taken against employees for violations of such prohibition. . . ." Pub. L. No. 100-690 tit. V, subtitle D, §5152 (a)(1)(A).

Chapter 4

Developing Substance Abuse Procedures

General Considerations

A drug free workplace cannot be achieved simply by setting lofty goals in a policy statement. Management must approach the goal of eradicating drugs in the workplace the same as it would any other business goal. Management must be willing to develop definitive procedures directed toward achieving a drug free workplace and, more important, it must consistently apply these procedures. An extensive collection of sample procedures appears in Appendix E, "Substance Abuse Procedures."

The importance of consistently applied procedures cannot be overstated. Procedures should respond to employees' concerns for fair treatment. Employees fear being treated harshly or arbitrarily, and experience indicates that their fears are not unfounded if they work for an employer that operates without written procedures. Those employers often deal with substance abuse on an ad hoc basis which results in an escalation of disruptive behavior until finally the impaired employee is discharged.[1] Employees are resentful when management treats certain individuals more harshly than others. They want to be assured that certain actions will result in certain reactions by management. Procedures answer those concerns because the procedures provide predictability. With procedures in place, employees are put on notice that management will not tolerate certain activities. Employees are also made fully aware of any penalties or programs that will result if they fail to meet management's standards. When the procedures are consistently applied and enforced, management will hear far fewer complaints of unfair or disparate treatment.

73

Procedures tend to alleviate discipline problems, many of which occur where management ignores its substance abuse problem. Employees are more likely to conform their behavior to meet management's standards when they are fully aware of what those standards are and how they can comply.

Procedures also provide guidance to managers and supervisors for the variety of situations they will encounter in the substance abuse program. Managers and supervisors will have confidence in their response to those situations because the procedures will have been thoughtfully considered and ratified in advance by management.

Management Support

Getting management support at the theoretical or policy statement stage is relatively simple, but getting management support at the procedural stage is another matter entirely. The procedural stage is the point at which the rhetoric ends and the work begins. In many cases, the commitment of management's time will be more difficult to obtain than financial support.

The effective implementation of procedures requires management support at every level. Top-level management support is critical, but it will not ensure the wholehearted implementation of procedures. The front-line managers must follow procedures on a daily basis and, consequently, the degree of their support will determine the success or failure of the procedural aspect of the substance abuse program.

Top-level management must provide the proper example. Research indicates that managers who support and implement procedures, regardless of their level of power, usually do so because they perceive a need for it.[2] Their perception is greatly affected by the intensity or ambivalence with which top management approaches implementation of the program. Top management, then, must concentrate on completely familiarizing "lower" managers with procedures and impressing upon them the importance of full implementation for the overall success of the program.

Written Procedures

If a written policy statement is important, written procedures are essential. In an area this complicated, written detailed procedures are crucial if the employer expects lower management and employees to comply. In addition, procedures that are written and explained to employees provide a defense for management against any litigation involving the substance abuse program. However, if management fails to comply with a written procedure, that procedure can be a valuable offensive weapon in an employee's lawsuit.

The key to writing successful procedures is simplicity. Employees have argued successfully in arbitration hearings that procedures must be understandable and not burdensome to comply with.[3] Nonetheless, procedures must be sufficiently specific. They must anticipate a variety of circumstances that may arise, and must equip management to address them. They should specifically define the substances and activities that are prohibited by the program and the criteria that define terms such as "impairment" and "substance abuse."[4] Moreover, the procedures should be easily understood and carefully written so that the supervisors implementing the procedures will be able to walk through the details effectively and accurately. If supervisors get confused or lost they will either not implement the program or, worse, will do it improperly and possibly illegally.

Communication and Education

Communication of procedures to all people affected by them is a more involved process than communication of the policy statement because of the greater specificity and detail. Consequently, the communication of procedures requires an education beyond the mere reading of the policy and procedure statements to employees. Top management must begin educating and training those who will be affected by the procedures long before they are implemented, a process that will be somewhat more involved for front-line management than for employees.

Although education and training will be dealt with in more detail in Chapter 5, "Substance Abuse Education and Training," it should be noted here that supervisors and employees must be taught the problems of substance abuse, the manner in which it affects their performance on the job, and the procedures that will be used to implement the substance abuse program. Comprehensive education will ensure that every employee is aware of the procedures and understands the purposes of the policy.

Date Certain

The implementation of procedures should occur on a "date certain" some time in the future. The process of management support, drafting the procedure, and educating all those affected by it should be carefully coordinated in advance and should climax at the date certain. Then, no one can claim to be caught off guard, and sufficient notice will have been given. As a result, front-line management will be prepared to implement the procedure and employees will have sufficient time to bring themselves into compliance, if necessary. The temptation of many employers is to spring a substance abuse program—particularly the drug testing—on employees and nail the offenders quickly and decisively in a blitzkrieg-type operation. This is a mistake. Successful substance abuse prevention must be thought of as a process—a long-term plan that knows no ending. Therefore, an employer should tell its employees about its substance abuse program, implement the program, and stick to it unwaveringly. If the policy is the skeleton, then the procedure is the muscle, nerve, and sinew that makes the substance abuse program work.

Guidelines for Developing Procedures

Initial Step: Summary

Procedural provisions may take a variety of forms, but they must adequately explain to employees how the substance abuse program will be run. Management may choose to begin its explanation of procedures with a summary. The summary should immediately follow the policy statement and preview the more detailed procedures that will follow. The summary will outline the procedures and cover the basic elements of the procedures that implement the employer's substance abuse policy. For instance, in the summary the employer will cover many of the following subjects:

- The prohibition against alcohol or drugs in the workplace;
- The employer's substance abuse education program;
- The applicant drug testing procedures;
- The employee drug testing procedures such as new employee testing, annual or biennial physical testing, for-cause testing, safety-sensitive position testing, post-accident testing, and rehabilitation testing;
- The outside contractor or vendor substance abuse program;
- The federal or state legal requirements; and/or
- Other provisions.

The employer has substantial latitude as to what its procedures will involve, but the following procedures should be considered:

Continuing Education

The employer should consider a continuing education program for all employees which would be presented on a periodic basis in an effort to keep employees aware of problems associated with drug and alcohol use and abuse. For some employers, education programs are mandatory. For instance, under certain federal laws and regulations, most notably the Drug Free Workplace Act of 1988, the employer must establish a drug free awareness program that informs employees of the dangers of drug abuse in the workplace, the employer's policy of maintaining a drug free environment, and any available counseling, rehabilitation, and assistance programs. The employer's education program under the Drug Free Workplace Act must also inform employees of the penalties that may be imposed for violation of the policy. As a result, many employers have implemented education and training programs for supervisors and employees alike. Without such an education program, many employers have found that employees lack understanding of the problem, and supervisors lack understanding of the employer's substance abuse program. Therefore, increasingly, employers are developing or purchasing continuing education programs that are presented to supervisors and employees on at least an annual basis.

Generally speaking, employers will develop continuing education programs for supervisors which cover subjects such as drug awareness and symptoms of drug use; recommended methods for dealing with suspected drug users; types and effects of drugs; symptoms of drug use and effects on performance and conduct; the relationship of the employee assistance program (EAP) to the drug testing program; the employer's substance abuse policy, procedure, and program; and other relevant treatment, rehabilitation, and confidentiality issues.

Education programs for employees usually concentrate on the types and effects of drugs; the symptoms of drug use and the effects on performance and conduct; the relationship of the EAP to the drug testing program; the employer's substance abuse policy, procedures, and program; and other relevant treatment, rehabilitation, and confidentiality issues.

Methods of education may take a variety of forms such as distribution of written materials, audio or video programs, consultant group discussions and presentations, lunch-time employee meetings, and/or employee drug awareness days.

Scope and Application

It is important that the employer spell out the scope and application of the substance abuse policy in the procedural section. Usually a substance abuse program will apply to all employees whether they are management, administrative, or hourly employees, and often temporary employees as well. However, some employers may find it necessary to apply their substance abuse policy differently to different groups of employees or outsiders for reasons that are unique to them. For example, many employers now require that outside contractors and vendors certify that they are in compliance with the particular employer's substance abuse program when the contractor's or vendor's employees are on the employer's property. Other employers, such as governmental contractors or governmental agencies, will find it necessary to apply certain aspects of their policy to certain employees, such as employees in sensitive positions, pilots, police officers, or nuclear plant operators, but not to others. It is important to spell out the scope and application of the policy so that an employee or other affected individual cannot later claim that he or she had no notice or are not covered by the policy.

Definition of Substance Abuse

Most employers find it useful to define the terms of substance abuse that they are dealing with or referring to in their policy. Usually these procedural sections are very broad and make no attempt to be all-inclusive for two reasons: new drugs of abuse may be developed over time, and the employer may not think of all of the particular drugs of abuse at the time the policy is written. Generally speaking, any drug or substance, including alcohol, that can be used or abused and that can affect job performance is a legitimate subject of inquiry and should be covered by the substance abuse policy and procedure.

Often the employer will either define substance abuse or explain what it means by "legal" and "illegal" drugs. Substance abuse is usually defined as reporting to work or working while under the influence of, using, or being impaired by alcohol or any other drug; chemical dependency on alcohol or other drugs where job performance or safety of employees is adversely affected; or the use of illegal drugs.

Illegal drugs are fairly easily defined as those drugs that are controlled substances included in Schedule I or II of Section 812 of Title 21 of the United States Code, the possession of which is unlawful under Section 841 of Title 21. Also, many employers will cite their state statutes, where applicable, which are usually recitations of federal law and regulations concerning control of substances. However, many other employers simply state that illegal drugs include those controlled substances under federal or state law which are not authorized for sale, possession, or use, and legal drugs which are obtained, used, or distributed illegally.

Increasingly, employers also have to deal with the problem of improper use of legal drugs. Therefore, many employers state that legal drugs include alcohol, medications prescribed by physicians, and over-the-counter medications. Employers then prohibit the use or abuse of such drugs to the extent that job performance or fitness for duty is adversely affected. Further, many employers require the employee to notify the supervisor when taking prescribed medication and upon request, furnish the supervisor with the physician's statement regarding the possible or probable side effects of the medication.

The explanation of terms, whether they be controlled substance, psychoactive substance, illegal drug, or legal drug, is important because employees, where possible, will invariably try to argue that some particular substance is not covered by the employer's policy. Therefore, it is important that the employer write the procedure as broad as possible concerning potentially abused substances and their connection with job performance.

Drug Testing

Any discussion of substance abuse programs inevitably leads to the subject of drug testing. No procedural section in a substance abuse program is complete without an explanation of drug testing.

Drug testing is probably the most effective tool available to reduce drug abuse in the workplace. It sends a clear message to applicants, employees, and supervisors alike that drug use will be actively fought by the employer. Ultimately, drug testing provides a deterrent effect that mere education will not. It encourages non-drug-using employees to remain drug free, while it provides strong incentive for drug users to stop.

Drug testing is also useful to detect users for purposes of referral or discipline. Individuals with serious drug problems are unlikely to involve themselves voluntarily in the substance abuse program and may have escaped the notice of their supervisors. Generally speaking, however, drug testing, or urine screening for the purposes of this discussion, should be viewed only as a "tool of proof" (albeit an effective one) in an overall substance abuse program. It is critically important not to make drug testing the focus of a substance abuse program. It should be viewed only as a necessary element of the program. Drug testing provides the proof of substance abuse. And, in spite of occasional protestations otherwise, an employer can rely on a confirmed positive drug test (confirmed by gas chromatography/mass spectrometry (GC/MS)) in making decisions on substance abuse. In addition, drug testing is the best stick developed to date in the usual carrot-and-stick approach of well-defined substance abuse programs. That is, if the employee does not take the carrot of rehabilitation and abstinence, the drug testing stick will prove his or her deviation from the program and subject the individual to discipline or termination.

Therefore, in most substance abuse programs, when it comes to drug testing, the question is not whether to include drug testing as a procedure in an employer's substance abuse program; the question involves such issues as whom to test, under what circumstances to test, and what to do with employees who test positive? These questions will be discussed below within the various categories of testing options available.

Applicant or Pre-Employment Testing

The employer's substance abuse program should always include the testing of applicants. Testing applicants will not cause morale problems because the employer and the applicant have not yet developed a working relationship. The drug testing of applicants allows the employer to avoid hiring a substance abusing employee, which will save the employer countless dollars and problems. In addition, existing employees will expect applicants to be held to the same or higher standards of the substance abuse program that they are, and will expect the employer to do everything possible to stop substance abusing individuals from entering the workplace. It should be reiterated that most employees do not use drugs. Therefore, applicant testing is the first line of defense to keep substance abusers out of the work force.

For employers subject to the National Labor Relations Act, it should be noted that the National Labor Relations Board has ruled that an employer must bargain prior to establishing drug and alcohol programs for current, unionized employees, but need not bargain prior to establishing testing programs that affect only job applicants. In contrast, the Supreme Court has ruled that employers subject to the Railway Labor Act can test their workers for drug and alcohol abuse without first engaging in negotiations with railway labor unions.[5]

Drug testing of applicants or pre-employment screening is widely accepted and widely implemented. As a matter of fact, applicant screening is probably the most utilized program for drug testing. An increasing number of companies throughout the United States test applicants, including a large percentage of the Fortune 500 companies. Furthermore, the federal government, whose employees have considerably more constitutional claims than private employees, has been authorized to develop and has implemented applicant testing programs in conjunction with an increasing array of federal statutes and regulations.[6]

Issues to be dealt with when testing applicants are as follows:

• Employment Policy—Testing of Applicants
• Notice/Posting
• Application Form/Medical History Questionnaire
• Consent and Release
• Collecting and Testing Procedures
• Contingent Employment
• Notification of Results and Confidentiality
• Opportunity to Contest Results
• Referral Options

The detailed procedures that are necessary concerning applicants are fairly straightforward.

Employment Policy—Testing of Applicants

The employer must establish that applicants are covered by the substance abuse policy, and that employment will be denied if the results of the drug screening test are positive. Also, many employers take the time to explain the company's substance abuse policy to each applicant for two reasons: so the applicant cannot later claim he or she was denied employment for reasons that were never explained; and because by explaining the substance abuse testing and policies to applicants and the reasons behind those policies, more of the public will be educated and informed concerning the problems of substance abuse.

Employer policies concerning applicants usually state that applicants will be tested as part of the application process, and that applicants will be advised of the testing requirements in detail and of the employer's substance abuse policy in general. Other employers provide for applicant testing as a part of routine pre-employment physical examinations. In most cases, the testing of applicants is very straightforward and relatively simple; nevertheless, it is extremely important to an employer's overall substance abuse program.

Notice/Posting

Many employers have found that by giving sufficient notice and/or posting of the fact that the employer subjects applicants to drug screening, substance abusers will refrain from seeking employment. To a certain extent this is probably true. However, many substance abusers have the attitude that they will not get caught, or believe they can refrain from using substances for a sufficient time to have the substances clear their systems, or substance abusers will attempt to beat the test. Nevertheless, notice and posting by means of signs or printed material may be a useful deterrent and certainly should be used in case the employer later needs to prove it gave notice.

Notices to applicants are very straightforward and usually state that "Applicants for employment will be required to undergo a drug screening test before consideration of employment," or "All applicants tentatively selected for this position will be required to submit to urinalysis to screen for illegal drug use prior to appointment."

Application Form/Medical History Questionnaire

Rarely do employers with substance abuse programs not make mention of the programs on the application form or the medical history questionnaire. The purpose of mentioning the substance abuse program and drug testing in the application or questionnaire is to provide notice to the applicant and to have the applicant acknowledge the notice and the fact that the program has been explained to him or her. Also, this is the best opportunity to insert a consent and release form. Since applicants sign application forms or medical history questionnaires, it is important for employers to use these forms effectively in order to document, at a minimum, the applicant's acknowledgement of the substance abuse program and drug testing.

Whereas the application form will provide an opportunity for the applicant to acknowledge the existence of, and his or her anticipated participation in the employer's substance abuse program, the medical history questionnaire is used for a variety of reasons. In addition to obtaining acknowledgement and consent, the medical history questionnaire, which should be studied carefully by the employer's medical personnel, may give indications of the employer's health problems related to substance abuse. For instance, if an applicant has been hospitalized frequently due to accidents, depression, or digestive tract or liver malfunction problems, the problem may be related to substance abuse. At any rate, an employer's medical history questionnaire should be studied thoroughly by health personnel in order to detect the potential for substance abuse among applicants.

Consent and Release

In order to perform a drug test, it is imperative that an employer obtain an informed consent from the applicant concerning this or any medical test. It is also imperative that the employer obtain a release from the applicant which will allow the laboratory to give the results of the test to the employer and the employer to take the appropriate action based on its substance abuse policy. Failure to obtain consent for the performance of a medical test subjects the employer and the laboratory to a "technical battery" for which they can be sued. Failure to obtain a release of liability for performing the test and releasing the results also could subject the employer and the laboratory to liability under various state statutes and/or common law principles concerning inappropriate taking of medical specimens, release of medical records, and possible invasion of privacy.[7]

It is not difficult, however, to avoid potential legal problems as long as the employer has a proper consent or release form. These forms should be *mandatory*. Consent or release forms, whether they are placed on the application, on the medical history questionnaire, or as a separate document, should always be included as part of the substance abuse policy and procedure. They should be signed and processed before the testing occurs. Additionally, many employers insist that these consent and release forms be witnessed.

The consent and release form should be as all-inclusive as possible. The form should state that the applicant understands that the employer has a substance abuse program and the details of the program have been explained to the applicant. The applicant should also be asked to consent freely and voluntarily to the request for urine or any other specimen or sample and to release the employer, the laboratory, their employees, agents, and contractors from any liability whatsoever arising from the request to furnish the urine or other specimen or sample. The applicant should be asked to consent to the appropriate chemical testing of the specimen or sample, give permission to the laboratory to release the test results to the employer, and yield to any decisions made concerning the application for employment or continued employment based on the results of the test.

The validity of consent and release forms is particularly important in dealing with minors or legal incompetents. In situations where minors are involved, such as substance abuse programs for schools or other educational institutions, the parent or legal guardian must sign the consent form. Likewise, in a situation where a legally incompetent person is to be tested, the legal guardian or personal legal representative must give consent and sign the form. Although these situations are not frequent except in educational institutions or student-work programs, they are an element that managers and substance abuse program administrators must take into account.

Failure to cover minors or legal incompetents in a consent and release form is a very serious mistake. Employers are advised to have their legal counsel develop and review consent and release forms to ensure that these forms meet all of the requirements of the locality involved.

Collection and Testing Procedures

These procedures will be discussed later in this chapter.

Contingent Employment

Many employers believe it is easiest to place the applicant/new employee in a contingent employment status until he or she has tested negative on the drug test or has been deemed able to meet "company medical standards." Employers vary as to whether they allow applicants/new employees to begin work prior to finding out the test results. In any case, if the applicant or new employee fails the drug test or is unable in any way to meet company medical standards, the employment relationship ends. If an employer takes the contingent employer approach, a simple statement in the procedural section will suffice. Employers often state that "acceptance for employment is contingent upon the determination that an applicant has successfully completed a drug screening test. No one shall be permitted to work until the results of the test have been obtained." An alternative is to state that "each applicant will be notified that appointment to the position will be contingent upon a negative drug test result."

In essence, employers often follow the contingent employment approach in order that they may easily terminate employment if the applicant tests positive. Otherwise, it is often troublesome to hire an employee, fill out the appropriate employer and governmental forms, put the employee to work and begin training, and then have to terminate the employee. The easiest approach is to offer the applicant employment contingent upon the results of the drug test, and not put the employee to work until the drug test results are known to be negative.

Notification of Results and Confidentiality

Notification of the results of the test is a critical aspect in the implementation of an employer's substance abuse program. How this information is handled, particularly when the results are positive, will influence how applicants and the public perceive the employer and its substance abuse program. In all cases, confidentiality should be maintained. Additionally, the employer should designate a specific individual or individuals to release the information to the applicant. Many employers utilize medical personnel or trained individuals in their personnel department to handle the release of any such confidential and sensitive information. The information should be released in person, not over the telephone, if at all possible.

If the results of the drug test are negative, then the process is fairly simple, and the employer's designated official informs the applicant of the negative test results and proceeds with the employment process. However, if the test results are positive, then the designated official should explain this fact to the applicant in conjunction with the employer's procedure and be willing to explain the results including review of the lab report that notes the drug involved and the confirmed positive result. If an employer's trained representative takes the time to explain the details involved with a confirmed positive result, the employer is much less likely to have to deal with the reactions of angry applicants or their families.

Furthermore, it is important that the employer deal directly with the applicant involved, and not the applicant's family members or friends, who may be upset with the test result. If an applicant who has been informed of a positive test result seeks legal counsel, then the employer's designated official should explain the testing procedure and the drug test results to the applicant's legal representative. It is also helpful in these circumstances for the employer to have a good working relationship with the laboratory in case further explanation is necessary. With these types of procedures arranged in advance, there usually is little difficulty in dealing with applicants concerning positive test results.

Where employers are not careful with the dissemination of the test results, they run the risk of being named in defamation, slander, or libel suits for any nonprivileged publication of the test results which may harm the reputation of the applicant. From a practical standpoint, it is not only unnecessary but extremely unwise to discuss test results with anyone other than the applicant.

In the employer's written procedures, confidentiality should be stressed in order to assure employees that the employer has taken every step it could to ensure confidentiality. In addition, confidentiality should be stressed so that employees involved in administering the program realize how important the subject is. Confidentiality should never be breached in substance abuse situations because to do so is to subject the employer to legal action. Furthermore, and perhaps more important, if the employer's managers or employees breach the confidentiality of applicants or others, it will undermine employees' confidence in the substance abuse program. Therefore, for legal and practical reasons, confidentiality should always be maintained.

Usually employers provide procedural sections that state that all information involving medical examinations and test results of any applicant will be treated as confidential medical information. Such information should only be accessible to those company officials and designated medical or professional persons with a valid need to know, and will not be provided to any other party without the written consent of the applicant, except pursuant to administrative or legal procedure or process. Other employers provide that test results will be kept strictly confidential and should be disclosed only to individuals such as medical officers, EAP administrators, designated management officials, or pursuant to court orders of competent jurisdiction. Often, test results, since they are medical tests, are subject to federal or state statutes or regulations providing for the confidentiality of results, and therefore, should be kept confidential.

Practically speaking, as long as an employer provides procedural safeguards regarding release of information of the test results on a very restricted basis, confidentiality should not be a problem. However, it is imperative that employers enforce this confidentiality requirement in order to maintain the integrity of the substance abuse program.

Opportunity to Contest Results

A number of employers, particularly government employers, believe that it is procedurally necessary to give an applicant the opportunity to contest positive test results. Although this subject will be discussed later in this chapter, suffice it to say that if the employer decides to give the applicant the opportunity to contest the positive results, it should be under very strict, controlled circumstances. An employer should never allow an applicant to bring in another specimen. A split sample (discussed later in this chapter) or the original sample *only* should be utilized.

Where an employer allows an applicant an opportunity to contest results, it is usually under two circumstances: utilization of a second specimen; or a second confirmation on the original specimen by a different laboratory. To give an applicant an opportunity to provide another specimen is ill-advised. As long as a proper chain of custody exists for the original specimen and as long as enough of the specimen has been retained by the laboratory for subsequent analysis, it is a bad idea to allow an applicant to provide a second specimen which may be either the applicant's specimen after the drugs have cleared his or her system or someone else's specimen. On the other hand, since licensed laboratories are required to maintain the positive specimen for at least one year,[8] it is permissible to allow either the original laboratory to conduct a second, confirmation test using GC/MS, or allow the preserved specimen to be tested by another laboratory, as long as the confirmation technique is by GC/MS and the proper chain of custody is maintained. Usually, if an employer gives the opportunity to contest the results, the confirmation should be performed by the original laboratory at the applicant's expense.

If the confirmation test is positive, and the applicant does not provide a satisfactory explanation for the results, then the applicant should again be informed of the results of the drug test and denied employment. On the other hand, if the results of the confirmation test are negative, the applicant should be reimbursed the cost of the additional test and the results of the initial positive test should not be used to deny employment.

The most likely situation where applicants will contest the test results is where they have a prescription for the particular drug that has been found in the test results. In such cases employers should provide an opportunity to discuss the matter with the applicant, review the prescription and even contact the prescribing physician concerning the prescription in order to determine its validity and accuracy. In such situations where an applicant has tested positive for codeine, for example, or some other medically used drug that would be detected in the drug screening process, an employer still retains the option of deciding if the applicant should be hired, particularly if the employer is concerned that the applicant's prescription drug may affect job performance.

Experience has shown that it is rare for applicants to contest the results and proceed with a second testing, but employers, particularly governmental employers, should consider the procedure to contest results in their substance abuse program.

Referral Options

A number of employers, in dealing with applicants who have tested positive, take the approach that the applicant will not be considered further. However, more enlightened employers, at a minimum, will refer the applicant to substance abuse treatment facilities and give the applicant an opportunity to do something about his or her substance abuse problem. Experience has shown that this referral procedure does not cost the employer anything, certainly is a goodwill measure, and occasionally results in the applicant seeking rehabilitation. This approach is particularly useful if the employer intends to reconsider the applicant at some future date. In that case, employers can either refer the applicant to rehabilitation facilities in the general area, or possibly give the applicant notice of his or her opportunity to reapply after some specified period of time.

It is usually helpful for employers to develop a list of referral agencies for applicants who test positive. It is even more useful for the employer to meet representatives from each of these referral agencies, which are usually governmental agencies, in order to reach an understanding of what the employer expects of the referral agency. In the process, the employer can begin to understand the rehabilitation programs available and determine if those programs meet the employer's standards for rehabilitation. Realizing that many of these agencies have limited resources, the employer should develop as large a referral list as possible in order to give willing applicants an opportunity to seek suitable rehabilitation.

Another option for employers is to allow a rejected applicant to reapply for a job and to resubmit to drug testing after a certain specified period of time, usually three to six months. In this case, the employer should stress that an applicant who undergoes rehabilitation will be considered more favorably than someone who simply reapplies after the specified period of time without being rehabilitated.

Many employers have developed referral notices which are signed by the employer and the applicant and which indicate that the applicant has tested positive on the screen test and will not be considered by the employer for employment at that time, but state that the applicant is given an opportunity to receive professional evaluation and/or the opportunity to enter a rehabilitation program at the applicant's expense at a facility approved by the employer. These referral notices formalize the rejection and referral process, encourage the applicant to seek rehabilitation for the substance abuse problem, and cover the employer from a legal standpoint if the employer's substance abuse program is ever questioned concerning the approach to rejection of applicants. More important, referral for rehabilitation is a humane way of approaching the rejection of an applicant for substance abuse reasons, and may be the impetus that leads to an applicant's seeking help.

Employee Testing

The most critical aspects of any written substance abuse procedures are the sections dealing with employee testing.

An increasing number of employers in the United States have implemented drug testing procedures for current employees. Most employers anticipate terrible problems, including deterioration of morale, sabotage, or extensive litigation, when they consider testing current employees. Rarely do such problems surface. If an employer develops a comprehensive substance abuse program, of which testing is only a part, and if the employer properly communicates the substance abuse program, current employees rarely have a problem with the concept of the program. It is important to realize that most people do not use drugs, particularly drugs of abuse. However, most employees are beginning to realize the destructive potential, lost productivity, and danger associated with fellow employees who are substance abusers. As a result, if the employees perceive that the employer has a fair and equitable substance abuse program, most will be in favor of the drug testing aspect of the program. In fact, in most cases employees are delighted that the employer has developed a substance abuse program including drug testing because they are fearful of the dangers caused by substance abusing employees in the workplace.

Other sections of this book deal with areas such as communication of the substance abuse program,[9] drug testing as a mandatory subject of bargaining and the nature of testing current employees in unionized companies, and the various requirements concerning drug testing of current employees imposed by federal and state constitutions, statutes, and regulations and the interpretations given these laws by the courts.[10] This portion of the chapter will begin by dealing with the types of current employee tests most commonly seen: mandatory, across-the-board testing; annual physical biennial, or periodic recurring testing; probationary employee testing; "safety-sensitive position" testing; "for-cause" testing; post-accident testing; contractor testing; and random testing. Also, this section will describe other specific procedural provisions related to testing.

Types of Current Testing

Mandatory, Across-the-Board Testing. Many employers, particularly smaller, private companies with 150 or fewer employees, have found that the most expeditious way to ascertain substance abuse compliance is to require mandatory, across-the-board testing of all employees. As long as the employer establishes a comprehensive substance abuse program and is willing to work with employees who have a problem with substance abuse, there is rarely any problem posed by this approach. It is perfectly legal for a private employer to test all of its employees, assuming there are no state or local statutes or ordinances against such a practice and provided the employer bargains prior to establishing drug and alcohol programs for currently unionized employees.[11] Oftentimes in order to begin a substance abuse program, to be in compliance with federal, state, or customer specification, or for other reasons, an employer will arrange a mandatory, across-the-board program. Usually employers who opt for this type of program desire to get their substance abuse program in place, deal with the employees who have a problem, if any, and then transform their program into an ongoing program with other forms of testing such as annual testing or for-cause testing. Mandatory, across-the-board testing programs for governmental employees are not seen as often on the federal or state level, but are more frequent on the county, local, or authority level, particularly for safely-sensitive positions such as police officer or firefighter.[12]

Annual Physical, Biennial, or Fitness for Duty. An increasing number of employers are recognizing the connection between substance abuse and health. As a result, many employers' substance abuse programs require drug testing during the annual physical of the employee. Also, an increasing number of employers, particularly public employers and construction industry firms, refer to the examinations as "fitness-for-duty" examinations. Many employers, particularly in the transportation or nuclear power industries, are required by federal regulation to drug test employees on a biennial basis or on a periodic recurring basis in accordance with required federal or state certification.[13]

Usually, private employers will state that drug tests will be performed on eligible employees as a part of annual physical examinations or periodic recurring physical examinations or biennial physical examinations where the examinations are required by law, regulation, or company policy, or routinely performed pursuant to company or location policy. Employers involved in the transportation industry, which is regulated by the Department of Transportation, are required to have biennial testing of drivers and periodic testing of pilots.[14]

Many public employers require annual medical examinations or physical examinations for all positions considered sensitive from a health and safety standpoint and positions that may directly affect public safety or employee safety. These annual examinations usually include drug testing, and the most usual employee categories subject to testing are police officers, firefighters, drivers of vehicles, or other such employees.[15]

Probationary Testing. A number of employers have developed probationary employee testing programs. The theory behind these programs is that an applicant may be able to temporarily abstain from using substances and thereby "beat the test." As a result, some employers have found it necessary to establish testing programs during a probationary period for new hires. The probationary period may last only for the first three months of the new employee's career, or it may last for 12 months. Probationary employee testing varies from being fixed at certain intervals, usually quarterly, to being done on a random basis any time during the probationary period.

"Safety-Sensitive Position" Testing. Increasingly, employers with employees in "safety-sensitive" positions are requiring drug testing of these employees on a much more frequent basis than other employees. Safety-sensitive positions may include airplane pilots, heavy machinery or equipment operators, railroad engineers, truck drivers, vehicle operators, police officers, firefighters, bus drivers, handlers of hazardous materials, workers involved with nuclear materials, employees involved in the drug interdiction effort, employers authorized to bear arms, employees with classified information, and employees whose work may involve national security.[16]

Safety-sensitive position testing is also required of certain government employees and federal contractors doing business with the government under various federal statutes and regulations.[17] Recently the Supreme Court ruled in several cases that employees involved with heavily regulated industries with safety concerns such as the railroad industry,[18] Customs Service employees seeking transfer or promotion to positions having a direct involvement in drug interdiction or positions requiring employees to carry firearms,[19] and employees in numerous other safety-sensitive positions[20] could be drug tested to assure that these employees were drug free and were not a threat to the safety and health of other employees or the public. The Supreme Court found that the individual employee's concerns for privacy rights were outweighed by the employer's concerns for safety and health.

Where employers have employees in safety-sensitive positions, the most expeditious way of handling drug testing is to define the positions that are subject to drug testing, notify the employees that they are involved in safety-sensitive positions, and carry out the employer's substance abuse program. Usually employees categorized in safety-sensitive positions are tested at least annually and often on a random basis.

"For-Cause" Testing. Most substance abuse programs involving drug testing have provisions providing for the testing of employees who are suspected of being impaired on the job, whose work performance has deteriorated, or who are suspected of substance abuse. Testing provisions on this basis are "for cause" since the employer has a reasonable suspicion that the employee may be impaired due to substance abuse.[21]

It is important that for-cause testing be implemented on a fair and equitable basis. Supervisors should be trained in recognizing symptoms of possible substance abuse as they relate to work performance. The more objective the criteria, the greater the likelihood of achieving the goals of the employer's substance abuse program and dealing with the potential substance abusing employee, and providing a sustainable case if the situation is challenged legally.[22] Examples of cause factors that indicate that the employee may be impaired are as follows:

- Sudden changes in work performance;
- Repeated failure to follow instruction or operating procedures;
- Violation of employer's safety policies;
- Unexplained significant deterioration in job performance;
- Excessive tardiness;
- Excessive absenteeism, particularly on Mondays and Fridays or after holidays;
- Significant change in personality (repeated abusive behavior, insolence, insubordination);
- Reliable report from other employees;
- Unexplained absences from normal work sites;
- Unusual behavior that cannot be readily explained;
- Changes in appearance and demeanor;
- Physical signs and symptoms such as reddened eyes or dilated pupils;
- Excessive cravings for water or sweets;
- Odor of alcohol or drugs;
- Slurred speech;
- Difficulty in motor coordination;

- Discovery or presence of substances in the employee's possession or near the employee's workplace;
- Other unusual behavior or work performance.

In all cases supervisors should be trained to recognize the above-listed or similar symptoms. Furthermore, the employer should establish a program for a confidential investigation to be undertaken if the supervisor has a reasonable suspicion that the employee may be impaired or using substances. The term "confidential investigation" is a "term of art" since the investigation should be "confidential" in accordance with earlier discussions of confidentiality, and "investigation" must be conducted in order to document properly the alleged behavior. Additionally, many employers put in safety steps such as requiring at least two supervisors or managers to acknowledge and sign before an employee may be tested under the for-cause criteria. For example, under Department of Transportation regulations, carriers are required to have "reasonable-cause" testing programs, where reasonable-cause conduct must be witnessed by two supervisors, or one supervisor if trained in the detection of drug use.[23]

Of all the different types of employee testing, for-cause testing based on a reasonable suspicion is the least controversial. Rarely will employers find for-cause testing to be a problem area because the testing is based on specific job performance or the effect of substance abuse on job performance in most cases. However, it is imperative that the employer establish the criteria for this type of testing, educate managers and employers on this type of testing, and implement the investigation procedure consistently and appropriately.

Post-Accident Testing. Although many employers view post-accident testing in the "for-cause" context and view the severity of the accident as a part of the consideration of whether to test for cause after the accident, an increasing number of other employers, particularly in the federal sector and in the transportation industry, have designated post-accident testing as a category standing alone.[24] A number of these employers have made drug testing mandatory after any accident, often in order to eliminate substance abuse as a possible contributing factor for liability reasons. Other employers have made post-accident testing mandatory in an effort to ascertain the extent of substance abuse involved in accidents in order to reduce workers' compensation claims to the individuals injured (if substance abuse was involved with the injured employee) or in order to diminish or eliminate damages for litigation resulting from accidents in the workers' compensation, third-party injury, or products liability areas.

Usually employers will set the criteria for post-accident testing based on the circumstances of the accident or unsafe act. Often the criteria may be testing after a death or personal injury requiring immediate hospitalization, damage to the employer's or others' property in excess of a certain number of dollars, or based on the required state or federal regulations. The Department of Transportation requires post-accident testing of drivers within 32 hours of any "reportable accident."[25] Often the term accidents need to be defined. In many cases it is relatively simple, for instance, after a train accident in the railroad industry or a plane crash in the airline industry, a vehicle accident for any employer, or any death or serious injury in the workplace. Other employers work with their insurance carriers in order to define where the line should be drawn on testing beyond the obvious. For instance, most employers do not drug test when an employee presents himself or herself to the facility's nurse for a Band-Aid on a cut the employee received in the workplace. On the other hand, for forklift collisions or property damage or near misses, many employers have determined they should use their discretion in considering drug testing, and work to make sure that the discretion exercised is consistently applied.

Contractor Testing. Recently, based on the development of federal statutes and regulations concerning private employers involved in business with the government, mandatory contractor testing programs are now being required of these private employers. Additionally, many private employers, particularly those who have subcontractors working for them and are covered under federal law, are requiring their contractors and vendors to impose substance abuse programs including drug testing on these other employers. (Contractor and vendor programs are discussed later in this chapter.)

The Drug Free Workplace Act of 1988[26] applies to employers with contracts from the federal government totaling $25,000 or more. Employers with contracts falling under this Act must publish a statement notifying employees that the unlawful possession or use of controlled substances is prohibited. The statement must also specify the action to be taken against employees for violation of the prohibition. The policy statement must require employees to notify the employer if they are convicted of a drug-related crime in the workplace. If the employee is convicted of such a crime, the employer must impose a sanction against the employee or require the satisfactory participation in a rehabilitation program. The employer is required to notify the contracting agency within ten days of learning of the employee's conviction. The employer is required to make a good-faith effort to maintain a drug free workplace. Employers covered by the Drug Free Workplace Act also must establish a "drug-free awareness program" that informs employees of the dangers of drug abuse in the workplace, the employer's policy of maintaining a drug free environment, and any available counseling, rehabilitation, and assistance programs. The program must inform employees of the penalties that may be imposed for violations of the policy. A government contractor may be suspended or debarred, or the contract terminated, if the contractor fails to carry out the requirements of this law. A contractor may also be sanctioned if enough of its employees are convicted of drug-related crimes to indicate failure to make a good-faith effort to provide a drug free workplace.[27] In addition, the Department of Defense has established federal acquisition regulations for a drug free work force. These regulations became effective October 31, 1988, for solicitations and contracts issued on or after that date. These regulations apply to all contractors with contracts involving access to classified information or any contract when the contracting officer determines that the clause is necessary for reasons of national security, or for the purpose of protecting the health and safety of those using the product or affected by the performance of the contract. In essence, this means that any employer involved in business with the Department of Defense must establish a substance abuse program in conformity with the federal regulations.

Under the Department of Defense regulations,[28] the contractor is required to institute a program designed to achieve a drug free workplace. These programs must include:

• Provisions for identifying drug users, including mandatory testing programs for positions creating a risk to the public health, safety, and national security. Although not specifically included in the regulations, the Department of Defense General Counsel has interpreted this provision to include mandatory random testing.[29] Additionally, a contractor may establish a discretionary program to test employees where

there is reasonable suspicion of drug use, where an employee
has been involved in an accident or unsafe practice, or as a
pre-employment requirement;
- Supervisory training to assist in identifying and addressing
  illegal drug use by employees;
- Provisions allowing self-referrals as well as supervisory referrals for treatment; and
- Employee assistance programs that must include education,
  counseling, rehabilitation, and coordination with available
  community resources.

In addition to the above legal requirements of contractors, it is
anticipated that many other federal and possibly state agencies may
require employers to establish substance abuse programs. It is
critical that the employer and its legal counsel review these statutes
and regulations as they are enacted or promulgated in order to
conform with these requirements in this rapidly changing field.

However, an employer that operates in conformity with many
of the provisions provided in this chapter should be reasonably well-
covered and in compliance with these laws and regulations. (See also
Appendices A, "Drugs of Abuse," C, "Model Policy, Procedure,
and Program," and F, "Substance Abuse Programs.") However,
employers that are involved in federal contract work or in other
employers' contracted substance abuse programs, should always
review those contracts on a regular basis, with their legal counsel in
order to assure compliance.

Random Testing. Random testing involves mandatory, unannounced drug testing whereby employees are required to submit to
the testing without any prior notice. In the past many employers
have shied away from using random testing because of its effect on
morale more than for legal reasons. In the courts, random testing
has the greatest likelihood of being challenged, particularly in a
federal constitutional context.[30] As a result, random testing has
acquired an undeserved bad name. Recently, more employers are
tending to use random testing in certain situations where it is
proving very effective as a deterrent to substance abuse on the job.
Further, since the courts have been ruling more favorably on the
random testing issue because of the deterrent effect it provides,
even more employers, including public employers, have been
implementing random testing programs. The usual categories of

random testing include: general random testing; probationary employee random testing; safety-sensitive position random testing; and post-rehabilitation random testing.

General random testing includes random testing imposed on the entire work force or a general population. This type of random testing is not particularly prevalent. Probationary employee random testing usually is used to detect substance abusers during the initial probationary period of employment, as was discussed earlier in this chapter. Safety-sensitive position random testing is utilized fairly extensively in safety-sensitive positions discussed above, and particularly with pilots, police officers, and firefighters. As was noted before, certain federal regulations require sensitive position testing in the defense areas and the transportation industry, both of which are fairly extensively regulated.[31]

Finally, the most prevalent use of random testing is in the post-rehabilitation area. It is held by many employers that post-rehabilitation random testing is essential in order to guarantee adherence to the employer's substance abuse program by an employer who has been a proven substance abuser but has agreed to go through the employer's rehabilitation program. The theory is that if the employer is willing to invest the time and money to rehabilitate the employee, then the employee must satisfy his or her part of the bargain and agree to random testing during a period of time after rehabilitation, usually for one year.

In most cases, an employer will require a returning rehabilitated employee to sign a surveillance agreement or random testing agreement where the employee agrees to random testing for a period of time, usually one year, and the employee agrees not to use alcohol or drugs during that period of time. These agreements usually state that the employee recognizes his or her obligation to meet the medical standards of the employer; they acknowledge the employee's identification as a user of controlled substances; the employee agrees to maintain abstinence from controlled substances unless medically prescribed; he or she agrees to submit to random testing during the prescribed period of time; and he or she agrees that refusal or failure to submit to the drug surveillance test, or a positive finding on a test, shall be cause for immediate discharge from the employment of the employer. Other provisions are often included in the agreements. These types of agreements are very common and are usually considered mandatory in dealing with rehabilitated employees once they return to work.

Usually in determining the categories of random testing, an employer will determine what its needs are. For instance, once the employer determines the categories of random testing to be implemented, such as random testing of sensitive positions, the employer will establish a procedure for testing these individuals randomly. Initially, the employer will determine the job categories to be tested, such as heavy equipment operators, pilots, and guards. This determination is usually based on the nature of the job description, the employee's duties, and the danger that could result from failure of the employee to discharge his or her duties adequately. Once the categories have been determined, it is important that the employer ensure that the selection process does not result in arbitrary, capricious, or discriminatory selections. For example, federal agencies must be able to justify their selection of positions as a neutral application of the selection criteria set forth, and agencies are absolutely prohibited from selecting positions for drug testing on the basis of a desire to test particular individual employees.[32] Further, federal rules for selecting individuals for random testing provide a variety of means of selection including selecting social security numbers at random by a computer, selecting individuals according to birth dates, or selecting based on the first letter in their surnames.

It is also important to recognize that random testing means unscheduled testing of the individuals in the jobs involved. If an employer schedules testing of employees the entire process will be undermined and the deterrent effect will be nullified.

Significantly, random testing provides the largest employee population sample on a continuing basis; it targets critical jobs and is therefore an effective deterrent to the use of substances; employees will not likely have time to mask or hide drug use since the tests are unannounced; and it usually has the greatest effect in reducing drug use in the workplace. However, random testing also creates the greatest negative morale or negative employee relations impact because employees often view it as an intrusion; it is the most often challenged element in an employer's substance abuse program; and it puts the greatest strain on the substance abuse program to make sure that all of the procedures, including those relating to confidentiality, are properly implemented.[33] In summary, although there are a number of minuses involved in random testing, it nevertheless has the greatest deterrent effect, particularly when used in safety-sensitive positions where the danger to persons and property is the greatest. Generally speaking, random testing is becoming a more acceptable form of testing and will probably be utilized more in the coming years.

Specific Procedural Provisions

Once an employer has articulated the types of current employee testing to be implemented, then certain other procedural elements must be detailed.

Notice and Employee Acknowledgment. It is imperative that current employees have the employer's substance abuse policy explained to them. They should be put on notice of its existence and told that it is a term and condition of their employment. Employers give notice to their employees concerning the substance abuse program including its testing requirement by a variety of means including distributing the policy and procedure to all employees affected, educating employees concerning substance abuse and the employer's substance abuse policy, posting the policy on bulletin boards, explaining the policy in employer newsletters or other publications and communications, mailing letters to the homes concerning the substance abuse policy and procedure, or even reviewing the substance abuse policy with employees and requiring them to sign a form acknowledging their understanding and review of the policy and procedure. Increasingly, employers are being required to give copies of the substance abuse policy to employees, particularly where such policies are mandated and regulated by federal law or regulation.[34]

Regardless of the method of communication, it is imperative that the employer communicate its substance abuse program by every possible means.

Constructive Confrontation and Voluntary Referral. In an effort to detect substance abuse and in order to avoid the detailed procedures involved with drug testing substance-abusing current employees, many employers use the strategy of "constructive confrontation." The essence of this procedure is that employees are asked to seek help for substance abuse voluntarily rather than being forced through the sanctions and possible discipline associated with violation of the substance abuse policy. It is important that all employees be forewarned that supervisors will approach those employees who show signs of substance abuse rather than waiting for the employees to become involved in the substance abuse program.

This method of initiating involvement is necessitated by the fact that employees rarely enter the procedures of the substance abuse program voluntarily because of the denial associated with substance abuse problems. Experience has shown that a supervisor may need to approach constructive confrontation gradually, including a period of informal discussion with the employee, although the supervisor's approach will often depend upon the employee and the circumstances involved. The constructive aspect of the supervisor's informal discussions should meet several standards. The supervisor should express emotional support and group concern for the employee's welfare. The supervisor should suggest that the employee's position will be maintained if improvement occurs in the future and should also point out an alternative course of behavior that the employee can take to regain satisfactory work performance. The supervisor's discussions should also include a confrontational aspect, however. The supervisor should emphasize management's expectations regarding the employee's work performance. The supervisor should point out where the employee is falling short of meeting these expectations, and should inform the employee that formal sanctions will follow if those expectations continue to go unmet. Finally, the supervisor should establish some distinctions between the employee and other employees who are meeting expectations, thus setting the stage for further sanctions, if needed.[35] If the employee's performance fails to improve and he or she does not voluntarily submit to the rehabilitative aspect of the program, the employee should be formally disciplined for poor performance. Discipline may include a written warning, suspension, mandatory participation in drug counseling, drug testing, or discharge, depending upon the employer's substance abuse program.

In addition, many employers have developed procedures encouraging voluntary referral to an EAP or rehabilitation program before referral to drug testing or the EAP becomes mandatory. Constructive confrontation and voluntary referral can be extremely useful in combination, particularly when the employee appears to have some performance problems and is anxious to avoid the stringent discipline of most substance abuse programs.

Consent and Release. It is imperative that a current employee sign a consent and release form prior to any drug screening test being administered. (Further discussion concerning the reasons for consent/release forms appears earlier in this chapter.)

In essence, it is important to obtain a consent and release of liability from a current employee for a drug test as it is from an applicant, if not more so. The employee must consent that the medical test be made; consent to the release of the information from the laboratory to the employer; and release the company employees, management, designated medical representative, the laboratory, and its agents from any and all claims or causes of action resulting from the test and any decisions resulting from the test.

In addition, many employers provide in their consent and release form a section where the employee may report any medications he or she is taking, the conditions for which the drugs are taken, and the prescribing physician. These employers also require consent to allow the employer to verify the submitted drug information with the prescribing physician. The theory behind this request is twofold. First, the employer takes the position that if a person is going to work on its premises he or she must remain drug free, and if the employee is forced to use drugs because of a medical condition, and that medical condition might affect the employee's work performance and potential safety and health, then the employer needs to know of the existence of any such condition. Second, the employer takes the attitude that the physician may or may not know all of the circumstances concerning employment and if the employer has the opportunity and the permission to discuss the circumstances with the prescribing physician, it may affect the treatment to the benefit of the employee, the employer, and the physician. For instance, if a physician is prescribing sleeping pills because an employee complains of an inability to sleep, and those sleeping pills are interfering with the work performance of the employee, whose job involves driving forklifts between expensive and dangerous machinery where other employees' lives are put in jeopardy by any impaired employee, then the physician may reconsider his or her position, or the employer may want to consider reassigning the employee to a less hazardous task. The point in obtaining this type of information is not to meddle, but to protect the safety and health of that particular employee and the employer's other workers.

Investigations. Usually, investigations are held in conjunction with for-cause testing. For the sake of documentation, it is important to have confidential investigation forms signed by the appropriate employer officials. (See "For-Cause Testing," earlier in this chapter.)

In most cases, employers develop investigation forms which are filled out by supervisors and state that the supervisor has observed the following conditions affecting the work of the particular employee which give rise to suspicion of substance abuse. Those conditions include sudden changes in work performance; repeated failure to follow instructions or operating procedures; violation of employer safety policies; discovery or presence of substances in an employee's possession; odor of alcohol and/or a residual odor peculiar to some controlled substance; unexplained and/or frequent absenteeism, personality changes, or disorientation; accidents; or injuries to persons or property.

Often, employers will implement a backup procedure for the investigation of for-cause determinations, using two supervisors instead of just one. The purpose is to avoid the appearance of witch hunting. Once cause is established and the drug test process is implemented, the investigation form becomes a part of the substance abuse or personnel file. Additionally, many employers require that some other written report be prepared, detailing the incident and including appropriate dates, times of the reported drug-related incidents or for-cause factors, reliable sources of information, the rationale leading to the test, findings of the test, and the action taken, in order to fully document the investigation and the follow-up procedures.

Drug Rings. Certain investigations lead to the inevitable conclusion that drug rings (coordinated drug-related activities) exist in the employer's facility or facilities. In most cases when a drug ring is suspected or discovered, there is a tendency on the part of untrained managers to panic or to fail to react at all. However, it is imperative that management deal with the situation aggressively as soon as it is discovered. Otherwise, the employer risks losing control of the situation and becoming liable for any unsafe or dangerous acts performed by substance abusing employees since the employer has been put on notice that a serious substance abuse problem exists.

There are a number of specific actions that management should take when drug rings are suspected or discovered. Ten recommendations for dealing with drug rings include the following: use experts; get organized; get the facts; be aggressive; consult police; review personnel information; train management; enforce the substance abuse program; test suspects; and document.

1. Use experts. Drug rings are serious business. It is not unusual in the workplace for participants of drug rings to be intimidating and potentially violent. Therefore, precaution should always

be taken and management should make every effort to use experts in the field of substance abuse, whether they be attorneys, police officers, or others. Attorneys are particularly adept at dealing with drug rings because usually they understand drug laws and the employer's substance abuse program. Furthermore, attorneys are familiar with the type of detailed investigations necessary in drug ring situations.

2. Get organized. A well-respected upper-level manager should be appointed to coordinate the employer's management team in responding to the drug ring situation. This manager also will be needed to direct the organization to respond to the expert's suggestions in a quick and decisive manner. Getting organized also involves selecting individuals who will be involved in the investigation, arranging for appropriate personnel and materials, and organizing paperwork.

3. Get the facts. It is imperative that the employer completely review the facts and circumstances that led to the suspicion or conclusion that a drug ring exists in the workplace. For example, if the information is based on someone coming forward, then that individual should be interviewed thoroughly, statements taken, information corroborated, and documentation made. Or, if the information is derived from arrests or tips from informants or law enforcement officials, all pertinent materials, legal documents (such as arrest records), or other information should be gathered as quickly as possible.

4. Be aggressive. Now is not the time to tarry. Management cannot afford to be faint-hearted about any potential drug ring situation. The consequences are too severe. The employer should thoroughly investigate the situation by interviewing all potential witnesses including management and nonmanagement employees, review documentation that may be appropriate, and otherwise leave no stone unturned in the investigation.

5. Consult police. Management should notify the police and consult narcotic intelligence officers to review the names of suspects and the incidents concerning drug use at or around the facility. Where criminal conduct is suspected or where illegal substances or drug paraphernalia have been discovered, law enforcement officials should always be involved in handling such materials. Supervisors should be warned not to become amateur drug investigators because the consequences are too serious. Again, use of experts who are familiar with these situations is important in order to eliminate costly mistakes.

6. Review personnel information. Personnel information significant to the investigation includes absenteeism rates, accident reports, disciplinary actions, employee complaints, or other such internal documents that might give clues concerning the individuals involved in drug activity. Usually managers find that as they review the existing personnel information, a clearer picture begins to emerge concerning the drug-related activity.

7. Train management. If managers at all levels have already been trained, then they should be retrained concerning for-cause drug testing and the dangers of substance abuse. If managers have not been trained previously, then an intensive education and training program should be implemented as quickly as possible along the guidelines discussed in Chapter 5, "Substance Abuse Education and Training."

8. Enforce the program. During the education and training program, supervisors should be taught about the substance abuse program with all of its intricacies. Further, management should ensure that all aspects of the substance abuse program are consistently applied to supervisors and other employees alike. If a comprehensive substance abuse program has been implemented at the employer's facility, use and enforcement of the substance abuse program will allow the employer to handle 99 percent of all substance abuse problems in the workplace including drug rings. Experience has shown that draconian tactics such as drug sniffing dogs or massive arrests are usually unnecessary if the employer properly uses its existing substance abuse program.

9. Test suspects. Suspects should be drug tested according to the rules of the substance abuse program. Drug testing is the proof that substance use or abuse exists. Substance abusing employees including drug ring participants will almost always deny substance use. However, if the employer actively enforces its substance abuse program and tests for cause, on a random basis, or in whichever way the program directs, the substance using or abusing employee usually will be detected quickly. Furthermore, once the employer starts testing, many employees will admit to substance use, and often some employees will not only confess, but will give detailed information on other substance users or pushers. Once the substance abusing employees have been detected, the employer's substance abuse program should direct management on how to handle the detected employees.

10. Document. It is imperative that every aspect of the substance abuse/drug ring investigation and actions taken be documented thoroughly. The purpose of the documentation is threefold:

to maintain the proper written records for equipping managers to make appropriate personnel decisions, to help support the efforts of law enforcement officials, and to minimize management's legal exposure. If the employer documents the existence of substance abuse or drug rings and accumulates evidence, including drugs, paraphernalia, and witness statements, then it is exceedingly unlikely that any personnel action would be successfully challenged in court.

Of course, there are alternatives to this approach: mass screenings of all employees, the use of undercover investigations, or the use of drug-sniffing dogs in the workplace. It is recommended that these alternatives be used only in the most extreme situations. All three of these activities often have a serious demoralizing effect on employees and tend to undermine the employer's substance abuse program. In most cases if an employer will implement its well-articulated substance abuse program, even the most serious drug rings can be handled effectively without unnecessary disruption of workplace operations. In unusual situations where there is workplace drug-related violence, management should go to any length to use police, drug sniffing dogs, or any other means available to root out the bad elements. However, these situations are extremely rare.

In conclusion, the vast majority of serious drug-related or drug ring situations in the workplace can be handled effectively by a well-articulated substance abuse program. The employer should always use experts, and management should always get organized, get the facts, be aggressive, consult the police, review personnel information, train management, enforce the substance abuse program, test suspects, and document everything.

Alcohol Testing. Many employers have found that alcohol is the most prevalent drug of abuse in the workplace. The general consensus is that urine screening for alcohol is impractical. Therefore, most employers use breathalyzers to detect alcohol use and blood tests for confirmation. Many employers try not to overlook the abuse of alcohol and the necessary investigation and testing procedures when writing the procedural aspect of their substance abuse policy.

Transportation of Impaired Employees. If, after a confidential investigation, the employer determines that the employee may be impaired and unable to transport himself or herself from the premises, it is always wise for the employer to arrange for transportation of the impaired employee. Therefore, the employer should arrange for transportation whenever possible for reasons of safety, liability, and common sense.[36]

Transportation of impaired employees may include a supervisor driving the employee home, calling a family member to pick up the employee at work, calling a taxi for the employee, or any other method to get the employee home or to medical treatment in order to avoid injury or property damage.

Collection and Testing Procedures. The procedure regarding collection of specimens and testing is critically important for the integrity of the substance abuse program. Many employers find it necessary to articulate the procedure involved with the collection and testing techniques in order to make it clear to employees that the procedure is very straightforward and not some strange process performed in a mysterious laboratory in some foreign land. Issues to be considered include: collection personnel; test kits (description and labeling); accuracy safeguards including observable voids, temperature/pH, and toilet bluing; tampering; split samples; chain of custody; lab selection; confirmation techniques; and drugs to be tested.

Collection Personnel. Usually the employer will specify either the employer's personnel authorized to participate in the collection procedure, or the laboratory where the employees will be directed to give specimens. Many employers use their medical department if one exists. Otherwise, employers will use the personnel department or some designated employee to be involved in the substance abuse program. It is important that the number of personnel involved be very restricted and kept to a minimum in order to maintain the integrity of the program.

Test Kits (Description and Labeling). Many employers have found that it is often useful to detail the equipment to be utilized such as the test kit, specimen cup, and labels and elaborate upon exactly what is expected of the applicant or employee. Some employers go to the extent of itemizing or walking through the process of identification, receipt of the specimen cup, production of the specimen, return of the specimen cup for the identification signature, description, and labeling, signing the chain of custody, and so forth. Other employers simply leave the procedure to the authorized personnel or laboratory.

Accuracy Safeguards. Assuring the accuracy of the specimen identification is a critical part of the substance abuse process. Many employers will detail the procedures for their authorized personnel or the laboratory to follow in collecting the specimens.[37]

1. Observable voids. A small number of employers utilize observable voids in the specimen collection procedure. This procedure, which involves the collection personnel actually watching the employee produce the urine sample, is usually embarrassing to the applicant or employee giving the specimen and often embarrassing to the authorized employer personnel or the laboratory personnel. Observable voids should only be utilized when the employer feels it is absolutely necessary.

However, with the increasing use of black-market urine, or where substance abusing employees purchase "clean" urine from non-substance-abusing employees, many employers are being forced under certain circumstances to utilize observable voids to assure that the specimen that is obtained is actually provided by the employee in question. Because of the development of sophisticated devices to mimic the delivery of a specimen, particularly in males, a combination of observable voids and checking the temperature and pH have become necessary in many situations, particularly with individuals who are reputedly involved in the black-market urine schemes.

2. Temperature/pH. In order to assure the accuracy of the specimen, particularly when the observable void procedure is not followed, many employers and laboratories provide, and the Health and Human Services regulations require,[38] that the specimen collection personnel check the temperature of the specimen once it is received and check the pH of the specimen. If the temperature and pH of the specimen are not within the prescribed limits as defined by either the employer, the laboratory, or the federal agency, the specimen should be rejected. This temperature and pH checking procedure should be explained to employees.

3. Toilet bluing. Experience has shown that another method of assuring accuracy is for the water in the toilet where the specimen will be given be treated with a bluing agent in order to prevent an applicant or employee from tampering with the specimen or adding water to increase the volume and dilute the concentration of the specimen.

Other employers, particularly federal employers, provide that if no bluing agent is available to deter specimen dilution, the collection site person should instruct the individual not to flush the toilet until the specimen is delivered to the collection site person. After the collection site person has possession of the specimen, the individual will be instructed to flush the toilet and to participate with the collection site person in completing the chain of custody procedures.[39]

Essentially, these accuracy safeguards are important for the overall implementation of the substance abuse program. If employees perceive that the substance abuse program, particularly the drug testing procedure, can be beaten, substance abusing employees will stop at nothing to beat the system.

Tampering. Most substance abuse procedures detail the effect of applicants or employees presenting tampered specimens. Usually the effect is to eliminate the applicant from consideration for employment, or consider the employee to have refused to cooperate with the testing procedure which normally results in discipline or discharge.

In addition to making every effort possible to minimize tampering, certain employers, in particular federal agencies, provide guidance on circumstances when observation may be required to prevent tampering. These regulations state generally that the employee or applicant may be required to provide a sample under observation if there is reason to believe that the employee or applicant may alter or substitute a urine specimen. The regulations go on to state that "for example, employers may wish to require observation when facts and circumstances suggest that the person to be tested (a) is an illegal drug user; (b) is under the influence of drugs at the time of the test; (c) has previously been confirmed by the agency to be an illegal drug user; (d) is seen to have equipment or implements used to tamper with urine samples; and (e) has recently been determined to have tampered with a sample."[40]

Private employers usually take the attitude that rather than simply requiring an observable void, or observing the submitting of the specimen, the employer will simply consider adulterated or unreadable samples, or samples that clearly are not authentic, to be considered evidence of the employee's failure to cooperate with the company policy. Usually these employers provide that the employee will be questioned concerning the adulterated sample according to the company policy, and if a satisfactory explanation is not provided, the employee is subject to disciplinary action up to and including termination.

Split Samples. Occasionally, employers will provide that applicants or employees present split samples, or two specimens at the same time. The circumstances where split samples are utilized with the most publicity include the 1988 Olympic Games and athletic competition in the nonemployment context, or in for-cause testing of current employees. Rarely are split samples utilized for applicants. The advantage of a split sample situation is that if the results of the original sample are brought into question, the split sample will provide the sufficient amount of specimen to enable the laboratory to test the second specimen and compare the results with the first specimen test results.

However, split sampling is not prescribed by the federal government regulations, particularly the Department of Transportation. The federal regulations require that employers test for the five major drugs listed in the DOT drug regulations. If an employer wants to test for some other drug, not covered by DOT regulations, the employer must obtain a second or split sample from the employee and base that request for the second sample on whatever other legal authority is available, since the employer cannot rely on the DOT regulations as a basis for the request.[41]

As a result, employers using split samples are the exception and not the rule.

Chain of Custody. Essentially, chain-of-custody procedures provide that first the specimen container shall be sealed with evidence tape in the presence of the person giving the specimen; the time and date and signature of the occupational nurse or specimen collector will be entered on the chain-of-custody form; in the presence of the person giving the specimen, the sealed specimen shall then be placed in a plastic chain-of-custody zip-lock bag and it shall also be sealed with evidence tape; the occupational nurse or collector will ensure that the appropriate chain-of-custody documentation is completed at the facility and by the courier receiving the specimen for the laboratory; and the courier will transfer the specimen to the independent lab for confirmation.[42]

Essentially, a chain-of-custody form lists the subject's name and social security number and has places for the employer's name, the temperature of the specimen, the sample date and time, and a list of any drugs or medication taken in the last week. Then the chain-of-custody form will specify that the sample was received from a certain individual by another individual, stating the date and time, for the original transmission (sample received from "employee" by "occupational nurse," on May 1, 1990 at 10:05 a.m.) Next the chain-of-custody form will indicate that the specimen was received from the occupational nurse by the courier at the particular time, and so forth. As long as the chain of custody is maintained from the employer to the lab and the laboratory personnel, its integrity should be above question.

However, the chain of custody does not end when the specimen is received by the laboratory. Most chain-of-custody forms will document that the specimen was received in referral by the laboratory by a particular individual at a certain date and time. Next the form will indicate whether the seals were intact and any comments that are deemed necessary by the laboratory personnel. The chain-of-custody form may also state that the specimen was tested by a named laboratory representative, the disposition of the sample (i.e., normal appearance with seals intact), and if it was tested positive, the storage location of the confirmed positive specimen. Furthermore, there may be a provision for returning the specimen should it ever be requested by the employer or the employee if it is in dispute.

Although this type of detail may appear burdensome, it is critical considering the sensitivity of the issue and the circumstances involved.

The responsibility for an accurate chain of custody rests on both the employer and the laboratory. The employer's responsibility is to ensure that the collecting personnel have the applicant or employee fill out the chain-of-custody documentation accurately and make sure that the chain-of-custody form is unquestionable in the transmission links that involve the employer, including transfer to the courier or laboratory. The chain of custody proves that the specimen given is the same as the specimen tested and the results reported. Any break in the chain of custody will invalidate the test results. Many employers leave the accuracy of the chain of custody to the laboratory. This is a mistake. Any good laboratory will refuse to accept a specimen where the chain of custody is not verified. Therefore, the accuracy of the chain of custody should be beyond dispute. The employer should specify and explain the chain of custody to applicants and employees in the substance abuse procedures and the collecting personnel should explain the chain of custody when the specimen is being given. Furthermore, the employer and its personnel should be familiar with the chain-of-custody forms, the importance of the chain of custody, and how the transmission operates.

Lab Selection. Most employers make reference to the laboratory selection process in the substance abuse procedures. Some employers will simply specify that the laboratory will be selected by the employer at its discretion. Other employers specify the particular laboratory to be used. In any event, it is the employer's responsibility to choose a certified laboratory for each of its locations. Laboratory certifications can be ascertained by checking the laboratory's state licensing, CLIA (Clinical Laboratories Improvement Act of 1967), or NIDA (National Institute of Drug Abuse)/HHS (Health and Human Services) certification program.[43]

Choosing a certified laboratory usually is not the difficult task it once was, because of the increasing federal regulations and the number of certification programs in this area. However, what any employer should seriously consider, above and beyond the laboratory qualifications issue, is the service that the employer wishes to request of the laboratory. If time is of the essence for the hiring procedure or for determining whether current employees have been engaged in substance abuse, then the employer should have a clear understanding about the turnaround time necessary for the laboratory. Many excellent laboratories now provide turnaround time of 24 hours for GC/MS-confirmed specimens. In any event, 48 hours should be the outside limit for turnaround time, particularly since a well-run, efficient laboratory should be oriented toward its customers' needs, which in most cases are very time-sensitive.

Confirmation Techniques. The procedure section in many employers' substance abuse programs specifies that all positive drug screens will be confirmed, and usually the procedure specifies a particular type of confirmation technique such as Gas Chromatography/Mass Spectrometry (GC/MS). The federal guidelines specify that all positive tests be confirmed by GC/MS and many other employer policies do the same.[44]

Drugs to be Tested. Many employers will specify the drugs to be tested in the drug testing procedures. Some employers state that the company or agency will determine the drugs to be tested. Other employers state that the drugs to be tested may vary depending upon the location. And still other employers list the specific drugs to be tested including the cutoff levels and concentrations. In most cases the drugs to be tested include, at a minimum, amphetamines, cocaine, marijuana, barbiturates, and the opiates. Additionally, a number of employers test for the benzodiazepines (Valium) and phencyclidine (PCP).[45]

Notification of Results and Confidentiality. Notification of results will be different for employees than for applicants. The employer should establish a definite and confidential chain of command for notification of results. Where the results are negative, the employer should consider having a detailed communication meeting with the employee to explain the employer's concerns and to provide back pay if the employee has been kept away from work at the employer's request. If the results are positive, the employer should have a detailed communication meeting with the employee, tell the employee what drug or drugs were discovered, and inform the employee of the sanctions for a positive test in accordance with the employer's substance abuse policy. These sanctions usually include: discipline; discharge; leave of absence; and/or required rehabilitation. Again, it is critical that the results of the test and the communication meetings remain confidential. No results should be released to any member of management except on a need-to-know basis. Further, results should never be released to outsiders without the written authorization of the employee.

Opportunity to Contest Results. From a legal standpoint, it is far more important to give current employees the opportunity to contest the results than applicants. In the private sector, this procedural right is optional and at the discretion of the employer. In the public sector, it should be considered prudent if not mandatory.[46] As with applicants, if the employee is given the opportunity to contest the results, it should be done either with a split sample or with a retest of the original specimen and never with a new specimen that the employee brings in. However, many employers also ensure that during the communication meeting when the employee is notified of the results, the employer makes a point to investigate all of the possible facts and circumstances surrounding the positive test result and give the substance abusing employee an opportunity to explain or refute the findings.

Many employers reserve for themselves the right to be flexible in interpreting the test data depending upon the circumstances. For instance, the military has learned through experience that occasionally officers or enlisted men may ingest spiked drinks or be fed marijuana brownies unknowingly. Although these occasions are rare, it is incumbent upon the public-sector employer to investigate the circumstances thoroughly, particularly when the alleged offending employee is vociferous in his or her protestations. The opportunity to contest is not as imperative in the private sector unless the employer decides to grant such rights or the private employer is required to grant such rights by statute, ordinance, or collective bargaining agreement.[47]

Rehabilitation Options. Any good substance abuse policy will go beyond termination of an employee who has been found to have a positive drug test. Therefore, options open to employers include referral to the employer's employee assistance program or referral directly to rehabilitation. These types of programs are discussed in Part Three of this book. However, it is important in the procedural section to spell out the employer's policy for dealing with rehabilitation options and time off for counseling.

For example, certain employers provide that work time lost will be paid according to eligibility for sick days, applicable short-term disability benefits, and eligible vacation pay while employees are engaged in rehabilitation or counseling. Other employers provide that employees will be allowed up to certain periods of time for counseling (one hour or more depending upon travel time), and have an excused absence for each counseling session, up to a certain amount of time. In general, many employers are relatively lenient in granting employees time off for counseling and rehabilitation, if the employees' prescribed program allows them to participate in outpatient counseling while they are working, and usually after they have received some sort of intensive rehabilitation counseling while away from work.

Medical Benefits. If the employee has opted to seek rehabilitation under the employer's policy and program, medical benefits may or may not be available depending upon the employer's program. As a result, many employers find it useful to include reference to the medical benefits program in the procedural section, including statements such as: "Medical benefits are provided in accordance with the Company's health insurance plan, and all other costs of treatment for rehabilitation will be the responsibility of the employee."[48]

Post-Rehabilitation Agreements. Any employer who offers rehabilitation to its employees should have a mechanism to handle return of the employee to the work force. Usually this mechanism takes the form of a "surveillance agreement" or a "last chance agreement" whereby the employee agrees to stay free of substances in consideration of the employer allowing him or her to return to work and maintain employment. Usually the agreements provide that if an employee abandons rehabilitation or tests positive during the period in question, he or she will be terminated. Experience has shown that it is counterproductive for employers to coddle recovering individuals and, whereas substance abusers should be given a chance at rehabilitation, that rehabilitation opportunity should be limited and not become a revolving door.

In most cases, last chance agreements provide elements similar to the following: "The employee promises to cooperate and partici- pate in the employer's counseling/rehabilitation program; the employee authorizes the counseling or rehabilitation representative to confer with the employer's officials regarding participation in the program, and including disclosure of medical/psychiatric evalua- tions; the employee states his or her understanding that upon return to work the employee will be subject to unscheduled drug or alcohol random testing and the failure to take such a test, or having a positive test result, will be grounds for termination; the employee acknowledges that his or her employment depends upon remaining drug-free; and the employee acknowledges the agreement does not alter the at-will nature of the employment." These agreements not only obtain the consent for tests and an understanding of the rela- tionship between the employee and the employer, but also they provide sufficient documentation for the employer if it becomes necessary to impose adverse disciplinary action. On the other hand, if the employee participates in the treatment program and remains drug-free, often an employer will destroy the agreement or elimi- nate it from the personnel records once the employee has success- fully completed the term of the agreement.

Employee Failure to Cooperate. Procedurally, it is important to state very clearly the effect of an employee's refusal to cooperate with any aspect of the employer's substance abuse program, includ- ing refusal to sign a consent form, refusal to agree to the drug test, refusal to seek rehabilitation if that option is available, and refusal to cooperate with the rehabilitation process. In almost all cases, the effect of an employee's failure to cooperate with the employer's substance abuse program is termination, although other disciplinary options are certainly available.

Disciplinary Options. Some employers prefer to make the disciplinary options available under the substance abuse policy completely free-standing and others choose to interrelate the sub- stance abuse policy with other employment policies such as rules and regulations and disciplinary policies. From a procedural stand- point, the employer should always reserve the right to discipline or terminate employees in accordance with that employer's disciplin- ary policies or civil service proceedings.

Management Communications with the EAP/Rehabilitation Counselor. Many employers have found it necessary from experience to stipulate that the employer reserves the right to communicate with the EAP or rehabilitation counselor in order to monitor the progress of the employee in rehabilitation. Although communications should not be widespread within the employer's management and every right of confidentiality of the employee during rehabilitation should be observed, adequate case management by the employer's personnel department or appropriate officials is helpful in ensuring that the employee's return to the work force occur in as smooth a manner as possible. Because rehabilitation counselors are always concerned about the confidentiality of their relationship with the employee/patient and because the employer's management is concerned that it have knowledge that the employee is cooperating with the program, some employers have required the employee to agree in writing to communications between the EAP/rehabilitation counselors and the employer. This is an area that will probably develop significantly over the next few years.

Effect on Personnel Records. Many employers have procedural sections stipulating that cooperation of the employee with the substance abuse program including successful completion of rehabilitation will have no adverse effect on the employee's personnel record. Further, some employers provide that once a period of time has passed, such as one year, after the successful completion of rehabilitation and the post-rehabilitation random testing program, all references to the substance abuse problem will be deleted from the employee's personnel file. This has the effect of wiping the slate clean for the employee.

Other employers, particularly public employers, provide that any personnel records or medical records dealing with substance abuse be kept strictly confidential and/or have limited access status for protection of privacy rights. Many employers have found that these procedures have a positive effect on the morale of employees and cause the employees to perceive the substance abuse program as one actually oriented towards rehabililtation rather than simply another form of discipline.

Aftercare Follow-Up. A growing number of employers have realized that aftercare is critical for the maintenance of a rehabilitated employee's sobriety. As a result, a number of employers provide for periodic, usually semi-annual or annual, communication meetings with the rehabilitated employee and his or her supervisor in order to gauge the progress of the rehabilitation of the employee. Some employers have found that aftercare follow-up is a cost-effective method of protecting the investment that the employer now has in the rehabilitation of the employee.

Certain employers provide that for a specified period of time (one to two years) after successful completion of rehabilitation and return to work, the employee will have periodic, confidential meetings with the company's EAP representative so that the employee's aftercare program can be evaluated. Employers also provide that the EAP representative will discuss the matter with the company president or other official if a problem exists and appropriate action will be taken according to the employer's policy. These policies also may provide that after the specified time period, so long as the employee has maintained compliance with the program, all records and references to the employee's substance abuse problem will be deleted from the records.

Other Procedural Issues

In most substance abuse policies, there are procedural issues that do not fit nicely into the aforementioned categories. Therefore, most employers place other procedural issues that are of interest to them in a miscellaneous category where they may add or delete matters as their substance abuse program evolves. Some of these issues may include: medical authorization review—prescription drugs; use of employer vehicles; entertainment functions; outside contractors and vendors; searches; criminal charges; employment-at-will statement; and severability.

Medical Authorization Review—Prescription Drugs

Through experience, a number of employers have determined that many physicians are notorious for not understanding substance abuse. Experience has indicated that medical professionals are quick to prescribe drugs that may affect work performance and behavior, and the reality is that substance abusers will deceive medical professionals into obtaining prescription drugs to which they become addicted. As a result, many employers reserve the right to counsel with the prescribing physician, refer the employee to the company physician for evaluation, and even overrule the prescribing physician if a pattern of substance abuse appears. Usually once the prescribing physician realizes that the employee may be a substance abuser, particularly where the employee is receiving multiple prescriptions from different physicians, the physician is often very cooperative with the employer's program. The basic philosophy of an employer under these circumstances is that the employer has a duty to maintain a safe and drug free workplace, and the employer is under an obligation to determine any circumstance that may cause an employee to become impaired that may affect the safety and health of the individual employee or other employees.

Use of Employer Vehicles

As their substance abuse programs have developed, some employers have found that they need to pay particular attention to employees who are authorized to drive, lease, or operate company vehicles or equipment. Although the development of procedural matters in this area initially came from concerns regarding liability to the employer caused by actions of employees who were driving while impaired due to alcohol or drugs, many other employers have determined that it is necessary to hold such employees to a higher standard of safety and conduct than employees who do not pose such safety risks to other employees and the public. As a result, a number of employers have adopted special procedures for dealing with employees who are authorized to operate vehicles or equipment in conjunction with their job duties.

An employer may state that substance abuse by employees who operate employer vehicles, which may include employer-owned, employer-leased, or short-term car rental vehicles, or the employee's own vehicle on company business, can create very serious risks for both themselves and members of the public. As a result, employers may provide that employees who operate such vehicles may be subject to disciplinary action up to and including termination of employment for conviction of driving the vehicle under the influence of alcohol or drugs. Further, many employers provide that the above provision applies regardless of whether the vehicle is being operated for personal or business use. These provisions usually require that any employee covered under these provisions report to their supervisor any citation alleging they were driving under the influence of alcohol or drugs, regardless of whether the offense may have occurred in the employee's vehicle, an employer-owned or leased vehicle, on personal business, or on company business. Usually it is also provided that failure to report such citations may result in disciplinary action up to and including termination of employment, and that the report must be made within five days of the citation.

Such provisions usually apply to traveling salespersons or even executives or top officials of the employer. However, this approach is being considered by an ever-increasing number of employers.

Employer Entertainment Functions

An increasing number of employers have begun restricting the use of alcohol, primarily at employer functions or during business entertainment of customers or clients. Some of the procedures that have developed have been an attempt to restrict expenditures. However, other policy and procedural developments in this area have been based on an employer's recognition that it appeared inconsistent to restrict or prohibit alcohol or other substance use of employees on one hand, and then openly encourage alcohol consumption at employer or corporate functions. As a result, there is an increasing trend to restrict or eliminate employer-sponsored events where alcohol is served.

Outside Contractors and Vendors

An increasing number of employers, including the federal government,[49] are requiring that outside contractors and vendors certify their compliance with the employer's substance abuse program or certify that the contractor or vendor has developed a drug free workplace program of its own. The form of this compliance and certification varies depending upon the substance abuse program of the employer.

Like employers covered by the contractor requirements of the Drug Free Workplace Act and Department of Defense regulations (reviewed earlier in this chapter) many other private employers have also begun implementing contractor and vendor programs. For example, certain private employers require that all contractors certify in writing to the employer that the contractor's employees having access to the employer's property have been tested or screened for drugs or other controlled substances within the last 12 months, and that the contractor's employees have tested negative for drugs. These employers also provide that all contracts, all purchase orders, or agreements with contractors of the employer, will be amended or written to include language of such contractor's certification regarding its employees' drug free condition. Other employers provide that on-site vendors and contractors whose employees have significant potential impact on the safety of the workplace should be required to have a compatible testing program as appropriate.

Searches

A number of employers use their substance abuse procedures to articulate their policy on searches of property on the employer's premises. For private employers, such a policy is a wise legal move, and since private employers have significant property rights, it is rarely a problem. Public employers, however, operate in a different constitutional realm and therefore are more restricted in how they may effectuate search policies. Usually in the public sector some reasonable suspicion is required, although recent court decisions have reduced this necessity.[50]

For private employers, the search policy is often used in conjunction with searches for contraband in employee lockers, lunch boxes, vehicles, and the like. Private employers, in particular, may establish programs for regular or random searches to determine the presence of alcohol or illegal drugs. These searches may be of the employer's property, lockers, or personal property brought onto the employer's property. Usually the employer provides that personnel who refuse such searches will be terminated. Additionally, prior to implementation of any search procedure, many employers communicate to employees that subjection to searches is a condition of employment, and employees are made to understand that they are subject to searches of personal or company property while on the employer's site. Certain employers specify that search procedures should be a carefully thought-out balance between individual rights and legitimate business concerns. Corporate officials should be consulted in order to ensure the lawfulness of search procedures and to minimize the impact on employee relations. Finally, many employers provide that when the search turns up contraband such as controlled substances, procedures should exist in order to transfer these materials to law enforcement officers and to cooperate fully with any criminal investigation.[51]

Criminal Charges

A number of employers have determined that because of arbitration and cases revoking discipline of employees who had been arrested for drug-related activities,[52] a specific procedure was necessary to cover criminal arrest and conviction situations. As a result, many employers specify that arrests or convictions for drug-related crimes should be investigated by the employer's personnel and will be a cause for testing. Furthermore, recent federal statutes and regulations[53] now require that federal contractors report any of their employees who have been convicted of drug-related crimes in the workplace and make affirmative efforts to maintain that convicted drug offenders do not work on federal projects. (See "Contractor Testing," earlier in this chapter.)

Employment-at-Will Statement

Because of the erosion of employment-at-will in a number of states, some employers are now specifying that their substance abuse policy, procedures, and program are not employment contracts and that the relationship between the employer and the employee is an "at-will" relationship. This procedural development is a relatively recent phenomenon, but if employment-at-will litigation continues at the pace that it has occurred recently, these employment-at-will statements will be found in written procedures more often. Usually an employer will state something to the effect that no part of the policy or any of the procedures thereunder is intended to affect the company's right to manage its workplace, to discipline its employees, or guarantee employment, continued employment, or terms and conditions of employment. Additionally, certain employers provide that because of the seriousness of substance abuse situations, the employer completely reserves the right to alter or change its policy or decisions on a given situation depending upon its investigation and the totality of the circumstances.[54] Finally, certain employers simply state that under no circumstances do any of the agreements, policies, procedures, or programs within the employer's substance abuse program constitute a contract that would in any way affect the employment-at-will relationship.

Severability

Because of the complicated nature of substance abuse policies and procedures, many employers are now adding severability clauses that in essence state that if any part of the policy is determined to be void or unenforceable under state or federal law, the remainder of the policy, to the extent possible, will remain in full force and effect.

In particular, public employers, particularly municipalities or authorities, will state that if any of the provisions of the employer's substance abuse program are held to be unconstitutional, or otherwise invalid by any court of competent jurisdiction, the decision of the court shall not affect or impair any of the remaining provisions.

Conclusion

Substance abuse procedures are the nuts and bolts of any employer's substance abuse program. Experience has shown that if an employer will develop very precise procedures for handling all aspects of the substance abuse program, there will be much less confusion, and much greater acceptance of the substance abuse program, so long as the procedures are consistently applied at all levels. Whether the substance abuse procedures deal with communication, education, drug testing, discipline, searches, or whatever, the fact that the employer has taken the time to develop precise procedures will go a long way toward ensuring the total acceptance of the substance abuse program. Whereas the substance abuse policy is the philosophy, the procedure is the mechanism that implements the policy and provides the framework leading to the program element, which sets the stage for the rehabilitation of the employee and his or her return to work.

Since this book was described earlier as a "how-to" book, examples have been selected from numerous private and public employers from around the country in order to illustrate all of the specific procedural sections that have been discussed in this chapter. These examples may be found in Appendix E. Appendix C contains a model policy, procedure, and program for the review of any interested employer.

Notes

1. Presnall, "Folklore and Facts About Employees With Alcoholism," *Journal of Occupational Medicine*, Vol. 9, 1967, 187–92.
2. Sonnenstahl & Trice, *Strategies for Employee Assistance Programs: The Crucial Balance* (Ithaca, N.Y.: ILR Press, 1986), 13–14.
3. *Northrup Worldwide Servs.*, 64 LA 742 (1975).
4. *Hoover Co.*, 77 LA 1287, 1290 (1982).
5. *Johnson-Bateman Co.*, 295 NLRB No. 26, 131 LRRM 1393 (1989); *Minneapolis Star Tribune*, 295 NLRB No. 63, 131 LRRM 1404 (1989); *Consolidated Rail Corp. v. Railway Labor Executives' Ass'n*, 491 U.S. ___, 131 LRRM 2601 (1989).

6. Executive Order No. 12,564, Drug Free Federal Workplace, 51 Fed. Reg. 32,889 (1986); Drug Free Workplace Act of 1988, Pub. L. No. 100-690, tit. V, subtitle D; Department of Transportation, Procedures for Transportation Workplace Drug Testing Programs, 53 Fed. Reg. 47,002 (1988) (to be codified at 49 C.F.R. §40); Department of Defense, Federal Acquisition Regulation Supplement; Drug-Free Work Force, 53 Fed. Reg. 37,763 (1988) (to be codified at 48 C.F.R. §§223 and 252); Department of Health & Human Services, Mandatory Guidelines for Federal Workplace Drug Testing Programs, 53 Fed. Reg. 11,970 (Apr. 1988); Office of Management & Budget, Government-Wide Implementation of the Drug-Free Workplace Act of 1988, 54 Fed. Reg. 4946 (1989).

7. *Kelley v. Schlumberger Technology Corp.*, 849 F.2d 41, 3 IER Cases 696 (1st Cir. 1988); *Hook v. Rothstein*, 281 S.C. 541, 316 S.E.2d 690 (S.C. Ct. App. 1984); *Pugsley v. Privette*, 220 Va. 892, 263 S.E.2d 69 (1980); Cal. Health & Safety Code §56.05 (West 1983); Minn. Stat. Ann. §181.954 (1987); Utah Code Ann. §34-38-13 (1987); Vt. Stat. Ann. tit. 21, §516 (1987).

8. Department of Health & Human Services, Mandatory Guidelines for Federal Workplace Drug Testing Programs, 53 Fed. Reg. 11,980 (Apr. 11, 1988).

9. Chapter 5.

10. Chapter 2.

11. *See, e.g.*, Conn. Acts 551, L1987, §2 (effective Oct. 1, 1987); Iowa Code, §730.52 (effective July 1, 1987); La. Rev. Stat. Ann. §23:1601(10)(A)(1987); Minn. Stat. §181.93(13) and 181.94(4) (effective Sept. 1, 1987); Mont. Code Ann. §39-2-304 (1987); Neb. Laws §2(8), L.B. 582, L. 1988 (1988); R.I. Gen. Laws §28-661(A-6) (effective July 1, 1987); Utah Code Ann. §34-38-9, 10, and 11 (1987); San Francisco, Cal., S.F. Mun. Code §300 A.1 (1985); *Johnson-Bateman Co.*, *supra* note 5.

12. *Lovvorn v. City of Chattanooga*, 647 F. Supp. 875, 1 IER Cases 1041 (E.D. Tenn. 1986), *aff'd*, 846 F.2d 1539, 3 IER Cases 673 (6th Cir. 1988). Most other decisions involving drug testing of public employees in situations where the employer has reasonable individualized suspicion of drug use include *Everett v. Napper*, 632 F. Supp. 1481, 1 IER Cases 1310 (N.D. Ga. 1986), *aff'd in part*, 833 F.2d 1507, 2 IER Cases 711 (11th Cir. 1987) (firefighters); *Transit Union Div. 241 v. Suscy*, 538 F.2d 1264 (7th Cir.), *cert. denied*, 429 U.S. 1029 (1976) (municipal bus drivers) and *Allen v. City of Marietta*, 601 F. Supp. 482 (N.D. Ga. 1986) (municipal utility employees).

13. Procedures for Transportation Workplace Drug Testing Programs, 53 Fed. Reg. 47,002 (1988) (to be codified at 49 C.F.R. §40); Proposed Rule, Nuclear Regulatory Commission Fitness-for-Duty Program, 53 Fed. Reg. 36,795-02 (1988) (to be codified at 10 C.F.R. Part 26).

14. The Federal Highway Administration mandates that truck drivers be subject to urinalysis biennially or periodically under 49 C.F.R. §391.05. The Federal Aviation Administration mandates periodic drug testing for its employees under §V, ¶B of Appendix 1 to 14 C.F.R. §121.

15. *Penny v. Kennedy*, 648 F. Supp. 815, 1 IER Cases 1047 (E.D. Tenn. 1986), *aff'd*, 846 F.2d 1563, 3 IER Cases 691, *vacated and reh'g en banc granted*, 862 F.2d 567, 3 IER Cases 1706 (6th Cir. 1988) (police); *Lovvorn v. City of Chattanooga*, 647 F. Supp. 875, 1 IER Cases 1041 (E.D. Tenn. 1986), *aff'd*, 846 F.2d 1539, 3 IER Cases 673, *vacated and reh'g en banc granted*, 861 F.2d 1388, 3 IER Cases 1706 (6th Cir. 1988) (firefighters); *Capua v. City of Plain-*

field, 643 F. Supp. 1507, 1 IER Cases 625 (D.N.J. 1986), *vacated and reh'g en banc granted,* 861 F.2d 1539, 3 IER Cases 673 (6th Cir. 1988) (firefighters and police); *Transport Workers Local 234 (Philadelphia) v. Southeastern Pa. Transp. Auth.,* 678 F. Supp. 543, 127 LRRM 2835 (E.D. Pa. 1988), *aff'd,* 863 F.2d 1110, 130 LRRM 2553 (3d Cir. 1988) (transportation workers).

16. Federal Aviation Administration, Anti-Drug Programs for Personnel Engaged in Specified Aviation Activities, 53 Fed. Reg. 47,024 (1988) (to be codified at 14 C.F.R. §§61, 63, 65, 121, and 135). Executive Order No. 12,564 of September 15, 1986, 51 Fed. Reg. 32,889 (1986), §7(d). Customs Directive on Drug Screening Program, Customs USA, Fiscal Year 1985, 113–14.

17. Department of Defense, Federal Acquisition Regulation Supplement; Drug-Free Work Force, 48 C.F.R. §§223 and 252; Customs Directive on Drug Screening Program, Customs USA, Fiscal Year 1985, 113–14; Procedures for Transportation Workplace Drug Testing Programs, 49 C.F.R. §40.1 (1988).

18. *Skinner v. Railway Labor Executives' Ass'n,* 489 U.S. ___, 4 IER Cases 224 (1989).

19. *Treasury Employees v. Von Rabb,* 489 U.S. ___, 4 IER Cases 246 (1989).

20. *Jones v. McKenzie,* 628 F. Supp. 1500, 1 IER Cases 1076 (D.D.C. 1986), *rev'd and vacated in part,* 833 F.2d 335, 2 IER Cases 1121 (D.C. Cir. 1987), *cert. denied sub nom. Jenkins v. Jones,* 490 U.S. ___, 4 IER Cases 352 (1989); *Copeland v. Philadelphia Police Dep't,* 840 F.2d 1139, 2 IER Cases 1825 (3d Cir. 1988), *cert. denied,* 490 U.S. ___, 4 IER Cases 352 (1989); *Alverado v. Washington Pub. Power Supply Sys.,* 111 Wash.2d 424, 759 P.2d 427, 3 IER Cases 769 (1988), *cert. denied,* 490 U.S. ___, 4 IER Cases 352 (1989).

21. In *O'Connor v. Ortega,* 480 U.S. 709, 1 IER Cases 1617 (1987), the Supreme Court distinguished between reasonable suspicion and probable cause in the context of workplace searches. The Court "conclude[d] that the 'special needs, beyond the normal need for law enforcement make the . . . probable-cause requirement impracticable,'. . . for legitimate work-related, noninvestigatory intrusions as well as investigations of work-related misconduct. . . . We hold, therefore, that public employer intrusions on the constitutionally protected privacy interests of government employees for noninvestigatory, work-related purposes, as well as for investigations of work-related misconduct, should be judged by the standard of reasonableness under all the circumstances. [Citation omitted.]" *Id.,* 1 IER Cases at 1623.

22. In *Times-Mirror Cable Television,* 87 LA 543 (Berns, 1986), the suspension of an employee after he was arrested at work during a police investigation of drug traffic was found by the arbitrator to have been without just cause where the employer made no attempt to investigate the situation before placing the employee on suspension. In *Boise Cascade Corp.,* a testing program which allowed testing upon reasonable cause or after an accident was found by Arbitrator Sam Kagel to violate a collective bargaining agreement with the Paperworkers. Kagel ruled the just cause requirement for discharge or discipline was violated because it placed the burden on the employee to demonstrate that there was no just cause for discharge or discipline by supplying a urine sample for purposes of being tested for drugs. *Nat'l Rep. Substance Abuse* (BNA), p. 5 (Jan. 21, 1987).

23. Controlled Substances Testing, 49 C.F.R. §391.99 (1988).

24. Federal Highway Administration Controlled Substances Testing, 53 Fed. Reg. 47,134 (1988) (to be codified at 49 C.F.R. §391.115, Post-Accident Testing Procedures). In *Skinner v. Railway Executives' Ass'n, supra* note 18, the

Supreme Court reviewed the Federal Railroad Administration's (FRA's) requirement of post-accident toxicological testing. After reviewing the governmental interest and the minimal privacy intrusion the Court found post-accident testing under the regulation proper. The Supreme Court rejected the contention that "less drastic and equally effective means" could be used instead of urine or blood tests. The Court stated that the reasonableness of a governmental activity does not necessarily turn upon the existence of less intrusive alternatives. The FRA expressly considered several alternatives to its drug-screening program and reasonably found them wanting. The Court, therefore, refused to "second-guess the reasonable conclusions drawn by the FRA after years of investigation. . . ." *Id.*, 4 IER Cases at 236 n.9.

25. Controlled Substances Testing, 49 C.F.R. §391.113 (1988).
26. Drug Free Workplace Act of 1988, Pub. L. No. 100-690 tit. V, subtitle D.
27. *Id.* §5152(b).
28. Department of Defense Federal Acquisition Regulation Supplement; Drug-Free Work Force, 48 C.F.R. §§223 and 252 (1988).
29. Potential DOD Contractors Warned on Drug Regulations, 248 Daily Lab. Rep. A-3 (BNA, Dec. 27, 1988).
30. *Lovvorn v. City of Chattanooga*, 647 F. Supp. 875, 1 IER Cases 1041 (E.D. Tenn. 1986), *aff'd*, 846 F.2d 1539, 3 IER Cases 673, *vacated and reh'g en banc granted*, 861 F.2d 1388, 3 IER Cases 1706 (6th Cir. 1988); *Treasury Employees v. Von Raab*, 489 U.S. ___, 4 IER Cases 246 (1989).
31. Department of Transportation, Procedures for Transportation Workplace Drug Testing Programs, 53 Fed. Reg. 47,002 (1988) (to be codified at 49 C.F.R. §40); Department of Defense, Federal Acquisition Regulation Supplement; Drug-Free Work Force, 53 Fed. Reg. 37,763 (1988) (to be codified at 48 C.F.R. §§223 and 252).
32. Establishing a Drug-Free Federal Workplace, FPM Letter 792-16 (Nov. 28, 1986), at 3(a)(3).
33. DuPont Corp., Substance Abuse Committee Report (Jan. 3, 1986), at 28–29.
34. Drug Free Workplace Act of 1988, Pub. L. No. 100-690 tit. V, subtitle D, §5152(a).
35. Sonnenstuhl & Trice, *supra* note 2, at 24–25.
36. *Dickinson v. Edwards*, 105 Wash.2d 457, 716 P.2d 814 (1986); *Greer v. Ferrizz*, 110 A.D.2d 815, 488 N.Y.S.2d 234 (1985); *Meany v. Newell*, 352 N.W.2d 779 (Minn. 1984); *Southern Bell v. Altman*, 183 Ga. App. 611, 359 S.E.2d 385 (1987).
37. Procedures for Transportation Workplace Drug Testing Programs, 49 C.F.R. §40.25 (1988); Department of Health & Human Services, Mandatory Guidelines for Federal Workplace Drug Testing Programs, 53 Fed. Reg. 11,980 (Apr. 11, 1988), subpart 2.2.
38. Department of Health & Human Services, Mandatory Guidelines for Federal Workplace Drug Testing Programs, 53 Fed. Reg. 11,970 (1988), subpart 2.2(f)(12), Integrity and Identity of Specimen.
39. Procedures for Transportation Workplace Drug Testing Programs, 49 C.F.R. §40.26(f)(9) (1988); Department of Health & Human Services, Mandatory Guidelines for Federal Workplace Drug Testing Programs, 53 Fed. Reg. 11,980 (Apr. 11, 1988), subpart 2.2(f)(9).
40. Establishing a Drug-Free Federal Workplace, FPM Letter 792-16 (Nov. 28, 1986), subpart 4(g)(3).

41. Procedures for Transportation Workplace Drug Testing Programs, 49 C.F.R. §40.21(b)–(c) (1988).
42. See example No. 1 in Appendix D, "Substance Abuse Procedures" at "Chain of Custody."
43. Clinical Laboratories Improvement Act of 1967, 43 U.S.C.A. 263a (West, 1982); Department of Health & Human Services, Mandatory Guidelines for Federal Workplace Drug Testing Programs, 53 Fed. Reg. 11,970 (1988), subpart C; Current List of Laboratories Which Meet Minimum Standards to Engage in Urine Drug Testing for Federal Agencies, 54 Fed. Reg. 13,661 (1989).
44. Department of Health & Human Services, Mandatory Guidelines for Federal Workplace Drug Testing Programs, 53 Fed. Reg. 11,970 (1988), subpart 2.4(f).
45. *Id.* Subpart 2.4(e) directs that "[the] following initial cutoff levels shall be used when screening specimens to determine whether they are negative for these file drugs or classes of drugs:

Drug	Initial Test Level (ng/ml)
Marijuana Metabolites	100
Cocaine Metabolites	300
Opiate Metabolites	300*
Phencyclidine	25
Amphetamines	1,000

*25 ng/ml if immunoassay specific for free morphine.

Subpart 2.(4)(f) sets these cutoff values for the confirmatory test:

Drug	Confirmatory Test Level (ng/ml)
Marijuana Metabolite[1]	15
Cocaine Metabolite[2]	150
Opiates	
Morphine	[1]300
Codeine	[2]300
Phencyclidine	25
Amphetamines	
Amphetamine	500
Methamphetamine	500

    [1]Delta-tetrahydrocannabinol-9-carboxylic acid.
    [2]Benzotecgonine.

46. *Id.* subpart 2.7; Procedures for Transportation Workplace Drug Testing Programs, 49 C.F.R. §40.33 (1988).
47. *See, e.g.*, Minn. Stat. §181.953(9) (1987); Vt. Stat. Ann. tit. 21, §515 (1987); 21 U.S.C.A. §515 (1987).
48. The Poe Corporation Substance Abuse Program (Aug. 15, 1988), ¶E(6).
49. Drug Free Workplace Act of 1988, Pub. L. No. 100-690 tit. V, subtitle D, §5152(a).

50. *O'Connor v. Ortega,* 480 U.S. 709, 1 IER Cases 1617 (1987). In *Skinner v. Railway Labor Executives Ass'n,* 489 U.S. ___, 4 IER Cases 224 (1989), the Supreme Court in reviewing the Federal Railroad Administration's post-accident drug testing program and the lack of individualized suspicion, concluded that "[i]n limited circumstances, where the privacy interests implicated by the search are minimal, and where an important governmental interest furthered by the intrusion would be placed in jeopardy by a requirement of individualized suspicion, a search may be reasonable despite the absence of such suspicion." *Id.,* 4 IER Cases at 234.

51. DuPont Corp., Substance Abuse Committee Report (Jan. 3, 1986), at 37; Fluor Daniel/Wolf Creek Project Chemical Substance Abuse Policy, 1.3.4, 6.44; Milliken & Co. Substance Abuse Prevention Process, ¶7.

52. *Crown Zellerbach Corp.,* 87 LA 1145 (Cohen, 1986). The discharge of an employee who refused to undergo a drug-screening test after she reported to work in an unfit condition was reduced to a suspension. *Board of Educ. of D.C.,* AAA Case No. 1639-0030-85H (Dec. 30, 1985). Discipline of grievants for off-premises use of drugs confirmed by screening was found to be in violation of the labor agreement which was limited to actions on school premises. The drug screen alone could not establish on-premises use. *Shell Oil Co.,* 87 LA 473 (Nicholas, 1986). The discharge of an employee for possession of marijuana was overturned where a single marijuana cigarette was found in his automobile. The arbitrator found that the employer had failed to prove he actually "possessed" the marijuana.

53. Drug Free Workplace Act of 1988, Pub. L. 100-690 tit. V, subtitle D, §5152(a)(1)(D); Office of Management & Budget, Government-wide Implementation of the Drug Free Workplace Act of 1988, 54 Fed. Reg. 4,946 (1989).

54. Milliken & Co. Substance Abuse Prevention Process, ¶7.

Chapter 5

Substance Abuse Education and Training

Education and training are critical if an employer expects the employees in its workplace to understand and abide by a substance abuse program. Failure to educate and train employees, and particularly supervisors, concerning the substance abuse program usually dooms the substance abuse program to failure itself. The programs fail because the employees are not informed of the dangers of drugs and alcohol, or what is expected of them, and the supervisors remain ignorant or insecure about the substance abuse program and therefore usually do nothing. As a result, top management may deceive itself into thinking it has a working substance abuse program, but in reality, it has a "paper program," which may look good on paper, but is empty in practice.

This situation does not have to exist. When an employer develops a comprehensive substance abuse program with extensive education and training the usual result is that the employees know what is expected and the supervisors understand the goals and objectives of the program, and know how to implement its policies and procedures. It should be emphasized that education in general is a lifelong process and, similarly, substance abuse education and training must be established on a regular and continuing basis if it is to be effective. The reasons are simple. People forget, and with turnover, new employees and supervisors in the work force cannot be held to the standards of the substance abuse program if it has not been explained to them. Substance abuse programs are actually an ongoing process, or a long-term, never-ending system for dealing with this problem. If there is any part of this process that must be emphasized, it is the education and training facet. Substance abuse in the workplace did not appear overnight and will not be eliminated overnight. Therefore, education and training on the dangers of substance abuse and the program for dealing with it are crucial for the long-term containment and ultimate elimination of the substance abuse menace.

This chapter addresses three concerns: the education and training of managers, education and training of employees, and differing types, effectiveness, and cost of education and training methods that employers may implement.

Management Education and Training

For a substance abuse program to work and in order to achieve the goals of a drug free workplace, it is imperative that management from the top down fully support and participate in the education and training. To ensure support for the employer's substance abuse program and its proper utilization, management must be familiar with the necessity of the program and the specifics of the plan implementation, and understand the manifestations of an employee's substance abuse. Substance abuse education and training should be designed to educate managers on the role of supervisors in the substance abuse program, the facts on substance abuse, the details of the employer's substance abuse program, and the managerial recognition and handling of substance abuse problems in the workplace.

Education and training should be geared toward direct line supervision. These supervisors have daily contact with their personnel and are most familiar with their employees' normal behavior and work performance patterns. However, since the program applies to every level of the employer's operations, every member of management should participate in the substance abuse education and training program. In particular, education and training should be designed to ensure that supervisors have the knowledge and ability to perform the behavioral observation and work performance evaluation necessary to enable them to initiate appropriate corrective action.

Role of Supervisors

It should be emphasized to supervisors in the education and training that their role, primarily, is to recognize behavioral, personality, and performance changes in employees which may indicate a need to refer the employees for professional evaluation. Recognition is by far the most important role of supervisors. Subsequent to recognition, supervisors should be trained concerning documentation of the behavior and performance observations; confrontation or intervention with the employee concerning the behavioral and performance problems; implementation of the details and specifics of the employer's substance abuse policy, procedures, and program; the rehabilitation aspect of the employer's substance abuse program if necessary; and the myriad of emotions and problems involved with an employee's post-rehabilitation and return to work.

A supervisor's role in an employer's substance abuse program is crucial to the effectiveness of the program. A supervisor who is well trained in the facts of substance abuse, the employer's substance abuse program, and the recognition and handling of substance abuse problems in the workplace, is an employer's best defense against substance abuse problems.

Facts of Substance Abuse

In any substance abuse education and training, it is fundamental to start with a presentation of the facts on substance abuse. This section of the program will usually describe the problems of substance abuse in general and in the workplace in particular, and the drugs of abuse. Further, a well-designed program will provide samples, pictures, and/or paraphernalia of drugs of abuse.

The problems associated with substance abuse are covered in Chapter 1, "Significance of Substance Abuse in the Workplace." Although many employers may take the problems of substance abuse for granted, it is important to explain in detail a number of the problems caused by substance abuse in order for the supervisors or others to begin to understand the overall problem. Also, many employers have found that when they are able to give examples, particularly examples from their own work force, such as deaths or accidents due to proven substance abuse, supervisors and employees alike can relate to the problem more readily.

Concerning drugs of abuse, it is important in any substance abuse education and training to present a detailed and factual explanation of what the drugs of abuse are, and the problems they cause. This session in the education and training usually includes a lot of "myth exploding." Many supervisors and employees, particularly those using drugs, have developed all sorts of peculiar ideas about drugs. For example, many people believe that amphetamines increase work productivity (which is possible in the short term) and have no long-term bad effects (which is absurd). Further, some people will convince themselves that cocaine makes them smarter and more capable of dealing with the demanding rigors of their particular job. The fact that rehabilitation centers are now overcrowded with cocaine and crack addicts is a good indication of just how ludicrous this idea is.

The usual drugs of abuse that are identified include alcohol, marijuana, cocaine and crack, the opiates including heroin and morphine, the hallucinogens including LSD and PCP, amphetamines ("speed"), barbiturates ("downers"), and increasingly, benzodiazepines including Valium, Librium, and Xanax. Facts and details concerning these drugs of abuse and the terminology of substance abuse are found in Appendix A "Drugs of Abuse" and Appendix B "Glossary of Substance Abuse Terminology."

Additionally, most substance abuse education and training now includes pictures of these drugs of abuse, and examples of drug paraphernalia such as marijuana water pipes, crack pipes, cocaine kits with mirrors and straws, marijuana cigarette rolling machines, and syringes for heroin and other drugs. In addition, a number of employers will request that law enforcement officials bring samples of the drugs so that employees, particularly supervisors, can observe them firsthand in order to be able to recognize them. Many law enforcement officials have the capacity of burning marijuana, for instance, so that supervisors will know what it smells like and be able to recognize its very distinctive odor for future reference. Experience has shown that while many supervisors may claim to be knowledgeable concerning substance abuse, usually they are not. Therefore, it is critical to have a detailed education and training program concerning what drugs you are concerned about, what they look like, and how they affect the body.

Many substance abuse education and training programs at this point will deal with the signs and symptoms of substance abuse in connection with the particular drugs. The following chart is often useful for a discussion concerning the signs and symptoms of substance abuse, although it is important to point out to the supervisors that they are responsible for noticing behavior and work performance changes, not for becoming amateur diagnosticians.

Warning Signs of Alcoholism

1. Bloodshot eyes
2. Morning sweats

3. Smell of liquor
4. Lowered inhibitions
5. Loss of balance and coordination
6. Slurred speech
7. Irritability
8. Depression

Symptoms Indicative of Marijuana Usage

1. Paranoid thoughts
2. Anxiety
3. Fear and withdrawal from social interaction
4. Unpleasant mood swings
5. Increased sensory awareness to music, touch, light, and social interaction
6. Impaired short-term memory

Symptoms Indicative of Other Drugs

Amphetamines
1. Dilated eye pupils
2. Trembling hands and feet, heavy perspiration
3. Paleness
4. Sleep difficulties, excitability
5. Talkativeness

Cocaine
1. Runny nose
2. Tremors
3. Nervousness and irritability
4. Anxiety
5. Decreased appetite

Hallucinogens (PCP, LSD)
1. Dilated eye pupils
2. Trembling hands and feet
3. Chills
4. Cold and sweaty palms
5. Decreased appetite
6. Anxiety
7. Disorientation
8. Slowed reflexes
9. Slurred speech

Methaqualone (Quaaludes)
1. Lowered inhibitions
2. Impaired physical coordination

3. Slurred speech
4. Impaired judgment

Heroin
1. Needle marks on arms, hands, knees, and abdomen
2. Flushing
3. Drowsiness
4. Itching
5. Decrease in physical activity

In addition to the facts, examples, and signs and symptoms of substance abuse, most education and training will detail the illegality of all of these substances. Although the education and training should be geared toward the particular jurisdiction where the facility is located, every jurisdiction in the United States has particular statutory prohibitions against the use of these substances in most circumstances.[1] Further, the federal government controls most of these substances through federal law and regulation in conjunction with the Controlled Substances Act.[2] The drugs of abuse as well as all other drugs regulated by the federal government (which is all drugs) are placed in various "schedules" from Schedules I through V, with Schedule I being the most heavily sanctioned. The schedules are organized in decreasing potential for abuse (I, highest to V, lowest). These schedules and their components appear in Appendix G.

Although alcohol is a so-called "legal" drug, there are numerous statutes and regulations dealing with alcohol, including the legal age for alcohol consumption, penalties for driving under the influence, and laws against providing alcohol to minors. Most if not all jurisdictions in the United States have laws dealing with these and various other issues concerning alcohol.[3] Additionally, although the illegal drugs of abuse are a much more exciting topic, alcohol abuse is far more prevalent than all of the other drugs combined.[4] Therefore, no education and training should ignore the effects of alcohol, the illegal or inappropriate use of alcohol, and the fact that it has no place in the workplace.

Employer Substance Abuse Programs

As a part of an employer's substance abuse education and training method, it is imperative that the supervisors and employees be educated concerning the employer's particular substance abuse program. Aspects of the employer's program that should be covered include: the employer's policy and philosophy concerning substance abuse; procedural details; the employer's program for handling substance abuse problems, whether it is an employee assistance program, a referral program, or other program; counseling opportunities such as the EAP, inpatient treatment, outpatient treatment, and community resources available to employees; return to work and aftercare programs; penalties for violating the substance abuse program; and requirements of federal and state law.

Substance Abuse Policy and Philosophy

It is important that supervisors be trained concerning the employer's substance abuse policy and the employer's philosophy behind that policy. In most cases the employer's philosophy is to create and maintain a drug free workplace. Further, it is important that supervisors understand that top management is committed to dealing with substance abuse problems and that supervisors are critical players. Additionally, some employers may have established substance abuse programs in conjunction with federal or state legal requirements such as those for federal contractors under the Drug Free Workplace Act, or Departments of Transportation or Defense regulatory requirements, or other laws.[5] In any event, the employer's basic substance abuse policy and philosophy should be explained in detail to the supervisors so that they will understand the program and philosophy thoroughly and realize that they are expected to comply with it.

Procedural Details

The bulk of any substance abuse program will deal with the procedural details that are involved. As was stated in Chapter 4, "Developing Substance Abuse Procedures," procedures are the nuts and bolts of any employer's substance abuse program. It is critical that supervisors understand the procedural details of the program and understand their role in effectuating the procedure, where necessary. Procedural details that commonly confuse supervisors include the drug testing procedures and the substance abuse documentation procedures.

Many employers find it is very useful to walk through the entire procedure of the substance abuse program including the portions dealing with applicants as well as employees so that supervisors have a feel for how the system operates. For instance, many employers provide laboratory personnel to explain the details of drug testing in conjunction with the employer's program. Further, most employers carefully review the documentation and paperwork involved with their particular substance abuse policy. Other employers include role playing in the education and training program so that supervisors can see themselves act out situations that may arise. Many employers also provide as much information in written form as possible to the supervisors so that the supervisors may study it on or off the job in order to more fully appreciate the complexity of substance abuse and the details of the employer's procedure.

Program

It is also important that the supervisors understand the employer's program for handling substance abuse. If an employer has an employee assistance program, the details of the program should be explained to the supervisors, and the supervisors should understand their role in directing employees to the EAP. If an employer has some other program for dealing with substance abuse, whether it is termination or referral to community resources, or whatever, then this program should be explained in detail to the supervisors. Additionally, many employers provide listings of typical questions and answers concerning substance abuse in general and the employer's substance abuse program in particular for the supervisors to take home and study.

Counseling Opportunities

Federal law requires that employers under certain circumstances[6] provide supervisors or employees with information about the various counseling opportunities available in the area. Where an employer has an employee assistance program, referral of a supervisor or employee to the EAP for counseling opportunities should constitute sufficient compliance with the federal statutes or regulations. Where the employer has no such program, it would be important that the employer establish lists of referral agencies such as state drug and alcohol units, vocational rehabilitation units, community drug and alcohol resources, and Veterans Administration hospitals or facilities. As far as the supervisors are concerned, where an employer is covered by federal or state law requiring education of employees on counseling opportunities, the supervisors should be made aware that this is a required element of the program and be given a list of counseling opportunities or referral agencies to which the supervisor can refer employees with substance abuse problems.

Return to Work and Aftercare

An often overlooked element of an employer's substance abuse program is what the supervisor does when the employee returns to work from rehabilitation. Usually so much time is spent discussing drug testing and identification of substance abusers that the subject of return to work and aftercare is often ignored. However, whether the employee is properly integrated into the work force once he or she has been rehabilitated is critical to the success of the substance abuse program. Supervisors should be trained concerning the employer's return-to-work program including how time away from work is handled, additional surveillance testing, interaction with the EAP personnel, and attendance at aftercare programs such as Alcoholics Anonymous. In addition, many employers have found it useful to educate supervisors concerning exactly what happens at rehabilitation facilities, so that the supervisors do not believe the employee has simply been on a vacation for 28 days prior to returning to work. This type of rehabilitation sensitivity training for supervisors is often very useful in expanding the supervisor's knowledge and appreciation of the complexity of substance abuse problems. Further, the supervisor may become much more useful in easing the return-to-work transition of the rehabilitated employee.

Penalties for Violating the Programs

An essential element of any employer's education and training program is ensuring that supervisors understand what the penalties will be for either supervisors or employees who violate the substance abuse program of the employer. The supervisors need to understand the circumstances under which an employee will be warned, tested, or terminated. Most employers' substance abuse policies should state very clearly under what circumstances discipline will be implemented. Additionally, federal law[7] requires that employers covered by certain statutes and regulations educate supervisors and employees concerning the penalties for violation of substance abuse policies where the federal government is involved directly or in a regulatory capacity. As a result, education of supervisors concerning the penalties for violating the substance abuse program should be considered mandatory.

Federal and State Law Requirements

Increasingly, employers' substance abuse policies and programs are being mandated or regulated under federal or state law. As a result, many employers have found it useful to educate their supervisors in the elements of their substance abuse programs which are required by law. It is unfair to the supervisor to impose responsibility for a substance abuse program on him or her and yet not explain that some of the requirements of the program may have been mandated by federal law, violation of which could subject the employer to debarment, suspension, termination, or prosecution. Further, when a supervisor realizes that certain aspects of the substance abuse program are required by law, he or she generally takes the program much more seriously.

Recognition and Handling of Substance Abuse Problems in the Workplace

Once supervisors have been educated and trained concerning the facts of substance abuse and the particular employer's substance abuse program, they must learn to recognize and handle substance abuse problems in the workplace. There are five basic areas with regard to recognition and handling about which the supervisor must be trained. They are: recognition (including use of a checklist); documentation; constructive confrontation; implementation; and rehabilitation and return to work.

Recognition

Probably the most critical role of a supervisor is to recognize the behavior and performance problems of his or her employees which indicate that the employee may be a substance abuser. However, it is not enough that the supervisor simply notice that "something is wrong" with the employee or that the employee is "not acting like himself." The supervisor must be trained on specific recognition factors and techniques in order to be able to work with his or her employees in a constructive manner. Most employers use some sort of checklist which lists factors concerning both behavior patterns and job performance in order to be as objective as possible. Almost any checklist may be used for both substance abuse recognition for drug testing purposes or in conjunction with referral to an employee assistance program, and the critical element is for the supervisor to be trained at both behavior and job performance recognition techniques.

The checklist below lists a variety of factors that a supervisor should be able to recognize in dealing with his or her employee if the employee begins to show behavior or job performance problems. It is important to realize that many behavior or job performance problems may not be caused by substance abuse. For instance, if a person is ill with some other disease such as diabetes, depression, or possibly even common ailments such as viruses, his or her performance will be affected. Also, financial problems or family problems can affect an employee's performance. However, where the behavioral change is noticeable to the supervisor or other employees on a more regular basis, these checklists may be useful in identifying problems so that the individual employee may be referred to an employee assistance program, or may be subject to drug testing, if necessary.

Employee Behavior Checklist for the Identification of the Troubled Employee

1. The checklist is to be used when you've become concerned about an employee's declining performance.
2. THIS CHECKLIST IS TO BE USED ONLY AS AN OBSERVATIONAL AID FOR THE MANAGER. IN NO EVENT SHOULD THIS DATA BE INCLUDED AS PART OF AN OFFICIAL FILE.
3. Where a combination of THREE (3) or more items appear on a continuous basis, this is a likely indication of a troubled employee.
   I. CURRENT BEHAVIORAL PATTERNS
      (Check those that best describe the current situation)
      A. EMPLOYEE'S APPEARANCE
         _____ sloppy
         _____ inappropriate clothing
      B. MOOD
         _____ withdrawn
         _____ sad
         _____ mood swings, high and low

_____ suspiciousness
_____ extreme sensitivity
_____ nervousness
_____ frequent irritability with others
_____ preoccupation with illness and death (morbidity)

C. ACTIONS
_____ physically assaultive (or threatening)
_____ unduly talkative
_____ exaggerated self-importance
_____ rigidity—inability to change plans with ease
_____ making incoherent or irrelevant statements on the job
_____ over-compliance with any routine (making it a ritual)
_____ frequent argumentativeness
_____ frequent outbursts of crying
_____ excessive amount of personal telephone time

II. JOB PERFORMANCE
A. ABSENTEEISM
_____ multiple instances of improper reporting of time off
_____ excessive sick leave
_____ repeated absences following a pattern
_____ excessive lateness in the morning, or upon returning from lunch
_____ peculiar and increasingly improbable excuses for absences
_____ high absenteeism rate for colds, flu, gastritis, general malaise, etc.
_____ frequent unscheduled short-term absences (with or without medical explanation)
_____ frequent use of unscheduled vacation time

B. "ON-THE-JOB" ABSENTEEISM
_____ continued absence from job location more than job requires
_____ frequent trips to water fountain or restroom
_____ long coffee breaks

C. ACCIDENTS
_____ physical complaints on the job
_____ accidents on the job
_____ accidents off the job

D. WORK PATTERNS AND PRODUCTION

_____ current work assignment requires more effort than previously taken

_____ work takes more time to produce

_____ difficulty in recalling instructions, understanding office procedures, etc.

_____ display of disinterest in work

_____ increased difficulty in handling complex assignments

_____ difficulty in recalling previous mistakes (although these have been brought to the employee's attention)

_____ general absentmindedness, forgetfulness

_____ alternate periods of high and low productivity

_____ coming to work in an intoxicated condition

_____ odor of drugs

_____ missed deadlines

_____ mistakes due to poor judgment

_____ outside complaints about the employee's work

_____ improbable excuses for these poor patterns

_____ carelessness

E. EMPLOYEE RELATIONSHIPS ON THE JOB

_____ over-reaction to real or imagined criticism

_____ wide swings in job morale

_____ borrowing money from co-workers

_____ unreasonable resentments against co-workers

_____ avoids co-workers

_____ repeated and compulsive criticism of the company

_____ persistent requests for job transfer

_____ unrealistic expectation for promotion

_____ abrasiveness with others (manager and/or co-workers)

F. WORK-RELATED RELATIONSHIPS IN THE COMMUNITY

_____ inappropriate behavior at company business meeting

_____ complaints from the community concerning the employee

Current Behavioral Patterns. In reviewing employee behavior patterns, supervisors should be made aware of the importance of detecting changes in the employee's appearance, mood, and actions. If an employee's appearance has markedly changed from being neat to being sloppy, or the employee begins to wear inappropriate clothing or has some other marked change in appearance, the supervisor should note that something may be affecting this change in the employee's behavior. Similarly, regarding the employee's mood, the supervisor normally will be trained concerning changes in the employee's mood, usually contrasting changes that may or may not be caused by substance abuse. For example, if the employee was once outgoing and now is withdrawn, if the employee who was once pleasant is now very sad, or more particularly, when the employee suffers from mood swings, such as alternating between high moods and low moods or excitement to depression, the supervisor should be taught to notice this type of behavior. Further, if an employee changes and becomes very suspicious, extremely sensitive, or excessively nervous, the supervisor should be trained to note these mood changes.

The supervisor should be trained to note if the employee appears frequently irritable with others in the workplace or becomes preoccupied with illness and death. It is not unusual for a substance abusing employee to act withdrawn, sad, or have mood swings when he or she is either using substances in the workplace or being affected by use of substances at home. Some supervisors report that an employee may be withdrawn and depressed prior to lunch and then after lunch appear very excited and happy. Investigation at times indicates that the employee is using substances during the lunch break and his or her mood is thereby affected afterward. Similarly, sensitivity, nervousness, and irritability are often associated with either drug use or withdrawal from drugs.

Supervisors should also be trained concerning the behavioral actions of their employees. For instance, when an employee becomes physically assaultive or threatening to a supervisor or employee, it is not unusual that substances may be involved. Similarly, when an employee becomes unduly talkative, or if he or she begins to develop an exaggerated sense of self-importance, it is possible that substances may be involved, particularly amphetamines, cocaine, or marijuana.

Other fairly typical behavioral patterns include rigidity or the inability to change plans with ease (loss of flexibility), or overcompliance with any routine, such as making the routine more a ritual. This type of fixed behavior usually indicates that the employee may be in serious condition and maintains the rigidity or ritual as a way of coping with his or her inability to deal with the usual changing circumstances in the workplace. In addition to talkativeness, if an employee begins to make incoherent or irrelevant statements on the job, he or she may be under the influence of psychoactive substances. Other actions include frequent argumentativeness, frequent outbursts of crying, or even uncontrollable laughter. Additionally, where an employee tends to make an excessive number of personal telephone calls, it may indicate that he or she is either in desperate need of some substances, or on the other hand, it may be that his or her personal life is a wreck. In any case, it is not for the supervisor to try to diagnose the problem of the employee, but to note the behavioral patterns listed above as typical of employees with substance abuse problems.

Job Performance. A more comfortable area of training for most supervisors is the area of job performance. Most supervisors have been trained concerning evaluation of job performance in conjunction with management skills training and specific instruction on personnel policies and disciplinary rules. As a result, the categories of job performance evaluation, including absenteeism, on-the-job absenteeism, accidents, work patterns and production, employee relationships on the job, and work-related relationships in the community are areas with which most supervisors are familiar. However, it is important that supervisors be trained to recognize the connection between normal or abnormal job performance and the potential for substance abuse.

Absenteeism is an example of a job performance problem that is very typical of substance abusers. For instance, substance abusers are often prone to multiple instances of improper reporting of time off and excessive sick leave. Similarly, substance abusers will often have repeated absences following a pattern, such as Monday and Friday absenteeism. Usually this indicates that the employee, who may get paid on Thursday, uses his or her paycheck on substances, goes on a bender through Sunday, and simply cannot handle work on Monday morning. Monday and Friday absenteeism are classic signs of alcoholism or other drug abuse.

Other indications of absenteeism-related performance problems include excessive tardiness in the morning or upon returning from lunch and peculiar and increasingly improbable excuses for absences. These types of absences may indicate that the employee is using substances on the job as well as away from the job. It is also typical of the type of deteriorating performance for an employee to have high absenteeism rates for colds, flu, gastritis, general malaise, and so on. Further, frequent unscheduled short-term absences, with or without medical explanation, may be an indication of substance abuse. Generally speaking, if a supervisor notices an employee who frequently seems to be sick for no apparent reason, then there may be a substance abuse problem. Furthermore, where an employee frequently uses unscheduled vacation time, the employee's spouse calls in with excuses, or where the employee frequently blames absences on problems at home, substance abuse may be indicated.

On-the-job absenteeism is usually extremely annoying to supervisors. However, a supervisor should look beyond his or her annoyance and recognize the connection between on-the-job absenteeism and possible substance abuse. For instance, if an employee has a continued absence from the job location more than the job would normally require, takes frequent trips to the water fountain or to the restroom, or takes long coffee breaks, the supervisor's suspicion should be aroused and substance abuse may be indicated.

Accidents are another type of performance problem which may suggest substance abuse. Where an employee has accidents or other incidents on the job, the supervisor receives unsafe work habit complaints about the employee from other employees, the employee makes complaints concerning the physical requirements of the job, or where the employee has accidents off the job, substance abuse may be indicated. The employer should identify safety-sensitive jobs in its workplace and pay special attention to the possibility of accidents or other incidents and the substance abuse of employees in these particular occupations.

Another significant indication of job performance problems that may be related to substance abuse is work patterns and production. Because a supervisor's primary job is to achieve production requirements, productivity is an area where the supervisor must be alert to job performance changes. For instance, common indications of possible substance abuse include situations where the current work assignment requires more effort than the employee has previously taken, or the work takes more time to produce. Further, where an employee has difficulty in recalling instructions or understanding operative procedures, substance abuse may be indicated. Similarly, where an employee previously has been interested in his or her work and now displays a disinterest in the work, there may be problems. Sometimes supervisors complain that employees seem to have tuned-out and that the employees experience increased difficulty in handling complex assignments and recalling previous mistakes (although these have been brought to the employee's attention previously), or that they exhibit general absentmindedness and forgetfulness. All of these employee symptoms may be indicators of substance abuse.

A classic sign of substance abuse is alternate periods of high and low productivity. This type of erratic work performance is fairly typical of employees who while on substances work very excitedly and then when withdrawing from substances, work lethargically with poor performance. More obvious signs involving work patterns and production problems include coming to work in an intoxicated condition or smelling of the odor of alcohol or other substances. Other indications may be mistakes due to poor judgment, carelessness, improbable excuses for these poor patterns, or even complaints about the employee's work from other employees. Although some supervisors deal with these types of problems daily, they must be trained to think of these problems as potential indications of substance abuse in the workplace.

A very significant indication of job performance problems is poor employee relationships on the job. Although no supervisor likes to manage based on hearsay, a supervisor must be trained to recognize the significance of employee relationships and employees' comments about one another in the workplace. For example, where employees have an overreaction to real or imagined criticism or employees indicate wide swings in morale, supervisors must be sensitive to the possibility of substance abuse. Further, when employees begin borrowing money from co-workers or certain employees appear to be cashing paychecks at the facility, substance abuse may be indicated. Borrowing money and paycheck cashing commonly have been found to indicate that drug dealing is occurring in the workplace.

Other indications of possible employee relationship problems are unreasonable resentments against co-workers or employee avoidance of co-workers. Other indications are repeated and compulsory criticism of the company, persistent requests for job transfers, or unrealistic expectations for promotion. Finally, where employees have a great abrasiveness with others, whether management or co-workers, there may be a substance abuse problem. It is not unusual for substance abusers to have human relations problems of their own either at home or in the workplace.

Finally, work-related relationships in the community must be considered in training supervisors concerning recognition of substance abuse. For instance, where the employee exhibits inappropriate behavior at employer business meetings or functions, or where the employer receives complaints from the community concerning the employee, substance abuse may be indicated. It is not unusual for substance abusers to act in a relatively well-behaved fashion in the workplace, but act abominably while on business trips or at company retreats. Similarly, when the employer receives word that the employee has been put in jail, has received a drunk driving charge, has been accused of child molestation, has been charged with passing bad checks, has filed for personal bankruptcy, or has other such problems, the supervisor should be trained to bring his information to management as a possible indication of substance abuse problems.

As was stated previously, it is important that the employer provide supervisors with extensive training concerning substance abuse recognition in order to deal effectively with substance abuse problems in the workplace. However, this recognition should be confined to identifying possible symptoms of substance abuse and bringing them to the attention of the employer's proper officials such as personnel department managers or the employee assistance program administrators. It is important that supervisors not try to play doctor or act like amateur diagnosticians. Supervisors should only be instructed to recognize behavior and job performance problems which may indicate substance abuse and then turn the situation and the information over to the experts to deal with the problem.

Documentation

Once supervisors have been trained to recognize possible substance-induced behavior and job performance problems, the next aspect of training should be documentation. Although any employer's substance abuse policy and procedure should contain extensive documentation requirements as discussed in Chapter 4, "Developing Substance Abuse Procedures," the necessity for documentation cannot be overemphasized. The education and training program should spend a significant amount of time explaining to the supervisors what documentation is required.

The documentation forms that are generally used may include a substance abuse checklist, as discussed above, a confidential investigation form, as discussed in Chapter 4, or a simple documentation form that lists the date, the behavior or incident, and any supervisory comments. Supervisors must learn that documentation should be dated and signed by the supervisor, and possibly reviewed, dated, and signed by the supervisor's superior in order to assure compliance with the employer's substance abuse policy. Further, supervisors should also understand that documentation is also designed to prevent potential harassment of employees by ill-intentioned supervisors, which is always a possibility.

Most employers require that supervisors cooperate with either the employer's personnel department or the EAP administrators in recognizing and documenting potential substance abuse problems. Until a supervisor is sufficiently comfortable with substance abuse investigations, he or she should work closely with these trained individuals not only to prevent deviation from, and inconsistency in application of, the substance abuse policy, but also to ensure that the documentation is properly completed. Often where drug testing is involved, many employers require that either two supervisors (or one supervisor thoroughly trained in recognition of substance abuse problems) cooperate in the recognition and documentation aspects of substance abuse investigations. In addition, certain federal regulations require two-supervisor investigations or an investigation by one trained supervisor on any for-cause drug testing situation.[8]

Confidentiality is critical in all substance abuse investigations including the recognition and documentation phases. Although confidentiality is discussed elsewhere,[9] it should always be emphasized to supervisors in order to avoid any possible morale or legal problems.

Constructive Confrontation

Supervisors should be trained in techniques of constructive confrontation once it has been concluded that the employee may have a substance abuse problem. Whether the term of art is intervention, counseling, or constructive confrontation, supervisors should be educated, possibly including role playing, in the employer's preferred techniques of confronting potential substance abusing employees with the suspected problem. Although constructive confrontation is discussed in Chapter 4, "Developing Substance Abuse Procedures," it may be helpful to reiterate: A supervisor or supervisors should meet with the employee privately and confidentially and discuss the particular behavior or job performance problems that have led to the meeting. The supervisors should be trained to explain the employer's substance abuse policy including the employee assistance program options if available or the supervisor should discuss the drug testing requirements if appropriate under the policy. The topics of the confidential meeting with the employee should be based on the employer's particular substance abuse policy and procedure format. Therefore, it should be stressed to supervisors that they should understand the employer's substance abuse policy thoroughly in order to be able to deal with employees effectively.

Program Implementation

Once a supervisor has been trained in constructive confrontation or intervention, the supervisor must be educated and trained concerning implementing the substance abuse program. If the employer has drug testing, the supervisor should understand the details of the employer's policy and should be able to direct the employee through the testing including the proper documentation and consent forms, and/or direct the employee to the employer's medical facility for the drug testing. Further, if the employer has an employee assistance program, the supervisor should be knowledgeable about EAP referral so that he or she can direct the employee to the EAP administrator or counselor for further help. Although it is natural to assume that supervisors should understand how the system works for a particular employer, experience has shown that until a supervisor is comfortable with the precise details of implementation of the substance abuse program the supervisor will not use the program effectively or supervisors will be inconsistent in the implementation of the program. Therefore, many employers use role playing or other modes of communication in order to assure that supervisors are comfortable with the implementation phase of the substance abuse program.

Rehabilitation and Return

Many supervisors view rehabilitation of substance abusing employees as a 28-day vacation. This is usually far from the case. Therefore, many employers find it useful to educate supervisors concerning what rehabilitation is all about. Some employers will take supervisors to the rehabilitation facility to see how it operates, or they will have rehabilitation and EAP personnel discuss the process of rehabilitation with the supervisors either in a group or individually. As a result, supervisors will usually obtain much greater sensitivity, and therefore will become much more capable of dealing with the employee when he or she returns to the workplace after rehabilitation.

In addition, supervisors should be trained concerning the employer's specific procedures for the return to work after rehabilitation. That is, an employer may require a drug test prior to re-entry into the work force or subsequent EAP counseling or aftercare programs which the supervisor should understand. Supervisors should be trained concerning any details such as scheduling changes that may vary from the employer's normal pattern for other employees, if the situation differs, even temporarily, for a rehabilitated employee who returns to work. Finally, supervisors should be reminded of the importance of confidentiality in working with the rehabilitated employee.

Employee Education and Training

It is very important that all employees covered by an employer's substance abuse policy be educated and trained concerning the facts on substance abuse and the employer's substance abuse policy, procedures, and program. Whereas it is mandatory to train supervisors concerning the recognition and handling of substance abuse problems, it is not imperative when it comes to education and training of other employees. Some employers, however, may include various aspects of recognition of signs of substance abuse and peer confrontation in conjunction with general education on the drugs of abuse and their various signs and symptoms.

Similar to supervisors, employees should be educated on the drugs of abuse including facts concerning drugs and alcohol, samples, pictures, and paraphernalia of drug use, the signs and symptoms of substance abuse, and the illegality of substance abuse. Many employers present the same program to employees concerning drugs of abuse that they present to supervisors. These employers reason that no employee can then complain that he or she was not given a full explanation of the various drugs that the employer is concerned about, or that supervisors are learning secret information. Further, many employers have found that most employees are extremely interested in substance abuse education for their own sake and because many employees have children who may be at risk.

Experience has shown that most employees are extremely grateful when employers take the time to explain the drugs of abuse and the signs and symptoms of substance abuse.

Most employers emphasize the facts of substance abuse and spend a considerable amount of time exploring the myths that many employees may hold about drugs. Experience has shown that this approach leads most employees to be much more open with their supervisors and top management than they otherwise might be. Many employers have discovered that once they open the conversation concerning substance abuse, since most employees do not use drugs, they will often come to the employer's supervisors and openly discuss drug and alcohol problems in the workplace, much to the surprise and enlightenment of the employer.

Many employers also discuss the illegality of drugs and alcohol and review the particular legal penalties in their jurisdiction. Often local police, state troopers, or narcotics officers are invited to make presentations to employees concerning the penalties for drug use. Some employers even utilize reformed drug criminals to speak to the employees about the problems and penalties associated with drug use. This "scared straight" concept has not been used very extensively, but will become more common as drug education programs become more sophisticated.

Another mandatory aspect of employee education and training is the review of the employer's substance abuse policy, procedures, and program. Employers review the substance abuse policy including the employer's philosophy, often in great detail, with the employees. Most employers also review the procedural details and the employer's referral or employee assistance program. Additionally, as may be required by law,[10] employers will review the counseling opportunities available to employees under their policy and the penalties for violating the rules of the program, up to and including termination. The education and training program should also discuss any rehabilitation, return to work, and aftercare programs which the employer provides.

Employers with employee assistance programs often have the EAP counselors or administrators educate the employees on this important benefit for the employees and often their families. A primary objective of this presentation is to urge employees and their families to use the EAP on a confidential basis prior to any required referral to the EAP under the employer's substance abuse policy. (EAP training is discussed at greater length in Chapter 7, "Employee Assistance Programs.")

The usual result of well-defined and well-presented employee substance abuse education and training is enlisting the aid and support of employees in working to achieve a drug free workplace. Once the employees understand that it is their responsibility as well as the employer's to work toward a drug free workplace, many will join the effort and cooperate wholeheartedly with the employer to achieve this goal.

Types, Effectiveness, and Cost of Education and Training

The type of education and training that is presented to supervisors and employees may vary depending upon the employer's substance abuse program. Experience has shown, however, that when an employer uses substance abuse professionals, whether EAP administrators, drug testing lab representatives, law enforcement officials, attorneys, or others, the program usually is much better received than if some appointed in-house official, without firsthand experience, attempts to explain an area in which his or her experience is limited. Also, a format that includes heavy use of audiovisuals is usually much better received than one that does not. Audiovisual presentations may include pictures, samples, or paraphernalia concerning alcohol and drugs of abuse, as well as copies of the employer's substance abuse policy and various other related documents.

Use of substance abuse professionals is very important. EAP professionals are able to elaborate upon the details of an employee assistance program, the benefits to the employee and his or her family, where appropriate, and the various positive aspects of an EAP. Further, they will be able to answer questions and relate personal substance abuse situations and experiences, whereas a nonprofessional or an inexperienced person is not capable of communicating such experience or information. Similarly, drug testing lab representatives can explain the details and procedures involved with drug testing and eliminate many of the myths in employees' and supervisors' perceptions of drug testing. These professionals often bring examples or have pictures of the drug testing apparatus, chain-of-custody forms, lab reports, and the like, which are helpful in explaining the drug testing procedures to the supervisors or the employees. Law enforcement personnel and attorneys are often able to articulate the illegal aspects of drugs of abuse and dispel the notions that substance abuse programs are unconstitutional invasions of privacy, often to the satisfaction of most supervisors and employees. Furthermore, law enforcement personnel are usually authorized to bring controlled substances into the workplace in order that supervisors or employees may see or smell substances of abuse firsthand.

Many employers have found that regardless of the type of program, whether by personal presentation, slide presentation, use of the myriad of videotapes currently available concerning substance abuse, or whatever, by using an informative and interesting format, the message concerning substance abuse and the employer's policy is communicated much better than simply by reading the policy or having some disinterested official lecture employees on the evils of drugs. It is suggested that employers be as creative as possible in developing substance abuse education and training.

The effectiveness of the employer's substance abuse education and training is inextricably related to the type and format of the program. If the substance abuse education and training is boring or threatening, supervisors and employees usually will not get the message. However, use of the type of programs described above has been shown to be very effective. The education and training for supervisors and employees provides the employer with a golden opportunity not only to get the message across concerning the employer's substance abuse program but also to enlighten the recipients of the larger problem of substance abuse in society. Further, when supervisors and employees take an interest in the substance abuse program, they are much more likely to cooperate with the program. This cooperation is directly related to the program's success.

The cost of education and training varies proportionately with the extent and sophistication of the program presented. Employers can obtain professionals who can present an excellent program which will be well-received by supervisors and employees at a reasonable cost. Prices can vary from a few hundred to a few thousand dollars depending on the size of the work force and the number of presentations required. Many employers have found that giving presentations to small groups of employees improves the effectiveness of the presentations. Often, outside EAP providers will include the cost of training in the overall cost of the EAP provided to the employer, so that additional costs of training are negligible. Whatever the precise cost, most employers have discovered that making the necessary financial commitment to ensure an excellent and well-received substance abuse education and training program is a wise investment.

Notes

1. *Alabama*: Ala. Code §§20-2-20–20-2-32 (1984); *Alaska*: Alaska Stat. §§11.71.100–11.71.195 (1983); *Arizona*: Ariz. Rev. Stat. Ann. §§36-2512–36-2516 (1986); *Arkansas*: Arkansas Uniform Controlled Substances Act, Ark. Stat. Ann. §§5-64-203–5-64-215 (1987); *California*: Uniform Controlled Substances Act, Cal. Health & Safety Code §§11054–11058 (West, 1975); *Colorado*: Colorado Controlled Substance Act, Colo. Rev. Stat. §§12-22-309–12-22-312 (1985); *Connecticut*: Conn. Gen. Stat. Ann. §210–242 (West, 1985); *Delaware*: Del. Code Ann. tit. 16, §§4713–4722 (1983); *District of Columbia*: District of Columbia Uniform Controlled Substances Act of 1981, D.C. Code Ann. §§33-513–33-522 (1988); *Florida*: Drug Abuse Prevention and Control Act, Fla. Stat. Ann. §893.03 (1976); *Georgia*: Controlled Substances Act, Ga. Code Ann. §§16-13-25–16-13-29 (1988); *Hawaii*: Haw. Rev. Stat. §§329-13–329-22 (1985); *Idaho*: Uniform Controlled Substances Act, Idaho Code §§37-2704–37-2713 (1977); *Illinois*: Illinois Controlled Substances Act, Ill. Rev. Stat. ch. 56 ½, §§1203–1212 (1985); *Indiana*: Indiana Uniform Controlled Substances Act, Ind. Code Ann. §§35-48-2-3–35-48-2-12 (West, 1985); *Iowa*: Iowa Code Ann. §§204.203–204.212 (1987); *Kansas*: Kansas Uniform Controlled Substances Act, Kan. Stat. Ann. §§65-4105–65-4113 (1985); *Kentucky*: Ky. Rev. Stat. §§218A.040–218A.130 (1982); *Louisiana*: Louisiana Controlled Dangerous Substances Statute, La. Rev. Stat. Ann. §40:964 (West, 1977); *Maine*: Me. Rev. Stat. Ann. tit. 17-A, §1102 (1983); *Maryland*: Uniform Controlled Substances Act, Md. Ann. Code art. 27, §279 (1987); *Massachusetts*: Mass. Gen. Laws Ann. ch. 94C, §3 (West, 1985); *Michigan*: Controlled Substances Act, Mich. Comp. Laws Ann. §§333.7210–333.7227 (West, 1980); *Minnesota*: Minn. Stat. Ann. §152.02 (West, 1989); *Mississippi*: Miss. Code Ann. §§41-29-113–41-29-121 (1981); *Missouri*: Narcotic Drug Act, Mo. Rev. Stat. §195.017 (1983); *Montana*: Dangerous Drug Act, Mont. Code Ann. §§50-32-201–50-32-232 (1987); *Nebraska*: Uniform Controlled Substances Act, Neb. Rev. Stat. §28-405 (1985); *Nevada*: Uniform Controlled Substances Act, Nev. Rev. Stat. §§453.166–453.206 (1986); *New Hampshire*: Controlled Drug Act, N.H. Rev. Stat. Ann. §318-B:1-b (1984); *New Jersey*: New Jersey Controlled Dangerous Substances Act, N.J. Stat. Ann. §§24:21-4–24:21-8.1 (West, 1940); *New Mexico*: Controlled Substances Act, N.M. Stat. Ann. §§30-31-1–30-31-41 (1978); *New York*: N.Y. Pub. Health Law §§3306 (Consol., 1985); *North Carolina*: Uniform Narcotic Drug Act, N.C. Gen. Stat. §§90:89–90:94 (1985); *North Dakota*: Uniform Controlled Substances Act, N.D. Cent. Code §§19-03.1-04–19-03.1-14 (1981); *Ohio*: Ohio Controlled Substances Act, Ohio Rev. Code Ann. §3719.41 (Page, 1988); *Oklahoma*: Uniform Controlled Dangerous Substances Act, Okla. Stat. Ann. tit. 63, §§2-203–2-212 (West, 1984); *Oregon*: Or. Rev. Stat. §475.005 (1987); *Pennsylvania*: Controlled Substance, Drug, Device and Cosmetic Act, 35 Pa. Cons. Stat. §780-104 (1977); *Rhode Island*: Rhode Island Uniform Controlled Substances Act, R.I. Gen. Laws §§21-28-2.03–21-28-2.07 (1982); *South Carolina*: S.C. Code Ann. §§44-53-180–270 (Law. Co-op., 1985) (Supp.

1988); *South Dakota*: S.D. Codified Laws Ann. §§34-20B-10–34-20B-26 (1986); *Tennessee*: Tennessee Drug Control Act, Tenn. Code Ann. §§39-6-405–39-6-416 (1982); *Texas*: Texas Controlled Substances Act, Tex. Rev. Civ. Stat. Ann. art. 4476-15 §§2.01–2.17 (Vernon, 1976); *Utah*: Utah Controlled Substances Act, Utah Code Ann. §58-37-4 (1986); *Vermont*: Vt. Stat. Ann. tit. 18, §4201 et seq. (1987); *Virginia*: Va. Code §§54.1-3444–3455 (1988); *Washington*: Controlled Substances Act, Wash. Rev. Code Ann. §§69:50:203–213 (1985); *West Virginia*: Uniform Controlled Substances Act, W. Va. Code §§60A2-203–213 (1989); *Wisconsin*: Uniform Controlled Substances Act, Wis. Stat. Ann. §§161.13–24 (West, 1989); *Wyoming*: Wyo. Stat. §§35-7-1011–35-7-1022 (1988).

2. Controlled Substances Act, Pub. L. No. 91-513 tit. II, 84 Stat. 1242 (1970 as amended). The controlled substances schedules are codified at 21 U.S.C.A. §812 (West, 1981), and are listed in Appendix G.

3. *Alabama*: Legal Drinking Age—Ala. Code §6-5-70 (1975), DUI—Ala. Code §32-5A-191 (1983), Furnishing to Minors—Ala. Code §§6-5-70–71 (1975); *Alaska*: Legal Drinking Age—Alaska Stat. §04.16.050 (1986), DUI—Alaska Stat. §§28.35.030–038 (1984), Furnishing to Minors—Alaska Stat. 04.16.051 (1986); *Arizona*: Legal Drinking Age—Ariz. Rev. Stat. Ann. §4-244 (1974), DUI—Ariz. Rev. Stat. Ann. §§28-691–694 (1988), Furnishing to Minors—Ariz. Rev. Stat. Ann. §4-241 (1974); *Arkansas*: Legal Drinking Age—Ark. Stat. Ann. §3-3-203 (1987), DUI—Ark. Stat. Ann. §§5-65-101–5-65-115 (1987), Furnishing to Minors—Ark. Stat. Ann. §§3-3-201 and 3-3-202 (1987); *California*: Legal Drinking Age—Cal. Bus. & Prof. Code §§25658–25667 (West, 1985), DUI—Cal. Veh. Code §§13351, 13352, 13954, and 23152–23229 (West, 1987), Furnishing to Minors—Cal. Bus. & Prof. Code §§25658–25667 (West, 1985); *Colorado*: Legal Drinking Age—Colo. Rev. Stat. §12-46-112 (1985), DUI—Colo. Rev. Stat. §42-4-1202 (1984), Furnishing to Minors—Colo. Rev. Stat. §§12-46–112.5 and 12-47-128 (1985); *Connecticut*: Legal Drinking Age—Conn. Gen. Stat. Ann. §30-86 (West, 1975), DUI—Conn. Gen. Stat. Ann. §14-227(a), (b), and (c) (West, 1987), Furnishing to Minors—Conn. Gen. Stat. Ann. §30-86 (West, 1975); *Delaware*: Legal Drinking Age—Del. Code Ann. tit. 4, §904 (1985), DUI—Del. Code Ann. tit. 21, §4177 (1985), Furnishing to Minors—Del. Code Ann. tit. 4, §904 (1985); *District of Columbia*: Legal Drinking Age—D.C. Code Ann. §§25-121 and 25-130 (1981), DUI—D.C. Code Ann. §40-716 (1981), Furnishing to Minors—D.C. Code Ann. §25-121 (1981); *Florida*: Legal Drinking Age—Fla. Stat. Ann. §562.111 (West, 1986), DUI—Fla. Stat. Ann. §§316.193–316.1934 (West, 1975), Furnishing to Minors—Fla. Stat. Ann. §562.11 (West, 1986); *Georgia*: Legal Drinking Age—Ga. Code Ann. §3-3-23 (1982), DUI—Ga. Code Ann. §40-6-391 (1985), Furnishing to Minors—Ga. Code Ann. §3-3-23 (1982); *Hawaii*: Legal Drinking Age—Haw. Rev. Stat. §281-101.5 (1985), DUI—Haw. Rev. Stat. §§291-4–291-5 (1985), Furnishing to Minors—Haw. Rev. Stat. §281-101.5 (1985); *Idaho*: Legal Drinking Age—Idaho Code §23-603 (1977), DUI—Idaho Code §§18-8004–18-8006 (1987), Furnishing to Minors—Idaho Code §§23-312 and 23-603 (1977); *Illinois*: Legal Drinking Age—Ill. Rev. Stat. ch. 43, tit. 134a (1986), DUI—Ill. Rev. Stat. ch. 95 ½, tit. 11-501–11.501.4 (1971), Furnishing to Minors—Ill. Rev. Stat. ch. 43, tit. 131 (1986); *Indiana*: Legal Drinking Age—Ind. Code Ann. §7.1-5-7-7 (West, 1984), DUI—Ind. Code Ann. §§9-11-2-1–9-11-2-6 and 9-11-3-1–9-11-3-4 (West, 1987), Furnishing to Minors—Ind. Code Ann. §7.1-5-7-8 (West, 1984); *Iowa*:

Legal Drinking Age—Iowa Code Ann. §123.3(33) (West, 1986), DUI—Iowa Code Ann. §321.72 (West, 1985), Furnishing to Minors—Iowa Code Ann. §123.47 (West, 1987); *Kansas*: Legal Drinking Age—Kan. Stat. Ann. §41-727 (1986), DUI—Kan. Stat. Ann. §8-1567 (1982), Furnishing to Minors—Kan. Stat. Ann. §§21-3610–21-3610b (1988); *Kentucky*: Legal Drinking Age—Ky. Rev. Stat. §244.085 (1981), DUI—Ky. Rev. Stat. §§189.520 and 189A.010–189A.130 (1989), Furnishing to Minors—Ky. Rev. Stat. §244.080 (1981); *Louisiana*: Legal Drinking Age—La. Rev. Stat. Ann. §§14:91–14:91.3 (West, 1986), DUI—La. Rev. Stat. Ann. §14:98 (West, 1986), Furnishing to Minors—La. Rev. Stat. Ann. §14.91–14.91.3 (West, 1986); *Maine*: Legal Drinking Age—Me. Rev. Stat. Ann. tit. 28-A, §2(20) (1988), DUI—Me. Rev. Stat. Ann. tit. 29, §§1311-A-1318 (1978), Furnishing to Minors—Me. Rev. Stat. Ann. tit. 28-A, §§354, 2079, and 2081 (1988); *Maryland*: Legal Drinking Age—Md. Ann. Code art. 2B, §118 (1987), DUI—Md. Transp. Code Ann. §21-902 (1987), Furnishing to Minors—Md. Ann. Code art. 2B §118 and art. 27 §401 (1987); *Massachusetts*: Legal Drinking Age—Mass. Gen. Laws Ann. ch. 138, §§34-34C (1981), DUI—Mass. Gen. Laws Ann. ch. 90, §§24L and 24N (1985), Furnishing to Minors—Mass. Gen. Laws Ann. ch. 138, §§34-34C (1981); *Michigan*: Legal Drinking Age—Mich. Comp. Laws Ann. §§436.33–436.33C (West, 1978), DUI—Mich. Comp. Laws Ann. §§257.625–257.625b (West, 1977), Furnishing to Minors—Mich. Comp. Laws Ann. §750.28 (West, 1968); *Minnesota*: Legal Drinking Age—Minn. Stat. Ann. §340A.503 (West, 1972), DUI—Minn. Stat. Ann. §169.121 (West, 1986), Furnishing to Minors—Minn. Stat. Ann. §§340A.502 and 340A.503 (West, 1972); *Mississippi*: Legal Drinking Age—Miss. Code Ann. §67-1-81 (1973), DUI—Miss. Code Ann. §§63-11-1–63-11-47 (1973); Furnishing to Minors—Miss. Code Ann. §67-1-81 (1973); *Missouri*: Legal Drinking Age—Mo. Rev. Stat. §311.310 (1963), DUI—Mo. Rev. Stat. §§577.010–577.040 (1979), Furnishing to Minors—Mo. Rev. Stat. §311.310 (1963); *Montana*: Legal Drinking Age—Mont. Code Ann. §16-6-305 (1987), DUI—Mont. Code Ann. §§61-8-401–61-8-408 (1987), Furnishing to Minors—Mont. Code Ann. §16-3-301 (1987); *Nebraska*: Legal Drinking Age—Neb. Rev. Stat. §53-180 (1988), DUI—Neb. Rev. Stat. §§39-669.07–39-669.08 (1988); Furnishing to Minors—Neb. Rev. Stat. §§53.180.00–53.180.03 (1988); *Nevada*: Legal Drinking Age—Nev. Rev. Stat. §202.020 (1986), DUI—Nev. Rev. Stat. §§484.379–484.394 (1986), Furnishing to Minors—Nev. Rev. Stat. §§202.030–202.060 (1986); *New Hampshire*: Legal Drinking Age—N.H. Rev. Stat. Ann. §175-6 (1977), DUI—N.H. Rev. Stat. Ann. §§265-82–265-82-b (1982), Furnishing to Minors—N.H. Rev. Stat. Ann. §175-6 (1977); *New Jersey*: Legal Drinking Age—N.J. Stat. Ann. §33:1-77 (West, 1940), DUI—N.J. Stat. Ann. §§39:4-50 and 39:4-51 (West, 1973), Furnishing to Minors—N.J. Stat. Ann. §33:1-77 (West, 1940), *New Mexico*: Legal Drinking Age—N.M. Stat. Ann. §§60-7b-1–60-7b-1.1 (1987), DUI—N.M. Stat. Ann. §66-8-102 (1987), Furnishing to Minors—N.M. Stat. Ann. §§60-7b-1–60-7b-11 (1987); *New York*: Legal Drinking Age—N.Y. Alco. Bev. Cont. Law §§65–65a (Consol., 1980) (Supp. 1988), DUI—N.Y. Veh. & Traf. Law §§1192–1194 (Consol., 1976), (Supp. 1988), Furnishing to Minors—N.Y. Alco. Bev. Cont. Law §65a (Consol., 1980) (Supp. 1988); *North Carolina*: Legal Drinking Age—N.C. Gen. Stat. §18B-302 (1983), DUI—N.C. Gen. Stat. §20-138.1 (1983), Furnishing to Minors—N.C. Gen. Stat. §18B-302 (1983); *North Dakota*: Legal Drinking Age—N.D. Cent. Code §5-01-09 (1987), DUI—

N.D. Cent. Code §39-08-01 (1987), Furnishing to Minors—N.D. Cent. Code §§5-01-09 and 5-02-06 (1987); *Ohio*: Legal Drinking Age—Ohio Rev. Code Ann. §§4301.63–4301.63.2 (Page, 1982), DUI—Ohio Rev. Code Ann. §4511.19 (Page, 1982), Furnishing to Minors—Ohio Rev. Code Ann. §4301.63.2 (Page, 1982); *Oklahoma*: Legal Drinking Age—Okla. Stat. Ann. tit. 21, §1215 (West, 1983), DUI—Okla. Stat. Ann. tit. 47, §761 (West, 1988), Furnishing to Minors—Okla. Stat. Ann. tit. 37, §§537 and 538 (West, 1953); *Oregon*: Legal Drinking Age—Or. Rev. Stat. §471.105 (1987), DUI—Or. Rev. Stat. §§813.010–813.160 (1987), Furnishing to Minors—Or. Rev. Stat. §471.410 (1987); *Pennsylvania*: Legal Drinking Age—18 Pa. Cons. Stat. §6308 (1983), DUI—75 Pa. Cons. Stat. §3731 (1977), Furnishing to Minors—18 Pa. Cons. Stat. §§6310–6310.1 (1983); *Rhode Island*: Legal Drinking Age—R.I. Gen. Laws §3-8-6 (1987), DUI—R.I. Gen. Laws §31-27-2 (1982), Furnishing to Minors—R.I. Gen. Laws §§3-8-11.1–3-8-11.2 (1987); *South Carolina*: Legal Drinking Age—S.C. Code Ann. §20-7-380 (Law. Co-op., 1985) (Supp. 1988), DUI—S.C. Code Ann. §§56-5-2930 and 56-5-2940 (Law. Co-op., 1977) (Supp. 1988), Furnishing to Minors—S.C. Code Ann. §61-13-287 (Law. Co-op., Supp. 1988); *South Dakota*: Legal Drinking Age—S.D. Codified Laws Ann. §35-9-2 (1986), DUI—S.D. Codified Laws Ann. §32-23-1 (1984), Furnishing to Minors—S.D. Codified Laws Ann. §35-9-1 (1986); *Tennessee*: Legal Drinking Age—Tenn. Code Ann. §1-3-113 (1985), DUI—Tenn. Code Ann. §§55-10-401 and 55-10-403 (1989), Furnishing to Minors—Tenn. Code Ann. §39-6-929 (1982); *Texas*: Legal Drinking Age—Tex. Alco. Bev. Code Ann. §§106.02–106.05 (Vernon, 1978), DUI—Tex. Civ. Code Ann. §6701 1-1 (Vernon, 1977), Furnishing to Minors—Tex. Alco. Bev. Code Ann. §§106.03 and 106.06 (Vernon, 1978); *Utah*: Legal Drinking Age—Utah Code Ann. §§32.A-12–13 (1986); DUI—Utah Code Ann. §§41-6-43–41-6-44.30 (1988), Furnishing to Minors—Utah Code Ann. §32A-12-8 (1986); *Vermont*: Legal Drinking Age—Vt. Stat. Ann. tit. 7, art. 657 (1988), DUI—Vt. Stat. Ann. tit. 23, art. 1201 and 1210 (1987), Furnishing to Minors—Vt. Stat. Ann. tit. 7, art. 658 (1988); *Virginia*: Legal Drinking Age—Va. Code §4-112 (1988), DUI—Va. Code §§18.2-266–18.2-273 (1987), Furnishing to Minors—Va. Code §4-112.1 (1988); *Washington*: Legal Drinking Age—Wash. Rev. Code Ann. §§66.44.290–66.44.291 (1985), DUI—Wash. Rev. Code Ann. §46.61.502 (1987), Furnishing to Minors—Wash. Rev. Code Ann. §66.44.270 (1985); *West Virginia*: Legal Drinking Age—W. Va. Code §60-3-22 (1989), DUI—W. Va. Code §17C-5-2 (1986), Furnishing to Minors—W. Va. Code §60-3-22 (1989); *Wisconsin*: Legal Drinking Age—Wis. Stat. Ann. §125.02(8M) (West, 1989), DUI—Wis. Stat. Ann. §§346.63–346.65 (West, 1971), Furnishing to Minors—Wis. Stat. Ann. §125.07 (West, 1989); *Wyoming*: Legal Drinking Age–Wyo. Stat. §12-6-101 (1986), DUI—Wyo. Stat. §31-5-233 (1984), Furnishing to Minors—Wyo. Stat. §§12-6-101 and 102 (1986).

4. The costs of alcohol abuse to society are higher than the costs of drug abuse, and alcohol use itself is more prevalent than the use of other drugs. Total costs to society of alcohol abuse for 1980 were calculated at $89.5 billion; costs attributed to the abuse of other drugs were $46.9 billion. A 1982 survey indicated 67.9% of young adults surveyed reported alcohol consumption during the previous month. In comparison, lower numbers in this age group reported using marijuana (27.4%) and cocaine (6.8%). Harwood, et al., *Economic Costs to Society of Alcohol and Drug Abuse and Mental Illness: 1980* (Research Triangle Park, N.C., Research Triangle Inst., 1984).

5. Drug Free Workplace Act of 1988, Pub. L. No. 100-690 tit. V, subtitle D, §§5152 and 5153; Department of Defense Federal Acquisition Regulation Supplement; Drug-Free Work Force, 53 Fed. Reg. 37,763 (1988) (to be codified at 48 C.F.R. §§223 and 252); Department of Transportation, Procedures for Transportation Workplace Drug Testing Programs, 53 Fed. Reg. 47,002 (1988) (to be codified at 49 C.F.R. §40); Executive Order No. 12,564, Drug Free Federal Workplace, 51 Fed. Reg. 32,889 (1986).

6. As a step toward certifying that it is creating a drug-free workplace, a federal contractor must "establish[   ] a drug-free awareness program to inform employees about— . . . any available drug counseling, rehabilitation, and employee assistance programs. . . ." Drug Free Workplace Act of 1988, Pub. L. No. 100-690 tit. V, subtitle D, §5152(a)(1)(B)(iii).

7. Under the Drug Free Workplace Act of 1988, contractors must "inform employees about— . . . the penalties that may be imposed upon employees for drug abuse violations. . . ." Pub. L. No. 100-690 tit. V, subtitle D, §5152(a)(1)(B)(iv).

8. Among the reasonable-cause testing criteria established by the Federal Highway Administration for motor carriers is the requirement that "[t]he conduct must be witnessed by at least two supervisors, if at all feasible. If only one supervisor is available, only one supervisor need witness the conduct. The witnesses must have received training in the detection of probable drug use by observing a person's behavior." (To be codified at 49 C.F.R. §391.99(c)). Controlled Substances Testing, 53 Fed. Reg. 47,153 (1988) (to be codified at 49 C.F.R. §§391 and 394).

9. Chapter 4.

10. Drug Free Workplace Act of 1988, Pub. L. No. 100-690 tit. V, subtitle D, 102 Stat. 4304; Department of Defense Federal Acquisition Regulation Supplement; Drug-Free Work Force, 53 Fed. Reg. 37,763 (1988) (to be codified at 48 C.F.R. §§223 and 252); Controlled Substances Testing, 53 Fed. Reg. 47,153 (1988) (to be codified at 49 C.F.R. §§391 and 394).

Part Three

Guidelines for Establishing Substance Abuse Programs

Chapter 6

Introduction to Substance Abuse Programs

An employer's substance abuse program depends upon the employer's philosophy toward its employees and its commitment to handling the treatable conditions from which substance abusing employees suffer. Although particular programs will be discussed in greater detail in Chapters 7 through 11 and model substance abuse programs are provided in Appendix C, "Model Policy, Procedure, and Program," and Appendix F, "Substance Abuse Programs," a brief summary of different kinds of programs is presented here. The different types of substance abuse programs that are considered here include the following:

- Disciplinary Programs
- Employee Assistance Programs (explored in greater depth in Chapter 7)
- Rehabilitation Referral Programs (covered more extensively in Chapter 8)
- Inpatient Rehabilitation Programs (also see Chapter 9)
- Outpatient Rehabilitation Programs (also see Chapter 10) and
- Aftercare and Long-Term Rehabilitation Programs (also see Chapter 11)

Disciplinary Programs

If an employer has a disciplinary or punitive philosophy toward substance abuse in the workplace and believes that substance abusing employees are the scourge of mankind and should be eliminated from the workplace, then the employer will probably terminate any employees detected abusing substances. However, not only is this an extremely unproductive program, but increasingly, federal and state legislation and regulation require that employers have more enlightened programs.[1] An example of a disciplinary program appears in Appendix F, "Substance Abuse Programs." Most employers have determined that the economics associated with rehabilitation are so significant that they cannot afford simply to terminate substance abusing employees. In short, employers have concluded that it is not cost-effective to terminate substance abusing employees without giving the employee a chance at rehabilitation. Usually employers have thousands of dollars worth of training and experience invested in employees. Therefore, to terminate such an employee without the benefit of a chance at rehabilitation and only run the risk of replacing that employee with another substance abuser does not seem to be very intelligent from a cost-effective, economics standpoint. As a result, strictly disciplinary or "test and fire" substance abuse programs will not be treated in a separate chapter, and will be handled only procedurally as listed in Appendix F.

Employee Assistance Programs

Although much more will be said about employee assistance programs, at this point it will suffice to say that EAPs are one of the most creative innovations in the field of substance abuse rehabilitation in the latter half of the twentieth century. The basic functions of an EAP are, first, to receive and evaluate the substance abusing employee; second, to direct the individual toward the most appropriate form of treatment, whether it is counseling, group therapy with support groups such as Alcoholics Anonymous, outpatient treatment programs, or inpatient treatment programs; and third, to coordinate the aftercare and follow-up program in order to help the individual maintain his or her sobriety. Statistics indicate that EAPs are an extremely cost-effective way to handle substance abuse in the work force. EAPs are now the preferred alternative of employers who are experienced in the field of substance abuse in the workplace and who are familiar with recently passed or recently issued federal statutes and regulations. EAPs will be discussed in depth in Chapter 7.

Rehabilitation Referral Programs

A large number of employers take the referral approach to deal with employees who have been identified as substance abusers. With this approach, an employer refers the substance abuser to community, county, state, or federal agencies that exist to handle individuals with alcohol and drug problems. Examples of these types of agencies are mental health centers, drug and alcohol centers, vocational rehabilitation centers, and local support groups such as Alcoholics Anonymous, Cocaine Anonymous, and Narcotics Anonymous. Rehabilitation referral programs will be discussed in greater detail in Chapter 8.

Inpatient Rehabilitation Programs

Many employers, particularly those who have had substance abuse programs for a long time, use inpatient rehabilitation programs extensively. The basic format for inpatient rehabilitation or hospitalization of alcoholics and addicts was developed based on the "Minnesota Experience" or the Minnesota Model. The basic assumptions of this model are that alcoholism is an illness which is no-fault, multiphasic, chronic, and similar in character to other forms of addiction which are grouped under the term chemical dependency. The basic treatment structure of most inpatient rehabilitation centers is that they are operated by a therapeutic community consisting of a multidisciplinary staff including physicians, psychiatrists, psychologists, addiction counselors, and nurse-practitioners. The philosophy of Alcoholics Anonymous (AA) is used extensively throughout inpatient treatment centers, and the strategy is to use task-oriented groups, peer groups, and didactic lectures for education about and treatment of substance abuse. Additionally, individual therapy and group therapy are used in conjunction with the AA Twelve Step program. The costs of these inpatient programs, as is true of most hospitalization in the country today, are extremely high. The average cost of inpatient treatment ranges between $4,000 and $15,000. Ironically, however, most employers' insurance programs are oriented to cover inpatient treatment rather than other less costly forms of treatment. Inpatient rehabilitation programs will be discussed in greater detail in Chapter 9.

Outpatient Rehabilitation Programs

Outpatient rehabilitation programs evolved out of the necessity to treat greater numbers of alcoholics and addicts at a reduced cost. Outpatient programs are usually much more flexible than inpatient programs with regard to length of the program and hours of involvement. The various outpatient treatment models include intensive day programs for 4 to 6 weeks, evening programs for 6 to 12 weeks, halfway house programs for a few weeks to several months, and long-term day programs for 12 to 16 months. A comparison of inpatient and outpatient programs deals with issues such as medical and psychiatric evaluations, detoxification discharge rates, success rates, the intensity of interventions, penetration into the workplace, insurance bias and developments, and cost effectiveness. By far the most significant issue is that with all other factors being equal, outpatient treatment programs are much more cost-effective than inpatient programs. The outpatient program structure generally is very similar to inpatient programming. Outpatient rehabilitation programs are discussed in greater detail in Chapter 10.

Aftercare and Long-Term Rehabilitation Programs

Aftercare deals with the transition period between formal rehabilitation, occurring in either inpatient or outpatient programs, and integration into the mainstream while participating in self-help groups to support sobriety. Long-term rehabilitation refers to the development of the individual's sobriety maintenance program through self-help groups such as Alcoholics Anonymous (AA), Narcotics Anonymous (NA), and Cocaine Anonymous (CA).

Aftercare deals with reintegration of the recovering employee to the workplace, the discussion of relapse potential, and the employer's role in relapse prevention. The different types of aftercare programs that exist include formal programs or support groups for the employee and the family and informal programs or self-help groups which include AA, NA, and CA. Finally, the relationship between aftercare and the employer's overall substance abuse program will be discussed in order to tie the entire substance abuse treatment, rehabilitation, and return to work process together. Aftercare and long-term rehabilitation programs are discussed at length in Chapter 11.

Conclusion

There are many resources available for an employer to use in establishing an effective substance abuse program. Generally speaking, if an employer follows the three principles of human resources in dealing with substance abuse and establishes a comprehensive policy, a detailed procedure, and the proper program for handling substance abusers, the employer will go a long way toward eradicating substance abuse in the workplace, and do its part in contributing toward a drug free America. The benefits of establishing a proper substance abuse policy, procedure, and program will also return far more to the employer and its employees than can be measured in dollars and cents.

Notes

1. For example, the Department of Transportation regulations require covered employers to have an EAP (49 C.F.R. Part 391.121). Likewise the Department of Defense regulations (48 C.F.R. Part 223) require the same. Several states have enacted laws requiring rehabilitation, see, e.g., Iowa Code §730.5 (1987); Me. Rev. Stat. Ann. tit. 26, §681 (1989); and 21 Vt. Stat. Ann. tit. 21, §511 (1988). The Drug Free Workplace Act of 1988, Pub. L. No. 100-690 tit. V, subtitle D, stops short of directing contractors to discharge employees convicted for violation of criminal drug statutes in the workplace; instead the Act allows the contractor the option of "requiring the satisfactory participation in a drug abuse assistance or rehabilitation program by, any employee who is so convicted. . . ." §5152(a)(1)(F). Drug testing regulations for the Federal Railroad Administration allow a return to service of an employee suspended for testing positive once the employee has successfully completed counseling or treatment under an EAP program. Random Drug Testing; amendments to Alcohol/Drug Regulations, 53 Fed. Reg. 47,102 (1988) (to be codified at 49 C.F.R. §§217, 219, and 219.605(e)).

Chapter 7

Employee Assistance Programs

An employee assistance program or EAP is a worksite-based counseling service program designed to assist in the identification and resolution of productivity problems associated with employees impaired by personal problems or concerns including, but not limited to health, alcohol, drug, family, marital, financial, legal, emotional, stress-related, or other personal problems that adversely affect employee job performance. The primary goals of an EAP are to: (1) identify employees whose personal problems are detrimental to job performance; (2) motivate these people to seek and accept help for their problems; (3) assess their problems and personal resources and develop a plan of action to help them; and (4) assist employees in obtaining the services they need, so that they might live healthy, productive lives.[1] Thus, EAPs are in essence a mechanism that connects the identification of substance abuse or the workplace problems with the employer's program for assessing the extent of the problem and directing the employee to rehabilitation. Further, the EAP functions to reintegrate the rehabilitated employee back into the workplace and acts as a monitoring vehicle for assuring compliance with the employer's substance abuse program. Whether the EAP achieves its goals depends on a number of factors which are discussed in this chapter.

It is a basic tenet of this work that a complete substance abuse program provides for counseling and rehabilitation. Further, employers who rehabilitate their employees can avoid many of the health, safety, and financial costs associated with substance abuse. Consequently, many employers have developed EAPs as separate, functioning departments in order to avoid or reduce these costs.

Generally speaking, EAPs have become increasingly popular and sophisticated as a modern human resources tool. Experience has demonstrated that they benefit not only those employees who are substance abusers, but ultimately the entire organization by

implementing employee education programs and supervisory training, raising awareness of substance abuse and other workplace
problems, and reducing the overall costs borne by the organization.
This chapter discusses the history and development of
employee assistance programs, guidelines for establishing EAPs,
the structure and functional analysis of EAPs, the administration of
EAPs, internal EAPs, external EAPs, qualifications of EAP counselors, the effectiveness of EAPs, the focus of an EAP (whether it is
to be broad brush or narrow in its implementation of a substance
abuse program), and preparing EAP policies.

History

Programs that provided assistance to employees in dealing with
personal problems emerged in the late nineteenth and early twentieth centuries. The first EAPs were prompted by a combination of
factors, including the temperance movement of the late nineteenth
and early twentieth centuries, the push for higher productivity, and
often genuine compassion for employees. Initially, the development of these programs was slow, and only a handful of companies
had them. In the 1950s there were still fewer than 50 such programs
in the United States. Since the mid-1970s, however, the number of
EAPs has exploded. Several experts have estimated that more than
10,000 EAPs of one form or another are operating in the United
States today. Indeed, a recent survey conducted in the summer of
1988 by the Bureau of Labor Statistics (hereinafter referred to as the
1988 BLS survey) estimates that EAPs are in place at as many as
300,000 establishments in the country. (This large disparity in estimates can be accounted for by the fact that many employers have
more than one "establishment" under the BLS definition.) In any
event, the BLS estimates that 31 percent of the 85,000,000 employees covered in the survey have access to some sort of EAP. In
addition, at the time of the survey, employers employing an additional 8.6 percent of the work force were considering establishing
EAPs.[2]
In the early part of the twentieth century a few businesses
established counseling programs for their employees.[3] Programs
were primarily designed to deal with emotional and mental problems, as well as problems associated with alcohol. Alcoholics Anonymous (AA) was founded in 1935, and in 1940 AA methods were

introduced at DuPont and Eastman Kodak. Other companies adopted occupational or industrial alcoholism programs at about the same time to combat the growing problems of alcoholism in the workplace. Between 1944 and 1948, companies such as Allis-Chalmers, Illinois Bell, Consolidated Edison, and Standard Oil initiated formal occupational alcoholism programs.

Many early programs dealt exclusively with alcoholism. After World War II, the Yale Center for Alcohol Studies, among others, was able to promote industrial alcoholism programs with business and labor leaders. Further, by the mid-1950s "there were approximately fifty to sixty industrial alcoholism programs in the United States," and in 1959 the National Council on Alcoholism (NCA, now known as the National Council on Alcoholism and Drug Dependence (NCADD)), which had been affiliated with Yale, began marketing services to employers associated with programs for alcoholics in 1959.[4] Supervisors were trained to recognize symptoms of alcoholism and to confront employees who exhibited these symptoms. Once confronted, an employee was given a choice between counseling and discharge.

In the late 1960s and early 1970s, many companies began broadening their alcoholism programs to include drug abuse problems. Progressive company programs began handling family problems, financial stress, and a variety of other personal problems that interfere with job performance. Some companies extended counseling services to employees' dependents.

In 1971 the federal government established the National Institute on Alcohol Abuse and Alcoholism (NIAAA). The NIAAA has provided a great deal of research, support, and financing for alcohol-related problems. It also has provided seed money for a number of EAPs.

Eventually, broader-based programs came to be called employee assistance programs. The term employee assistance program is one of fairly recent vintage. The term "employee assistance" was first used by the NIAAA to distinguish its programs from those of the NCA. The term came into common use after the publication of James T. Wrich's book, *The Employee Assistance Program*, in 1980.[5] Since that time the term has come to describe not just substance abuse programs, but programs assisting employees with a wide variety of personal problems.

By 1972, 25 percent of the Fortune 500 companies reported that they had EAPs, and by 1979 the figure had risen to 57.7 percent.[6] It is impossible to calculate with certainty how many EAPs exist today, but as was stated earlier, experts indicate that more than 10,000 companies have EAPs in operation in the United States today.

The 1988 BLS survey concluded that the larger the business establishment, the more likely it was to have an EAP. For example, 70 percent of the nation's largest establishments—those with 1,000 employees or more—had EAPs, versus only about 9 percent of the smallest establishments—those with fewer than 50 workers. Because these small workplaces form the overwhelming majority of the nation's establishments—more than 90 percent—only 7 percent of establishments overall had employee assistance programs. The small establishments, on the other hand, employ only about 35 percent of all workers. Hence, proportionately more employees currently work in establishments that have EAPs.[7]

Guidelines for Establishing EAPs

Although EAPs come in a variety of forms, certain basic components are essential to the establishment of any successful program: complete management support, a well-defined program policy, a qualified EAP director and staff, supervisory training, employee education, short-term counseling services, and a proper referral system that maintains confidentiality. Furthermore, employers must become familiar with federal laws that may affect the design of their EAPs.

Management Support

It is no understatement that, in order for an EAP to be successful, management support for the EAP must be complete. The 1988 BLS survey revealed that 9 out of 10 EAPs were management sponsored. The remainder were sponsored by a union or by both management and union.[8] Top-level management support is essential, but so is the support of front-line management.

Employees' perception of the EAP's importance, as well as management's commitment to it, is significantly influenced by outward manifestations of management support. In addition to articulated commitment, management support must also be financial. The amount of financial support will be discussed more fully later but it must be stressed that the company must be willing to fund the EAP at an adequate level from the outset. The financial commitment a company must make in order to maintain a good EAP depends in large part on the size of the company. Some experts contend that adequate funding requires one full-time EAP staff member for every 3,500 to 4,000 employees, including services for employees' families.[9] Other sources suggest a full-time EAP coordinator for every 1,800 to 2,000 employees.[10] Smaller companies may use the services of outside contractors to establish and maintain their EAPs. The relative merits of internal and external EAPs are also discussed later in this chapter.

Program Policy

A written program policy is essential because it sets forth the roles of those who will implement the EAP. Without a clear, written policy, neither supervisors nor employees will know what to expect from the EAP procedures. A written policy will increase employee confidence in the program and will encourage supervisors to confront employees whose performance is impaired.

The EAP policy should be consistent with the company's existing policies regarding performance, discipline, and medical practices. The policy should clearly set forth management's commitment to the EAP, its purposes, and procedures to be followed. Specific policy provisions should be written within the context of a company's personnel policy manual. The preparation of EAP policies will be discussed at length later in this chapter. Examples of EAP policies and programs may be found in Appendix C, "Model Policy, Procedure, and Program" and Appendix F, "Substance Abuse Programs."

EAP Staff

The EAP staff is charged with managing and coordinating the EAP. The responsibilities include seeing that the EAP policies and procedures are implemented throughout the employer's facilities. Staff must also educate supervisors to be aware of their role in the program and see that employees who need the services receive them. Even where EAP services are contracted out, someone in management should be assigned to monitor and coordinate EAP activities to ensure that the EAP contractor has the necessary organizational knowledge and influence.

According to the 1988 BLS survey, EAPs that were internally run typically had very few staff employees assigned to run them. Not unexpectedly, the number assigned usually depended on the size of the establishment. Not many of the establishments with fewer than 10 workers had an employee staffing their assistance program. BLS concluded that counseling, referral, and other services were probably provided by managerial personnel. In contrast, almost all the firms with 5,000 workers or more with EAPs had some staff assigned to the program, including 46 percent that had 2 to 4 employees on the EAP staff and 39 percent that had 5 employees or more on the program staff.[11]

An EAP should be staffed by qualified professionals such as clinically licensed psychologists, psychiatrists, certified employee assistance professionals (CEAP), certified addiction counselors (CAC), social workers, and psychiatric nurses. The necessity of employing qualified personnel cannot be overemphasized. Unqualified counselors will not only be of little benefit to the employees who use their services, but may also expose the employer to liability for failure to properly diagnose and refer employees. The staff should also consist of persons with good administrative and communication skills who can integrate with the company as a whole.

Supervisory Training

Unless supervisors are well informed of the program policy, believe that management supports it, and understand how to carry out their functions properly, an EAP will be less than successful. Supervisory training is usually run by the EAP staff whether the EAP is maintained internally or by an outside contractor. Supervisors must be made aware of the policy and its importance. They must also be instructed on their roles in implementing the policy. A supervisor's primary role is to determine when a problem may exist based on job performance, confront the employee with the problem, and refer the employee to the EAP for assistance. The supervisor's role is critical since improperly confronted employees may feel threatened and thus become more difficult if not impossible to assist. Diagnosis and treatment of the problem, however, should be left to professionals accessible through the EAP. Finally, supervisors must be advised on how their functions within the program can be blended with their other supervisory responsibilities.

Employee Education

Employee education should be designed to accomplish two goals. The first is to make employees aware of the availability of the EAP. To accomplish this the employer should develop and disseminate information about the various services available, how an employee can make contact with the services, their procedures, costs, and other similar information.

An equally important goal is to remove any social stigma from using an EAP. Many employees may be discouraged from using the EAP if they view it as a public admission that there is something wrong with them. Therefore the education component of the program should stress both the confidential nature of the program and the fact that it is designed to assist otherwise normal persons who have problems with which they are unable to cope. Only through wide dissemination of information, such as posters, brochures, notices in company newsletters, and home mailings can this information become available to the greatest number of employees.[12]

Short-Term Counseling Service

Whether the employer adopts an internal EAP, contracts with an external service, or uses a community resource network, the EAP should provide some form of short-term counseling. Some EAPs provide only preliminary assessment, and refer the employee to appropriate professionals for further counseling and treatment. Many internal programs provide counseling themselves. The type of initial counseling will depend on the type of EAP adopted by the company, which is itself often determined by the size of the company. An EAP should, at the very least, have individuals with sufficient training to counsel initially with employees in order that they might be referred to the proper professional.

Methods of Referral

Voluntary Referral

The most effective and desirable means of referral is for the employee to seek help on his or her own. The recognition of the problem by the individual is the first step in the process of controlling the problem and receiving the proper rehabilitation. Employees who voluntarily enter programs should not have their participation divulged to management. At the same time, employees should not be allowed to perceive the EAP as a shield to make them immune from disciplinary procedures for substandard job performance or for violation of company rules.

Management Referral/Constructive Confrontation

Often called constructive confrontation or intervention, this approach is primarily used by supervisors and managers to encourage workers who deny the existence of a problem to seek help. Management referral may include confronting employees with specific instances of unacceptable behavior or job performance the continuation of which could lead to formal discipline. It may also include the supervisor or manager reminding the employee of the existence of the program. Finally, if these attempts fail, mandatory participation in and satisfactory completion of the program might be required. As was discussed above, it is critical that supervisors receive sufficient training in constructive confrontation techniques to ensure maximum employee cooperation.

Peer Referral

Peer referral may or may not be used in conjunction with management referrals. This method can often be used in situations where employees are not subject to regular supervision. Participants (nonsupervising employees) learn to identify problems and how to intervene when necessary. Sometimes they are trained in small groups about various aspects of alcohol and drug abuse, from signs of abuse through types of available treatment.

The touchstone of any successful program is employee trust. Identifying those who need help is difficult at best. Unless confidentiality is maintained, employees who are substance abusers will be extremely reluctant to avail themselves of the EAP. Peer referral training must emphasize the necessity of maintaining strict confidentiality. The EAP must not be perceived as a police agency for the employer to use as a tool for disciplining employees. Likewise, employees' problems should not be allowed to be an acceptable topic of workplace conversation. Unless employees believe that they can use the EAP without adverse consequences, they will avoid the program and its effectiveness will be lost.

Federal Government Requirements

Recent federal laws and regulations require many federal contractors to maintain EAPs. The most widely applicable statute, the Drug Free Workplace Act of 1988, part of the landmark Anti-Drug Abuse Act of 1988,[13] which applies to all contractors with contracts of $25,000 or more, does not require employers to adopt EAPs per se. However, it does require a contractor to establish a drug free awareness program to inform employees of the dangers of drug abuse in the workplace, the employer's policy of maintaining a drug free workplace, and the availability of drug counseling, rehabilitation, and employee assistance programs, if any.[14] If an employee is convicted of a drug offense connected with his or her employment, the contractor must, among other things, impose a sanction on the convicted employee, which may include discharge, or require the employee to satisfy rehabilitation requirements.[15]

Other federal laws and regulations go further and require establishment of EAPs. The Department of Transportation through the Federal Highway Administration has adopted strict drug testing regulations. These regulations also require motor carriers to adopt EAPs that educate drivers on the hazards of drugs and educate supervisors on the same hazards and on how to detect drug use or abuse.[16] They require that the carrier include at least 60 minutes of training on these subjects.[17]

The Federal Aviation Administration also has adopted regulations that require EAPs to perform an educational function.[18] These requirements are much more detailed than those of the Federal Highway Administration. Each EAP education program (which may be internal or contracted for) must display and distribute informational material and provide information on community service hot lines for employee assistance. The regulation also requires a significant amount of training for employees.

The Department of Defense has gone even further. In regulations issued in 1988,[19] the DOD requires contractors to adopt EAPs "emphasizing high level direction, education, counseling, rehabilitation, and coordination with available community resources."[20] The regulations also require supervisory training and provisions for referrals to treatment.[21]

Analysis and Function of EAPs

Whereas the structure of EAPs varies widely from internal to external in operations, and from narrow range to broad brush in coverage, the functions of EAPs contain certain common elements. Of the many functions of an EAP, the seven most common include identification, education, motivation, assessment, assistance, prevention, and program effectiveness assessment.

EAPs function in a manner so that they can identify those employees who need help, that is, employees whose personal problems are detrimental to their job performance. Identification is accomplished by a number of means such as voluntary referral, supervisory identification or referral, and peer referral. Second, it is the usual function of the EAP to educate and train supervisors and employees on the purposes of the EAP and the assistance it can provide so that EAP-related problems can be more easily identified and handled appropriately. Third, the EAP operates to motivate these employees to seek and accept help. Well-trained EAP staff usually are excellent motivators. Also, clearly defined EAP policies and procedures in conjunction with personnel or disciplinary procedures are useful for motivating the employee to seek and accept help.

Fourth, the typical EAP contains a mechanism for assessment of the employee's problem in order that the employee can be directed to the best source of assistance, whether it is Alcoholics Anonymous, inpatient treatment, outpatient treatment, professional counseling, or whatever is deemed necessary.

Fifth, especially in the area of substance abuse, the EAP must be able to assist employees in getting the services they need. The EAP should always provide a source for rehabilitation of the employee, which is a primary goal of any EAP.

Sixth, the typical EAP will stress prevention of relapses into substance abuse. The EAP should establish an aftercare or follow-up program with the rehabilitated employee in order to continue to assess and assist the employee. Particularly where the problem is substance abuse, an individual's aftercare program is critical to maintaining recovery. The EAP staff can usually be of great assistance in follow-up aftercare by maintaining contact with the individual and his or her recovery program. Further, a growing number of EAPs are concerned with wellness programs in which they emphasize the benefits of good health habits including proper diet and exercise.

Finally, analysis of an EAP must include examination of its effectiveness in performing its basic functions. The ultimate goals of all EAPs remain fundamentally the same: recognizing the personal problem affecting job performance and doing something to correct the problem. EAP staff should always be concerned with how well they are helping the employer create and maintain an environment in which employees' personal problems are not having a significant impact on job performance.

Administration of EAPs

Responsibility for the EAP must rest with an individual high enough in the organization to ensure sufficient resources for its support and to maintain the visibility of the program. Only then can the EAP be assured of the involvement of senior management and, where appropriate, union leadership, in sustaining the program. For instance, if an internal EAP exists, the primary EAP administrator should report to the company president, vice president of human resources, or equivalent. Where an external EAP exists under contract, a company official should be assigned as liaison between a highly placed individual such as the president or vice president of human resources and the EAP contractor. Studies have shown that the maintenance of a liaison and the importance placed on the EAP in terms of its contact with upper management have a direct relationship on the effectiveness of the EAP.[22]

The physical location of the EAP depends on the structure of the program and whether the program is provided internally or on an external basis by an EAP contractor. In any event, the physical location of the EAP should facilitate easy access by employees, and at the same time ensure confidentiality.[23] The standards for employee alcoholism and/or assistance programs developed by the Association of Labor-Management Administrators and Consultants on Alcoholism (recently renamed Employee Assistance Professionals Association, Inc., or EAPA) and other organizations say this about confidentiality:

1.2 Confidentiality

Written rules will be established specifying how records are to be maintained, for what length of time, who will have access to them, which information will be released to whom, and under what conditions, and what use, if any, can be made of records for purposes of research, evaluation and reports. Client records maintained by an EAP should never become part of an employee's personnel file. Adherence to Federal regulations on confidentiality of alcohol and drug abuse records (42 CFR Part 2) is required of Programs even indirectly receiving Federal funds.[24]

Thus, recordkeeping must be maintained in such a way as to ensure confidentiality while facilitating case management and follow-up and providing ready access to statistical information.[25]

The employer should review medical and disability insurance benefits to ensure that those plans adequately cover diagnosis and treatment for alcohol and drug problems. Where feasible, the standards recommend that insurance coverage include outpatient and day treatment care. In all, the employer should do everything possible to integrate the EAP with its medical and disability benefits.[26]

Furthermore, if an external EAP is used, indemnification and other legal responsibilities should be addressed in the provider agreement. In any case, the employer should purchase adequate coverage to ensure the company and the EAP staff against malpractice and other liability claims.[27]

The EAP staff should have managerial and administrative experience. In addition, the staff should be skilled in identifying problems, interviewing, motivating, referring employees, and, where appropriate, in counseling and related fields. It is essential that the EAP staff have experience and expertise in dealing with alcohol-related problems.[28]

The EAP must have an adequate education component. Employees and their families should be informed about the EAP and the services it offers. This information should be continually updated. It is especially important that information be made available to new employees and their families. The employer should have a major commitment to ongoing education about drug and alcohol use, alcoholism, and addiction. Management and, where appropriate, union representatives should be thoroughly informed about their key role in using the EAP services. Orientation for them should be updated regularly.[29] It is essential that supervisors be trained to confront employees only with performance problems and to refer troubled employees to the EAP staff to address the underlying personal problems.

The EAP should also network with community resources on alcohol treatment. These resources include Alcoholics Anonymous, Al-Anon, Alateen, Cocaine Anonymous, Narcotics Anonymous, other self-help groups, and health care community services and professionals.[30]

Finally, the entire EAP process should be monitored on a systematic basis. It should be reviewed periodically and evaluated objectively. At a minimum, the standards provide that there should be an annual review of the EAP's performance.[31]

Internal EAPs

EAPs fall broadly into two categories: the in-house or internal model, in which significant portions of the EAP are performed by the employer, and the outside or external model, in which most or all of these functions are contracted out. The internal model was developed as the basic EAP in the 1970s, but external contracting began emerging in that same decade.

Analysis

Traditionally, the internal model is characterized by having a manager maintain the program. This person usually works closely with the human resources and medical departments of the company. Typically, the persons in charge of the internal EAP will be specially qualified in the areas of substance abuse treatment and program administration. Responsibilities will include training supervisors, maintaining the employee education program, and working with managers and employees to screen and make initial referrals to community resources. In some internal programs, counseling is provided by qualified employees.

Whether the employer uses an internal EAP or contracts with an external resource often depends on the size and needs of the company. Internal EAPs are most commonly found in large companies. It has been stated that a full-time internal EAP coordinator will work at capacity with a work force of between 1,800 and 2,000 employees.[32] This is not to say, however, that all large companies use the internal model. Many large companies contract out these services. While it is difficult to obtain figures, it is generally felt that the internal model becomes less cost-effective the smaller the employer, although this depends in great part on the scope of services provided and the readiness of the work force to use the EAP.

The advantages of the internal EAP are several. The first is accessibility. When employees or their supervisors have an EAP available on site, they are able to use its services more readily. Second, management may be better able to control actual operations and costs of the program, since those administering the program are directly under management supervision. Third, management has better access to data regarding the program's effectiveness. Fourth, the internal EAP may be more attuned to the company's needs because of its location within the company. Since the persons responsible for the EAP are employees of the company and work full time with the company and its employees, they normally would have a deeper understanding of the working environment. The internal EAP is also more readily placed in the chain of communications between management and employees.

Fifth, the internal EAP may be more adaptable to geographic changes in the organization particularly when the employer locates facilities in remote areas. Where external EAP services are not readily available, many companies feel that an internal EAP manifests an expression of concern for the welfare of its employees which is more visible and tangible when it is housed internally.

There are some disadvantages to the internal model. First, it requires a higher degree of management commitment to ensure proper operation of the program. The EAP administrators are under the supervision of the company's management, who may not have sufficient expertise or motivation to ensure that they are performing their jobs properly. Use of an external EAP (assuming that a good one is chosen) releases management from the need to involve itself in the day-to-day workings of the program.

Second, employees may perceive an internal EAP as lacking confidentiality. This in large part depends on the corporate culture of the organization. If employees believe that the records maintained by the internal EAP are somehow available to others within the corporation, they will be less willing to use the program.

Finally, there is the issue of cost effectiveness. As was pointed out above, the internal model is usually more cost-effective in large companies. But even in large companies, internal EAPs are usually in place only where there are large concentrations of employees. Where employees are spread out geographically, internal programs are usually not very cost-effective. Cost effectiveness is addressed more fully later in this chapter.

Examples

The following are examples of internal EAPs:

DuPont Co.

One of the earliest assistance programs in America began in the 1940s at DuPont. Members of the DuPont family became interested in the newly founded Alcoholics Anonymous program and instituted these methods within the DuPont Company as a program to help employees troubled with alcoholism. Early in the program, Alcoholics Anonymous was the only method of treatment available. As other programs became available to help employees with other substance abuse problems, DuPont quickly added these treatments to the employee benefits package.

DuPont's program does not attempt to provide counseling for financial problems, marital difficulties, or legal problems, choosing instead to concentrate on substance abuse matters. The program offers three methods of treatment: the standard Alcoholics Anonymous model; inpatient treatment facilities with the person away from work and the everyday environment; and an intensive outpatient treatment program. The outpatient program is particularly designed for the person in the early stages of a problem, with the person continuing his or her daily work routine and going to the treatment program at night.

The DuPont program is available to all employees, eligible dependents, pensioners, survivors of pensioners, and dependents of pensioners. As with most programs, involvement with the EAP at DuPont may be initiated by the employee voluntarily seeking help, a supervisor or manager requesting the help of the program with an individual employee, or the spouse of a troubled employee.

CSX, Inc.

CSX, Inc., through its subsidiary, CSX Transportation, Inc., is one of the country's largest rail carriers. CSX has developed a sophisticated substance abuse policy in cooperation with its union. Like most successful programs, it emphasizes rehabilitation.

The structure of CSX's internal program provides systemwide coverage. The program is fully staffed with qualified counselors. The program director reports directly to the vice president of risk management, thus providing the program with substantial clout within CSX. The program operates independently but in cooperation with management to ensure credibility and improve acceptance among employees.

The program's philosophy is based upon encouraging employees to seek help voluntarily before job performance becomes unacceptable. Voluntary referral is facilitated by direction provided by supervisors, union representatives, Operation Red Block (the railroad's company-union substance abuse program) team members, and even family members. During ensuing treatment, the employee remains on the job unless circumstances require otherwise. If taken out of the work force, the employee will be returned as soon as rehabilitation makes this possible. The decision to return such an employee to work is made in conjunction with CSX's chief medical officer who must ensure that the company's medical standards are met.

The program also provides services to certain employees who have violated the company's rules prohibiting alcohol and drug use or possession on the job or reporting for work under the influence of such substances. In some situations, employees who violate these rules may choose program participation to avoid discipline. However, the services provided differ from other referrals inasmuch as EAP counselors continually monitor rehabilitation, and the determination of whether the employee may return to work is made by operating management. In addition, a comprehensive medical examination is required.

EAP counselors also evaluate employees who are identified as substance abusers through drug testing. The drug testing may accompany routine physicals given by the company, for-cause testing, testing pursuant to agreements with employees, and other physical examinations as directed by the medical department. In all cases, employees found to be chemically dependent must successfully complete rehabilitation before returning to work.

The internal program structure also allows EAP counselors to assist supervisors in making referral determinations to the EAP concerning individual employees. This assistance is in addition to ongoing training which is given to supervisors to improve their abilities to recognize troubled employees. The close relationship between counselors and supervisors is consistent with the program's objectives of early identification and prevention.

CSX's internal EAP is designed to provide assistance to employees in resolving any problem, substance abuse or otherwise, that adversely affects job performance. Counseling is provided at no cost to employees and much of inpatient care costs are covered by the company's health insurance.

Company officials report that CSX has benefited from the EAP by rehabilitating employees, thus reducing absenteeism, personal injuries, and accidents. By both humanistic and good business standards, the EAP has improved CSX.

External EAPs

Since the 1970s, a growing number of companies have begun to contract with outside organizations to provide EAP services. These outside organizations or external EAPs may be either for-profit or nonprofit. They often provide a wide range of services, including education and supervisory training as well as referral to appropriate health professionals. Many of the organizations employ their own professional counselors. While the EAP organization is located away from the employer, the external EAP's employees may provide services on the employer's premises or at an external EAP office where troubled employees may be referred.

Usually the external EAP is provided as part of the employer's benefit program. The cost of services provided by the external EAP, to the extent that they are not picked up by the employer, are often covered by insurance. The external EAP usually reports to a company official who acts as the liaison with top management.

Analysis

There exist a number of advantages to the external EAP model. First, a good external EAP provider will have expertise drawn from working with a wide range of employers whose employees have different problems. The service typically has more individuals working for it, thus providing a larger pool of expertise than could be found in a single individual working within the company.

The second advantage is flexibility and location. An external EAP may be able to take its services directly to employers' various facilities. Some external EAP providers are multistate, regional, or even national in scope, and thus are able to deliver their services to a broader geographic area.

Third, external EAPs may also enhance the employee's perception of confidentiality concerning his or her problems. Since the external EAP personnel are not employees of the employer, the employees are more apt to believe that the information provided to the EAP personnel will not be leaked to the company. This being the case, they are more likely to use the EAP.

Finally, the most obvious advantage of the external EAP is the economy of scale. Small employers that could not otherwise afford to employ such professionals for their few employees can use an organization that has broad-based expertise. This expertise can be tapped affordably since the cost is being shared by many other employers. The 1988 BLS study revealed that about half of all business *establishments* (as opposed to companies) contracted out for EAPs. It concluded that small establishments generally use contracted-out programs. For example, 63.8 percent of establishments surveyed with 50 to 99 employees contracted out but only 40.7 percent of those with more than 5,000 employees did so.[33]

Through the 1970s and 1980s the internal versus external EAP decision usually was made on the premise that large employers had internal EAPs and small employers had external EAPs. However, this is becoming less and less the case. As the sophistication of EAP professionals rises and the costs of health care increase, many larger employers are turning to external EAP providers to handle the myriad of administrative, training, and treatment details associated with EAPs and managed health care. Further, as the federal and state governments continue to require EAPs for employers they regulate as part of the drug free workplace programs, there will continue to be an increase in the development of specialized external EAP providers in the coming years.

Contracting out an EAP, although it is quick and easy, may result in significant loss of control. Managers often feel that by using this approach, they need not concern themselves with the day-to-day operations of the EAP. While this is an advantage in one sense, there also is a disadvantage since management lacks control over the operations of the EAP. The employer is less likely to be able to judge the effectiveness of an external EAP than it would one based on the internal model.

In addition, the employer may be less likely to be able to structure the EAP to conform to its particular needs. Many employers have felt that by contracting out the services they might isolate themselves from medical malpractice suits and other liabilities. Whether this is in fact the case is not clear. In fact, the employer may expose itself to more liability because it has less control over the persons actually providing the service. Employers should strive to work closely with the external EAP provider to avoid these problems.

Any employer considering an external EAP should also consider its funding and fee structure. The following questions, reprinted from the August 1985 issue of *Personnel Administrator*,[34] should be asked:

1. How does the vendor distribute overhead among clients?
2. What percentage of the fee is overhead and what percentage is attributable to direct service?
3. Does vendor receive public funds or grants? What percentage of income is federal/state grant based? How secure is long-term funding?
4. How are fee increases determined?
5. When are first-year installation costs recouped?
6. How does vendor provide for funding of lost business?

7. How long is fee structure guaranteed? What is projected fee structure for second and third years? Will fees increase or decrease if employee use increases?
8. Are there any unlisted service charges? If so, itemize.
9. Is fee based on number of total employees or cost per projected use?
10. Is there any limitation on number or length of visits as a cost reduction measure? If so, itemize.
11. Who determines when employee treatment is to be discontinued?
12. Are there any charges for after-hour or holiday visits?

Examples

The following are two examples of successfully implemented EAPs using external providers.

Richmond Employee Assistance Program

The Richmond Employee Assistance Program (REAP) was formed by six employers in the Richmond, Virginia, area who were concerned with the effect of unaddressed employee problems that negatively affected job performance. The employers found that by joining together for the purposes of contracting with an external EAP provider, the cost of an EAP became affordable. Since 1981, the group has grown from 6 to 23 employers which range in size from 50 to 5,000 employees. Approximately 13,000 employees are now served by the consortium. REAP is governed by a board of directors whose responsibility is to monitor the EAP's services and act as a liaison between member employers and the EAP provider.

In addition to cost, a motivating factor in the choice of an external EAP provider was confidentiality. Most members of REAP have a small number of employees. Informal discussions among employees and reports to the personnel department concerning troubled employees were perceived as potentially compromising the confidentiality of troubled employees. Use of an external EAP has allowed member employers to avoid the appearance of violating confidentiality since employees are assessed and treated through the EAP.

The Richmond EAP offers eligible employees and their family members referral, counseling, and prevention/education services. REAP reports that the most common problems that the EAP staff sees are emotional and mental problems, not substance abuse.

However, the EAP provides members with advice in developing drug policies, including implementation of urine testing programs. Other areas covered by the EAP include marital and family problems, problems connected with children and aging, financial counseling, and eating disorders.

REAP is staffed by three clinical social workers and one staff member with a master's degree in rehabilitation counseling. The office is centrally located to be convenient to all members' employees. The cost of the EAP is reasonable at $14.00 per employee per year. So for $8,400 a year, an employer of 600 employees has its counseling needs covered. Communications are provided to employees by both the employer and the EAP provider. The utilization rate of eligible employees is reported to be about 6.5 percent. REAP also provides member employers with policy and program development, publicity, and program evaluation. Furthermore, management training is provided to ensure that company supervisors are able to recognize troubled employees and properly refer them to REAP.

An interesting aspect of REAP is that the program serves employees in both the public and private sectors. REAP's apparent success in meeting the needs of such a diverse client base provides an excellent example of the effectiveness and flexibility available through an external EAP.

Metropolitan Police Department

The Metropolitan Police Department (MPD) in Washington, D.C., adopted an employee assistance program which is essentially external but has some characteristics of an internal EAP. Similar to other external EAPs, the program consists of EAP counselors who assess and diagnose referrals and, depending on the circumstances, engage in short-term counseling (up to six months) or refer the employee for appropriate treatment. However, like an internal program, some of the counseling services use department police who have experienced similar problems and have received some training in counseling and group therapy. Fellow police are used in the program to bridge the gap between police officers and EAP counselors who may not be as familiar with the special needs of police officers, while maintaining the added confidentiality the EAP hoped to achieve by having an external structure.

The MPD/EAP is designed to assist officers and support personnel with many personal problems. The primary purpose of the EAP is stated to be the prevention of work-related incidents that may adversely affect job performance. Stress-related problems that are addressed by the EAP include marital/family, emotional, financial, alcohol and drug abuse, and legal problems. Family members of employees are also eligible for assistance in some situations.

Similar to most external EAPs, program functions are allocated among the employer, the EAP, and community treatment and rehabilitation resources. The role of the MPD (which consists of management, employees, and the union) includes identifying troubled employees, motivating them, and referring them to the EAP. The EAP's role includes training and education of supervisors and employees, case consultation, problem assessment and diagnosis, referral for treatment, follow-up, reintroduction into the workplace, and providing feedback for monitoring program effectiveness. The role of community resources is to provide treatment, counseling and rehabilitation services, and feedback.

Alcohol abuse is a major target of the MPD/EAP. The program is designed so that EAP professionals decide the type of treatment an employee should receive. Types of treatment include inpatient, outpatient, or support group participation. When inpatient treatment is recommended, a provider is chosen based on the employee's insurance and ability to pay for treatment, the program's ability to offer education, family treatment, aftercare/follow-up, and AA participation. Distance from the employee's home is also an important factor since family involvement is encouraged.

A unique aspect of the MPD/EAP is the use of peer counselors. The program's developer found through experience with other law enforcement organizations that peer counselors were most effective in identifying officers with problems and in motivating them to seek further assistance. Also, peer counselor participation was found very effective in group therapy/support activities related to critical incidents (e.g., shootings) and aftercare programs. To ensure that peer counselors are properly qualified, the program establishes formal procedures for their selection and training.

The training program for MPD supervisors includes a five-step program for successful confrontation of troubled employees. The five steps include recognizing that a problem exists, documenting poor performance or other job-related problems, confronting the troubled employee with performance problems including dealing with employee denial and giving discipline when necessary, referring the troubled employee to the EAP counselor, and assisting with reintegration of the rehabilitated employee back into the workplace. Supervisors are encouraged to call EAP counselors for assistance. The EAP stresses that the supervisors' role in employee education and early diagnosis is essential to the program's success.

The MPD/EAP also provides for quarterly statistical reports to be submitted to the chief of police for evaluation of the EAP. Information that is monitored includes the number, participation rates, and participant evaluations for training and informational seminars and support groups; the number and extent of participation of program clients; methods of referral utilized; relationship of client to the program (i.e., extent of participation, attitude, and responsiveness); primary diagnosis; clients' sex; locations of treatment; disposition of the cases (i.e., successfully completed, ongoing); telephone hot line use; and performance evaluation of the EAP staff. Also, reports are prepared for each program participant detailing performance from one year prior to treatment until one year after treatment to determine the EAP's effectiveness.

Qualifications of EAP Counselors

There is no universally adopted licensing procedure for EAP professionals. The Employee Assistance Professionals Association, Inc. (EAPA), (formerly the Association of Labor Management Administrators and Consultants on Alcoholism, Inc. (ALMACA)), has developed a written examination for EAP professionals. This test was first given in 1987. Those who pass the examination receive the credential of Certified Employee Assistance Professional (CEAP). The purpose of the examination is to provide a standard requisite knowledge of EAPs and to monitor the level of knowledge required for certification. It also recognizes formally those individuals who meet the eligibility requirements. Finally, it assists persons in identifying qualified employee assistance programs. The examination covers work organization, human resources, EAP policy and administration, EAP direct services, chemical dependency and addiction, and personnel and psychological problems. (Appendix H contains the EAPA (or ALMACA) Code of Professional Conduct for Certified Employee Assistance Professionals.)

In addition the Employee Assistance Society of North America (EASNA) is in the process of establishing different credentials and minimum standards for four categories of EAP professionals. These are employee assistance administrator, employee assistance consultant, employee assistance assessment and referral specialist, and employee assistance referral agent. (The proposed Code of Ethics for EASNA is also contained in Appendix H.)

Many degreed professionals also provide EAP services. These are licensed psychiatrists and psychologists, social workers, professional counselors, and human resource professionals. It is very likely that as the field of employee assistance programs develops, certification and licensing standards will become more strict.

Effectiveness of EAPs

There is no disagreement that EAPs provide a valuable benefit for employees. Further, the consensus of opinion from employers who have EAPs is that the programs are financially beneficial to their companies.[35] Until recently hard data were difficult to come by, and the research that had been conducted showed varying degrees of effectiveness. One reason for the variance according to research conducted by Hazelden Research Services is the lack of quantifiable data available to evaluate EAPs.[36] However, even in the face of sparse research at this time, it is difficult to dispute the conclusion that EAPs benefit program sponsors. Current research shows that measures of effectiveness are being attempted and can be grouped into three distinct categories: administrative factors, cost effectiveness (including direct and indirect cost reductions), and subjective factors.

Administration and Process

The initial determination of an EAP's effectiveness should be related to the program's administration and process.[37] As was described before, development of an effective EAP requires a substantial commitment of time, effort, and resources. It is during the development stage that administrative functions, including scheduling and methods of evaluating the EAP, are established. As was stated by one expert, "an EAP should be custom designed for its specific workplace."[38] This expert suggests that particular attention must be given to proper staffing. EAP staff members are directly responsible for effective administration and proper counseling and referral of employees. Without sufficient expertise in both management and professional skills, troubled employees can be given inappropriate care which increases health care costs.

There are many important administrative factors in addition to staffing. Is necessary information being communicated to employees? Are counseling and referral services being provided properly? Are employees satisfied and using the EAP? Is management receiving necessary feedback to determine other aspects of the EAP's effectiveness? Assessments of the program should begin early and continue throughout the program's administration.

Cost Effectiveness

In this era of skyrocketing health care costs, cost must be a major factor determining effectiveness.[39] The first step in determining cost effectiveness of an EAP is determining its baseline operational costs. In a survey conducted by Coopers & Lybrand[40] of 140 industrial and 60 service firms, the responses from employers who had EAPs regarding the cost per employee per year ranged as follows:

Under $1.00	5%
$1–$10	10%
$10–$20	37%
$20–$30	18%
Over $30	13%
Other	17%

The study emphasized that these costs are highly dependent on employee utilization rates. Other national surveys have placed the average annual cost per employer in a range from $10 to $36.[41] Georgia Power, which uses a broad brush external EAP, reports the annual cost of the program to be $210,000[42] for 15,000 employees, a cost of approximately $14 per employee.

The cost of an EAP will also vary depending on the range of services offered, the structure of the program, and the geographical coverage. Internal programs involve greater start-up costs due to staffing, office space, and materials. However, with amortization these costs eventually may compare favorably to the per employee cost of a contracted, externally provided EAP. External EAP providers also vary the cost per employee depending on the total number of employees and the estimated participation rate. Furthermore, the cost of both internal and external EAPs will depend on the extent and range of services provided to employees. For example, will the program be limited to substance abuse treatment or will other personal problems such as marital problems be covered? Will family members be eligible for participation? Generally, the wider the range of services provided the more the EAP will cost.

Finally, geographical distribution of the work force will directly affect the cost of the EAP. If the employees are concentrated in a small geographical area, the costs will be much less than if employees are scattered over a multistate or international area.

Direct Cost Reductions

After determining the baseline cost, the second step is to determine savings that result from the EAP. The most easily quantified data reflecting the effectiveness of an EAP relates to direct costs such as health benefits. For example, such data include the cost of health care and disability claims, the cost of accidents and on-the-job injuries, and the cost of worker's and unemployment compensation. Savings may be calculated from two perspectives. First, cost comparisons can be made of individual EAP participants as they progress through the program. Second, the costs attributable to reductions in accidents and injuries involving EAP participants, as compared with employers who do not participate in the EAP, can be tracked.

EAPs that are narrowly constructed to focus on alcohol and drug abuse treatment have been the most frequently studied programs in terms of health and medical costs. These studies have also provided the most objective data for supporting a finding of direct cost savings for employers. As was previously mentioned, a common method is to compare medical costs of EAP participants before, during, and after participation. For example, one study of the treatment of alcoholics found "positive net savings" ranging from $405 to $9,400 per treated individual by the end of the third year of treatment.[43] These cost savings can then be compared with the costs of operating the EAP to determine cost effectiveness. A summary of results of several EAP cost impact studies compiled by Hazelden Research Services shows significant direct cost reductions and is included in Table 1.[44]

Several employer-sponsors have also reported direct cost reductions due to reduced accidents and injuries and reduced workers' compensation payments. Phillips Petroleum calculated that its EAP saved more than $8 million annually due in great part to

Table 1 EAP Cost-Impact Studies

SOURCE	TYPE OF COMPANY	SAMPLE CHARACTER-ISTICS (N)	TYPE OF EAP	TYPE OF TREATMENT	LENGTH OF FOLLOW-UP	CRITERIA	OUTCOME
Heyman, 1976	4 large service and manufacturing	162	Alcoholism			Self-reported work performance	67% of coerced clients and 33% of voluntary clients improved
Manello, 1979	7 railroads	1,571	Alcoholism			"Return to adequate work levels"	"About 70% of those who accepted treatment were successfully rehabilitated"
Milstead-O'Keefe, 1980	10 companies in community Agency of Labor Management	13 women alcoholics	Broad Brush			5 measures of work performance	Success rate equaled "71–88% across the work performance criteria"
Presnall, 1980	Not given	167 problem drinking men	Alcoholism			Amount of drinking, absenteeism	73/167 improved, decrease from 47–61 work shifts lost annually prior to treatment to 12–21 work shifts lost annually after treatment, depending on drinking outcome
Foote, et al., 1978	4 companies	Company A (N = 343) Company B (N = 22) Company C (N = 57) Company D (N = 159) mainly men	Broad Brush		13 months after referral	Absenteeism	Company A: no data; Company B: increase from 244 to 298 average hours annually; Company C: decrease from 307 to 133; Company D: decrease from 628 to 492

continues

Table 1   continued

SOURCE	TYPE OF COMPANY	SAMPLE CHARACTER-ISTICS (N)	TYPE OF EAP	TYPE OF TREATMENT	LENGTH OF FOLLOW-UP	CRITERIA	OUTCOME
Foote, et al., (cont'd)	4 companies	Company A (N = 343) Company B (N = 22) Company C (N = 57) Company D (N = 159) mainly men	Broad Brush		13 months after referral	Disciplines	Company A: decrease from .6 to .5 average number annually; Company B: decrease from 1.1 to .7; Company C: decrease from 1.0 to .2; Company D: decrease from 1.6 to .7
						Grievances	Company A: no data; Company B: decrease from .2 to 0 average number annually; Company C: decrease from .1 to 0; Company D: decrease from 1.4 to .9
						On-the-job accidents	Company A: decrease from 2.3 to 1.7 average number annually; Company B: decrease from 1 to .9; Company C: decrease from .3 to 0; Company D: no data
						Visits to medical unit	Company A: decrease from 7.3 to 5.9 average number annually

Chopra, et al., 1979	Not given	86 coerced clients and 100 voluntary clients (all men)	Alcoholism	Three-week inpatient program	Maximum of 14 months	Amount paid in worker's compensation benefits — Company A: decrease from $163 to $124 average annually; Company B: decrease from $320 to $237; Company C: decrease from $130 to $5
						Amount paid in sickness and accident benefits — Company A: increase from $425 to $679 average annually; Company B: increase from $123 to $205; Company C: decrease from $2,035 to $824; Company D: increase from $593 to $629
						Abstinence — 48% of coerced and 34% of voluntary clients reported abstinence
Freedberg & Johnson, 1980	200 businesses & industries	370 coerced clients and 58 voluntary clients	Alcoholism	Three-week inpatient program followed by 80–90 hours of aftercare	12 months	Abstinence — 31% of coerced and 36% of voluntary clients reported abstinence; 32% and 21% reported improvement
						Work status — 15% of coerced and 7% of voluntary were fired
						Ontario Problem Assessment Battery — "Significant improvement"
						Supervisor's Rating Form — "Significant Improvement"

continues

Table 1 continued

SOURCE	TYPE OF COMPANY	SAMPLE CHARACTER- ISTICS (N)	TYPE OF EAP	TYPE OF TREATMENT	LENGTH OF FOLLOW-UP	CRITERIA	OUTCOME
Anony- mous, 1980	Illinois Bell	752 referred problem drinkers with at least 5 years of employment before and after referral	Alcoholism	Varied; hospital re- commended for 50%	At least one year	Abstinence	58% reported abstinence; 19% reported improvement
						Supervisor's ratings	Prior to referral 90% had fair to poor ratings. After referral 66% had good ratings
						Disability claims	Decreased by 52%
						Off-duty accidents requiring >7-day absence	Decreased by 42.4%
						On-duty accidents	Decreased by 61.4%
Schram, et al., 1978	3 companies	206 referred problem drinkers	Alcoholism	Varied; inpatient rec- ommended for 10%	3–30 months	Job retention	83.3% remained employed in the company
					12–30 months	Treatment outcome	38.3% successfully completed treatment or were still actively involved in treatment

Hazelden Studies

SOURCE	SAMPLE TYPE OF COMPANY	SAMPLE CHARACTER-ISTICS (N)	TYPE OF EAP	TYPE OF TREATMENT	LENGTH OF FOLLOW-UP	CRITERIA	OUTCOME
Spicer, Barnett, & Kliner, 1979	Referrals from many companies to a treatment center (Hazelden)	N = 191 (Mostly males)	N/A	4-week residential treatment	12 months	Self-reported alcohol use	69% abstinence (compared with 62% in total patient population)
						Self-reported drug use	78% abstinence (compared with 70% in total patient population)
						Self-reported improvement in: relationship with spouse, general physical health, self-image, ability to manage finances	78–91% reported improvement
						Self-reported improvement in job performance	85% reported improvement
						A.A. attendance >1 × week	58% reported improvement
						Self-reported improvement in overall quality of life	59% reported improvement

continues

Table 1   continued

SOURCE	TYPE OF COMPANY	SAMPLE CHARACTER-ISTICS (N)	TYPE OF EAP	TYPE OF TREATMENT	LENGTH OF FOLLOW-UP	CRITERIA	OUTCOME
Hazelden, 1981	Hennepin County Employees	N = 109 EAP Clients 63% women 37% men	Broad Brush	Varied; only 48% referred to inpatient treatment	4 months	Self-reported: quality of work	46% improved
						quantity of work	35% improved
						relationship with co-workers	33% improved
						relationship with supervisors	32% improved
						# of times arrived to work late	Decrease from 196 times to 61 times total
						# of time left work early	Decrease from 120 times to 43 times
						# times used health insurance plan	Decrease from 96 to 90
						sick days	Decrease from 158 to 126
						medical leave days	Increase from 41 to 75
						accidents on job	No change (2)
						times used Workers' Compensation	Decrease from 8 to 0
						short-term disability	No change (0)

Source: Reprinted with permission from J. Spicer and P. Owen, "Finding the Bottom Line: The Cost-Impact of Employee-Assistance and Chemical Dependency Treatment Programs," Hazelden Research Services, p. 58–61 (undated).

reduced accidents and injuries.[45] The Foote Survey reported a decrease in the average amounts paid annually in workers' compensation benefits. One surveyed company decreased its average annual payments from $163 to $124 per employee. Another company decreased its average annual payments from $320 to $237 per employee. A third company decreased its average annual payments from $130 to $5 per employee.[46]

Indirect Cost Reductions

Indirect cost savings are more difficult to determine. Such savings result from reduced turnover and reduced paid and unpaid absences. Another factor that may reflect indirect cost savings is improvement in productivity. Methodology is critical to the validity of the analysis of indirect costs. The data are somewhat subjective, and the integrity of the analysis may be suspect due to the self-interest of companies who are reporting the success of their respective programs. However, a sound approach was developed by Saint Vincent Health Center for use in determining indirect cost savings attributable to its EAP.[47]

The Saint Vincent study focused on employee turnover, sick time, and unpaid time off. The cost of employee turnover consisted of replacement costs for the estimated 19 employees who, but for the EAP, would have lost their jobs due to poor performance related to personal problems. Replacement costs included recruiting, on-the-job training, orientation, and development. The savings in turnover costs alone was calculated to be $11,400.

Savings attributable to reduced use of paid sick time were calculated by comparing use before and after counseling. Statistical analysis revealed a 10 percent reduction in the use of paid sick time. Using an average hourly rate, annual savings were determined. The study noted that additional cost savings resulting from reduced overtime and replacement costs (e.g., costs associated with putting a replacement on the job including costs of hiring, training, benefits, and lost productivity) also accrued but were not included in the calculation. The savings from a reduction in unpaid sick time was calculated in a similar manner. The annual savings in paid and unpaid sick time was $2,449.

Subjective Factors

Savings that result from subjective factors such as improved job performance, higher morale, better discipline, fewer grievances, and greater EAP participation and rehabilitation rates are the most difficult to quantify and express in terms of cost. Another factor which may result in savings that are difficult to measure is the number of claims filed for health insurance, workers' compensation, and unemployment compensation. Consequently, analysis of these factors tends to focus on their value as "indicators," rather than proof, of program effectiveness. A study performed by Burlington-Northern on its EAP's impact on job performance[48] used the following indicators: attendance factors, insurance utilization rates, accident rates, grievance activities, changes in performance ratings, and assessments of whether an individual's job was in jeopardy. Many indicators showed significant improvement after employee par-

Table 2   Burlington-Northern EAP Study Job Performance Changes (In percentages)

INDICATORS (PREVIOUS MONTH)	AT INTAKE[1] (N = 646)	AT 3 MONTHS FOLLOW-UP (N = 501)	AT 12 MONTHS FOLLOW-UP (N = 464)
Used health insurance	17	8	5
Arrived late for work	17	5	3
Left work early	13	4	3
Took sick days	18	7	8
Used medical leave	4	1	2
Had an accident on the job	2	1	1
Used short-term disability	1	1	1
Used worker's compensation	1	1	1
Absent for other reasons	13	4	14
Filed a grievance	1	—	—
Job Performance Ratings (Previous Month)			
Improved	2	45	39
Stayed the same	41	22	23
Worsened	28	2	3
Unknown	28	31	35
Job In Jeopardy			
Yes	25	7	4
No	48	65	63
Unknown	27	28	33

Note. These differences between intake and follow-up responses were statistically significant at the .01 level for a matched group of 225 clients completing both the intake and three month follow-up forms.

[1]In order to increase the sample size, intake data were included on a 12-month sample of clients: July 1982–June 1983.

Source: Reprinted with permission from J. Spicer and P. Owen, "Finding the Bottom Line: The Cost-Impact of Employee-Assistance and Chemical Dependency Treatment Programs," Hazelden Research Services, p. 48 (undated).

ticipation in the program (See Table 2). These factors do not measure monetary cost, but improvement or deterioration of certain conditions over time.

Many other employer-sponsors who conclude that EAPs are effective base their conclusions on improvements in subjective factors. For example, United Airlines reported improved job performance of program participants as rated by supervisors. The supervisors rated performance on an 11-point scale from −5 to +5. The average rating improvement was 3.5 points.[49] Kimberly-Clark reported a 43 percent decrease in absenteeism and 70 percent reduction in accidents among program participants.[50] General Motors and Reynolds Metals reported drops in absenteeism of 40 percent and 80 percent, respectively.[51] A survey reported in *Risk Management* found a 68 percent decline in sickness disability cases, a 23 percent decrease in the use of health benefits, and a 33 percent reduction in accident benefit claims for substance abusers participating in EAPs.[52] AT&T reported reductions of 78 percent in companywide absenteeism, 87 percent in absence due to disability, 81 percent in on-duty accidents, and 58 percent in off-duty accidents for participants in EAPs.[53] Disability claims at Illinois Bell dropped 52 percent after the start of its EAP and on-duty accidents decreased by almost 62 percent.

A Model for Evaluating an EAP

Exhibit 1 is constructed to help an employer-sponsor evaluate the effectiveness of its EAP. The exhibit is the skeleton of an evaluation program; specific objectives and ways of measuring whether they have been achieved must be determined by the employer.

Administrative Factors

The initial focus when evaluating an EAP should be the program's administration. Although quite subjective in many respects, it is essential to determine if an EAP is being managed and operated effectively in order to give meaning to the more quantifiable cost factors. Maintaining effective administration is the cornerstone of achieving an effective EAP. This model approach identifies three specific areas of inquiry within the general category of administrative factors: operations, service, and information processing.

Exhibit 1   Evaluation Model of an EAP's Effectiveness

	[EXAMPLES OF] SPECIFIC OBJECTIVES	OBJECTIVES ACHIEVED?	COMMENTS

I. Administrative Factors
A. Operations
  1. Review EAP
    Policy/Procedure
	• Review action schedules
	• Review meeting preparation—assignment of review responsibilities
	• Review current P/P
	• Review proposed changes to P/P
	• Analysis of input from function areas
	• Review composition of committee members (executive commitment)
	• Develop, implement, and analyze employee surveys
	• Review communications within the committee and with the organization—evaluate substance and timeliness		

2. Personnel	• Annual individual performance appraisals—set objectives • Performance appraisal of EAP's internal "teams" or functional subunits—establish team performance standards • Manpower planning audits/skills inventories • Review budget performance/cost control • Review asset management (purchase, lease, operation, maintenance) for equipment and facilities • Evaluate professional competence using independent certification • Review availability of and participation in various training and continuing education programs		

continues

3. Community Networking
- Review breadth and substance of community contacts
- Review contact categories including other EAPs, external programs, publicly funded resources, information resources, etc.
- Review accessibility of community networking information
- Review performance of individuals/teams assigned with responsibility for developing community contacts
- Survey community contacts' perception of EAP and its personnel

4. Employee Survey
- Analyze survey results
- Review design and substance of survey
- Track survey frequency and employee participation
- Develop action plan for modifications
- Review utilization of external survey construction expertise

B. Services
1. Utilization
- Define terms and data sources
- Track employee use with sufficient information to determine characteristics affecting use
- Collect comparative data through literature or survey
- Differentiate between levels of use and whether referral was required

2. Communications
- Review all forms of communications to employees about the EAP
- Review timing and communication medium
- Review feedback on whether proper information is being communicated and whether communication techniques are effective
- Review effectiveness of employee education programs
- Review quality profile for counseling, referral, accessibility, personnel, and timeliness

Exhibit 1   continued

[EXAMPLES OF] SPECIFIC OBJECTIVES	OBJECTIVES ACHIEVED?	COMMENTS
3. Recovery Rate		
• Define terms and data sources • Categorize by source problem and extent of recovery • Collect comparative data from literature and survey results • Review action schedules for internal audits • Review accuracy of records		
C. Information Processing		
• Review confidentiality of record retention process and communication procedures • Review timeliness of accessing recorded information • Review record format • Legal assessment of information processing		

II. Direct Cost Reductions
A. Savings in—
1. Health care costs
2. Mental health care costs
3. Accident costs
 (on-duty)
 (off-duty)

TOTAL COMPANY				EAP PARTICIPANTS ONLY			
THIS YEAR	LAST YEAR	DOLLAR CHANGE	% CHANGE	THIS YEAR	LAST YEAR	DOLLAR CHANGE	% CHANGE

continues

4. Injury costs
   (on-duty)
   (off-duty)
5. Workers' compensation
6. Unemployment compensation

III. Indirect Cost Reductions
A. Savings in—
   1. Turnover cost
      [No. of replacements saved × replacement cost/employee]
      Replacement cost:
         Recruiting
         Orientation
         Training
         Lost productivity
   2. Absenteeism (EAP Participants)
      a. Paid
         [no. of hours × average hourly rate]
      b. Unpaid
         [no. of hours × replacement cost]
         Replacement cost:
            Hourly rate of replacement
            Overtime
            Lost productivity
   3. Productivity
      [Evaluation is dependent on employer productivity measurements.]

Exhibit 1   continued

	[EXAMPLES OF] SPECIFIC OBJECTIVES	OBJECTIVES ACHIEVED?	COMMENTS

IV. Subjective Factors
  A. EAP Participants Only
    1. Job Performance
	• Establish frequency of analysis
	• Statistically analyze job performance data
	• Review data summary and establish action plans		

2. Morale	• Review various survey data to develop morale index • Develop and implement morale surveys • Develop alternative measures of morale, for example, participation in employee suggestion programs		
3. Discipline	• Summarize disciplinary data by category and characteristics of the employee • Develop standard disciplinary profiles for measuring deviation • Review management training on the subject of discipline • Conduct procedural review of disciplinary procedures		
4. Grievances	• Summarize grievance data by category and characteristics of the employee • Review grievance data with Labor Relations management officials		
5. EAP Participation Rate	• Review methods of initial referral to the EAP • Review number of phone contacts • Review number of management inquiries • Review number of requests for information • Review number of in person contacts • Review number of repeat in person contacts		

6. Recovery Rate
- Review participants' range of services used
- Review number of referrals to external resources
- Collect comparative data from literature and surveys
- Define terms including levels of recovery and types of source problems
- Collect comparative data from literature and surveys

B. Total Company

1. Job Performance
- Establish frequency of analysis
- Statistically analyze job performance data
- Review data summary and establish action plans
- Review various survey data to develop morale index

2. Morale
- Develop and implement morale surveys
- Develop alternative measures of morale, for example, participation in employee suggestion programs

3. Discipline
- Summarize disciplinary data by category and characteristics of the employee
- Develop standard disciplinary profiles for measuring deviation
- Review management training on the subject of discipline
- Conduct procedural review of disciplinary procedures

4. Grievances
- Summarize grievance data by category and characteristics of the employee
- Review grievance data with Labor Relations management officials

Evaluation of operational considerations will indicate how well an EAP is being managed. A proper place to begin this analysis is a review of policies and procedures. Policy reviews should be conducted at least annually and include input from all areas of the organization. To expedite the process, surveys may be used for data collection. In addition, an agenda committee composed of representatives of each functional division of an organization may be given responsibility for identifying areas of concern and proposed revisions to be presented at the annual evaluation. These may be the same employees with liaison responsibilities between their respective functional areas and the EAP. Due to the fundamental directions derived from the policy, the annual evaluation should be chaired by the highest level executive with direct responsibility for the EAP. Furthermore, when changes are made, effective and timely communication of the changes to all employees must be a top priority of the review process.

Evaluation of the personnel who work for the EAP is another important factor reflecting the effectiveness of the EAP. In addition to the annual evaluation of each individual's performance, performance standards for functionally related groups within the EAP should be set and reviewed. This process should also include an audit of current skills inventory and planning to anticipate future skills requirements and how these skills will be acquired. Employees with budget responsibilities should be evaluated on their success in meeting budget objectives and controlling costs. Similarly, employees with responsibility for the operation and maintenance of assets (e.g., computers and medical equipment) or physical facilities should be evaluated on success in achieving performance standards in these areas.

A critical factor in the evaluation of individuals who work in the EAP is to determine professional competence. With development of certifying boards for EAP professionals, this evaluation should be made with their assistance. In addition, participation in continuing education and training should be mandatory for all EAP personnel. Records establishing education and training needs and documenting employee participation should be maintained.

Community networking is also an important factor which may indicate the effectiveness of an EAP. Most EAPs are structured to take advantage of available external resources in the service of program participants. Thus, objectives should be established which assign individual responsibility for establishing contacts and developing effective relationships with external resources. This can be accomplished by setting individual performance standards or developing a team approach with shared accountability for developing these contacts. An additional method of monitoring the effectiveness of networking is to survey the community resources regarding their perception of the EAP.

Another effective evaluation technique is to design a survey which elicits EAP participants' perception of the program's success in achieving objectives. The survey may be conducted annually or administered to individuals at specific stages of participation in the EAP. The content of the survey should mirror the administrative factors which are chosen for evaluating the EAP.

The second area of inquiry regarding administrative factors focuses on the quality of services. One indication of an EAP's effectiveness is the use rate by employees and others eligible to participate. Care should be taken to define what is meant by "use" to ensure consistency in data collection. It may be helpful to define several levels of participation. This information tends to become more useful over time as trends are established. Use rates can also be compared to other EAPs as a reflection of effectiveness. Similar to use rates, referral rates should also be tracked because they may indicate the effectiveness of the EAP.

Measuring the effectiveness of communications, although difficult, is essential to an accurate evaluation of the quality of services provided by an EAP. In addition to substantive content, evaluation of communications should include establishing a schedule for making written and other communications to employees. The schedule should ensure broad coverage of relevant information such as the types of services available through the EAP and how the services can be accessed. Ease of accessibility has been found to be a major contributing factor to the success of many EAPs. In addition, periodic surveys requesting employee feedback should be made to determine whether employees are actually "getting the message." Education, a highly specialized form of communication, should be conducted for all employees on an annual basis. This will provide a forum to emphasize the purpose of the EAP and availability of services under the EAP and provide an easily monitored method to ensure that all employees are exposed to the program.

The evaluation of services provided by the EAP must also include the quality as perceived by employees. Specific quality factors include the quality of counseling by EAP personnel and referrals, the accessibility of program services such as counseling referral services, information, and EAP personnel, and the timeliness of services. Perceived as well as actual program confidentiality are essential for a successful EAP and consequently must be continually monitored and included in the evaluation of service effectiveness.

The recovery rate of program participants is without question a measure of an EAP's effectiveness and reflects to some degree the quality of services provided. Recovery information, however, must be viewed in the proper context. Similar to use and referral data, recovery information must be precisely defined to ensure that proper comparisons are being made. Recovery rates should be identified specifically in terms of the source problem and extent of recovery required to be labeled as such.

The third area of administrative factors involves an evaluation of the effectiveness of information processing. Its importance to determining an EAP's effectiveness speaks for itself since accurate and timely information creates the basis for and is clearly involved in all aspects of this model approach. Data collection and recordkeeping methods should be reviewed annually. This review should include both an operational review to ensure the mechanics of recordkeeping are meeting the EAP's needs but also to ensure that the proper type of information is being collected. Other factors which must be reviewed are timeliness and accuracy of information processing. In addition, procedures may be helpful to provide for the continuing update of certain summary information which is used in day-to-day operations. These summaries can be used as the basis of action plans, and the evaluation process should include review of both the substance of these plans and the effectiveness of implementation. Finally, due to swift changes in federal and state laws regarding confidentiality, periodic reviews of the EAP's information processing should be made by legal counsel.

Objective factors that may be quantified are used in evaluation by comparing changes over time. This year or current period is compared to last year or a preceding period. Actual changes are calculated and expressed in actual amount of change and percentage change. The quality of quantitative data as a reflection of EAP performance may improve as more data are collected and experienced trends are established in the use of the EAP over time.

Factors related to direct cost reductions should be reviewed on a total company basis and using only EAP participants. Costs to be tracked may include health care costs, mental health care costs,

costs due to accidents both on and off the job, injury costs both on and off the job, workers' compensation claims, and unemployment compensation claims.

Factors related to indirect cost reductions should be evaluated in a manner similar to the evaluation of direct cost reductions. However, due to the greater difficulty in quantifying these costs, particular care should be taken to document how individual cost subfactors are calculated. This is necessary to ensure consistent comparisons over time. For example, turnover costs are calculated by estimating the cost of recruiting, orienting, and training replacements and the cost of the resulting lost productivity. Absenteeism can be calculated by determining the number of hours and multiplying by an average wage. The cost of replacing an employee while absent including the wage of the replacement employee, overtime, and lost productivity should also be included. Detailed records should be made regarding methodology and identification of specific cost components used in each of these calculations.

Indirect cost reductions attributable to changes in productivity should also be monitored. Productivity may be measured for the company as a whole or for EAP participants only, or both. Although the specifics of how productivity is determined may be unique to each business, productivity trends and estimated costs may be valid indicators of EAP performance.

Purely subjective factors are evaluated similar to administrative factors. Thus, objectives are set for each factor, a determination is made of whether the objective has been achieved, and a review is conducted and report made regarding performance based on these objectives. Examples of purely subjective factors include job performance, morale, the company's experience issuing discipline and processing grievances, program participation rate, recovery rates, and a review of changes in the number of claims related to health insurance, disability, workers' compensation, and unemployment compensation.

One tool that has been used successfully to collect information regarding employee perceptions of the EAP is a survey. The survey should include questions designed to discover the awareness among employees of the program and program services, evaluation of the quality and breadth of services provided, identification of services used, perceived confidentiality, and general feelings about the program including its success. Specific questions may be included soliciting responses from managers and supervisors to evaluate the effectiveness of their role in the program.

Improving Cost Effectiveness: New Approaches

New approaches to improve the cost effectiveness of EAPs are currently being developed. One new approach has been termed "managed care." David Levine, vice president for managed care at Human Affairs International (an external EAP contractor) was reported to have described managed care as an EAP which includes gatekeeping, preferred provider agreements, utilization review, case management, and insurance claims review.[54] Gatekeeping refers to the function which encourages employees to use the EAP's assessment and referral services, thereby giving the EAP control over referral decisions, extent of treatment, and, consequently, costs. Preferred provider agreements give employees better coverage for using the "preferred" treatment facility. Preferred facilities charge less as a result of economies of scale.

Owens-Illinois is a corporate employer which has successfully adopted managed care.[55] Cost controls included in its managed care program are limits on the number of chemical dependency treatments each employee is eligible to receive and a progressive decrease in coverage after the initial treatment. Also, to qualify for full benefits employees must participate in the EAP and follow through on treatment programs. Owens-Illinois reported a 46 percent savings in program costs resulting from the managed care approach.

Another recently emerging approach is for an employer to differentiate between employees with good and poor health habits. Control Data Corporation found in a study of 15,000 employees that "a typical 40-year-old man who smokes two packs a day, does not exercise, does not wear seat belts and is 30 percent overweight would cost his employer $1,282 in medical bills in 1988, more than twice the $631 of someone the same age with better habits. Not counted are productivity losses."[56] This finding was consistent with complaints from healthy employees that they were subsidizing unhealthy employees. CDC responded by providing employees with healthy habits more extensive health care coverage. Thus, an employee with poor habits was given a strong incentive to improve his or her health habits. Most initiatives of this type increase benefits for healthy employees rather than reduce benefits for others. Also, the programs commonly address only modifiable behavior like smoking and drinking. Circle K Corporation, which recently proposed dropping all health care coverage for employees with problems related to alcohol, drugs, or AIDS, was highly criticized for its severe approach.[57]

Data currently available strongly suggest that EAPs do in fact effectively reduce employer costs in addition to providing employees with a valuable benefit.[58] As the popularity and perceived success of EAPs continue, more and better studies will continue to be conducted to verify their effectiveness.[59] However, in spite of the current lack of extensive research, it may be safely concluded that "employee assistance and alcoholism treatment programs are a sound investment and do have a strong effect on the 'bottom line.'"[60]

Focus of EAPs

The first EAPs were directed almost exclusively to the problem of alcohol abuse and alcoholism. Today, many EAPs still focus on alcohol and drug abuse. Alcohol abuse is still considered by most employers as the number-one problem among its troubled employees.

Over the past decade or so, many "broad brush" EAPs have been established. These cover addictions to drugs and alcohol, and also overeating and sex addictions. They seek to assist employees with a wide range of mental health and emotional problems, including those experienced by an employee going through a divorce or coping with the loss of a loved one. A broad brush EAP may deal with any issues that affect the employee such as marital problems, family problems, alcohol and drug problems, obesity, depression, stress, interpersonal problems, gambling, legal matters, or financial and job problems. Finally, those programs are increasingly addressing problems of employees' family members by helping the employee cope with the problems, or directly assisting the family member, or both.

Additionally, an increasing number of employers are looking into so-called wellness programs. These programs are commonly designed to complement existing EAPs, and emphasize a preventive approach and a focus on how to become and remain healthier. A 1989 report of the National Chamber Foundation reported that "more physically fit individuals experience [less] work absenteeism, and employer initiatives that increase the level of physical activity among the work force may indeed have a positive effect on employee absenteeism."[61] Wellness programs help employees to avoid illness in the first place.

Employers who support such programs believe that healthier employees will be more productive. Not only will they miss fewer days because of illness, but they will be able to perform their jobs on a higher level since both their mental and physical capabilities will be increased. There are several types of these programs. These include health care profile programs, where employees are assessed and advised on how to conduct their lives in order to become healthier. They also include programs covering smoking cessation, control of high blood pressure, weight reduction, nutrition, stress management, back problem prevention, and off-site injury prevention. Table 3, taken from the Coopers & Lybrand survey,[62] illustrates the broad range of services that modern EAPs/wellness programs provide.

Wellness programs clearly are directed at a bottom line issue— health costs. By some estimates the annual costs of health care may reach $1 trillion by the turn of the century.[63] Much of this cost will be borne by business. Programs that reduce illness in employees may significantly reduce these direct costs as well as increase productivity.

Preparing EAP Policies

An employer should always articulate its employee assistance program policy in a written format. In each EAP policy, an employer will want to discuss the details of its particular EAP and explain how it fits in with the rest of the employer's substance abuse program. (See Appendix F, "Substance Abuse Programs," for examples of EAP policies.) Certain basic policy considerations will be considered here, including the following:

- Philosophy and recognition
- Purpose and function
- Coverage
- Nondiscrimination provision
- Reference to EAP provider
- Educational program component
- Voluntary referral
- Management referral

Table 3

EAPs are not only one of the fastest growing employee benefits, but the coverages they provide are growing in scope and breadth. Many traditional EAPs began simply as a referral system for alcoholism and grew to meet the demands of such problem areas as chemical dependency, mental problems, and marital and family problems. Today, many EAPs cater to a host of employee problems.
Question: Does your company's EAP provide assistance in the following areas?
Question: Is this service provided internally or externally?

	YES	NO	EXTERNAL	INTERNAL	BOTH
Traditional					
Drug/Alcohol Abuse	38 (95%)	0 (0%)	27 (68%)	4 (10%)	5 (13%)
Marital/Family					
Problems	37 (93%)	2 (5%)	26 (65%)	4 (10%)	4 (10%)
Mental Disorders	38 (90%)	2 (5%)	24 (60%)	4 (10%)	6 (15%)
Financial Problems					
Counseling	33 (83%)	5 (13%)	27 (68%)	2 (5%)	1 (3%)
Time Management	13 (33%)	24 (60%)	7 (18%)	3 (8%)	2 (5%)
New					
Mental Health					
Counseling	36 (90%)	2 (5%)	23 (58%)	4 (10%)	5 (13%)
Dependent Care					
Problems	35 (88%)	3 (8%)	23 (58%)	5 (13%)	4 (10%)
Bereavement					
Counseling	35 (88%)	3 (8%)	24 (60%)	4 (10%)	3 (8%)
Stress Management	34 (85%)	3 (8%)	21 (53%)	6 (15%)	4 (10%)
Community Services					
Referral	32 (80%)	4 (10%)	18 (45%)	10 (25%)	1 (3%)
Eating Disorders	30 (75%)	8 (20%)	23 (58%)	3 (8%)	1 (3%)
24 Hour Crisis Hotline	29 (73%)	9 (23%)	22 (55%)	3 (8%)	1 (3%)
Weight Control	25 (63%)	12 (30%)	15 (38%)	4 (10%)	3 (8%)
Health Education	21 (53%)	16 (40%)	12 (30%)	6 (15%)	3 (8%)
Lunch-time					
Counseling &					
Lectures	21 (53%)	17 (43%)	10 (25%)	8 (20%)	2 (5%)
Smoking Cessation	20 (50%)	17 (43%)	10 (25%)	8 (15%)	2 (5%)
Exploratory					
Directions					
Health Risk					
Screenings	8 (20%)	28 (70%)	3 (8%)	3 (8%)	1 (3%)
AIDS Support Group					
Meetings	4 (10%)	32 (80%)	2 (5%)	0 (0%)	1 (3%)
Other					

—EAP will deal with any problem
—Lending library, support groups

Source: Reprinted with permission from Coopers & Lybrand, *Employee Assistance Program Survey Results* (undated), p. 8.

- Confidentiality
- Medical records
- Right to discipline
- Relationship to substance abuse program/drug testing
- Management follow-up condition
- Medical/disability benefits
- Medical leave/work scheduling policy
- Cooperation with counselors
- Return-to-work procedures
- Aftercare/follow-up.

Philosophy and Recognition

In the beginning of the EAP policy, it is appropriate for the employer to state its philosophy concerning the EAP and its recognition that personal problems can affect job performance. Usually in this section employers state that they recognize that alcoholism, drug abuse, and psychological adjustment problems are treatable conditions. Usually employers also state that the EAP exists for the purpose of helping employees whose work performance or behavior is being adversely affected by certain non-work-related problems. Employers also state that it is in the best interests of both the employee and the employer that referral to the EAP or to professional assistance be voluntary and in lieu of disciplinary action. In essence, the primary purpose of this section of the policy is for management to acknowledge that problems may exist, state that it is willing to assist employees with these problems, and urge employees to use the program and facilities to solve these problems.

Purpose and Function

Usually this section explains the EAP in greater detail by describing the purpose of the EAP and its function. This section usually states that EAPs are primarily designed to help employees and their families with any problem that causes, or may cause, unacceptable job performance by the employee. Examples of some problems include not only substance abuse, but legal, financial, personal problems, psychological or psychiatric disorders, gambling, overeating, and marital/family problems. Usually it is stated that the problem may not be job-related, but eventually will affect job performance. Further, most employers state that the intent of the policy is to rehabilitate the employee, not to take punitive action. Furthermore, employers often state in the policy that EAP coordinators will help employees with personal problems by offering advice and providing referrals to outside rehabilitative services or agencies.

Coverage of EAP

At this point the employer needs to state whether the EAP serves the employee or the employee and the employee's family. Usually a simple statement is sufficient. Sometimes employers determine that it is necessary to state that services are extended to the immediate family, and the policy defines whether adult children, former spouses, stepchildren, etc., are included.

Nondiscrimination Provision

Many employers feel that it is necessary, particularly in order to encourage voluntary participation in the EAP, to state that participation in the EAP will not be used against the employee. This so-called nondiscrimination provision is sometimes useful in assuring employees of the good intentions of the EAP and as an inducement to encourage otherwise reluctant employees to participate. Essentially these provisions state that no employee will have his or her job security or promotional opportunity jeopardized by a request for counseling or a referral to the EAP.

Reference to EAP Provider

Many employers feel that it is important to designate in the policy who the EAP provider is. For instance, if the EAP provider is an internal program, the employer will list the contact person. If the EAP provider is an external EAP contractor, it is helpful to state the name of the EAP provider and its telephone number and address. Further, some employers explain the process of contacting the EAP provider, particularly where external EAPs are involved.

Educational Program Components

Particularly in conjunction with federal requirements, the EAP policy will explain the education and training programs that will be provided, the counseling services available, and the other assistance available to employees seeking rehabilitative services in general and through use of medical insurance. Often employers will use the EAP counselors to train employees and managers concerning the substance abuse portion of their program and all other aspects of the EAP. This section of the policy allows the employer to introduce the education, training, and counseling programs that will be delivered to the employees.

Voluntary Referral

Ideally, referral to the EAP will be on a voluntary basis. Although few things in this world, particularly regarding substance abuse, are handled voluntarily, experience has shown that some employees and their dependents will use an EAP on a voluntary and confidential basis if given an opportunity. As a result, the employer should state that the employees may avail themselves of the EAP services at any time they feel the need to seek help with a problem that is causing or may cause their job performance to decline. Usually the employer also explains the process for voluntary referral and contact with the EAP official or representative.

Management Referral

The management or medical referral component of the EAP is the policy that authorizes management to force an employee into the EAP for evaluation upon the threat of that employee losing his or her job. Usually these policies state that management referral is based on observation and documentation of deteriorating job performance by supervisory or medical personnel, or a positive result of a drug test, or both.

Confidentiality

The issue of confidentiality is always covered in EAP policies, primarily to assure the participating employees that their problems will not be broadcast to the world. However, it is important that the employer leave itself some room because it may be required to divulge some of the confidential information to appropriate courts of law or law enforcement officers, or others, as the needs arise. In any case, confidentiality is important and should be stressed in these policies to the extent possible.

Medical Records

Many employers specify that the medical records associated with the EAP will be kept confidential to the extent possible. This policy statement usually has a reassuring effect on employees.

Right to Discipline

In many cases an employer will reserve the right to implement discipline so that the EAP cannot serve as a shield for the employee against the employer's disciplinary or personnel policies and procedures. The EAP policy should articulate the employer's intentions where rehabilitation and discipline are concerned.

Relationship to Substance Abuse Program/Drug Testing

In this section of the policy the employer usually will specify that any employee who tests positive on a drug test will be referred to the EAP. Although the referral procedure is usually the same as the management or medical referral, many employers use this section as an opportunity to expand upon the connection between drug testing and the EAP.

Management Follow-Up Condition

In the past many employers have made the mistake of turning employees over to the EAP and then forgetting about them. In most substance abuse programs today, employers realize the importance of maintaining contact with the employee and the EAP during the counseling sessions primarily when the referral to the EAP has been mandatory or management-directed. As a result, employers will state in the policy that acceptance of EAP services by the employee including treatment and/or counseling shall necessitate management to follow up with the EAP regarding the employee's progress and/or completion of treatment and any aftercare procedures. Employers usually state that all details are strictly confidential and managers shall only be concerned with a satisfactory completion of each phase of rehabilitation. Further, employers indicate that all decisions regarding counseling and/or treatment shall be made by a joint decision of management and the EAP. This concept of a managed EAP is considered very useful in assuring employers that the employees will not use the EAP as a revolving door or to avoid discipline or termination because of substance abuse or other problems.

Medical/Disability Benefits

Most employers have linked the substance abuse or other counseling services inherently related with an EAP to their medical or disability insurance plans. As a result, these employers refer to those plans in the EAP policy. This has two effects. First, it puts the EAP in the proper context, that it is health- and benefit-related. Second, it indicates that the employer is concerned enough with the personal problems of the employees to have covered treatment of these problems in the medical and disability insurance policies.

Medical Leave/Work Scheduling Policy

Often an employer will link EAP counseling with the personnel policies covering leaves of absence, particularly medical leaves of absence. The purpose of this linkage is to assure employees that treatment for substance abuse or other EAP-covered problems will not be used to penalize the employee in terms of pay, seniority, or benefits. Again, this approach emphasizes the benefits of the EAP program and usually has a positive effect on the morale of employees, who then realize that they will be allowed to deal with these personal problems without being severely penalized.

Cooperation with Counselors

Usually employers state that if an employee refuses to cooperate with the counselors of the EAP in any aspect of treatment after having been referred to the program because of testing positive for drugs or after being referred by management, the employee may be disciplined or terminated for violation of the company policy and for failing to meet company medical standards. This policy makes it very clear to the employee that the carrot is rehabilitation through the EAP and the stick is discipline or termination for failure to cooperate. Although this appears to be an obvious policy, it is important to state it very clearly. Because the employer maintains the ability to discipline the employee for failure to cooperate, the EAP cannot be considered a safe haven from discipline.

Return-to-Work Procedures

In many instances an employer will allow the employee to continue participation in the EAP counseling or rehabilitation and return to work. Particularly where the employer's EAP encourages outpatient rehabilitation, return to work is viewed as part of the rehabilitation therapy and is encouraged. As a result, particularly in drug-related situations, the employer will want to safeguard itself and other employees and clients by requiring surveillance or random testing of the employee who has previously tested positive under the substance abuse program. As a result, the EAP policy needs to make it clear that if the employee strays from the treatment regimen and tests positive for drugs, he or she will be terminated. Again, this type of policy allows the employer to maintain control over the employee's actions in its workplace.

However, many employers also provide that once the return-to-work procedures have been successfully completed, including the time period stated in the surveillance agreement, and the employee has either been released from the EAP or has satisfied all of the treatment criteria, the employee may return to regular employment status. This procedure gives the employee a goal to work toward which also is important in any rehabilitation treatment regimen. For example, many employers provide that if the employee satisfactorily completes the EAP or other rehabilitation, returns to work for a period of time, satisfactorily performs the job, and remains drug free for a period of time (usually a year), then the employer will destroy the disciplinary records concerning the substance abuse incident and return the employee to full regular employment status.

Aftercare/Follow-Up

Increasingly, employers are requiring EAP staff members to maintain contact with the employee during the aftercare phase of the employee's rehabilitation. This required follow-up may continue for several years in order to maintain compliance with the rehabilitation program. Recognizing that recovery is a lifetime commitment rather than simply a periodic cleansing, many employers are continuing to monitor the aftercare of rehabilitated employees in an effort to ensure compliance with the rehabilitation program. Other employers are requiring follow-up on the employee's aftercare program in order to study the success of the EAP program. In these latter cases, aftercare follow-up is usually voluntary rather than mandatory.[64]

Conclusion

Employee assistance programs have become the program of choice for most employers with well-designed substance abuse programs. EAPs are the mechanisms that connect identification of the substance abuse problem with treatment, rehabilitation, and return to work. Although EAPs have evolved significantly over the last ten years, their primary goals remain the same: to identify employees with problems, motivate these employees to seek and accept help, assess these problems and personal resources, and develop a plan of action to assist employees in getting the services they need so that they may be rehabilitated to live healthy, productive lives. The achievement of these goals is certainly possible under any well-defined and properly implemented EAP.

Notes

1. Resource One, *Employee Assistance Program Employee Checklist* (Greenville, S.C.: Resource One, 1989), 3.
2. U.S. Department of Labor, Bureau of Labor Statistics, *Survey of Employer Anti-drug Programs* (Report 760, January 1989).
3. *See, generally,* Bureau of National Affairs, Inc., *Employee Assistance Programs: Benefits, Problems, and Prospects.* BNA Special Report (Washington, D.C., BNA, 1987), 9.
4. Sonnenstuhl & Trice, *Strategies for Employee Assistance Programs: The Crucial Balance* (Ithaca, N.Y.: ILR Press, 1986), 5.
5. Wrich, *The Employee Assistance Program* (Minneapolis, Minn.: Hazelden Foundation, 1980).
6. BNA Special Report, *supra* note 3, at 10.
7. U.S. Department of Labor, *supra* note 2.
8. *Id.*
9. Masi, *Designing Employee Assistance Programs* (New York, American Management Association, 1984), 24.
10. BNA Special Report, *supra* note 3, at 100.
11. *Id.*
12. *See, generally,* Sonnenstuhl & Trice, *supra* note 4, at 17.
13. Pub. L. No. 100-690 tit. V, subtitle D.
14. Section 2(a)(2).
15. Section 2(a)(5).
16. 49 C.F.R. §391.119–123.

17. The pertinent text of the regulations is as follows:
§391.119 Employee Assistance Program (EAP).

(a) Every motor carrier shall establish an EAP program. The EAP program shall, as a minimum, include—

(1) An educational and training component for drivers which addresses controlled substances;

(2) An education and training component for supervisory personnel which addresses controlled substances; and

(3) A written statement, on file and available for inspection, at the motor carrier's principal place of business, outlining the motor carrier's EAP.
§391.121 EAP Training Program.

(a) Each EAP shall consist of an effective training program for the motor carrier's supervisory personnel and all drivers.

(b) The training program must include at least the following elements:

(1) The effects and consequences of controlled substance use on personal health, safety, and the work environment;

(2) The manifestations and behavioral causes that may indicate controlled substance use or abuse; and

(3) Documentation of training given to drivers and motor carrier supervisory personnel.

(d) EAP training programs for all drivers and supervisory personnel must consist of at least 60 minutes of training.
§391.123 Aftercare Monitoring.

After returning to work, drivers who test positive must continue in any aftercare program and be subject to follow-up testing for not longer than 60 months following return to work.

18. 14 C.F.R. §121.457 Appendix I (VIII). The pertinent text of the regulation is as follows:

VIII. Employee Assistance Program (EAP).

The employer shall provide an EAP for employees. The employer may establish the EAP as a part of its internal personnel services or the employer may contract with an entity that will provide EAP services to an employee. Each EAP must include education and training on drug use for employees and training for supervisors making determinations for testing of employees based on reasonable cause.

A. *EAP Education Program.* Each EAP education program must include at least the following elements: display and distribution of informational material; display and distribution of a community service hot-line telephone number for employee assistance; and display and distribution of the employer's policy regarding drug use in the workplace.

B. *EAP Training Program.* Each employer shall implement a reasonable program of initial training for employees. The employee training program must include at least the following elements: The effects and consequences of drug use on personal health, safety, and work environment; the manifestations and behavioral clues that may indicate drug use and abuse; and documentation of training given to employees and employer's supervisory personnel. The employer's supervisory personnel who will determine when an employee is subject to testing based on reasonable cause shall receive specific training on the specific, contemporaneous physical, behavioral, and performance indicators of probable drug use in addition to the training specified above. The employer shall ensure that supervisors who will make reasonable cause determinations receive at least 60 minutes of initial training. The employer shall implement a reasonable recurrent training program for supervisory personnel making reasonable cause determinations during subsequent years. The employer shall identify the employee and supervise EAP training in the employer's drug testing plan submitted to the FAA for approval.

19. 48 C.F.R. §25.223.

20. 48 C.F.R. §25.223(c)(1).

21. The pertinent text of the regulation is as follows:

(c) Contractor programs shall include the following, or appropriate alternatives:

(1) Employee assistance programs emphasizing high level direction, education, counseling, rehabilitation, and coordination with available community resources;

(2) Supervisory training to assist in identifying and addressing illegal drug use by Contractor employees;

(3) Provision for self-referrals as well as supervisory referrals to treatment with maximum respect for individual confidentiality consistent with safety and security issues;

(4) Provision for identifying illegal drug users, including testing on a controlled and carefully monitored basis. Employee drug testing programs shall be established taking account of the following . . . .

22. Blum & Roman, "Internal vs. External EAPs," in BNA Special Report, *supra* note 3, at 95–104.

23. *Standards for Employee Alcoholism and/or Assistance Programs*, (Arlington, Va.: Employee Assistance Professionals Association, undated).

24. *Id.* §1.2.

25. *Id.* §2.3.

26. *Id.* §2.4.

27. *Id.* §2.5.

28. *Id.* §2.6.

29. *Id.* §§3.1–3.3.

30. A list of available support groups appears in Chapter 9.

31. *Standards for Employee Alcoholism and/or Assistance Programs*, *supra* note 23, at §5.2.

32. *Supra* note 22, at 100.

33. U.S. Department of Labor, *supra* note 2.

34. American Society for Personnel Administration, Alexandria, VA.

35. BNA Special Report, *supra* note 3, at 25. *See also* Cangianelli, "The Navy's Employee Assistance Program Today, Local Command Programs," Mar. 1990, 16; "McDonnell Douglas Corporation's EAP Produces Hard Data," *Almacan*, Aug. 1989, 19–26.

36. Spicer & Owen, *Finding the Bottom Line: The Cost-Impact of Employee Assistance & Chemical Dependency Treatment Programs* (Center City, Minn.: Hazelden Foundation, undated), 41–50.

37. Masi, *Drug Free Workplace: A Guide for Supervisors* (Washington, D.C.: Buraff Publications, 1987).

38. Wrich, "Beyond Testing: Coping With Drugs at Work," *Harv. Bus. Rev.*, 1988, 120. James T. Wrich is president of employee assistance services for Parkside Medical Services Corporation and past director of United Airlines' EAP.

39. Weiss, "Cutting the Cost of Substance Abuse Treatment," *Compensation & Benefits Rev.*, May–June 1987, 37–44.

40. Coopers & Lybrand, *Employee Assistance Program Survey Results* (undated), 3.

41. BNA Special Report, *supra* note 3, at 30.

42. *Id.* at 105–9.

43. National Institute on Alcohol Abuse & Alcoholism, "Alcoholism Treatment Impact on Total Health Care Utilization and Costs," reprinted in *Medical Care*, January 1987.

44. Spicer & Owen, *supra* note 36, Appendix 2, "Summary of Selected EAP Cost-Impact Research."

45. Wrich, *supra* note 38, at 120.

46. *See* Table 1 in this chapter.

47. Hermann, "An Employee Assistance Program Pays Off," *Hosp. Mag.*, Feb. 1978, 34–36.

48. Spicer & Owen, *supra* note 36, at 48.

49. Wrich, *supra* note 38.

50. *Id.*

51. *Employee Assistance Programs: Drugs, Alcohol and Other Problems.* (Chicago, Ill.: Commerce Clearing House, 1986), 22.

52. Weinstein, "Successful Approaches to Helping Troubled Employees," *Risk Mgmt.*, June 1988, 70–71.

53. Wrich, *supra* note 38, at 72.

54. *Employee Assistance Programs Praised in Battle Against Substance Abuse*, 201 Daily Lab. Rep. (BNA), Oct. 20, 1987, at A-4-6.

55. *Id.*

56. Kramon, "New Incentives to Take Care," *N.Y. Times*, Mar. 21, 1989, at D-2.

57. *Id.*

58. Wrich, *supra* note 38.

59. *See* "McDonnell Douglas Corporation's EAP Produces Hard Data," *Almacan*, Aug. 1989, 19–26.

60. Spicer & Owen, *supra* note 36, at 50.

61. *Employer Initiatives to Reduce Substance Abuse*, a study prepared by S. Sullivan and N.S. Bagby, National Chamber Foundation, 1989, 17.

62. Coopers & Lybrand, *supra* note 40, at 8.

63. Franz, "Promoting Wellness & Disease Prevention in EAPs," *Almacan*, Nov. 1987.

64. See Appendix F, "Substance Abuse Programs."

Chapter 8

Rehabilitation Referral Programs

Until recently, an employer's decision to begin a substance abuse program was purely voluntary. Employers who began programs typically were motivated by a combination of good business judgment and altruistic feelings for employees.[1] This situation has changed. Although still in an early stage of development, federal laws already *require* certain employers to provide employees with information regarding substance abuse, its policies regarding substance abuse, and available rehabilitation resources in their community.[2] It is only a matter of time before state laws follow suit.[3]

Description and Development

An alternative available to employers who choose not to develop a comprehensive program is to institute a rehabilitation referral program (RRP). RRP is an in-house service developed by an employer whereby troubled employees are referred to drug and alcohol abuse treatment and rehabilitation programs available in the community. Initial referral is the only service provided. The advantage of an RRP is low cost or, usually, no cost; however, there are also substantial shortcomings in the effectiveness of RRPs as compared to EAPs.

Information Gathering and Communications

Development of a successful RRP requires more than simply collecting names of treatment programs in the community. The functions of available programs, cost, availability of services, and identity of contact persons must also be determined. Furthermore, once information is collected, it must be effectively communicated to employees so they can take advantage of it. Responsibility for information collection and communications must be assigned. Typically, responsibility is given to the personnel or medical department. In addition, some amount of supervisory training is necessary to ensure that troubled employees can be identified and properly encouraged to seek the assistance of the RRP.

Employers must strive to ensure that employees are properly referred. Proper referral requires that the employer have a general idea of what the employee's problem is so that referral can be made to the proper program. As will be discussed later in this chapter, most treatment and rehabilitation programs are tailored to meet the needs of people who have a certain category or subcategory of problems; for example, teenage alcoholics.

However, supervisors should not attempt to become amateur diagnosticians. The inquiry into the employee's problem need only be of such depth to ensure proper referral. Also, the employer should always attempt to offer employees at least two referral alternatives and leave the final choice to the employee. In addition to improving the potential that the employee will identify the best available program for his or her needs, by providing alternatives the employer may limit liability which might arise from a single source referral.

Referral Information

Referral information is readily available. The fact is that prevention, treatment, and rehabilitation programs have been and are available in most communities; however, only as a result of the growing national concern regarding alcohol and drug abuse are these programs now becoming visible. Available programs include those offered by both private and public institutions, but, practically speaking, it is the publicly supported institutions that are the main focus of most RRPs. Public programs are most affordable for employees who have limited medical insurance and financial resources and who cannot afford alternative treatment and rehabilitation programs.

The cost of available programs will be critical to their usefulness in an RRP. Clearly, employees will participate only if they can afford the program. Many programs that address less severe problems are free to all participants. Such programs might include education and some counseling. Publicly supported programs that do charge participants typically charge according to ability to pay. Thus, an individual with substantial financial resources may find very little difference in the cost of public and private programs while other participants may receive totally free treatment.

However, this is not to imply that the quality of a program is dependent on the program's cost. One study in which addiction counselors were asked to recommend treatment centers showed a wide range of treatment costs charged by the recommended programs. Typical costs ranged from $2,310 to $8,000.[4] Furthermore, one commentator believes that employers simply have not become sufficiently educated on the subject to substance abuse treatment and rehabilitation to know whether a particular program is providing a good service for the amount charged.[5] He argues that inappropriate tax write-offs for employers (i.e., uncapped insurance premium deductions) encourage a laissez-faire attitude about the cost of rehabilitation. He also believes that insurance providers are partly to blame because of their failure to establish firm price guidelines.

In the public sector, alcohol and drug abuse programs are supported at the federal, state, and local levels. Due to the continuing effort to move more treatment facilities into community settings, state and local governments administer most programs which actually provide services to participants.[6] Federal support is usually limited to policy formulation and financial assistance with exceptions such as programs run by the Veterans Administration.[7] In some cases, public funds are granted to nonprofit private organizations which provide treatment and rehabilitation services. Commonly, this occurs where there is no duplication of services and provision of a public program is not feasible.

Rehabilitation Program Formats

At state and local levels, responsibility for substance abuse treatment and rehabilitation is commonly held by the agency which also administers mental health and vocational rehabilitation programs. Centralized administration of programs may assist employers who implement RRPs due to increased and easier accessibility to referral information. However, centralized administration may also cause some problems. For example, if mental health officials are operating the substance abuse treatment and rehabilitation programs the programs will tend to be administered according to a mental health program model. Such models are often inappropriate, inefficient, or ineffective for substance abusers. Further, personnel selection may be inappropriate. Because of emphasis on the mental health functions, professionals are assigned to mental health programs while substance abuse programs are staffed with social workers who are not specially trained in substance abuse counseling and treatment. A similar problem occurs when the agency is headed by vocational rehabilitation professionals. The effect may be that treatment may be downplayed in favor of job-related rehabilitation activities. When these related areas of treatment and rehabilitation are combined for administrative purposes, program directors must ensure that the integrity and effectiveness of each program is maintained. Thus, comprehensive public programs should be developed so that the subprograms targeted at specific problems can take advantage of each other's resources without compromising any other subprogram's ability to meet the needs of its targeted clients. An analysis of these relationships among available programs can assist an employer in providing the most effective RRP for its employees.

Mental Health Format

The mental health format focuses on treatment of psychological problems. This format has traditionally excluded alcoholism as a primary focus of treatment. Rather, alcoholism has been treated as a secondary or symptomatic condition of mental illness. Treatment of drug addiction has been approached similarly. Mental health treatment attempts to discover the nature of the mental problem whereas substance abuse treatment begins with the problem identified, that is, addiction, and thus moves directly into treatment and rehabilitation. While mental health programs deal with the complexity of mental disorders, substance abuse treatment focuses more on behavior.

More recently, mental health programs have been expanding to accommodate the unique requirements of substance abuse treatment. Programs are now being offered which include evaluation assessment, drug screening, psychiatric assessment, nursing assessment, individual sessions, and group therapy support sessions. Further, social workers are being used rather than psychiatrists and psychologists to provide treatment at reduced costs. Although this has financial benefits, it is questionable whether social workers who have not been trained in substance abuse and addiction behavior can effectively provide the necessary treatment.

Substance Abuse Format

Treatment and rehabilitation programs designed in the substance abuse format focus solely on alcoholism and other drug dependencies as chronic, progressive diseases. All aspects of the chronic disease are treated using an interdisciplinary team made up of physicians, nurses, chemical dependency counselors, clergy counselors, psychiatrists, clinical psychologists, and other health care professionals. The programs are designed so that patients learn to become responsible for their own actions and include substantial emphasis on group therapy. Further, aftercare is regarded as a vital element in the substance abuse format.

The substance abuse format includes provision for detoxification. Commonly, detoxification facilities are supported partially or completely by public funding. Currently, the major weaknesses of the substance abuse format come from the lack of adequate funding. Lack of funds has kept treatment resources from meeting demand and has limited the number of available qualified substance abuse professionals. Further, there are insufficient funds to support adequate aftercare programs. Thus, although maintaining its contribution to short-term substance abuse treatment, this format currently is falling short of offering the long-term solutions that are necessary. It is probable that public funding for these programs will increase and it is almost assured that employers and the public in general will come to rely on these programs more and more.

Vocation Rehabilitation Format

Although often administered under agencies that are responsible for mental health, vocation rehabilitation programs provide a unique service to impaired individuals. The vocation rehabilitation format focuses almost exclusively on the chronically unemployed. The format consists of job skills analysis, aptitude testing, retraining, and occupational rehabilitation. These program elements often overlap with and consequently must accommodate substance abuse treatment. The value of the vocation rehabilitation format, even in the context of substance abuse, is unquestioned; however, the format orientation simply does not focus enough on substance abuse problems to begin to be able to meet the treatment needs of alcohol and drug abusers.

Public Funding and Legislation

Public Support of Treatment and Rehabilitation Programs

To better understand the current structure and availability of publicly funded substance abuse treatment and rehabilitation programs, employers should understand how and why such programs developed. Substance abuse and its effect on individuals, their families, and society have long been matters of public concern in the United States. Few people are aware that the first cocaine epidemic in America occurred about 100 years ago at the turn of the century. A combination of public outrage resulting from the realization of cocaine's destructive effect and enactment of laws prohibiting use operated effectively to extinguish recreational demand.[8] Consistent with this approach, the reaction of the government to alcohol and drug abuse was to enact laws restricting or prohibiting use and possession.[9] However, this approach failed to comprehend and address the many causes and problems associated with substance abuse. As society's experience with substance abuse increased, it became apparent that the government's role in dealing with these problems had to expand. The expanded approach was based in substantial part on the recognition that too little was known about the treatment and prevention of drug abuse, that the success of substance abuse efforts was dependent on the coordination of education, treatment, rehabilitation, and training efforts with law enforcement efforts, and that the overall effectiveness of substance abuse programs required the joint and cooperative efforts of federal, state, and local governments.[10]

In the mid-1980s, cocaine again emerged as the vehicle elevating the public's awareness and concern regarding drug abuse. Epidemic cocaine abuse reported among groups ranging from urban professionals to ghetto youth and punctuated by the cocaine-related deaths of highly visible celebrities and professional and college athletes sparked intense concern. In addition, the public has become frighteningly aware of the emergence and growing availability of crack, the highly addictive smokable form of cocaine, which is spreading from urban to rural areas and with it a consequential increase in crime rates. Grassroots organizations such as the National Federation of Parents for Drug-Free Youth and the Parents' Resource Institute for Drug Education (PRIDE) have formed with community support to attack the problems of substance abuse through education and other preventative programs. The result is a new sense of urgency to find solutions to substance abuse problems. Thus, the general public is becoming increasingly involved in efforts to combat substance abuse.

Federal Support

Federal involvement in substance abuse education, prevention, and treatment has been ongoing for nearly 20 years. Concern regarding reports of widespread drug abuse during the late 1960s and 1970s led to the enactment of several key pieces of federal legislation targeting substance abuse. In 1968 the Alcoholic and Narcotic Rehabilitation Act was enacted which provided funds for programs supporting treatment and rehabilitation of alcohol and drug abusers through community mental health programs.[11] In 1970 the Comprehensive Alcohol Abuse and Alcoholism Prevention, Treatment, and Rehabilitation Act provided additional funding for state and local programs focusing on alcohol treatment and rehabilitation.[12] A similar bill targeting drug abuse, entitled the Drug Abuse Office and Treatment Act, was passed in 1972.[13] Congress also established the National Institute on Alcohol Abuse and Alcoholism (NIAAA) and the National Institute on Drug Abuse (NIDA). These institutes were given responsibilities in their respective areas to provide public information, administer grant programs, and assist in development of research, substance abuse prevention programs, and training. The NIAAA and NIDA were combined in 1974 with the National Institute of Mental Health under the Alcohol, Drug Abuse, and Mental Health Administration (ADAMHA) to become the Department of Health and Human Services' leading agency dealing with substance abuse and mental health issues.[14]

In 1981, ADAMHA became authorized to grant federal funds to states in a combined block grant covering alcohol and drug abuse treatment and rehabilitation programs. Although few regulations were imposed on states with regard to administering the funds, three requirements were imposed. At least 35 percent had to be spent on alcohol abuse programs, at least 35 percent on drug abuse programs, and at least 20 percent on prevention and early intervention programs designed to discourage abuse of alcohol and drugs. The Department of Health and Human Services reports that since 1982 states have used grants to support the following programs:

- Both inpatient and outpatient alcohol and drug detoxification programs and counseling
- Alcohol and drug abuse prevention programming including school presentations, classes on responsible decision-making, and training programs for teachers
- Community outpatient treatment programs for families and youth experiencing difficulties due to alcohol or drug abuse[15]

More recently, Congress enacted the Anti-Drug Abuse Act of 1988.[16] In addition to imposing requirements on certain employers to establish substance abuse programs, the law launches a broad attack on substance abuse. The bill creates block grants and extends existing block grants for treatment and rehabilitation of substance abusers, construction of treatment facilities, maintenance of group homes for recovering substance abusers, and research on community-based alcohol and drug abuse treatment programs. One objective of the bill's funding provisions is to reduce the amount of time persons have to wait for drug abuse treatment due to lack of available treatment resources.

Title III of the bill addresses drug and alcohol abuse education and prevention. This section provides for the development of innovative programs dealing with alcohol abuse and its effect on the alcoholics' families, particularly children. Provisions also include extensive drug abuse education programs. The target groups for the programs include women, infants, and children in certain food subsidy programs, children in public schools, community-based volunteer drug abuse education and prevention activities, participants in youth gangs, and runaway and homeless youth.

In 1989, the NIAAA and NIDA published a national listing of alcohol and drug abuse facilities titled *The National Directory of Drug Abuse and Alcoholism Treatment and Prevention Programs.*[17] The listing includes about 8,689 federal, state, local, and private facilities listed according to state. Information includes name, city, address, telephone number, and types of services offered. This publication is a valuable tool for persons seeking referral information.

Despite growing publicity regarding government interest in subtance abuse problems, employers considering use of an RRP must understand that the availability of treatment under public programs is becoming harder to obtain. This situation is attributable to two major factors. First, there are less government funds available for public programs. Reviewing the period 1977 through 1986, one study finds that annual federal financial support for state and local substance abuse programs dropped from $583.3 million to $235.1 million.[18] Second, the public's increased use of drugs and its increased awareness of subtance abuse problems and the availability of publicly provided treatment and rehabilitation have resulted in increased program use. This puts additional pressure on increasingly sparse program resources. The result is that the availability of services is not meeting the current demand. The practical effect on employers who rely on RRPs is that their employees may not be able to obtain necessary services or treatment because of unavailability.

Program Structures

The structures of publicly supported treatment and rehabilitation programs are similar to treatments available through EAPs. The difference is that an employer can choose which programs fit its and its employees' needs when it operates its own EAP. With an RRP, the employer and employees are limited to programs that are already operating outside the workplace.

Generally speaking, program structures can be grouped into inpatient, outpatient, support group, and aftercare categories.

Inpatient Programs

Inpatient programs require participants to be admitted for full-time treatment. Inpatient treatment is common where acute detoxification is necessary or where other medical or psychiatric complications accompany the substance abuse problem. (Detoxification is the management of alcohol or drug withdrawal reactions, and is the most acute and dangerous phase of recovery). Typically, states operate free-standing detoxification units for alcohol and drug abuse. Admission to these facilities may result from self-referral, family referral, or forced participation by law enforcement and the courts. Inpatient treatment may also be undertaken if the person requires constant supervision, such as when the addiction is severe or participation is involuntary.

Like all treatment programs, the duration of inpatient treatment depends on the nature and severity of the individual's problems and the available financial resources. However, inpatient treatment is relatively expensive and publicly provided programs typically have few beds available. For example, in Georgia there are only 125 beds available in public facilities for acute treatment.[19] In South Carolina, the only public inpatient facility has 20 beds.[20] Consequently, patients having the most medically and financially critical needs face a great shortage of available treatment programs.

Similar to inpatient programs are residential programs where participants live in a rehabilitation community during treatment. Unlike inpatient programs, a residential program may allow the patient contacts or activities outside the facility during treatment, depending on the program and the individual's problem. Also similar to inpatient programs, residential programs are relatively expensive and are readily available at private facilities if the patient can afford the treatment.[21] Inpatient rehabilitation programs are more fully discussed in Chapter 9.

Outpatient Programs

Outpatient programs allow participants to live at home while receiving treatment. Outpatient treatment is far less expensive than inpatient treatment and many experts in the field believe there are advantages to treating an individual who remains in his or her normal environment. Outpatient programs are also growing in popularity among insurance providers due to lower costs. Publicly available programs may be conducted by clinics and state and local agencies specializing in treatment of particular problems.

Typical of such programs is the four-four-four program. This program consists of treatment four hours a night, four days a week for four weeks. This schedule allows a participant to continue working and to live at home where family support can be maintained. Some physicians believe, however, that outpatient programs are effective only in early stages of addiction and that more severe addictions must be treated in an environment where the patient can get away and concentrate on the problem.[22]

Other settings are also available for outpatient treatment. Community-based halfway houses, quarterway houses, and recovery homes provide residence for recovering alcoholics without spouses or family homes of their own. These facilities provide food, shelter, and supportive services for ambulatory and mentally competent persons. Outpatient rehabilitation programs are discussed in greater detail in Chapter 10.

Support Groups

Support groups and other self-help groups are another form of available treatment. Alcoholics Anonymous, Narcotics Anonymous, and Cocaine Anonymous are probably most widely known. Total abstention is the goal of these programs. These groups operate on the belief that continuous support from and to others with the same problem can help the individual to maintain sobriety.[23] These programs' self-help approach to rehabilitation incorporates a spiritual (but not religious) involvement. In addition, they focus on establishing organization and a structured direction for addicts to assist them in getting control of their behavior. The programs also provide an alcohol/drug free social environment for recovering substance abusers. However, as with outpatient treatment, support groups cannot give the intensive treatment necessary for initial treatment of severe alcohol and drug abuse.

More recently, self-help programs have been broadened to include assistance to nonaddicted family members who are attempting to cope with the addiction of a loved one. Such support groups include Al-Anon for spouses of alcoholics and Alateen for children of alcoholics.

Aftercare

Aftercare refers to programs designed to follow up after initial treatment and rehabilitation to assist with successful reintegration of the individual into everyday life and prevent relapses. The object of these programs is to reinforce corrected lifestyle patterns and encourage participation in other support group programs. Providing aftercare is critical since so many of the causal elements that existed during the period of substance abuse remain when the patient returns to his or her previous environment. Aftercare commonly includes family counseling to assist family members in dealing with and supporting the recovering patient.

A disadvantage of RRPs is that since the employer has been involved in referral only and not treatment, the employer is in a poor position to participate effectively in aftercare. An EAP provides an employer with professional guidance during the aftercare period and with the necessary information regarding an individual's rehabilitation in order to support the recovery process and reentry into the workplace. This information will probably be unavailable to the employer who uses an RRP. Various aspects of aftercare rehabilitation programs are examined at greater length in Chapter 11.

Conclusion

In summary, rehabilitation referral programs can help employers to meet legal requirements and business needs and provide troubled employees with helpful assistance. However, the overall benefits from RRPs are limited. An RRP is best suited for the employer with limited resources or one which uses the RRP as an initial step until a more comprehensive program can be developed.

The RRP should strive to ensure proper referral. This is accomplished in part by training supervisors to recognize troubled employees and to encourage these employees to seek assistance from the employer's RRP coordinator in contacting available treatment facilities. The RRP coordinator must be informed of the various treatment and rehabilitation programs available to employees and be able to effectively communicate this information. A properly designed and administered RRP can be an economical and effective mechanism for matching troubled employees with available treatment and rehabilitation programs thereby benefiting both the employee and the employer.

Notes

1. Bureau of National Affairs, Inc., *Employee Assistance Programs: Benefits, Problems, and Prospects.* Special Report. (Washington, D.C., BNA, 1987), 9.
2. Drug Free Workplace Act of 1988, Pub. L. No. 100-690 tit. V, subtitle D.
3. *See, e.g.,* Georgia Drug Free Workplace Act, Ga. Code Ann. §50-24-1 et seq.
4. Flanagan, "Sobering Facts on Rehabilitation" ("Counselors' Choice Chart"), *Forbes*, Mar. 9, 1987, 141.
5. Cohen, "Why Subsidize Expensive Private Drug Care?," *N.Y. Times*, June 6, 1988, at C-23.
6. Pub. L. No. 100-690, §2501, Evaluation of the Veterans Administration Inpatient and Outpatient Drug and Alcohol Treatment Programs.
7. Klebe, *Drugs and Alcohol Abuse: Prevention, Treatment, and Education* (Washington, D.C.: Congressional Research Office, Library of Congress, December 1986).

8. Steinhaus, "Cocaine Intoxication," Paper Presented at the Second International Symposium on Anesthesia History, London, 1987; Musto, "Lessons of the First Cocaine Epidemic," *Wall Street J.*, June 11, 1986, at 30.
9. Harrison Narcotic Act of 1914, 38 Stat. 785.
10. Drug Abuse Prevention, Treatment and Rehabilitation Act, 21 U.S.C. §1101.
11. Pub. L. No. 90-574.
12. Pub. L. No. 91-616.
13. Pub. L. No. 92-255.
14. *See* Klebe, *supra* note 7.
15. *Id.*
16. Pub. L. No. 100-690.
17. National Institute on Drug Abuse (NIDA), *National Directory of Drug Abuse and Alcoholism Treatment and Prevention Programs* (Washington, D.C.: NIDA, 1989) (DHHS Publication No. (ADM) 89-1603).
18. *See* Klebe, *supra* note 7, Table 2, at 8.
19. A & D Regional Plan Capacity (service area analysis) (compiled in 1989).
20. Behre, "State's Student Referrals for Drugs Rise 16 Percent," *Greenville-[S.C.] Piedmont*, Sept. 8, 1988, at C-2.
21. Alsop, "Drug and Alcohol Clinics Vie for Patients," *Wall Street J.*, Nov. 14, 1988, at B-12.
22. Coggins & Collier, "Day Treatment in the Workplace," *EAP Digest*, May/June 1985, 19–26.
23. Masi, *Drug Free Workplace: A Guide for Supervisors*, (Washington, D.C.: Buraff Publications, 1987), 110–13.

Chapter 9

Inpatient Rehabilitation Programs

History and Development

Through the centuries, alcoholics have usually been considered morally weak, insane, or possessed by the devil. Since insane asylums have existed, their populations have always had a large number of chronic alcoholics. Until recently, alcoholics, particularly chronic, debilitated alcoholics, were considered hopeless by most of the medical profession and were confined to mental institutions or long-term alcoholic hospitals/sanitoriums. Even into the middle of the twentieth century, the medical profession experimented on chronic alcoholics with belladonna treatment (poison therapy) or electroshock therapy.

Additionally, the attitude toward alcoholics, and later toward addicts, was that these people were perverted, weak, immoral, or socially irresponsible. Why else would a person drink himself or herself to oblivion, even after repeated hospitalizations or institutionalizations, loss of job, loss of family, and loss of everything of significance in a modern civilized society? Furthermore, the thought that alcoholics could be educated rather than lectured and moralized had not occurred to the many dedicated physicians and clergy who spent untold, thankless hours dealing with these poeple.

Fortunately, the situation today is dramatically different from what it was a few short years ago. There has always been some hope for alcoholics. Countless numbers of alcoholics have found recovery and sobriety through the church. Today, thousands of individuals are fortunate enough to receive treatment for their alcohol or drug addiction from hospitals or inpatient treatment programs. All of the modern American inpatient treatment programs base their recovery programs on the principles of Alcoholics Anonymous (AA).

Alcoholics Anonymous (AA) was founded in 1935 and was (and is) based on the spiritual foundation of turning the problem of addiction over to a Higher Power. The only purpose of the members of AA was to stay sober and help other alcoholics who had a desire to stop drinking. The principles of a spiritual foundation and working with others were developed by the two individuals who founded AA, based on the ideas, thoughts, and other group workings of admitted alcoholics around the Northeast and Midwestern part of the United States, particularly in New York and Ohio.

The fundamentals of Alcoholics Anonymous were published in 1939 in the book *Alcoholics Anonymous*, or the "Big Book," as it is called by AA members.[1] The first 164 pages of the Big Book consist of the principles of AA. The remaining 397 pages (hence the term Big Book) consist of stories about the alcoholics who were some of the early members of AA, as well as appendices and other materials. Chapter V of the Big Book introduces the Twelve Steps of the AA Recovery Program. (The Twelve Steps are found in Appendix I, "Alcoholics Anonymous Materials" of this book, along with other pertinent AA materials.) These Twelve Steps have become the cornerstone of all modern treatment programs that exist today. The Twelve Steps are used in such recovery programs as those for alcoholics (AA), narcotic addicts (Narcotics Anonymous, or NA), cocaine addicts (Cocaine Anonymous, or CA), overeaters (Overeaters Anonymous, or OA), gamblers (Gamblers Anonymous, or GA), people with emotional problems (Emotions Anonymous, or EA) and in Alanon, Alateen, and Adult Children of Alcoholics (ACoA). These other groups simply substitute the word or words for their particular problem for the term alcohol in the AA Twelve Steps, but otherwise the wording is essentially the same.

The importance of the AA Twelve Step recovery program is that it is a very specific, itemized, proven recovery program that is utilized almost universally in inpatient and outpatient addictive disease rehabilitation centers in the United States and in other parts of the world. Perhaps someday someone will discover a scientific cure for addiction, or a better recovery program; but for now the AA Twelve Step program is used so extensively by rehabilitation programs that any official inpatient or outpatient program that purports not to use the AA principles and Twelve Step program would be highly suspect.

There is almost universal agreement that the standard for inpatient treatment programs against which all other inpatient rehabilitation programs are judged is the Minnesota Model. The

Minnesota Model "has recently come to mean treatment based on combining the philosophies of the medical community, AA, and mental health practitioners, that is, the so-called multidisciplinary team treatment process."[2] Although there is more to the Minnesota Model than inpatient rehabilitation, the Model's development since the late 1940s has had such a profound influence on the structure of inpatient rehabilitation programs that it will be discussed briefly in connection with the evolution of present inpatient treatment programs in the United States.

Daniel J. Anderson, Ph. D., has authored an excellent book that discusses the origins and development of the Minnesota Model as well as other inpatient treatment models in the United States.[3] Essentially, the Minnesota Model began with a new attitude of treating the disease of alcoholism along with the "start-up of three new specialized treatment centers for alcoholics."[4] These three hospitals, according to Dr. Anderson, were started relatively independently and included Pioneer House in 1948, Hazelden in 1949, and Willmar State Hospital in 1950. As Dr. Anderson stated: "Each was designed to become a model of effective, economical treatment. Each was heavily influenced by the thinking of a relatively small group of recovered alcoholics, all members of Alcoholics Anonymous. One facility, Willmar State Hospital, had been admitting alcoholics for custodial care for over 30 years along with mental patients; now it would try to make a radical departure from psychiatric tradition, from the conventional understanding of alcoholism. The other two centers were both modest test projects, initially. Pioneer House was supported by a large city welfare department while Hazelden was a private non-profit foundation supported mainly by local businesses and industry."[5] Although the Minnesota Model began with the initiation of three alcoholism hospitals, since then, the term Hazelden has become synonymous with the term Minnesota Model and as stated earlier, is considered the "gold standard against which all other places can be measured."[6] It is noteworthy that Hazelden presently is not just a hospital in Minnesota. Hazelden is a dynamic organization that includes 12 substance abuse rehabilitation centers in Minnesota and Wisconsin as well as an Education Material Division which provides a full range of educational materials including more than 1,000 addiction-related books, pamphlets, films, audio and video cassettes, and specialty items, all of which can be ordered by mail.[7]

According to Dr. Anderson, a conceptual revolution took place regarding the treatment of alcoholism at Willmar State Hospital which began the process that became the Minnesota Model. As

Dr. Anderson stated, "It was 1950. Other than a brief medical detoxification period, there was no alcoholism program at this facility. Alcoholic patients were kept in locked wards, some of them mixed in with psychiatric patients. The staff was inadequately trained and budgets were extremely modest."[8] From this rather dreary beginning, a new set of basic assumptions evolved which have had the effect of completely transforming alcoholism treatment approaches into what exists today. The eight basic assumptions that evolved out of Willmar State Hospital and led to the development of the theoretical concepts that created the Minnesota Experience are reviewed briefly: First, alcoholism exists. It was discovered that there was tremendous denial or lack of acknowledgement that alcoholism was the problem suffered by individuals in all sorts of socioeconomic ranges. Although this concept seems elementary today, in 1950 it was revolutionary.[9] Second, alcoholism is an illness. The Minnesota researchers determined that somehow alcoholism was an illness because they realized about their alcoholic patients that "despite the repeated occurrence of drinking-related problems or disabilities, they continued to use alcohol." They concluded that "[t]his behavior . . . probably resulted because alcoholics had both a pathological dependence upon alcohol and a loss of control over their ability to regulate the ingestion of the drug."[10] The researchers concluded that "[i]t was this chronically dysfunctional behavior associated with drinking that was initially viewed as the illness of alcoholism . . . [t]hus, then as well as now, the loss of control of the drinking behavior plus the continued pathological dependence upon alcohol, despite its negative effects, was the essence of the hypothesis that alcoholism is in fact an illness."[11]

Third, alcoholism is a no-fault illness. Researchers concluded that since alcoholism was an illness or a disease, "the alcoholic cannot be held personally responsible for being an alcoholic."[12] As Anderson stated, "[i]n effect, we made alcoholism a no-fault illness in the sense that the assignment of personal blame or fault is untenable and unnecessary in the treatment environment."[13] Fourth, alcoholism is a multiphasic illness. It was observed by the researchers that the various aspects of alcoholism "included various physical, psychological, social, and spiritual problems in addition to the continuing and ongoing pathological need to use alcohol despite the loss of control phenomenon."[14] As a result, the researchers began to conclude that all of these factors needed to be treated. Fifth, alcoholism is a chronic, primary illness. Previously, the medical profession had viewed alcoholism as nothing more than a symptom of some other underlying condition."[15] However, the Minnesota researchers developed the concept that "alcoholism was an independent, primary and chronic condition."[16] As Anderson concludes: "It meant that we would treat the *alcoholism* as the primary condition and not something else."[17] Although this concept may also seem fundamental today, in 1950 this was an extraordinary idea.

Sixth, the basic presumption in the 1950s was that motivation was very important and that alcoholics *must* be motivated before they can possibly be helped. This idea was one of the fundamental concepts of Alcoholics Anonymous in connection with alcoholics "hitting" bottom before they could be helped. However, continued research by the Minnesota researchers determined that initial motivation treatment is unrelated to outcome. The researchers found that "[p]robate court-committed alcoholics did as well as alcoholics voluntarily coming into the treatment center!"[18] As Anderson stated, "The conclusion that we had to draw was simply that almost all alcoholics had locked-in resistance and that few initially are able to admit and accept their alcoholism. It seemed that denial and resistance were symptomatic of the illness whether the alcoholics were coerced into treatment or came voluntarily."[19] The Minnesota researchers concluded that "even outright denial and resistance to intervention could be treated successfully and that initial motivation for treatment was not necessary since it was not found to be related to patient outcome."[20] The interpretative idea here is that there are a number of motivating factors in any alcoholic's or addict's life that will force or motivate an alcoholic to seek treatment and maintain sobriety. These factors include employer pressures, family pressures, legal pressures, or medical pressures.

Seventh, education about alcoholism must begin in the community. The Minnesota researchers determined that "[m]ost members of the community were ignorant of the basic symptoms of alcoholism and tended to deny the presence of the condition by using almost the identical mental mechanism the alcoholics utilized. Thus it was necessary to develop highly specialized community education information programs. These special education programs focused mainly on families and employers. They dealt directly with helping people to become aware of conflicting cultural attitudes about alcoholism as well as the signs and symptoms of the condition and techniques for encouraging or even coercing alcoholics into treatment at earlier stages of the condition."[21]

Eighth, and finally, the concept of chemical dependency evolved. It was discovered at Willmar State Hospital that individuals identified as alcoholics might also be dually addicted to other prescription medications or narcotics. The researchers found that "[w]omen, especially, were found to be harmfully dependent not only on alcohol but on other prescription medications as well."[22] As a result, the idea evolved that "many people are multiply addicted to or use any number of mood-altering substances, either simultaneously or successively and experience harmful consequences as a result."[23] In essence, the researchers concluded that multiply addicted individuals could receive treatment in the same "basic program framework" as the alcoholics. It was further discovered that "addiction-prone people are vulnerable to many different mood altering substances and must be on guard against almost all forms of self-medication involving such substances."[24] As a result, the term "chemical dependency" more accurately described the spectrum of addiction and became a more appropriate term.

Once the basic assumptions had been established for the Minnesota Model, the substance abuse treatment program structure and strategies were developed. The Minnesota researchers and clinicians developed a "caring versus curing model" program structure based upon the philosophy of Alcoholics Anonymous within a therapeutic community by a multidisciplinary staff. The reason for developing a caring versus a curing model was that "[s]ince there was no hope . . . of getting at any underlying direct cause of alcoholism, it was decided that the focus would be on caring rather than curing."[25] Therefore the focus of the Minnesota clinicians as well as other substance abuse programs is on the triggers or immediate causes of the condition. Since alcoholism could not be cured, the goal became "[t]o help the alcoholic learn to live and cope with this chronic condition."[26]

The Minnesota researchers concluded that the AA philosophy "was the only viable new approach to alcoholism that seemed worth exploring."[27] Or as Anderson stated, "It was no accident that our basic program philosophy came very close to matching the concepts contained in the Twelve Steps of the Alcoholics Anonymous program."[28] Additionally, AA members in the Minnesota area cooperated with the hospitals in an effort to work with other recovering alcoholics and thereby help themselves. This cooperative venture was critical in establishing some of the basic tenets of the substance abuse recovery program, that is, that recovering people could very effectively work with one another toward the shared goal of sobriety.

The concept of a therapeutic community was developed based on the idea that a separate community should exist for chemically dependent patients and because the patients would be there for a relatively short duration. Therefore, "[w]hat emerged was the concept of a completely structured and disciplined environment utilizing a number of meaningful patient activities intended to produce positive behavioral changes."[29]

Finally, a multidisciplinary staff evolved in order to deal with the many aspects of this multiphasic disease. The idea here was to treat the whole illness rather than portions of it. Anderson stated, "Gradually, we selected for the treatment team various professional members of the regular psychiatric hospital staff. This group included physicians, social workers, psychologists, nurses, and clergy, as well as psychiatric aids. To properly utilize the philosophy of Alcoholics Anonymous, we also needed on the staff one or more recovered alcoholics who were practicing members of AA. These people were needed to act as what were originally termed 'counselors on alcoholism' to work directly with the patients. Not only were these recovering alcoholics needed to communicate the philosophy of AA, it was also hoped they would act as role models for the patients."[30] The result was the multidisciplinary staff and the evolution of the comprehensive alcoholism treatment program which has become the model for modern inpatient substance abuse treatment programs.

As the programs of the Minnesota Model evolved, new treatment strategies were developed. These included task-oriented groups, peer groups, and didactic lectures. The task-oriented groups were formulated based on the influence of AA communication strategies. Anderson stated, "[I]t was discovered that one of the most powerful therapeutic effects on our patients came not from the professional staff but from the interaction of patients with our new Counselors on Alcoholism [recovering AA members]." These groups encouraged open and honest discussion of a person's alcoholic disease and personal problems. As a result, the goal of these task-oriented group meetings was to help patients "resolve personal problems and assist in decision-making as these were directly related to their alcoholism."[31] Another interesting strategy which has been incorporated into practically all current treatment programs was the utilization of peer groups. The researchers learned that in the controlled environment, informal meetings and gatherings of recovering individuals had an extremely therapeutic effect. According to Anderson, "This finding that, somehow, sick, disturbed people could help each other in small peer groups without the benefit of professional assistance surprised us very much. . . . [w]ithout the influence of the A.A. oriented counselors, we probably would never have made the remarkable discovery that when a group of fellow suffers joins together in a controlled environment to share their common chronic problems, positive changes take place. People who can't help themselves *can* help each other."[32] Finally, didactic lectures were utilized based on the fact that the fellowship of AA is in many ways a didactic teaching program. In AA, it is not unusual for older members to teach the Twelve Steps to newer members in a "mini-lecture" format. Therefore, in addition to an informal lecturing system from the recovering counselors at the Minnesota hospital, a formalized lecture program was instituted on various aspects of the recovery process.[33]

Systematic program elements were developed for the Minnesota model which have been translated into practically all substance abuse treatment programs in current use today. These systematic program elements include admission, assessment, multidisciplinary staff meetings, general program track, and individualized prescriptive track.[34] After an initial detoxification, the chemically dependent patients were admitted to a primary care inpatient program. The admission structure was relatively simple and was essentially the same as entering the hospital. Following the admission, the patient was assessed in terms of diagnosis and individual patient needs. Following assessment and determination of staff availability, an individualized plan for treatment was developed. This patient plan was developed by the patient treatment staff in the multidiscipline staff meetings. This team approach has become the hallmark of most present inpatient treatment programs. Final assessment and development of the individual patient plan, a general program track, and an individualized prescriptive track was developed for each patient. The general program track included the group meetings, lectures, and AA meetings. The individualized prescriptive track consisted of assignment of the individual to a counselor and psychiatrist or psychologist, treatment of dual addiction or possibly other psychological or psychiatric disorders, and development of particularized recreational or occupational program tracks. The result was that a treatment plan was developed for each individual based on the multidisciplinary evaluation and assessment of the individual in order to effectuate as thorough a treatment plan as possible.[35]

Inpatient Treatment Models

There are four basic inpatient treatment models that treat substance abusers: detoxification, traditional psychiatric programs, behavior modification therapy, and a comprehensive alcoholic treatment model.[36]

Detoxification

For many years alcoholics were put into jail where they would suffer the pains of withdrawal without medical supervision. Everyone has heard the story of the "town drunk" who was put into jail to "sleep it off." Unfortunately, many chronic alcoholics had such severe withdrawal symptoms, including deliriums tremens, that a number of them died. Congress passed the Comprehensive Alcohol Abuse and Alcoholism Prevention, Treatment, and Rehabilitation Act of 1970,[37] and "a new era of humane treatment rather than criminal punishment began for thousands of alcoholics throughout the United States."[38] As a result of community pressure and the availability of federal funds, many states have adopted some form of the model legislation, Uniform Intoxication and Treatment Act. "This model legislation *decriminalizes* public drunkenness and under its provisions governmental agencies are no longer obliged to arrest inebriates. They are obliged, however, to provide some form of alternative treatment."[39] Because of this legislation and a number of other factors, including changing public attitudes, communities began the management of acute detoxification and withdrawal.[40]

The detoxification procedure occurs in a hospital setting with physicians and nurse-practitioners. Usually the detoxification centers, whether they are associated with a state-run facility or a private hospital, operate on a 24-hour basis and provide immediate medical evaluation; supervision of the intoxicated person by properly trained medical/nursing staff (but not necessarily physicians or nurses) until the patient is no longer incapacitated by the effects of alcohol; evaluation of medical, psychological, and social needs, leading to the development of a plan of continuing care; and effective transportation services.[41] The detoxification centers vary depending on their orientation. State-run facilities generally manage the individual through the medical crisis associated with detoxification and withdrawal and then release the individual to the public in the discharge procedure. Unfortunately, the individual might not be released to any treatment facility because of his or her low socioeconomic status and lack of funds, unavailability of openings at public treatment facilities, or the refusal of the individual to participate in any treatment program. Also, many jurisdictions only allow admission into the detoxification center by an individual a certain number of times per year. Therefore, if an individual has used up his or her quota, he or she may be forced to detoxify in the public domain. On the other hand, public or private detoxification centers associated with inpatient treatment facilities are oriented toward immediate transfer of the individual to the inpatient admission process once detoxification has been completed.

Regardless of the detoxification setting, practically all programs, in addition to handling the medical emergency, will at least provide an orientation to physical rehabilitation, education about alcohol (or drugs), possibly individual counseling or group therapy, and usually introduction to Alcoholics Anonymous or Narcotics Anonymous sessions.[42]

Traditional Psychiatric Programs

Other than jail, psychiatric institutions or mental health facilities have been the primary recipients of the alcoholic population for many years. Currently, a large number of alcoholics and addicts are admitted to psychiatric institutions for a variety of reasons, including insurance coverage. Within the psychological/psychiatric model of behavior pathology, Dr. Anderson states that "alcoholism is usually viewed as one of any number of maladaptive ways of dealing with life's stresses and is best regarded as a symptom of such maladaptation. Thus, regardless of which theoretical psychological formulation is made, the condition of problem drinking is usually viewed as a symptom of some other more primary psychiatric condition which requires treatment."[43] While many patients may have a dual diagnosis of alcoholism or addiction with some psychiatric or psychological problem such as depression, schizophrenia, or psychosis, often the primary problem is simply addictive disease. As a result, where psychological/psychiatric disorders may present themselves to the psychiatric institution, the underlying cause of these presentations very probably is alcoholism or drug addiction. According to Dr. Anderson, "[w]ith great frequency, alcoholics have a talent for sabotaging therapeutic relationships."[44] As a result, although a psychiatric/psychological treatment program may be necessary for a substance abuser, it alone may not be sufficient to deal with the individual's problem.

Behavior Modification Therapy

Behavior modification therapy is "based on the assumption that drinking is a learned behavior pattern involving social situations and customs, emotional and cognitive experiences, personal expectations and reinforcing conditions. . . . A general goal of behavior modification would be to try to reverse such a learned drinking pattern."[45]

One aspect of behavior modification is known as aversion therapy. "This model is designed to associate the sight, smell, taste, or thought of alcohol with a very unpleasant experience. A variety of chemical techniques have been used to induce nausea if alcohol is taken. According to a recent survey, there is no conclusive evidence for or against chemical aversion therapy at the present time, says Dr. Anderson."[46] An additional behavior modification aversion therapy involves electrical aversion therapy, using painful electric shock associated with drinking. The efficacy of this type of treatment is extremely doubtful. Other aversion therapy includes reviewing tragic scenes of alcohol-induced fatal accidents or other such mental shock treatments. The effectiveness of these types of therapy is questionable as well.[47]

Other more positive behavior modification techniques include relaxation training, stress reduction, or assertiveness training, which focus on relieving the stresses that may induce the addictive personality to abuse alcohol or drugs. These behavior modification techniques are often extremely useful in giving the alcoholic or addictive patient the tools to cope with the various stresses of life.

Comprehensive Alcoholism Treatment Model

This treatment model is equivalent to the Minnesota Model. As Anderson stated, "The basic assumption underlying this model is that alcoholism is a chronic, usually progressive illness which requires a caring rather than a curing model of treatment. From this perspective, alcoholism is viewed as a chronic, multiphasic illness which can be successfully arrested if all of the essential needs of the alcoholic are met and a comprehensive continuum of care plan is developed and adhered to by the client."[48] In the comprehensive alcoholism treatment model, a multidisciplinary staff assesses, manages, and treats the individual patient. This multidisciplinary staff is composed of physicians, psychiatrists, psychologists, nurse practitioners, certified addiction counselors, recovering alcoholics and addicts, and others. A general and specific treatment plan is developed for the individual based primarily on group therapy and the AA philosophy, and specifically concerning the patient's individual needs. Those individual needs may include the necessity of psychiatric treatment for depression, schizophrenia, or other psychiatric illnesses, psychological behavior modification techniques to deal with life's stresses and other problems, or other treatment strategies that can be "integrated into this model on an 'as needed' basis."[49] Practically all of the inpatient treatment facilities in the United States presently operate based on the comprehensive alcoholism treatment model. Probably the most widely known facility of this type is the Betty Ford Center located on the campus of the Eisenhower Medical Center, Rancho Mirage, California. This multidisciplinary, comprehensive approach based on the principles of Alcoholics Anonymous has been found to be extremely successful and is the approach of choice for inpatient treatment programs.

Basic Elements of Inpatient Program Structure

An employer should always carefully research the treatment program of the inpatient provider that has been selected for its employees. It is important for the employer to have a basic understanding of the elements of inpatient treatment programs so it knows what to expect of the treatment provider and of the employee who attends a particular inpatient treatment facility.

Reference guides to help employers begin this research list such elements as the extent of the treatment center's facilities, the length of treatment, the cost, insurance coverage, age limitations, type of programs, Joint Hospital Accreditation Committee accreditation, and licensing.

There are a number of basic elements in any inpatient treatment program: admission, detoxification, assessment, education, group therapy, AA/NA meetings, individual therapy, peer relations, recreational therapy, occupational therapy, family therapy, and aftercare therapy. The Sample Weekly Schedule shown in

Addendum 1 at the end of this chapter illustrates that inpatient programs aim to integrate all of these elements into an effective, comprehensive treatment.

Admission

During the admission procedure, the employee will be asked to complete numerous forms including insurance forms, consent release forms, and guarantee of payment forms. The admission procedures are usually highly structured and formal, and in many respects are very similar to entering the hospital for any other purpose. However, one aspect of admissions in substance abuse facilities is different. These hospitals will carefully scrutinize all materials brought into the hospital so as to ensure that the patient does not bring alcohol or drugs or any other dangerous or potentially harmful materials into their facility. Inpatient treatment providers are particularly sensitive to the threat of suicides by substance abusers suffering through withdrawal. Therefore, razors, hair blow-dryers, belts, and other potentially dangerous items may be confiscated and stored until release.

Insurance Coverage

A very important element of inpatient treatment is insurance coverage. Practically every inpatient facility has its program oriented toward third-party insurance coverage. As a result, practically every inpatient facility provides for a 28-day stay, which is the maximum length of stay covered by many policies. It is not unusual for a patient to be discharged after 28 days if that is the limit on the insurance coverage and the individual is unwilling to pay for further treatment.

Detoxification

Inpatient facilities vary as to whether they handle acutely intoxicated individuals in a detoxification setting. Usually, most inpatient facilities will either have a detoxification unit or will work in conjunction with some acute-care hospital that provides this service and then transfers the individual for the remainder of the substance abuse treatment.

Assessment

An inpatient facility staff member will evaluate the patient's problem and develop a treatment program. The elements of assessment include medical examination, psychiatric/psychological evaluation, determination of length of stay, development of a treatment team, assignment of counselors, determination of the general treatment program, and creation of an individualized program.

If an individual has received a medical examination during detoxification at another facility, the inpatient facility may or may not perform a subsequent medical examination. At a minimum, urine screens are performed to determine that the individual is indeed drug free. If the individual suffers from end-stage alcoholism (severe alcoholism which if untreated will lead to death) and requires constant medical supervision such as continuation of the detoxification procedure by use of long-acting barbiturates, or care for other medical complications such as hepatitis, sclerosis, high blood pressure, or concomitant diabetes, a medical plan will be developed based on an extensive medical history of the individual. Additionally, a psychiatric/psychological evaluation will be performed on the patient in order to ascertain any concomitant psychiatric or psychological disorders which may need to be treated as well. The length of stay in the inpatient treatment program will usually be determined by the extent of presenting problems. That is, if the presenting problem is alcohol abuse, the length of stay will probably be 28 days, as covered by insurance. However, if the addiction involves longer-acting prescription drugs, such as the benzodiazepines (e.g., Valium, Xanax), then the length of stay may be several weeks longer because of the risk of withdrawal at a much later date due to the long half-life of these drugs. Furthermore, if the diagnosis presented includes psychiatric dysfunction such as schizophrenia or depression, the length of stay may be extended in order to deal with these attendant complications.

The treatment team will be developed based on the diagnosis of the individual. Counselors and team members will be assigned to the particular patient based on the problems presented and the availability of staff. Additionally, the treatment team will develop the general treatment program which will include group therapy, lectures, and other general materials based on the philosophy of the particular program, and an individualized treatment program based on the presenting problems of the patient. These individualized programs may include psychotherapy, behavior modification techniques, recreational, occupational, or vocational therapy, or extensive family therapy. Once the individual's program is developed, the physician and counselor will meet with the patient to discuss the treatment program regime.

Education

It is surprising how little most people know about alcoholism or addictive disease. As a result, an extensive amount of time is spent using films, videotapes, lectures, Big Book[51] study groups, and audio tapes. Literature review and discussion groups review the physiological and psychological aspects of substance abuse. The education process also introduces the patient to self-help groups which are usually conducted by the alcohol and drug counselors. Practically all of the inpatient treatment programs provide substance abuse literature such as the Big Book and various other AA-related publications for review by the patients while they are in treatment.

Group Therapy

Group therapy or group psychotherapy is used extensively by most inpatient treatment facilities. These groups are usually run by physicians and/or counselors and often meet several times a week. Although in many cases patients will complain that they are not accustomed to discussing their substance abuse and their personal problems in front of other people, and prefer individual discussions, group discussions are used extensively, to force the individual to confront his or her problems and deal with them more openly.

The major benefit of group psychotherapy is that it breaks down the perception that most substance abusers have that their problems are unique. As a result, in groups the patient hears how other individuals have similar problems and through the group identification process, the patient acquires hope and a sense of cohesiveness or belonging. Additionally, the individual receives feedback from other group members. For example, it is not unusual for a patient to express overconfidence that he or she will never be tempted to drink or take drugs again. Other patients who have similarly deceived themselves can explain their experience, and the entire group benefits. The net result of this sharing of experiences is that a sense of being able to help develops, which raises the self-esteem of members of the group and provides crucial intervention for the individual members. Similarly, emotional circumstances that have led patients to have slips after attempts at abstinence will be discussed in the group meeting. For instance, an individual member of the group may have a pattern of withdrawal rather than talking to the group about what is troubling him or her. If the individual learns through practice to be able to ventilate the pain and anger in the group without reprisal or retaliation, it can help to prevent the individual from withdrawing and drinking or drugging rather than ventilating this pain and anger in the future.[52] Many therapists agree that forcing the individual to participate in group settings facilities the opening up and sharing of suppressed feelings, and that by ventilating these feelings, the individual's recovery begins to take place. Furthermore, group participation allows the individual to become more comfortable in subsequent AA and NA meetings, and by participating in these meetings during and after treatment, the individual's continuing recovery will be enhanced.

AA/NA Meetings

Practically all inpatient treatment facilities require patients to attend Alcoholics Anonymous (AA), Cocaine Anonymous (CA), or Narcotics Anonymous (NA) meetings while they are in treatment. These meetings may be held at the treatment facility or in the community nearby. It is not unusual for the treatment facility to fill a bus with recovering patients and take them to the AA, CA, or NA meeting in the local community, require them to attend, and transport them back to the inpatient facility at the completion of the meeting. This forced attendance at these self-help group meetings sets the stage for subsequent aftercare attendance at these meetings, which is critical for continued recovery.

Individual Therapy

As an adjunct to group therapy, most inpatient facilities arrange for individual psychotherapy with the attending physician or psychiatrist. There may even be different types of individual psychotherapy including meetings with the psychiatrist, meetings with the recovering counselor (certified addiction counselor), or individual therapy meetings with occupational and vocational rehabilitation therapists. These individual therapy meetings allow the patient to develop the personal side of recovery with the trained specialist. Furthermore, they allow the inpatient treatment provider to explore other areas of concern for the individual which may not be apparent during group therapy meetings. Additionally, where the presenting problem may be psychiatric or psychological as well as addiction-oriented, the trained clinician will be able to deal with the presenting psychiatric problem in a more traditional way.

Peer Relations

Peer groups or peer relations are critically important in the overall recovery process. It has been found that the relationships between recovering individuals who can share their experiences away from counselors or clinicians have a marked therapeutic effect. Furthermore, the opportunity to develop peer relations not only gets the message across that the individual is not alone in fighting the addictive disease, but also sets the stage for aftercare recovery and attendance at subsequent AA, CA, or NA meetings.

Recreational Therapy

Many inpatient facilities take the approach that the physical rehabilitation of the individual is extremely important for the overall treatment of the patient. As a result, as long as the patient is physically able, some form of recreational therapy or exercise, such as walking, swimming, basketball, volleyball, or other light sports, may be required.

Occupational Therapy

Certain patients may be in need of occupational or vocational rehabilitation. Particularly when the patient may be without a job upon release from treatment, the inpatient treatment facility may arrange for occupational therapy through occupational evaluation or vocational counseling in order to prepare the individual for job seeking upon discharge from the facility. Realizing that return to work after treatment has a tremendous therapeutic value, many treatment providers now are coordinating much more with the employer or its EAP provider in order to ease the transition from treatment back to work.[53] In this situation, counseling may help prepare the patient to return to his or her job.

Family Therapy

Practically all inpatient treatment facilities now recognize the importance of family therapy. Realizing that "[t]he alcoholic is like a tornado roaring his way through the lives of others,"[54] therapists are working with entire families who suffer from a member's alcoholism. Many treatment facilities now offer family programs in order to orient the family or significant others to the concept of addictive disease and what the family can expect of the individual upon release from the treatment facility.

Aftercare Therapy

An increasing number of inpatient treatment facilities have developed aftercare therapy programs. Usually these programs take the form of continued group meetings over a period of time after discharge, or individual counseling arrangements with the treatment facility's staff. Also, a number of treatment facilities engage in follow-up to determine the success of the patient's efforts to maintain his or her recovery and to offer additional suggestions on recovery. This subject will be discussed in greater detail in Chapter 11, "Aftercare and Long-Term Rehabilitation Programs."

Costs and Effectiveness

A standard 28-day patient rehabilitation program in 1986 cost between $4,000 and $15,000.[55] The cost of inpatient treatment facilities is usually broken down based on the components, such as hospital bed and board, individual psychotherapy, group therapy, and pharmacy requirements. All inpatient programs are designed to be covered by third-party insurance, Medicare, or Medicaid.

The effectiveness of inpatient treatment programs often depends more on the individual than on the program. It has been stated that "[a]lcoholics recover not because we treat them but because they heal themselves. Staying sober is not a process of simply becoming detoxified, but often becomes the work of several years or in a few cases even a lifetime."[56] However, many inpatient facilities will attempt to ascertain the maintained recovery rate at one-, three-, and five-year intervals, depending on the extensiveness of their follow-up studies. Most inpatient treatment facilities will claim success rates from 50 percent to 85 percent. However, it should be pointed out that there is no known cure for alcoholism or drug addiction. An employer may be very helpful in encouraging an individual's recovery and maintenance of sobriety with a little understanding of the recovery process.[57] But an addicted person's recovery really depends on the individual.

Conclusion

Most inpatient recovery programs in the United States follow the Minnesota Model of the comprehensive alcoholism treatment program. This Model assumes that alcoholism is a chronic, usually progressive illness that requires a caring rather than a curing model of treatment. Most treatment facilities view alcoholism in this context as a multiphasic illness that, according to Daniel J. Anderson, Ph.D., "can be successfully arrested if all of the essential needs of the alcoholic are met and a comprehensive continuum of care plan is developed and adhered to" by the patient.[58] The multidisciplinary inpatient team approach based on the Model developed by the Minnesota hospitals has revolutionized treatment of alcoholics and addicts in the middle to late 20th century. Practically all inpatient programs are involved in a hospital setting and are paid for by third-party insurance carriers or by government health programs. Whether the length of stay and cost involved in such programs are worthwhile will be discussed in subsequent chapters.

Addendum 1

Sample Weekly Schedule

INPATIENT TREATMENT PROGRAM

MONDAY		TUESDAY	
7:00–7:30 AM	Wakeup Call/Dress	7:00–7:30 AM	Wakeup Call/Dress
7:15–7:30	Meditation	7:15–7:30	Meditation
7:30–8:00	Breakfast	7:30–8:00	Breakfast
8:00–9:55	Dr./Staff Team Rounds/Study Peer Group Time	8:00–9:00	Study Period
		9:00–10:25	Lectures/Video/ Films
10:00–11:25	Lectures/Video/ Films	10:30–11:25	Individual Counseling/Free Time
11:30–12:00 PM	Lunch		
12:15–1:15	Individual Counseling— Clinician Recreational Therapy/Free Time	11:30–12:00 PM	Lunch
		12:30–2:00	Group Therapy
		2:05–3:00	Men's Meeting/ Women's Meeting
1:30–3:00	Group Therapy	2:30–3:30	Acceptance Group (Assigned by Counselor)
3:05–4:00	Grief Group		
3:05–4:30	Individual Counseling— Counselor Recreational Therapy/Physical Conditioning	3:05–4:30	Individual Counseling
		4:30–5:00	Dinner
		5:30–6:00	Free Time
		6:00–6:30	Listening Group
4:30–5:00	Dinner	6:30–7:00	Twelve Steps Tape Group
5:00–6:00	Free Time		
6:00–6:30	Listening Group	7:00–9:00	Outside AA/NA Meeting
6:30–7:00	Twelve Steps Tape Group	8:00–9:00	Rap Session
7:15–7:45	Relaxation Group (Optional)	9:00–12:00 AM	Free Time/Retire or
7:00–7:45	Prepare for AA/NA Meeting	10:45–11:45	Optional Meeting/ Discussion
7:45–9:00	AA Meeting	12:00 AM	Retire
7:45–9:00	Prescription Drug Meeting		
9:00–9:45	Visiting/Peer Group		
9:45–12:00 AM	Recreational Therapy/Free Time/Retire or		
10:45–11:45	Optional AA/NA Meeting/Discussion		
12:00 AM	Retire		

WEDNESDAY		THURSDAY	
7:00–7:30 AM	Wakeup Call/Dress	7:00–7:30 AM	Wakeup Call/Dress
7:15–7:30	Meditation	7:15–7:30	Meditation
7:30–8:00	Breakfast	7:30–8:00	Breakfast
8:00–9:55	Dr./Staff Team	8:00–9:00	Study Period
	Rounds/Study	9:00–10:30	Lectures/Video/
10:00–11:25	Lectures/Video/		Films
	Films	10:30–11:25	Individual
11:00–12:00 PM	Lunch		Counseling/
12:15–1:25	Individual		Recreation
	Counseling/Free	11:30–12:00 PM	Lunch
	Time or	12:30–2:00	Group Therapy
12:15–1:25	Reading/Study	2:05–4:30	Individual
1:30–3:00	Group Therapy		Counseling/
3:05–4:30	Individual		Occupational
	Counseling		Therapy
	Recreational	2:30–3:15	Fourth Step
	Therapy/Physical		Workshop
	Conditioning		(Assigned by
3:10–4:30	Parents'		Counselor)
	Communication	3:05–4:00	Grief Group
	Group	4:30–5:00	Dinner
	Spouse	5:30–6:00	Free Time
	Communication	5:30–6:00	Listening Group
	Group	6:00–6:30	Twelve Steps Tape
4:30–5:00	Dinner—Families		Group
	Invited	7:00–9:00	Outside AA/NA
	Participating in		Meeting
	Programs	8:00–9:00	Rap Session
5:30–6:25	Visiting/Peer Group	9:00–12:00 AM	Free Time/Retire
6:30–7:45	Family Education	10:45–11:45	Optional Meeting/
	Lecture		Discussion
7:45–8:00	Prepare for AA	12:00 AM	Retire
	Meeting		
8:00–9:00	AA Meeting/NA		
	Meeting		
9:00–10:00	Visiting		
9:00–10:30	Recreational		
	Therapy		
10:00–12:00 AM	Free Time/Retire		
10:45–11:45	Optional Meeting/		
	Discussion		
12:00 AM	Retire		

FRIDAY	
7:00–7:30 AM	Wakeup Call/Dress
7:15–7:30	Meditation
7:30–8:00	Breakfast
8:00–9:55	Dr./Staff Team Rounds/Study
10:00–11:25	Lectures/Video/Films
11:30–12:00 PM	Lunch
12:15–1:25	Individual Counseling/Recreational or Occupational Therapy
1:30–3:00	Group Therapy
3:05–4:30	Individual Counseling/Recreational Therapy/Physical Conditioning or Discharge Period
3:05–5:00	
4:30–5:00	Dinner
5:30–6:00	Free Time
6:00–7:00	Inside AA Meeting
7:30–8:00	Free Time
8:00–9:00	NA Meeting (Cafeteria)
8:00–9:00	AA Tape Meeting (Solarium)
9:00–9:30	Social with NA Members
9:30–11:00	Recreational Therapy/Free Time/Retire
12:00–1:00 AM	Optional Meeting/Discussion
1:00	Retire

SATURDAY	
8:00–8:30 AM	Wakeup Call/Dress
8:00–8:30	Meditation
8:30–9:00	Breakfast
9:00–10:25	Dr./Staff Rounds/Study
10:30–11:30	Film Series (Families Invited)
11:30–12:00 PM	Lunch
11:30–2:00	Visiting Hours
12:00–3:00	Recreational Activities
3:00–4:00	AA/NA Meeting
4:00–4:30	Dinner
5:00–5:30	Free Time
5:30–7:00	Study (Patients' Rooms)
7:00–10:00	Outside AA Meeting
8:00–9:00	Tape Meeting
8:30–10:00	Study
10:00–12:00	Free Time/Retire
11:00–12:00 AM	Optional Moonlighters' AA Meeting
12:00–1:00	Optional Meeting/Discussion
1:00	Retire

SUNDAY

7:30–8:00 AM	Wakeup Call/Dress
7:30–7:45	Meditation
8:00–8:30	Breakfast
8:30–9:45	Dr./Staff Rounds
9:45–10:30	Sunday Services (Families Invited)
9:45–11:00	Second Step Group (Those not Attending Sunday Services)
11:00–11:30	Free Time
11:30–12:00 PM	Lunch
12:30–1:00	Free Time
1:00–2:00	Orientation (New Patients)
12:30–4:00	Recreational Activities
3:00–9:00	Visiting Hours
4:00–4:30	Dinner
5:00–5:15	Prepare for AA/NA Meeting
5:15–6:30	Open AA/NA Meeting (Families Invited) (Gym)
8:30–9:00	(Meds)
9:00	Patients' AA Meeting
9:00–12:00 AM	Free Time/Retire
10:45–11:45	Optional Meeting/ Discussion
12:00	Retire

Notes

1. *Alcoholics Anonymous*, 3d ed. (New York: Alcoholics Anonymous World Services, 1976).
2. Sunshine & Wright, *The 100 Best Treatment Centers for Alcoholism and Drug Abuse* (New York: Avon Books, 1988), 207.
3. Anderson, *Perspectives on Treatment: The Minnesota Experience* (Center City, Minn.: Hazelden Foundation, 1981). This monograph was adapted from the following by D.J. Anderson: "Alcoholism Treatment in Minnesota: Three Decades of Program Development," Presented at the International Conference on Alcoholism, Bath, England, September 21, 1980, reproduced from the *Proceedings of the ALC*, by permission of M.T.P. Press, 1980; and "Inpatient Alcoholism Treatment Models in the U.S.A.," *Proceedings of the Eisenhower Medical Center and the California Society for the Treatment of Alcoholism/Other Drug Dependencies* (Rancho Mirage, Cal.: Eisenhower Medical Center, 1981).
4. *Id.* at 6.
5. *Id.* at 6–7.
6. Sunshine & Wright, *supra* note 2, at 207.
7. Hazelden Educational Material, Pleasant Valley Road, Box 176, Center City, MN 55012 (1-800-328-9000). Hazelden is known to have the finest and most extensive array of educational materials on substance abuse.
8. Anderson, *supra* note 3, at 7.
9. *Id.* at 7–8.
10. *Id.* at 8–9.
11. *Id.* at 9, citing U.S. Department of Health, Education & Welfare, and National Institute on Alcohol and Alcohol Abuse, *Third Special Report to the U.S. Congress on Alcohol and Health*, from the Secretary of Health, Education and Welfare, June 1978 (Technical Support Document).
12. *Id.* at 9, citing Royce, *Alcohol and Responsibility*, (Center City, Minn., Hazelden Foundation, 1979).
13. *Id.* at 9.
14. *Id.* at 10.
15. *Id.* at 11.
16. *Id.* at 10.
17. *Id.* at 10–11.
18. *Id.* at 11.
19. *Id.* at 12.
20. *Id.*
21. *Id.* at 12–13.
22. *Id.* at 13–14.
23. *Id.* at 14.
24. *Id.*, citing Heilman, *Dynamics of Drug Dependency* (Center City, Minn., Hazelden Foundation, 1980) (reprinted from *Minnesota Medicine*, Mar. 1973); and Peele, *The Addiction Experience*, (Center City, Minn., Hazelden Foundation, 1975).
25. *Id.* at 15.
26. *Id.*
27. *Id.* at 16.
28. *Id.* at 15–16.

29. *Id.* at 17.
30. *Id.* at 18.
31. *Id.* at 19.
32. *Id.* at 20.
33. *Id.* at 20–21.
34. *Id.* at 21–24.
35. *Id.*
36. *Id.* at 33–54.
37. Pub. L. No. 91-616, 84 Stat. 1848 (1970).
38. Anderson, *supra* note 3, at 33.
39. *Id.*, citing National Conference of Commissioners on Uniform State Laws, *Uniform Alcoholism and Intoxication Treatment Act*, Eightieth Annual Conference, Vail, Colorado, 1978.
40. *Id.* at 33.
41. *Id.* at 34.
42. *Id.* at 35.
43. *Id.* at 36.
44. *Id.*
45. *Id.* at 37.
46. *Id.* at 38.
47. *Id.*
48. *Id.* at 39.
49. *Id.*
50. Hart, *Rehab: A Comprehensive Guide to Recommended Drug-Alcohol Treatment Centers in the United States* (New York: Harper & Row, 1988); Sunshine & Wright, *supra* note 2; Moore, ed., *Roads to Recovery: A National Directory of Alcohol and Drug Addiction Treatment Centers* (New York: Collier, 1985).
51. *Supra* note 1.
52. *Service B Handbook* (New Canaan, Conn.: Silver Hill Foundation, 1985).
53. Ronan & Reichman, "Back to Work Vocational Recovery," *Almacan*, March 1987, 10; Abrams, "An Employer's Role in Relapse Prevention," *Almacan*, July 1987, 20; Miller, "Job Reintegration and Aftercare of the Recovering Worker," *Almacan*, Aug. 1986, 20.
54. *Alcoholics Anonymous*, *supra* note 1, at 82.
55. Miller & Hester, "In-patient Alcoholism Treatment-True Benefits?" *Am. Psychologist* 41 1986, 794; Sunshine & Wright, *supra* note 2; Hart, *supra* note 50.
56. Vaillant, *The Natural History of Alcoholism* (Cambridge: Harvard Univ. Press, 1983), 314.
57. See Chapter 11, "Aftercare and Long-Term Rehabilitation Programs."
58. Anderson, *supra* note 3, at 39.

Chapter 10

Outpatient Rehabilitation Programs

History and Development

The history and development of outpatient rehabilitation programs is considerably more obscure than that of inpatient programs. For many years alcoholics and addicts were treated alongside mental patients in highly regimented hospital settings. Outpatient rehabilitation programs evolved because of the different mode of treatment by psychiatrists and, later on, the difference in costs associated with outpatient versus inpatient treatment.

Since before the time of Sigmund Freud, psychiatrists have dealt with patients who suffered from mental or possibly substance abuse-related disorders, and who were not harmful to others in the doctor's office or in another nonhospital setting. For years, psychiatrists and psychologists have treated many individuals for schizophrenia, paranoia, manic depressive illness, bipolar disease, or other mental health problems, whereas the primary illness probably was substance abuse. This is the case today as well. (This is not to say that all psychiatric problems are related to substance abuse, but experience has shown that once the addictive disorder is recognized and treated, many of the accompanying psychiatric problems disappear.)

The result of this tradition of dealing with nonviolent patients was the development of substance abuse treatment in an outpatient setting. With the advent of Alcoholics Anonymous in 1935 and its emphasis on group interaction, plus the additional development of group therapy, particularly from the behavior modification school of thought, outpatient treatment began to resemble the emerging systems of inpatient care with the combination of individual psychotherapy and group psychotherapy, but outside of the hospital setting.

Another consideration that led to the development of outpatient rehabilitation programs was cost. Many patients particularly those who attended early AA-type meetings, found the expense associated with inpatient hospitalization to be prohibitive. As a result, outpatient programs began to develop based on the AA group therapy model.

Many of these outpatient programs were very loosely organized until, over time, experience with the inpatient Minnesota Model interdisciplinary treatment team concept became more widely known. Then many outpatient programs began to resemble inpatient programs with the multidisciplinary approach. The major distinction was that they were conducted in a nonhospital setting.

The basic problem in the development of outpatient treatment programs has been the lack of insurance coverage. Therefore, outpatient treatment has not been used as extensively as inpatient treatment. Further, the common belief existed that substance abuse rehabilitation could not be received in any setting other than in the hospital. Experience has proven this contention to be a myth. As will be discussed later in this chapter, outpatient treatment programs are as effective for many patients as inpatient treatment programs and considerably less expensive. Furthermore, an increasing number of governmental and corporate entities are opting for the outpatient treatment modality, primarily because of cost considerations.

Of course, outpatient treatment is not suitable for every patient. As will be discussed later in this chapter, some individuals, particularly those with serious medical or psychiatric problems, are better treated in a hospital setting. However, with the increasing emphasis on treatment of substance abusing employees in the workplace, as opposed to strictly disciplinary approaches to drug and alcohol problems, the outpatient alternative has been rapidly gaining popularity throughout the country and the expansion of the outpatient alternative is likely to continue.

Outpatient-Inpatient Format Differences

Characteristically, there are a number of basic format differences between outpatient and inpatient rehabilitation programs. These differences include flexibility, nighttime residence, length of program, hours of involvement, and job conflicts.

Flexibility

As was discussed previously, one of the fundamental problems with inpatient programming is the rigidity required by the hospital setting. On the other hand, flexibility regarding length of program, hours of involvement, and program format are all characteristic of outpatient programs.

Nighttime Residence

By definition, inpatient programs include round-the-clock care. Some outpatient programs provide a place for participants to spend the night and some do not. For instance, if an individual has been released from an inpatient setting and allowed to return to work, but either has no home to go to or is in a work release setting due to penal considerations, an outpatient halfway house may provide not only the nighttime residence for the individual, but also characteristic outpatient programming, access to AA or NA meetings, and probaby transportation services. On the other hand, one great advantage of outpatient programs is that an individual may attend programs during the day or evening and still be able to stay at home at night. Therapists who favor outpatient programs argue that removing a patient completely from his or her family and community for a minimum 28-day period is disadvantageous to the therapy of the individual, since the individual will still be required to learn to cope with his family and community after the initial substance abuse treatment is received. As a result, proponents of outpatient care argue that it is more therapeutic for the individual to remain at home at night and receive outpatient treatment either during the day or in the early evening, and therefore not only deal with the individual's substance abuse problems, but also the family and community problems inevitably associated with substance abuse.

Length of Program

Outpatient programs have much more flexibility concerning the length of the program; program length can be adjusted to suit the individual or individuals involved. An outpatient program may be an intensive day program, which in essence is an alternative to inpatient hospitalization. It may be an evening program, which allows the individual to remain at work during the day and attend rehabilitation in the evening and either return home at night or stay in the program's halfway house. These programs may last six to twelve weeks. Finally, the outpatient program may operate as a long-term day program, in which case the individual receives long-term counseling over an extended period of time, but also remains on the job. These programs can last three to four months.

Hours of Involvement

The hours of patient involvement in outpatient programs can be extremely flexible depending upon the program. The program may be structured to operate during the day, during the early evening, during the later evening, or even late at night or early in the morning in order to treat individuals who work on second or third shifts.

Job Conflicts

In an inpatient setting, the individual is forced to leave his or her job and check into the hospital. Outpatient programs make it possible to continue working during treatment. Although intensive outpatient day programs are necessary for some patients, many outpatient programs are scheduled around work so that they conflict as little as possible. Usually where the outpatient programming is coordinated with the employer's EAP, job conflicts can be kept to a minimum.

Outpatient Treatment Models

There are four basic types of outpatient treatment models, which vary based on length of the program and the hours of involvement: intensive day program, evening program, halfway house program, and long-term day program.

Intensive Day Programs

This type of program is essentially an alternative to the 28-day inpatient treatment model. These programs evolved from two considerations: cost and time away from family and community. It is inherently cheaper to operate a day program in an outpatient setting which does not require individuals to be housed around the clock.

Further, many individuals, particularly single mothers, cannot afford to leave their families or children for a month at a time. As a result, intensive day programs were developed to run five to seven days per week.

These programs operate essentially the same as full-service inpatient programs in that they provide individual and group therapy, education, medical, psychiatric, and psychological evaluation, usually operate on a treatment team basis, and provide recreational and occupational therapy, family programs, and aftercare. These day programs are usually staffed by medical professionals, certified addiction counselors, and nurse-practitioners, among others.

An excellent example of the use of day treatment programs as opposed to inpatient treatment programs is given by the United Technologies Corporation's (UT) day treatment program.[1] As was reported by Bensinger and Pilkington, the United Technologies Corporation's EAP officials noted that between 1975 and 1980 there was an increase in the number of employees who were self-referred but who wanted alternatives to 28-day inpatient alcoholism treatment. UT also noticed that "between 1975 and 1980 the average length of stay of patients *doubled*; the average cost per patient treated *tripled*; and treatment outcome did not change."[2] After extensive research, UT cited a number of reasons, including the following, for using outpatient treatment for employed alcoholics:

> "By not taking him (the employee) out of his home, community, and work role as alternative treatment approaches must, outpatient treatment is uniquely able to build, educate, and utilize the social support network surrounding the patient as part of his extended clinical experience. . . . [O]utpatient treatment reduces the stigmatization by the worker and those around him." In addition hospitalization often triggers regressive features, which may not be helpful for every patient. Hospitalization also blocks resumption of personal, job, and family responsibilities, which may counter treatment goals. Finally, while helpful to some, extended inpatient hospitalization was proven to be unresponsive to client profile changes observed in United Technologies' EAP.[3]

As a result, UT developed a day treatment program which runs 5½ days per week. Clients are required to attend outside AA meetings in their home area in addition to the two per week they attend in the day treatment program. When the day program was instituted, 64 percent of the referrals were self-initiated and the "remaining 36% of the clients were referred by management because of deteriorating job performance."[4]

At the end of 12 months of operation of the UT program, the study reported that the "program substantiates that day treatment is a viable and often preferable form of treatment for alcoholism for employed individuals and their families. Day treatment proved effective both as a first treatment intervention and in instances of relapse. Evidence to date indicates that many alcoholics who are gainfully employed do not necessarily require inpatient hospitalization of four to five weeks' duration. In this study group, most employees and their families preferred day treatment and many are entering treatment at a significantly earlier stage than they did when inpatient treatment was the only option. Although it is premature to attempt to predict the optimal application of day treatment, at this time it is clear that it is an effective option."[5]

Evening Programs

These types of programs are typically provided for individuals or employees whose substance abuse may be a problem, but not to the extent that it requires removal from work such as in inpatient programs or the intensive day outpatient programs. Evening programs usually run six to eight weeks, at approximately eight to ten hours per week. Characteristically, they operate between 6:00 P.M. and 9:00 P.M., three to five days per week, with additional AA or NA meetings required. Patients are usually provided individual therapy, family therapy, group therapy, AA/NA meetings, extensive education including lectures, videos, films, and audiotapes and peer group interaction. Evening programs often require frequent random urinalysis in order to ensure sobriety and compliance with the program. Where alcohol is the problem, random breathalyzer tests are also administered.

It should be stressed that in most cases the patients in evening outpatient programs are those whose substance abuse has not reached the point where they are unable to perform their jobs. However, their substance abuse has interfered with their life or job performance to the point where treatment is necessary.

Halfway House Programs

These types of programs are often used as an interim measure between inpatient rehabilitation and return to work, family, and community. Halfway house programs are also used in penal situations. For example, an individual who has been convicted of two or three DUIs or DWIs (Driving Under the Influence or Driving While Intoxicated) may be required to go to inpatient treatment, and upon the successful completion of the treatment, be required to remain in a halfway house, closely supervised, in the evening for several months as an alternative to incarceration. Other individuals completing inpatient treatment may opt for a halfway house program because they have no home to return to due to marital, financial, or legal problems.

In essence, the halfway house program allows an individual to work or seek work during the day and participate in the halfway house program in the evening. These programs are usually not very expensive, but usually include some individual therapy, some group therapy, participation in AA or NA meetings, and possibly some occupational or vocational rehabilitation counseling. Patient stays at halfway houses vary from several days to several months. Although a certain number are run by private concerns, most halfway houses are run by the state, county, or community government.

Long-Term Day Programs

These programs typically provide for individuals who may have a substance abuse problem which is not so severe that they are required to take extensive time off from work. These programs typically involve two or more individual counseling sessions per week, several hours of group therapy and substance abuse education per week, and evening AA or NA meetings after work. In most cases the employer will arrange for time off during the day for the employee to attend counseling sessions. Typically, these programs may operate three days a week for one or two hours per session. Additionally, these programs will usually require attendance at AA or NA meetings either at lunch time or in the evening.

Long-term day programs typically involve individual and group counseling, substance abuse education, occupational or vocational rehabilitation therapy, family counseling, peer groups, and aftercare. Although typically these programs do not involve extensive use of medical personnel, they do have medical or psychiatric personnel available as needed. These programs usually operate for three to four months and are particularly adept at involving the family and setting up special aftercare programming in order to help the patient to deal with work, family, and the community after receiving his or her initial substance abuse treatment.

Basic Elements of Program Structure

The basic elements of the outpatient program structure include detoxification, admission, assessment, education, AA or NA meetings, individual therapy, peer relations, recreational therapy, occupational therapy, family programs, and aftercare. Two sample programs are described in the addenda at the end of this chapter. The first is a six-week evening treatment program. The second is a long-term (12-week) day program.

Detoxification

While detoxification typically is not undertaken by outpatient facilities, outpatient rehabilitation programs of any significance have some working relationship with a detoxification center. As a matter of fact, most outpatient facilities require that the patient be detoxified before entering the program.

However, there is an increasing movement towards detoxifying addicted patients, particularly alcoholics, in an outpatient setting. Recent studies indicate that "outpatient medical detoxification is an effective, safe, and low-cost treatment for patients with mild-to-moderate symptoms of alcohol withdrawal."[6] As a result, particularly considering the cost factors, outpatient detoxification will probably be on the increase in the years to come, particularly in mild-to-moderate alcohol and possibly drug withdrawal situations.

Admission

The admission procedures for outpatient rehabilitation are essentially the same as for inpatient rehabilitation. In many cases, third-party insurance covers the outpatient treatment program. Admission may include filling out a number of government or insurance forms, consent forms, and other paperwork. Additionally, as a part of the admission procedures, most providers present an orientation for the patient and his or her family or signficant others.

Assessment

As in the inpatient program, most outpatient programs provide a medical, psychological, and/or psychiatric assessment of the patient. Depending on the diagnosis and the patient's mental and psychological health, a treatment plan is developed by the treatment team. The treatment team in an outpatient setting will consist of medical practitioners, psychiatrists or psychologists, addiction counselors, nurse-practitioners, and others. The team will determine the length of treatment and type of program. For instance, if the individual has not been allowed to return to work, he or she will probably be enrolled in a day outpatient program. If the individual is allowed to remain at work, the staff may determine that an evening or long-term day program may be sufficient. Similarly, the treatment team devises a general treatment program and an individual treatment program based on the needs of the patient. The general treatment program will consist of the substance abuse education, group therapy, AA or NA meetings, recreational therapy, and other general group programming. The individual treatment program will consist of individual therapy with the psychiatrist, psychologist, and addiction counselor as well as any particularized recreational or occupational therapy and family therapy.

Education

Particularly in an outpatient setting, substance abuse education is critically important. Most outpatient facilities make extensive use of recovering physicians, the recovering community, videotape materials, films, audio materials, and reading materials. Also, because the patients in an outpatient setting are usually not as medically debilitated as patients in inpatient settings, the individuals are perceived as being more receptive to the educational materials that are provided. A number of examples of educational materials are presented in the outpatient models described later in this chapter.

AA/NA Meetings

Outpatient programs make extensive use of AA and NA meetings as part of the treatment program. As in inpatient settings, AA and NA meetings are a requirement of the outpatient program. These meetings may be held at lunch time, in the evenings, at the outpatient facility or away from the facility. It is also not unusual for the outpatient providers to require that the individuals get proof of attendance at AA or NA meetings. Usually members of the AA or NA groups are more than willing to oblige, even though anonymity is a critical part of the philosophy of these groups.

Individual Therapy

An individual therapy program will be developed depending upon the patient's needs. The individual in outpatient treatment may require therapy from a psychiatrist, a psychologist, and/or the addiction counselor.

Peer Relations

Peer relationships are facilitated by the more informal nature of most outpatient programs. Individual patients may decide to ride together to the outpatient facilities or to AA or NA meetings, they may study the substance abuse educational materials together, or they may just visit with one another and share information. In all of these cases, the peer relations that develop are important for the maintenance of sobriety.

Recreational Therapy

Depending on the nature of the outpatient program, recreational therapy may or may not be provided. In intensive day programs, it is usually part of the program. In the evening or long-term day programs, it will probably not be provided, but will be encouraged by the program providers.

Occupational Therapy

Outpatient rehabilitation programs are particularly adept at occupational or vocational counseling. Because outpatient providers interact on a day-to-day basis with EAP providers and other employers, they normally are much more tuned in to the business world than many hospital providers. Many outpatient treatment centers provide an occupational therapist to work with the patient either concerning his or her current job problems or concerning getting a new job.

Family Program

Outpatient programs are usually very adept at family therapy and at working on family aspects of substance abuse concurrently with the individual's substance abuse problem. Most outpatient programs emphasize the importance of family therapy and are likely to be involved with various aspects of the family from the very beginning, since the patient is returning home in the evenings in most cases and is relating family problems to his or her individual counselor and to the group. Most programs have extensive family programs including individual family therapy; family group therapy; intervention therapy between the individual and his or her family, guided by the counselor; and suggested or required attendance at Al-Anon or Alateen for family members.

Aftercare

Because of the unique nature of the outpatient provider/patient relationship, outpatient treatment providers are usually particularly adept at developing excellent aftercare programs. Usually the outpatient providers will arrange a long-term aftercare relationship with the patient so that the patient's recovery will continue over an extended period of time on a monitored basis, and so that the provider may assist the patient in handling the various crises to recovery that occur after the more intensive substance abuse treatment program ends.

Outpatient vs. Inpatient Effectiveness

Debate has waged for years in the recovery community concerning the effectiveness of inpatient versus outpatient rehabilitation efforts. The areas considered here for comparison include medical, psychiatric, and detoxification situations; penetration into the workplace; discharge rates; success rates; long- versus shorter-term programs; more or less intensive interventions; socioeconomic types of patients; cost; and insurance bias.

Medical, Psychiatric, and Detoxification Situations

There is little doubt in the recovery community that when the patient has a severe medical or psychiatric emergency, whether it be withdrawal seizures or cocaine psychosis, an inpatient setting is appropriate.

In most detoxification situations, particularly where the medical practitioner deems it necessary to detoxify an individual with longer-acting barbiturates, a hospital setting is appropriate. On the other hand, as reported earlier in this chapter, recent studies indicate that outpatient treatment is an effective and low cost method for those patients with mild-to-moderate symptoms of alcohol withdrawal.[7] As a matter of fact, one study reported that the detoxification costs were substantially greater for inpatients than for outpatients ($3,319 to $3,665 for inpatients versus $175 to $388 for outpatients).[8] Whereas experts in the recovery field have often believed that inpatient settings were required for detoxification (unless patients detoxify themselves at home), there is some suggestion that in the future, detoxification, particularly in patients with mild-to-moderate alcohol withdrawal, will occur more on an outpatient basis than has existed in the last several decades.

Penetration Into the Workplace

Recent studies have indicated that where employers make outpatient rehabilitation available to employees, the percentage of voluntary referrals tends to increase, thus allowing treatment to penetrate more deeply into the workplace. As noted earlier in this chapter, when the United Technologies Corporation established its day treatment program, 64 percent of all the referrals to the outpatient program were self-initiated.[9] The primary reason for this increased voluntary participation is that outpatient programs cause much less disruption of the family life and community responsibilities of an individual than do inpatient programs.

Discharge Rates

There exists a myth that outpatients are more likely than inpatients to leave treatment prematurely. However, a 1985 study by the Chemical Abuse/Addiction Treatment Outcome Registry (CATOR) in Minnesota[10] indicated that the rate of full discharge from treatment is virtually identical for inpatients (78%) and outpatients (77%). This study was based on the discharge status of 11,902 CATOR-III patients which consisted of 9,922 inpatients and 1,980 outpatients.

Success Rates

Researchers generally believe that outpatient treatment programs are just as effective as inpatient treatment programs.[11] In 1981, the Hazelden Foundation completed an impressive comparison study of inpatient/outpatient outcomes for the treatment of alcoholism. The Foundation compared 80 outpatients with 959 inpatients who were in its program in 1981. The results of the study were published in a pamphlet entitled "Apples and Oranges."[12]

The conclusions reached by the study suggest that "simplistic comparisons of inpatient and outpatient programs should be avoided."[13] Research has indicated that the populations of alcoholics in inpatient and outpatient facilities are not identical. Usually, patients being treated in inpatient facilities are more severely affected by alcoholism. As a result, "[t]he tested populations are sufficiently different that simple comparisons are not conclusive."[14]

However, studies that attempt to compare outcome rates of inpatient and outpatient treatments consistently find no significant difference. Table 1 shows inpatient and outpatient rehabilitation results after one year.

Table 1
Inpatient and Outpatient
Rehabilitation Results

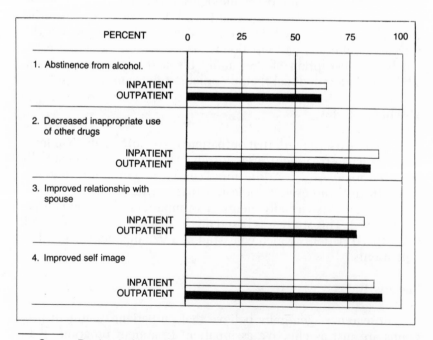

Source: Reprinted with permission from J. Spicer et al., "Apples and Oranges—A Comparison of Inpatient and Outpatient Programs (Center City, Minn.: Hazelden Foundation, copyright © 1981).

As the chart indicates, the success rates of inpatient versus outpatient treatment were judged to be virtually identical.

Longer vs. Shorter Programs

Miller and Hester made an extensive study of the research concerning comparisons of inpatient and outpatient rehabilitation programs or residential over nonresidental settings "for longer over shorter inpatient programs, or for more intensive over less intensive interventions in treating alcohol abuse."[15] Based on their review of the literature, they concluded that although there is a presumption that longer treatment programs have a greater impact than shorter-term programs, no empirical studies indicated this to be true whether in an inpatient or an outpatient setting. Similarly, the study found that neither more nor less intensive intervention affected the outcome and success of the rehabilitation whether the patient was in an inpatient or outpatient setting.

Interestingly, the socioeconomic profile of a patient was found to be a more accurate predictor of success when studying setting, length, and intensity of a treatment program, although certainly not in the way that most commentators in the area perceived the situation to be. In reviewing predictor studies, the researchers indicated that "[e]ven in the absence of overall differences in treatment outcome between inpatient and outpatient settings, it is possible that certain types of clients derive differential benefits (or harm) from being treated in these alternative settings. This is the central issue in matching clients to optimal treatment approaches [citation omitted]."[16] After extensive review of the materials and research data, it was concluded that "[a]vailable data . . . suggest that indicators of severity and social stability may be predictive of differential response to alternative treatment settings. The direction of findings is reasonably consistent: Most severe and less socially stable alcoholics seem to fare better in inpatient (or more intensive) treatment, whereas among less severe and more socially stable (married, employed) alcoholics, outpatient (and less intensive) treatment yields more favorable outcomes than inpatient treatment. When heterogeneous populations of alcoholics are averaged together, the consistent finding is of comparable (or better) outcomes from outpatient as opposed to residential (inpatient) treatment."[17]

It is significant that this review of the research indicates a certain irony: The employed, married individual who seeks substance abuse treatment is often referred to inpatient rehabilitation, which he or she does not necessarily need. The studies indicate that the socially stable individual is usually more successful and adaptive to the outpatient rehabilitation setting. However, his or her insurance often only covers treatment in the inpatient setting. On the other hand, the socially unstable individual (the homeless person and the unemployed person) is usually much more in need of inpatient rehabilitation than his or her socially stable counterpart. This individual usually has no insurance and therefore is unable to pay for the inpatient rehabilitation services, and consequently, usually does not receive such services. This situation seems counterproductive to the efficient handling of substance abuse problems. However, it surely will take time for such circumstances to be rectified.

Cost

Outpatient rehabilitation costs two-thirds to 90 percent less than traditional inpatient substance abuse rehabilitation.[18] The primary reason outpatient rehabilitation is less expensive than inpatient rehabilitation is that the enormous staff and facility costs associated with hospitalization are nonexistent in outpatient situations. The average cost of outpatient rehabilitation is between $1,500 and $4,000, depending on the length of stay, the intensity, and the number of hours in the program.

Studies by a number of researchers have indicated that in comparison studies the success rates of patients in inpatient and outpatient rehabilitation are virtually identical, although the cost effectiveness of the outpatient rehabilitation far exceeds that of inpatient treatment.[19] In their study, Miller and Hester commented that "[t]he truly substantial differences between residential and nonresidential treatment of alcoholism are to be found in the cost of each approach. A routine course of inpatient alcoholism treatment now commonly costs between $4,000 and $15,000. By contrast, a course of outpatient treatment of the length indicated by research to be optimal would average less than 10% of this cost, even if delivered by fully credentialized professionals at prevailing private practice rates. Self-help and paraprofessional interventions can be still more cost effective [citations omitted]."[20]

Miller and Hester continue, "Given a reasonably clear picture of equal benefits regardless of setting, nonresidential treatment offers many advantages including substantially lower cost and less intrusion into the individual's life and work patterns." Further, "[u]nnecessary placement in residential treatment may foster continued superfluous use of expensive health care resources."[21]

Insurance Bias

In spite of the increasing body of research indicating the cost effectiveness of outpatient rehabilitation, insurance carriers thus far are much more inclined to cover inpatient than outpatient rehabilitation. This situation is extremely expensive for the employer, the employee, the insurance carrier, and the government.

In 1983, the Office of Technology Assessment of the United States Congress stated that "many alcoholism treatment services are not cost effective—i.e., there are less expensive ways of providing treatment than are reflected in current reimbursement policy. However, reimbursement systems, particularly the Medicare, Medicaid programs have overwhelmingly emphasized the most expensive treatment services—inpatient, medically based treatment."[22]

However, employers and insurance carriers are slowly becoming more inclined to use outpatient rehabilitation for their substance abusing employees, particularly for alcoholics or addicts who do not require hospitalization for medical purposes. For example, in a rare departure from usual practice, Kentucky Blue Cross and Blue Shield established an intensive outpatient program (IOP) for chemical dependency in June 1989. The press releases about this program indicated that it was the first of its kind in the state and possibly the only such program offered by a national insurer.[23] The reasons cited for establishing the program were significantly reduced costs and less disruption to the patient-recipients' lives.[24] The cost of this program was estimated to be about $2,000 per patient. The reports on the program noted, "Alternatives to inpatient care for substance and alcohol abuse become more important as healthcare costs continue to rise."[25]

Additionally, around the country, communities and insurers are beginning to establish outpatient programs to reduce costs without reducing the effectiveness of the treatment.[26] Many employers are requiring employees to attend outpatient rehabilitation where possible, and are requiring the insurance carriers to write coverage for outpatient rehabilitation. In spite of insurance industry practices, which are exceedingly resistant to change, the increasingly frequent employer demand to shift from inpatient to outpatient treatment is leading to decreased medical costs while maintaining substantially equivalent success in substance abuse rehabilitation.

It has been suggested that if inpatient substance abuse rehabilitation continues to remain at such extraordinarily expensive rates, then the government should put a cap on the reimbursement of inpatient rehabilitation where the government is involved. For example, one commentator has written, "In fact, the Government could pay for such treatment simply by reforming the irrational and wasteful system of public subsidies for private drug rehabilitation. A simple cap of $6,000 per treatment for drug addiction would save not only billions of dollars in lost tax revenues, but countless lives as well."[27]

Because of the cost effectiveness of outpatient rehabilitation and the increasing pressure on reducing health care costs, more employers will be requiring outpatient rehabilitation in preference to inpatient rehabilitation for substance abuse in the future.

Conclusion

In summary, outpatient programs provide competent rehabilitation opportunities for the vast majority of individuals in need of substance abuse treatment. Clearly, the most appropriate patient for outpatient rehabilitation is the socially stable (employed, married) individual. However, third-party insurance carriers who offer coverage, primarily for employed individuals, have a bias and preference for inpatient providers over outpatient providers. The socially unstable (unemployed) individual is probably in greater need of inpatient rehabilitation but, ironically, cannot afford it.

Outpatient programs have been proven to be a cost-effective method of rehabilitation with treatment results equal to those of inpatient treatment. As a result, it is recommended that employers review their insurance coverage to create a preference for outpatient programs where medical complications are not sufficient to require hospitalization of the individual.

Addendum 1

Sample Evening Outpatient Treatment Program

Six weeks, three evenings per week

All patients will attend at least ten AA and/or NA meetings during the six-week program in addition to the meetings attended by the group.

WEEK 1
Tuesday: 6:00 p.m.–9:00 p.m.
(A) Introduction of patients/counselor
(B) Program overview
(C) Expectations: Patients and Counselor
(D) Rules: Attendance, AA/NA Meetings
(E) Discuss reasons for being in program
(F) Leave early if necessary. This is a time to build trust and rapport.
Wednesday: 6:00 p.m.–9:00 p.m.
6:00–7:00 p.m.: Update on patients
Video: "Alcoholism: Early Diagnosis and Management: Parts 1 and 2"
Handout: "Characteristics of an Alcoholic"
7:30–9:00 p.m. Group Therapy: Explanation of AA, Steps, Promises, Traditions, Chips, Give out schedules and (AA attendance) cards to be signed
Audio Tape: "What to Expect from AA"
Thursday: 6:00 p.m.–9:00 p.m.
6:00–7:00 p.m.: Update on patients
Speaker: Dr. Ted W.—Slide Presentation on the Disease Concept
7:30–9:00 p.m.: Group Therapy
Video: "12 Steps of AA"

WEEK 2
Tuesday: 6:00 p.m.–9:00 p.m.
6:00–7:30 p.m.: Update on patients
Video: "Chalk Talk"
Handouts: "Symptoms of Alcoholism"
7:30–9:00 p.m.: Attend AA meeting in community
Wednesday: 6:00 p.m.–9:00 p.m.
6:00–7:30 p.m.: Update on patients
Handout: "Do You Have a Problem"
Introduction: "Step One"
Handout: "Step One: If You Love Me"
7:30–9:00 p.m.: Group Therapy
Thursday: 6:00 p.m.–9:00 p.m.
6:00 p.m.–7:30 p.m.: Update on patients
Topic: "Drugs and Alcohol from a Physiological Point of View"
Speaker: Pharmacologist Dr. Joe F. will lecture on depressants, stimulants, hallucinogens, marijuana, and the addictability of various drugs.
7:30–9:00 p.m.: Group Therapy
Read from the *Twelve Steps and Twelve Traditions—Step 1.* Give out homework assignment on Step 1.
Audio Tape: "Powerlessness and Unmanageability"

WEEK 3
Tuesday: 6:00 p.m.–9:00 p.m.
  6:00–7:30 p.m.: Update on
  patients
  Topic: "Alcoholism: A Family
  Disease"
  Explain the Family Trap
  Audio Tapes:
  (1) "What About the Children"
  (2) "Family Forgiveness"
  7:30–9:00 p.m.: Attend AA
  meeting in community
Wednesday: 6:00 p.m.–9:00 p.m.
  6:00–7:30 p.m.: Update on
  patients
  Video: "CoDependency"
  Audio Tapes:
  (1) "Detaching with Love"
  (2) "The Healthy Family"
  7:30–9:00 p.m.: Group Therapy
  Discuss homework assignment
  from last Thursday
Thursday: 6:00 p.m.–9:00 p.m.
  6:00–7:30 p.m.: Speaker: Al-
  Anon—JoAnn G.
  7:30–9:00 p.m.: Group therapy

WEEK 4
Tuesday: 6:00 p.m.–9:00 p.m.
  6:00–7:30 p.m.: Discussion
  Topic: "Denial"
  Videos:
  (1) "Denial"
  (2) "One Day at a Time"
  7:30–9:00 p.m.: Group Therapy
  Lecture: Speaker: Psychologist
  Dr. Don G.
  Topic: "Psychological
  Dependency"
Thursday: 6:00 p.m.–9:00 p.m.
  6:00–7:30 p.m.: Lecture/
  Discussion
  Speaker: Certified Addiction
  Counselor Cindy B.
  Topic: "Communication"
  7:30–9:00 p.m.: Group Therapy
  Video: "Coping with
  Unmanageability"

WEEK 5
Tuesday: 6:00 p.m.–9:00 p.m.
  6:00–7:30 p.m.: Group Therapy
  Topic: Step 3
  Video: Step 3
  Take turns reading from the
  Twelve and Twelve—Discuss
  Topic: "Drugs"
  Video: Nightmare of Cocaine"
  Audio Tapes:
  (1) "Are We Really Letting Go"
  (2) "Spiritual Awakening"
  (3) "Spirituality in Recovery"
  (4) "Spirituality and Religion"
  7:30–9:00 p.m.: Attend AA
  meeting in community
Wednesday: 6:00 p.m.–9:00 p.m.
  6:00–7:30 p.m.: Group Therapy
  Topics: "Spirituality," "Feelings"
  Video: "Spiritual Awakening"
  Handout: "Whole Person Wheel"
  Audio: "Feelings"
  7:30–9:00 p.m.: Lecture
  Speaker: Lecture: Rev. Bob M.
  Topic: "Spirituality"
Thursday: 6:00 p.m.–9:00 p.m.
  6:00–7:30 p.m.: Group Therapy
  Topic: "Guilt"
  Video: "Guilt"
  7:30–9:00 p.m.: Lecture/
  Discussion
  Speaker: Dr. Peter B.
  Topic: "Guilt, Resentments,
  Anger"

WEEK 6
Tuesday: 6:00 p.m.–9:00 p.m.
  6:00–7:30 p.m.: Group Therapy
  Topic: "How to Manage Stress
  and Cope"
  Video: "Coping with
  Unmanageability"
  Audio:
  (1) "Working with a Program of
  Change"
  (2) "Rx for Health"
  7:30–9:00 p.m.: Attend AA
  meeting in community
Wednesday: 6:00 p.m.–9:00 p.m.
  6:00–7:30 p.m.: Group Therapy
  Video: "Self-Help Groups and
  Treatment"
  Audio Tape: "Why Relapse—
  Why the Revolving Door"
  7:30–9:00 p.m.: Lecture/
  Discussion
  Speaker: Dr. Chuck R.
  Topic: "Relapse"
Thursday: 6:00 p.m.–9:00 p.m.
  6:00–7:30 p.m.: Group Therapy
  Topic: "Sharing What Was
  Learned in Program"
  7:30–9:00 p.m.: Social Function
  Snacks and Soft drinks

Addendum 2

Sample Long-Term Day Outpatient Treatment Program

12 Weeks
2 or more individual counseling sessions per week
1 two-hour session per week: Group Therapy and Substance Abuse Education
90 AA and/or NA meetings—mandatory

WEEK 1
A. Introduction of patients/counselor
B. Program overview
C. Expectations: Patients/counselor
D. Rules: Attendance/AA/NA meetings
E. Discussion: Why each member is in the program
F. Handout on group therapy
G. Explain briefly what AA is all about. Briefly discuss (1) Steps, (2) Traditions, (3) Promises, (4) Chips
H. Handout: AA/NA Schedules
I. Audio: "What to Expect from AA"

WEEK 2
A. Update on patients
B. Video: (1) "Alcoholism: Early Diagnosis and Management: Parts 1 and 2"
(2) "Group Dynamics"
(3) "12 Steps of AA"
C. Handout: "Characteristics of an Alcoholic"
D. Audio Tape: "Guilt"
E. Speaker: Dr. Peter B.
Lecture: "Anger, Resentments, Guilt"

WEEK 3
A. Handouts: (1) "Symptoms of Alcoholism"
(2) "Powerlessness/ Unmanageability" (Homework)
B. Video: (1) "Step One"
(2) "Powerlessness and Unmanageability"
C. Speaker: Dr. Ted W.
Lecture: Slide Presentation on Disease Concept

WEEK 4
A. Handouts: (1) Johns Hopkins Questionnaire
(2) Addiction and Recovery Chart
B. Video: "Chalk Talk"
C. Discuss homework assignment on Powerlessness and Unmanageability

WEEK 5
A. Speaker: Pharmacologist Dr. Joe F.
   Lecture: "Drugs and Alcohol from a Physiological Point of View"
B. Audio: "Introduction from *Twelve and Twelve.*" Discussion

WEEK 8
A. (1) Audio: Step 2
      (a) From the "*Twelve and Twelve*"
      (b) "Step 2"
      (c) "Ya, but"
      (d) "Recovery is Forever, Our Big Ego"
   (2) Higher Power, Managing, Manipulating, and Intellectualizing
B. Video: (1) "Denial"
          (2) "Step 2"

WEEK 6
Alcoholism is a family disease
A. Video: "If You Love Me"
B. Discuss: Family Trap
C. Audio: (1) "What About the Children"
          (2) "Family Forgiveness"

WEEK 9
Speaker: Psychologist Dr. Don G.
Lecture: "Psychological Dependence"

WEEK 7
A. Video: "Co-Dependency"
B. Audio: (1) "Symptoms of Co-Dependency"
          (2) "Detaching with Love"
          (3) "The Healthy Family"
          (4) "Spousoholics"
C. Speakers: Al-Anon: JoAnn G./Ann P.

WEEK 10
A. Speaker: Certified Addiction Counselor Cindy B.
   Lecture: "Communication"
B. Video: "Coping with Unmanageability"

WEEK 11
Drugs and Step 3
A. Video: (1) "The Nightmare of
        Cocaine"
    (2) Step 3
Handout: "The Drug Quiz: Drugs
        and Cocaine,
        Marijuana"
B. Audio: (1) Step 3—Reading from
        "Twelve and Twelve"
    (2) "Are We Really
        Letting Go"
    (3) "Spiritual Awakening"
    (4) "Spirituality and
        Religion"
    (5) "Spirituality in
        Recovery"
    (6) "The Real Drug
        Problem"
    (7) "The Cocaine
        Experience"
    (8) "Cocaine"
    (9) "Drugs at Your
        Doorstep"
    (10) "Alcoholism and Drug
        Addiction"
    (11) "Treating the Cocaine
        Abuser"
    (12) "You and God Are a
        Majority"
C. Speaker: Rev. Bob M.
    Lecture: "Spirituality"

WEEK 12
A. Video: (1) "Coping with
        Unmanageability"
    (2) "Self-Help Groups and
        Treatment"
    (3) "How to Sabotage Your
        Treatment"
B. Audio: (1) "Working a Program of
        Change"
    (2) "Rx for Health"
    (3) "Why Relapse—Why
        the Revolving Door"
    (4) "Anonymity"
    (5) "Humility"
    (6) "Getting Better,
        Coping with Stress"
    (7) "Essentials of
        Recovery"
    (8) "Gratitude and
        Sobriety"
C. Speaker: Dr. Chuck R.
    Lecture: "Relapse"

Notes

1. Bensinger & Pilkington, "An Alternative Method in the Treatment of Alcoholism: The United Technologies Corporation Day Treatment Program," 25 *J. Occupational Med.*, 1983, 300–303.
2. *Id.* at 300.
3. *Id.* at 301, citing Schram, Mandell, & Archer, *Workers Who Drink* (Lexington, Mass: Lexington Books, 1970), 53; Baekeland, "Evaluation of Treatment Methods in Chronic Alcoholism," in Kissin & Begleiter, eds., *Treatment and Rehabilitation of the Chronic Alcoholic* (New York: Plenum Press, 1977), 395; Ruger, "Various Regressive Processes and Their Prognostic Value in Inpatient Group Psychotherapy," 30 *Int'l Group Psychotherapy*, 1980, 95–105.
4. Bensinger & Pilkington, at 302.
5. *Id.* at 303.
6. Hayashida, et al., "Comparative Effectiveness and Costs of Inpatient and Outpatient Detoxification of Patients With Mild-to-Moderate Alcohol Withdrawal Syndrome," 320 *New Eng. J. Med.* 1989, 358–365, 358.
7. *Id.*
8. *Id.*
9. Bensinger & Pilkington, *supra* note 1, at 302; Miller & Hester, "In-patient Alcoholism Treatment—Who Benefits?," *Am. Psychologist*, 1986, 794–805, 802.
10. Hoffman, Belille, & McKenna, *CATOR: Chemical Abuse/Addiction Treatment Outcome Registry, 1985 Report* (St. Paul, Minn.: Medical Education & Research Foundation, 1985).
11. Miller & Hester, *supra* note 9; Spicer, et al., "Apples and Oranges—A Comparison of Inpatient and Outpatient Programs (Center City, Minn.: Hazelden Foundation, 1981).
12. Spicer, et al., *supra* note 11; see also Southeast Council on Alcoholism & Drug Problems, *Out-patient or In-patient: Which Is More Successful?*, (Downey, Calif.: Southeast Council on Alcoholism & Drug Problems, [1982]).
13. Spicer, et al., *supra* note 11.
14. Southeast Council on Alcoholism & Drug Problems, *supra* note 12.
15. Miller & Hester, *supra* note 9, at 794.
16. *Id.* at 801.
17. *Id.*
18. *Id.* at 802.
19. Longabaugh, et al., "Cost Effectiveness of Alcoholism Treatment in Partial vs. Inpatient Settings: Six Month Outcomes," 44 *J. of Stud. on Alcohol*, 1983, 1049–1071; Miller & Hester, *supra* note 9.
20. Miller & Hester, *supra* note 9, at 802.
21. *Id.*
22. U.S. Congress, Office of Technology Assessment, *The Effectiveness and Cost of Alcoholism Treatment* (Washington, D.C.: U.S. Congress, Office of Technology Assessment, 1983), 66, cited in Miller & Hester, *supra* note 9, at 803.
23. *Nat'l Rep. on Substance Abuse.* (BNA) May 24, 1989, 2–3.
24. *Id.* at 2.
25. *Id.*
26. Wenzel, "Outpatient Program Combats Alcohol and Drug Abuse," *The [Columbia, S.C.] State*, Feb. 20, 1989.
27. Cohen, "Why Subsidize Expensive Private Drug Care?," *New York Times*, June 6, 1988.

Chapter 11

Aftercare and Long-Term Rehabilitation Programs

Aftercare Defined

Aftercare essentially is the recovery support that should follow inpatient or outpatient rehabilitation. The purpose of aftercare is to ensure the individual's long-term maintenance of sobriety or recovery, usually through self-help groups such as Alcoholics Anonymous and Narcotics Anonymous.

Experience has shown that when the employer monitors and assures compliance with an employee's aftercare program, the return on the rehabilitation investment is much greater than if there is no follow-up. As a result, an increasing number of employers, usually through their EAPs, are striving to support and coordinate the employee's aftercare rehabilitation program as a way of protecting their investment.

Aftercare is the continuation of the recovery process begun in inpatient or outpatient treatment for the chemically dependent individual and his or her family. Aftercare is basically a transition period between treatment and the long-term recovery effort. The significance of the aftercare process is that it inherently recognizes the need for the recovering individual to establish a pattern of long-term recovery, including attendance at self-help group meetings such as AA or NA in order to maintain abstinence and sobriety. Aftercare programs also recognize the importance of family participation in such groups as Al-Anon, ACoA, and Alateen for the family member's own sake, and in order to help family members to understand the nature of addiction and its effect on the individual.

The aftercare process or the development of a long-term program is essential for substance abuse recovery. Too often in our contemporary society the attitude is that if we take a pill, we will be cured. Similarly, the substance abuser may believe that after participation in some form of treatment, he or she will be cured of alcoholism or drug addiction. This could not be further from the truth. The fact about dealing with alcoholism and drug addiction is that it is a long-term process that takes constant vigilance on the part of the employee to maintain his or her sobriety. It is also important to the process that the employer remain consistent in applying the substance abuse rules.

Usually the extent of aftercare depends on the needs of the recovering employee.[1] In most cases, aftercare programs will consist of structured activities that complement and support rehabilitation treatments. Such activities include meetings of support groups in connection with the rehabilitation facility, vocational rehabilitation sessions with the recovering employee, individual psychotherapy sessions, if necessary, and required participation in self-help group meetings such as Alcoholics Anonymous (AA) or Narcotics Anonymous (NA). The goal of aftercare and all substance abuse treatment is to orient the individual toward a recovery path, particularly for the first, critical year.

One commentator on aftercare discusses the subject as follows:

> The objective of aftercare is to assist the recovering person in remaining substance free; in essence, to establish the foundation for a lifelong plan of recovery. Aftercare relies on support groups to guide recovering employees through a period of transition, with a gradual introduction to and increased involvement in self-help groups. As a comparison, support groups are transitional, therapeutic, intensive, motivational, educational, organized activities to promote personal change required for recovery. Self-help groups are long term, stabilizing, maintenance-oriented with caring and sharing group activities having no explicit or implicit therapeutic intent. Both support and self-help groups are significant to recovering employees returning to and keeping their jobs.[2]

Relapse Potential

Understanding the significance of aftercare and long-term rehabilitation through self-help groups may be best accomplished by understanding the nature of relapse.[3] By their very nature, alcoholism and addiction have been described as a progressive, relapsing, often fatal disease of which there is no known cure. It has been suggested that "relapse to alcoholic drinking reflects conditioned behavior, not a capricious desire or a simple response to psychological conflict."[4] There is also a physiological and psychological craving for alcohol or drugs that exists in the alcoholic or addict that is little understood. For instance, "conditioned alcoholic craving vanishes in treatment units and behavioral laboratories only to return unexpectedly at some unforeseen point in the alcoholic's future."[5] As has been described by one researcher, "[f]or any alcoholic there may be several or a whole battery of critical cues or signals. By rule of generalization, any critical cues can spread like the tentacles of a vine over a whole range of analogs, and this may account for the growing frequency of bouts or for the development of a pattern of continuous inebriation."[6] Researchers have written extensively about the psychological, pharmacological, behavioral, genetic, and other factors that are associated with addiction and cause relapse.[7] However, at the risk of oversimplification it must be stated that in order to prevent relapses, a recovering individual should avoid the people, places, and things that were associated with the individual's prior alcohol or drug use. Recovery involves a change of behavior, not just a medical or physiological readjustment. It is important that a recovering person learn to avoid the people with whom he or she used to use alcohol or drugs, places where the substance abuse occurred, and the things or other stresses that trigger substance abuse in order to increase the chances of recovery and decrease the chances of relapse. Fortunately, recovery is as progressive as addiction.[8] As a result, if the employee is encouraged to substitute support and self-help groups, different people, different places, and different things in his or her everyday life for the people, places, and things that trigger drug use, the chances of relapse are diminished.

One researcher presents the following advice concerning aftercare and relapse:

> There is a consensus in the professional literature that aftercare is a key aspect to preventing relapse in alcohol and drug-dependent persons. Since the recovering employee must continue with personal and work stresses associated with job reentry, relapse rates are particularly high within the first three months of aftercare. Thereafter, the probability of remaining sober/abstinent stabilizes for the first year. Persons receiving comprehensive aftercare generally show greater sobriety/abstinence rates at six and 12 month follow-ups. Attendance in at least eight aftercare sessions has been significantly associated with greater work adjustment for recovering persons. This adjustment has been cited in the form of fewer job changes, greater length of time on jobs, less lost time from work, and employment at a higher socioeconomic level. Without comprehensive aftercare, the investments of money, time, and energy by the employer, EAP, treatment center, and recovering employee may have been wasted.[9]

Employer's Role in Relapse Prevention

Understanding that relapse is almost an inherent part of addiction and that aftercare is important for the maintenance of sobriety, an employer should understand its role in relapse prevention. First, the employer must understand "enabling systems." For every chemically dependent individual, there is an elaborate, sometimes unconscious enabling system, a group of people—family members, employers, co-workers, etc.—a social and career network that allows someone to continue using alcohol and/or drugs while not allowing that person to suffer the consequences of this use. "Enablers are people who 'clean up messes,' look the other way, justify, rationalize, and in essence rescue the chemically dependent person."[10] Understanding that enabling systems exist for all addicted or chemically dependent individuals, employers should realize that "you can kill somebody with kindness."[11] However, if an employer takes the position that the substance abuse program rules apply to all employees, and that the rules will be consistently applied, then the employer may remove itself from the enabling system and force the recovering employee to comply with the rules. This attitude is not harsh; it is realistic and it may save the employee's life.

Furthermore, "[e]mployers are deemed to be even more powerful than family members in their ability to help active addicts overcome the consequences of their drug use. The job we have, the work we do, defines us and gives our lives meaning. It is the last thing we want to lose. Employers who have a keen understanding of the addiction process can be the central figure in the recovery process."[12] The employer should continue to make it very clear to the recovering employee that his or her job is on the line and that if he or she abides by the substance abuse program rules, the job may be maintained. On the other hand, the employer should make it clear to the recovering employee that deviation from the rules will have dire employment consequences. Again, this very straightforward approach may save the employee's life.

The employee who returns from treatment will be experiencing a number of stressful factors upon re-entry into the workplace. It is certainly possible for the employer to be compassionate while being stern in the enforcement of its substance abuse program rules. The following list of suggestions has been given to employers in order to assist the employer in dealing with a returning recovering employee:

1. Respect the employee's confidentiality. Let the employee decide how co-worker inquiries should be answered;
2. Make provisions for general workplace awareness and knowledge of substance abuse problems and the disease recovery process;
3. Communicate directly or indirectly to the employee your awareness that the treatment-to-work transition can be difficult at times;
4. Remind the employee how much he or she was missed during the approved sick leave and that his or her job was retained because of his or her value;
5. Check with the employee periodically to see "how things are going;"
6. Be relaxed when interacting with the employee;
7. Cooperate as much as possible with the EAP and treatment center during aftercare;
8. Let the employee know explicitly what is expected of his or her job performance. This may require refamiliarization and/or introduction to new job conditions (new projects, etc.); and
9. Do not regard the employee as he or she was before but rather as he or she is now. [13]

Formal Programs—Support Groups

Employee Programs

The employee's formal aftercare program will usually include support groups created by the inpatient or outpatient rehabilitation center in a transition setting. For example, an inpatient or outpatient facility may arrange for the employee to return once a week for one to three months after discharge so that the treatment staff will be able to monitor the progress of the individual and make suggestions for a more productive recovery. After discharge and for an initial period of time, some employees will deem it beneficial to revisit the treatment facility in order to touch base with the counselors and recovering friends. Confirming these relationships helps build a bridge between the treatment experience and the ultimate goal of the employee returning to a normal life. These types of support groups, which may include counselors, other patients, alumni of the treatment facility, and others, are classic aftercare programs.

Other forms of aftercare provided by a treatment facility may include keeping in contact with the participants by telephone, requiring attendance at a certain number of aftercare sessions which are regularly scheduled for discharged patients in various geographical areas, requesting that former patients return to the center several times over a 6-to 12-month period for special programs, and having alumni of the treatment facility maintain personal contact with the discharged individual to encourage attendance at AA or NA meetings in their geographical area.

Aftercare programming may also include vocational rehabilitation counseling in order to ease the individual back into the job or the job market, or in certain cases, a continuation of individual counseling or psychotherapy. Finally, the major thrust of aftercare is always to encourage the discharged individuals to develop a regular pattern of attending self-help group meetings such as Alcoholics Anonymous and Narcotics Anonymous. Most rehabilitation professionals agree that failure of the individual to attend AA or NA postdischarge for at least a certain period of time significantly decreases the chances of continued sobriety.

Family Programs

Many treatment facilities attempt to develop family programs in order to assist not only the substance abusing individual in dealing with family problems they are certain to have, but also to help family members break the co-dependent enabling system that invariably has been established in families of substance abusers. Many family programs last for at least a short period of time postdischarge, or at a minimum, the treatment staff encourages the family members to attend Al-Anon, Alateen, or other groups in order to deal with the addiction problem that has affected them as well.

Sample Program

An abbreviated description of a sample aftercare program that might be used by a treatment facility and its discharged patients is illustrated in Exhibit 1.

Informal Programs—Self-Help Groups

Alcoholics Anonymous

Alcoholics Anonymous or AA is best described by its own preamble:

Exhibit 1   Sample Aftercare Program

ACTIVITY	PROCESS
1. First two weeks after discharge from XYZ Treatment Facility	A. Active participation in AA B. Participation in aftercare at XYZ location weekly C. Phone counseling six times weekly D. Family participation in Al-Anon E. Family phone counseling as needed
2. Approximately two weeks after discharge, return to XYZ for two-day weekend program	Examination of participant's current status with respect to alcohol or other drugs, recharge and refreshment via group therapy activities. Family may attend and participate as therapy staff or family thinks necessary.
3. Next 10-week period	A. Active participation in AA B. Participation in aftercare at XYZ location weekly C. Phone counseling six times weekly D. Family participation in Al-Anon E. Family phone counseling as needed

Source: Adapted from Beech Hill Hospital and the Hurricane Island Outward Bound School, "An Innovative Approach to Adolescent Alcohol Abuse and Alcoholism." April 1984.

Alcoholics Anonymous is a fellowship of men and women who share their experience, strength and hope with each other that they may solve their common problem and help others to recover from alcoholism.

The only requirement for membership is a desire to stop drinking. There are no dues or fees for AA membership; we are self-supporting through our own contributions. AA is not allied with any sect, denomination, politics, organization or institution; does not wish to engage in any controversy, neither endorses nor opposes any causes.

Our primary purpose is to stay sober and help other alcoholics to achieve sobriety.[14]

Although not all recovering individuals require lifelong participation in AA, experience has shown that participation in AA for a certain amount of time is important if the individual wants to have a better than even chance of remaining drug or alcohol free, and from an employment perspective, maintaining acceptable job performance.

As was discussed previously, AA has as its basic tenets "The Twelve Step Program for Recovery" (see Appendix I, "Alcoholics Anonymous Materials"). These steps require among other things that members admit they are powerless over alcohol and that their life has become unmanageable (Step 1), that they came to believe that a power greater than themselves could restore them to sanity (Step 2), and that they made a decision to turn their will and their lives over to the care of a God as they understand Him (Step 3).[15] These are the basic action steps. The other steps show the individual how to put the program for recovery to work, such as taking a moral inventory (Step 4), making amends to others (Step 9), and working with other alcoholics (Step 12).

Several of the significant aspects of the AA program are that it requires an individual to be honest with himself or herself about the alcohol problem, it acknowledges alcoholism (or drug addiction) as a disease and not a moral weakness or a psychological problem, it functions based on group therapy and working with others, and it urges the individual not to plan for forever, but to take it easy (easy does it) and proceed one day at a time. The general attitude of AA members is that the individual is sick with a disease over which he or she has no control, and there is hope for prevention one day at a time, if the individual will attend meetings and work with other members of the program. AA members believe that the individual is not unique with this problem of alcoholism or addiction, that millions of other alcoholics have the same incurable disease, and that if the individual will work the twelve steps, work with other alcoholics, and not drink, there will be a daily reprieve from the debilitating effects of alcohol or other drugs. The AA program is a call to action. Members believe that it works if they work it, and that although they are not responsible for their disease, they are responsible for their own recovery.

The AA message is very powerful to millions of Americans who attend AA meetings every day. There is a strong spiritual and ritualistic element to AA, but it is not like a cult. Members attend meetings for their own sobriety—no one else's. The 12 traditions of AA (see Appendix I, "Alcoholics Anonymous Materials") enumerate how the members should relate among themselves, in other AA groups, and to the public. Some of the more famous of these traditions include the traditions that the only requirement for AA membership is the desire to stop drinking (Tradition 3), that every AA group ought to be fully self-supporting, declining outside contributions (Tradition 7), that AA has no opinion on outside issues (Tradition 10), that the public relations policy is based on attraction rather than promotion and maintaining anonymity at the level of press, radio, and films (Tradition 11), and that "anonymity is the spiritual foundation of all our traditions, ever reminding us to place principles before personalities" (Tradition 12.)[16]

There is a tremendous amount of hope generated in AA. Hope is one thing that any debilitated alcoholic or addict needs. The hope of AA is best shown in what are called "the promises."

AA members meet in groups that vary in size, but it is often stated that when any two AA members are together, a group meeting can occur. AA was started in 1935 by two recovering alcoholics, Bill W. and Dr. Bob S. At latest count there were two million members worldwide. Recently, a number of books have been written chronicling the history of Alcoholics Anonymous and various aspects of its development, makeup, simplicity, and complexity.[17]

It is difficult to prove how well AA works or why it works so well for those members who praise its success. However, there has been some intuitive research and comment on the subject. George Vaillant in his book, *The Natural History of Alcoholism*,[18] offers the proposition that alcoholism, like any disease, has a natural history and a natural progression. Vaillant's essential thesis, based on considerable research, is that "alcoholics recover not because we treat them but because they heal themselves. Staying sober is not a process of simply becoming detoxified but often becomes the work of several years or in a few cases even of a lifetime."[19] Vaillant contends that the task of a clinician "is to provide emergency medical care, shelter, detoxification, and understanding until self-healing takes place."[20] According to Vaillant's research, it is safe to conclude that AA encourages "self-healing" and enables the individual to break the ingrained habit of alcohol abuse because it deals with each of the four components necesaary for recovery: "(1) offering the patient a nonchemical substitute for dependency for alcohol, (2) reminding him ritually that even one drink can lead to pain and relapse, (3) repairing the social and medical damage that he has experienced, and (4) restoring self-esteem."[21]

Vaillant writes:

> Self-help groups, of which Alcoholics Anonymous is one model, offer the simplest way of providing the alcoholic with all four components referred to above. First, the continuous hope, the gentle peer support, and the selected exposure to the most stable recovery provide the alcoholic with a ritualized substitute dependency, and a substitute for lost drinking companions. Second, like the best behavior therapy, AA meetings not only go on daily, especially on weekends

and holidays, but also singlemindedly underscore the special ways that alcoholics delude themselves. Thus, in a ritual manner, AA allows the alcoholic, who might unconsciously be driven to relapse, to remain conscious of this danger. Third, belonging to a group of caring individuals who have found solutions to the typical problems that beset the newly sober alcoholic alleviates loneliness. Fourth, the opportunity to identify with helpers who once were equally disabled and the opportunity to help others stay sober enhances self-worth.[22]

What this means to the recovering employee is clear—AA, or some clearly identifiable self-help group, can greatly assist the recovery process begun with treatment. And, although many researchers love to knock AA because it is nonscientific, most individuals who deal in the substance abuse area believe that something does not have to be scientific to work. As will be seen in the other self-help groups, all of them are modeled on the basic AA Twelve Step Program.

Al-Anon and Alateen

Al-Anon was founded by Lois W., wife of AA's co-founder, Bill W. Al-Anon was developed as a twelve-step support group program for spouses, "significant others," and relatives of alcoholics either recovering or as yet not recovering. Meetings of Al-Anon groups are held to give comfort to the participants and to assist them in learning how to live comfortably in spite of the effects of alcoholism, and to grow spiritually by the 12 steps of Alcoholics Anonymous. Significantly, while a number of participants originally may have come to Al-Anon to help the alcoholic, these individuals usually come to the conclusion that their own thinking has to change before they can make a new and successful approach to the problem of living, and particularly living with an alcoholic or an addict. In Al-Anon individuals learn to deal with their own anxiety, anger, denial, obsessions, and feelings of guilt. They come to realize that much of their discomfort comes from their own attitude, not just from the problems caused by the alcoholic or addict. Participants work to change their own attitude and learn about responsibilities to themselves. They also work to discover feelings of self-worth, love, and their own spirituality. As a result, the focus of their personal and emotional lives is lifted from the alcoholic and placed where they do have some power, over their own lives.

As one long-term member of Al-Anon puts it, "Those of us who turn to Al-Anon have often done so with despair. We feel cheated out of a loving companion, unloved, unwanted, and alone. Some of us are domineering, self-righteous, arrogant, and smug. We come because we want and need help. We learn in Al-Anon to submerge our own ego for the good of all, for all of us are equal in the fellowship."[23]

Al-Anon groups have now proliferated throughout the United States and other parts of the world. As an offshoot of Al-Anon, Alateen was developed for the teenage family members of alcoholics and addicts. These self-help groups also operate on the principle that it is not the fault of alcoholics or addicts that they are the way they are or act the way they do. The emphasis in Al-Anon and Alateen is that the individual recognize his or her own self-worth, and in doing so become more able to deal with the family member who has the disease of alcoholism and/or addiction. AA's twelfth tradition, "Anonymity is the spiritual foundation of all our Traditions, ever reminding us to place principles above personalities,"[24] is one of the fundamental principles of Al-Anon and Alateen as well.

Adult Children of Alcoholics (ACoA)

Adult Children of Alcoholics (ACoA) is a self-help group which is a form of Al-Anon. Individuals in this group meet to discuss the problems they have as adults which were caused by or related to growing up in alcoholic families. As public awareness has increased,[25] this group has grown extensively throughout the country. The most succinct explanation of ACoA is provided by the National Association for Children of Alcoholics[26] (NACoA) in its charter statement shown in Exhibit 2.

Narcotics Anonymous and Cocaine Anonymous

Narcotics Anonymous (NA) is based on the principle that individuals addicted to narcotics have a problem fundamentally similar to that of alcoholics. The difference is simply the drug of choice, that is, narcotics instead of alcohol. Cocaine Anonymous (CA) operates on the same principle, with the drug of choice being cocaine. Although members of either NA or CA would agree that addiction is addiction, regardless of the drug involved, individuals in each of these groups usually find they can relate better to other individuals who have had the same problem with similar drugs either instead of or in addition to alcohol.

Exhibit 2

NACoA CHARTER STATEMENT

THE FOLLOWING FACTS ABOUT CHILDREN OF ALCOHOLICS (CoAs) HAVE BEEN ESTABLISHED:

- Alcoholism and other drug problems are our nation's number one health problem. It has a devastating affect on our nation's families and costs our country billions of dollars annually.
- One out of three families currently reports alcohol abuse by a family member.
- An estimated 28 million Americans are children of alcoholics (CoAs); 7 million are under 18 years old.
- More than half of all alcoholics have an alcoholic parent.
- Children of alcoholics are prone to experiencing a wide range of psychological difficulties, including learning disabilities, anxiety, shame, eating disorders, and compulsive achieving.
- Children of alcoholics often develop characteristics which can persist throughout adulthood:
  inability to trust
  extreme need to control
  excessive sense of responsibility
  denial of feelings
- Children of alcoholics are at the highest risk for child abuse: physical, sexual and emotional.

NACoA HAS BEEN FOUNDED TO SUPPORT AND SERVE AS A RESOURCE FOR CoAs OF ALL AGES AND THOSE WHO ARE IN A POSITION TO HELP THEM.

1. We believe that children of alcoholics of all ages have a common bond.
2. We define children of alcoholics as those people who have been impacted by the alcoholism or other drug dependence of a parent, or another adult filling the parental role. This results in a recognizable, diagnosable, and treatable condition which can be passed from one generation to the next.
3. Despite the widespread recognition and acceptance of alcoholism as a family illness, children of alcoholics continue to be ignored, misdiagnosed, and undertreated.
4. COAs deserve the understanding, information and help they need to break out of their isolation and silence.
5. The numbers of COAs and the severity of emotional, physical, and spiritual problems that can be caused by parental alcoholism are compelling reasons for increasing and improving services.
6. The problems of COAs cannot be dealt with simply within individual families or the alcoholism field alone. They should be the concern of the entire community.
7. Young, adolescent and adult COAs have the right to specific remedial and preventive services, whether or not the alcoholic parent or the rest of the family seeks help.
8. As a national association, we will direct our efforts to meet the special needs of all ethnic minorities and other underserved populations.
9. The traditional mental health approach is not sufficient for COAs when it fails to recognize and treat the specificity of their condition.
10. We recognize the healing value of participation in self-help groups for those affected by alcoholism.
11. We recognize that the abuse of other drugs by a parent and other addictive behaviors which create family dysfunction can have a serious impact on children similar to that seen in COAs. The effects of these family dysfunctions are often passed from one generation to the next.
12. This association was founded on a spirit of unity, compassion, and deep concern for all those affected by alcoholism.

Exhibit 2   continued

THE NATIONAL ASSOCIATION FOR CHILDREN OF ALCOHOLICS HAS TWELVE
GOALS:
1. To increase public and professional awareness, understanding, and recognition of the
   needs of COAs of all ages.
2. To advocate policies and accessible services addressing the unique problems arising
   from being the child of an alcoholic, particularly in the area of prevention.
3. To protect the rights of children to live in a safe and healthy environment.
4. To involve the entire community, especially schools, business and industry, human
   services, mental health, medical, religious, and law enforcement professions.
5. To help existing alcoholism programs initiate primary and comprehensive services for
   COAs staffed by professionals specifically trained to meet the needs of COAs.
6. To support school-based programs which acknowledge and address the problems of
   COAs.
7. To create a network which will promote the exchange of information and resources.
8. To encourage clinical and biomedical research related to COA issues.
9. To advocate funding from public and private sources.
10. To encourage training for professionals in issues related to COAs.
11. To develop professional guidelines for those who work with COAs.
12. To offer support to professionals who are themselves COAs.

Source: Reprinted with permission from the National Association for Children of
Alcoholics, South Laguna, CA.

NA's description of itself is as follows:

> N.A. is a nonprofit fellowship or society of men and women for
> whom drugs have become a major problem. We are recovering
> addicts, meet regularly to help each other stay clean. This is a
> program of complete abstinence from all drugs. There is only "one"
> requirement for membership, the honest desire to stop using. There
> are no musts in N.A. but we suggest that you keep an open mind and
> give yourself a break. Our program is a set of principles written so
> simply that we can follow them in our daily lives. The most important
> thing about them is that "they work."
> There are no strings attached to N.A. We are not affiliated with
> any other organizations, we have no leaders, no initiation fees or
> dues, no pledges to sign, no promises to make to anyone. We are not
> connected with any political, religious, or law enforcement groups,
> and are under no surveillance at any time. Anyone may join us
> regardless of age, race, color, creed, religion, or lack of religion.
> We are not interested in what or how much you used or who your
> connections were, what you have done in the past, how much or how
> little you have, but only what you want to do about your problem and
> how we can help. The newcomer is the most important person at any
> meeting, because we can only keep what we have by giving it away.
> We have learned from our group experience that those who keep
> coming to our meetings regularly stay clean.[27]

Cocaine Anonymous is similar to AA and NA and has a national
organization as well.[28]

Other Self-Help Groups

There are numerous other self-help groups that deal with various problems or afflictions. The primary concern of the employer is to know about the existence of these groups and to work with the employer's EAP representative to develop a sense of understanding when the EAP refers an individual to one or more of these groups. Some of the other better-known self-help groups include Overeaters Anonymous (OA)[29] and Gamblers Anonymous.[30] These groups focus attention on particular problems such as overeating, anorexia/bulimia, gambling problems, and other emotional problems that may not be associated with substance abuse.

Relationship to Employer Programs

Once an employer has invested time, energy, and money into a comprehensive substance abuse program, it is wasteful not to coordinate the employee's aftercare into the employer's overall program. There are several thoughts that an employer should keep in mind when integrating aftercare and long-term rehabilitation of the employee into the employer's overall substance abuse program.

Coordination Through EAP

Rather than the top managers and supervisors attempting to keep track of the details of the aftercare of every employee, the proper place for such tracking is with the employee assistance provider, whether internal or external. The EAP provider serves as the most logical contact person for the employee returning to work after rehabilitation. The EAP provider knows the employer's substance abuse program, knows of the circumstances of the employee's rehabilitation, knows what to expect from the recovery program of an employee, and is particularly trained and well versed in the various problems that arise in any employee's recovery. Therefore, the employer should look to the EAP provider to coordinate the employee's aftercare with the employer's substance abuse program. Where there is no EAP provider, the employer should appoint a personnel or medical department employee to coordinate such efforts.

Flexible Scheduling

Most employers have found that flexible work scheduling arrangements should be allowed in order to accommodate the employee's aftercare. However, some employers expect returning employees to adhere rigidly to all company rules. This approach is not realistic, particularly considering the fact that the employee in most cases has suffered through a major life crisis and would benefit from a little flexibility. More enlightened employers work with the EAP provider, the personnel department, the employee's supervisor, and any others involved in scheduling to accommodate aftercare counseling, group therapy, individual therapy, or any other aspects of continued rehabilitation. Normally this flexibility is only necessary for a few months at most and the return to the employer on such flexibility is usually substantial.

90 Meetings in 90 Days

The requirement for postrehabilitation attendance at 90 meetings in 90 days is a very practical one. Most recovering individuals recognize that unless an individual goes immediately from formalized rehabilitation to a regular long-term rehabilitation program such as attending AA or NA on a consistent basis, the odds are that the person will abuse substances again. If this occurs, the employer's investment in the employee's rehabilitation may have been wasted. As a result, many employers in conjunction with the EAP provider require that the employee attend 90 AA or NA meetings in 90 days, or some other reasonable number of meetings, in order to assure that the employee sticks with the aftercare and long-term recovery program.

Return to Treatment

A recent development in aftercare approaches includes allowing employees to return to treatment if they feel their sobriety is being threatened. Although an initial assumption might be that the employee wishes to return to treatment in order to avoid a drug test or because he or she is violating the employer's substance abuse program, many employees are motivated solely by their desire to maintain their sobriety. When it is determined that the employee is actively attempting to follow a recovery program, but is having extreme difficulty because of a variety of factors such as continued withdrawal symptoms, family problems, legal problems, or other problems, a number of employers allow the employee to return to treatment particularly for periodic weekend-type rehabilitation in an effort to support the sobriety program. A large number of inpatient and outpatient rehabilitation centers have established aftercare programs that allow the recovering individual to check in for a day or for several days in order to get "refresher" rehabilitation treatment. From a substance abuse coverage or insurance standpoint, this is usually considered continuing treatment rather than a new treatment.

Enforcement of Substance Abuse Program

Regardless of the flexibility that the employer might allow a recovering employee in some areas during the aftercare period, the employer should always consistently enforce its substance abuse program. Flexibility should not include compromising the integrity of the program for employees who are returning to work from rehabilitation. Consistent enforcement particularly applies to drug testing. An employer should never allow a rehabilitated employee to avoid a drug test or to otherwise escape from the substance abuse program. Since denial is such a significant element in the disease of addiction, an employer should not be deluded by a recovering employee into thinking that the rules should not apply to him or her. It is not inconsistent for the employer on one hand to exercise flexibility in dealing with the recovering individual in terms of aftercare or long-term rehabilitation, and on the other hand to enforce the detailed policies and procedures of the substance abuse program as it applies to all employees, whether they are recovering or not. Finally, most employers make sure that the substance abuse program is explained in its entirety to returning, recovering employees so that there will be no question that the rules apply to them as well.

Conclusion

The extent of aftercare or involvement in self-help groups as part of a long-term rehabilitation program is often a determining factor in whether an employee maintains sobriety and adheres to an employer's substance abuse program. An employer that allows an employee to be reintegrated into the workplace by properly using aftercare rehabilitation and an employer who understands its role in relapse prevention for recovering employees will be of great assistance to the recovering employee.

Notes

1. Miller, "Job Reintegration and Aftercare of the Recovering Worker," *Almacan*, Aug. 1986, 12–16.
2. *Id.* at 13.
3. Brownell, et al., "Understanding and Preventing Relapse," 41 *Am. Psychologist*, 1986, 765–782.
4. Vaillant, *The Natural History of Alcoholism: Causes, Patterns, and Paths to Recovery* (Cambridge: Harvard Univ. Press, 1983), at 177.
5. *Id.* at 176–177.
6. Keller, "On the Loss of Control Phenomenon in Alcoholism," 67 *Brit. J. of Addictions*, 1972, 153–166, 161, cited in Vaillant, *supra* note 4, at 177.
7. Vaillant, *supra* note 4, at 180. See also: Gorski & Miller, *Staying Sober: A Guide for Relapse Prevention*, (Independence, Mo., Independence Press, 1986); Blum et al., "Allelic Association of Human Dopamine D_2 Receptor Gene in Alcoholism," 263 *J. Am. Med. A.*, Apr. 18, 1990, 2055–2060.
8. Vaillant, *supra* note 4, at 314–315; Abrams, "An Employer's Role in Relapse Prevention," *Almacan*, July 1987, 20–22.
9. Miller, *supra* note 1, at 13; Miller cites these works: Marlatl & Gordon, eds., *Relapse Prevention* (New York: Guilford Press, 1985); Ahles, et al., "Impact of Aftercare Arrangements on the Maintenance of Treatment Success in Abusive Drinkers," 8 *Addictive Behaviors*, 1983, 53–58; McAuley, "The Effectiveness of an Out-Patient Aftercare Group with Previously Hospitalized Alcoholics," 12 *Brit. J. Soc. Work*, 1982, 35–46; Costello, "Alcoholism Aftercare and Outcome: Cross-lagged Panel and Parts Analyses," 33 *Brit. J. of Addictions*, 1980, 49–53; Vannicelli, "Impact of Aftercare in the Treatment of Alcoholics," 39 *J. Stud. on Alcohol*, 1978, 1875–1886; Chavapil, et al., "Outpatient Aftercare as a Factor in Treatment Outcome: A Pilot Study," 39 *J. of Stud. of Alcohol*, 1978, 540–544; Pokorny, et al., "Effectiveness of Extended Aftercare in the Treatment of Alcoholism," 34 *Q. J. of Stud. on Alcoholism*, 1973, 435–443.
10. Abrams, *supra* note 8, at 20.
11. *Id.*
12. *Id.* at 21.
13. Miller, *supra* note 1, at 16. Miller cites a 1985 personal conversation with Rick Scolette, Director of Family and Children's Services, Ithaca, N.Y.
14. Kurtz, *AA: The Story* (San Francisco: Harper & Row, 1988), at 158 (this is a revised edition of *Not-God: A History of Alcoholics Anonymous*).
15. *Alcoholics Anonymous*, 3d ed. (New York: Alcoholics Anonymous World Services, 1976), at 58–59.
16. *Id.* at 564.
17. Robertson, *Getting Better: Inside Alcoholics Anonymous* (New York: William Morrow & Co., 1988); Kurtz, *supra* note 14.
18. Vaillant, *supra* note 4.

19. *Id.* at 314.
20. *Id.*
21. *Id.* at 300.
22. *Id.* at 301.
23. Browne, Personal communications. Director, Program Services, Resource One, Inc., Greenville, S.C., June 1989.
24. *Alcoholics Anonymous, supra* note 15, at 564.
25. Marlin, *Hope: New Choices and Strategies for Adult Children of Alcoholics* (New York: Harper & Row, 1988).
26. NACoA, 31582 Coast Highway, Suite B, South Laguna, CA 92677, (714) 499-3889.
27. *Narcotics Anonymous,* 3d ed. (Van Nuys, Cal.: National Headquarters for Narcotics Anonymous, 1984). The complete address for Narcotics Anonymous is: World Service Office, National Headquarters for Narcotics Anonymous, 16155 Wyandotte St., Van Nuys, CA 91406; (818) 780-3951.
28. Cocaine Anonymous, World Services, Inc., 6125 Washington Blvd., Suite 202, Culver City, CA 90230; (213) 839-1141.
29. Overeaters Anonymous, 4025 Spencer St., Suite 203, Torrance, CA 90503. Mailing Address: P.O. Box 92870, Los Angeles, CA 90009; (213) 657-6252. Also note the American Anorexia/Bulimia Association, 133 Cedar Lane, Teaneck, NJ 07666; (201) 836-1800.
30. Gamblers Anonymous, 1543 W. Olympic, Suite 533, Los Angeles, CA 90017; (213) 386-8789.

Chapter 12

Summary and Conclusion

The problem of substance abuse in the workplace is a mirror image of the problem of substance abuse in society; that is, it is reaching epidemic proportions. The costs to business and government of workplace substance abuse is running in the hundreds of billions of dollars every year. Because of the initiatives of a number of employers through the years, some success is being achieved in conquering the problem of substance abuse in the workplace. Success is evidenced by employers who have cut some of these costs and have returned rehabilitated workers into the work force. Additionally, government initiatives have been made recently that not only address the problem in society in general, but also are beginning to assist business in waging the war for a drug free American workplace.

The legal issues surrounding employer-sponsored substance abuse programs have cleared up considerably in the last year. The Supreme Court has cleared the way for drug testing in all the cases it has reviewed thus far. Although there are still many legal issues concerning substance abuse programs which are making their way through the legal system, the right of business and government to maintain a drug free workplace is becoming clearer with every decision. If an employer develops a clear policy, procedure, and program, the legal problems encountered will be minimal. Adherence to the legal principles and to the guidelines for establishing substance abuse programs discussed in this work should assist practitioners in the substance abuse field in designing individualized employer programs that are both workable and understandable.

When an employer develops a clear policy and comprehensive procedural guidelines and properly trains managers and supervisors, the process for establishing a workable substance abuse program is well underway. Much work and thought needs to go into developing the policy and procedures of any employer's substance abuse program. The procedural detail is critical, not only from a legal standpoint, but also from a practical standpoint. Procedures must be understandable. If the managers and employees understand the company's substance abuse philosophy and the details of its program, they will be more prone to work within the program and usually will support it wholeheartedly. The importance of education concerning substance abuse matters cannot be overstressed. It is often said that the cardinal rule of employee relations is communication. This is particularly true regarding substance abuse matters. Since many people fear drugs, it is important that an employer clearly explain its substance abuse program and its efforts to keep its workplace drug free. With proper communication, both the managers and employees will feel that the substance abuse program is their own and will work actively to enforce it.

Many employers are beginning to understand that rehabilitation of substance abusing employees is a realistic and cost-effective goal. With the advent of employee assistance programs (EAPs), a mechanism now exists for coordinating substance abuse identification, rehabilitation, and return to work. The primary goals of an employee assistance program are to identify employees whose personal problems are detrimental to job performance, to motivate these people to seek and accept help, to assess their problem and personal resources, and to develop a plan of action to assist employees in getting the service they need so that they might live healthy, productive lives. EAPs can be very effective in reducing direct and indirect costs to the employer and have the net effect not only of lowering costs, but also returning rehabilitated—and far more productive—employees to the workplace. These goals can be achieved by the proper establishment of either an internally or externally located employee assistance program.

The choice of program structure will depend on the nature of the employer's business and its perceived needs. EAPs generally are tending toward a broad orientation rather than handling only substance abuse problems; it is becoming more common to find EAPs that also handle marital, legal, financial, and other problems.

An alternative to EAPs is the rehabilitation referral program. These programs refer employees who have substance abuse problems to federal, state, or local rehabilitation agencies. Generally these programs, whether oriented toward mental health, substance abuse, or vocational rehabilitation, are administered by well-meaning and qualified professionals. However, often the resources and expertise are lacking to coordinate the employees rehabilitation effectively within the context of the employer's overall substance abuse program. Many of these agencies are swamped with referrals from the general public in addition to employer referrals. It is often questionable how effective the effort to rehabilitate employees will be under these circumstances.

In most circumstances where a representative of the employer has counseled an individual employee, the decision will be made whether to refer the individual to an inpatient or an outpatient rehabilitation program. Inpatient programs evolved from the antiquated methods employed by mental institutions and sanitoriums into a much more humane, practical, and effective approach. Based on the Minnesota Model, most of these inpatient programs deal with addiction as a chronic multiphasic primary disorder and usually approach the chemical dependency problem head-on. Inpatient programs use a multidisciplinary team approach to addiction by coordinating the efforts of physicians, psychiatrists, addiction counselors, nurse-practitioners, and others. In most cases a treatment program is devised for the substance abuser consisting of individual therapy, group therapy, didactic lectures, peer group interaction, and other elements depending on the problems of the individual. Most inpatient programs are based on a 28-day hospitalization and usually are covered by a third-party insurance carrier. However, the effectiveness of hospitalization has been questioned more frequently in recent years by the government, employers, and others primarily because of the significant costs involved.

Outpatient rehabilitation programs evolved because of the need to treat a greater number of individuals at a lower cost. These programs operate on basically the same treatment format as inpatient programs but their models of administration vary considerably. The most frequently seen outpatient rehabilitation models include intensive day programs, evening programs, halfway house programs, and long-term day programs. The primary differences between inpatient and outpatient rehabilitation programs have been analyzed in terms of medical, psychiatric, and detoxification situations, discharge rates, success rates, length and intensity of treatment, socioeconomic types of patients, penetration in the workplace, insurance bias, and cost effectiveness. The basic conclusion from these comparisons is that in the vast majority of cases, outpatient treatment programs are just as effective as inpatient treatment programs at substantially less cost. Therefore, employers are urged to consider increasing the use of outpatient programs to handle substance abuse problems in the workplace.

Finally, aftercare and long-term rehabilitation programs are necessary if troubled employees are to reintegrate successfully into the workplace. The basic principles of all modern substance abuse treatment programs are based on the Twelve Step recovery program of Alcoholics Anonymous. In addition, the format of self-help groups including Narcotics Anonymous, Cocaine Anonymous, Al-Anon, Alateen, Adult Children of Alcoholics, Overeaters Anonymous, and Gamblers Anonymous are based primarily on the AA format and Twelve Steps. As employee assistance programs continue to grow, it is safe to predict that employers and EAP providers will have more contact with all of these other self-help groups than they have had in the past.

The war against drugs and the battle to obtain a drug free workplace are only beginning to be waged seriously. As more employers decide to develop substance abuse programs or are required by federal and state governments to do so, it is hoped that the ideas expressed in this work will be useful to those who want to win that war.

Appendices

Appendix A

DRUGS OF ABUSE

Descriptions and Effects of Commonly Abused Drugs

ALCOHOL—ETHYL (BEVERAGE) ALCOHOL

<u>Code Names</u>

booze, hooch, brewskis, drink

<u>Description</u>

A central nervous system sedative, beverage alcohol is a clear liquid produced by fermentation and distillation from agricultural products. 0.6 oz. of pure ethyl alcohol (1.5 oz. of 80 proof liquor) is a normal dose of beverage alcohol. This is the amount of alcohol present in a standard bar drink, a 12 oz. container of beer, and a 5 oz. glass of wine.

<u>Short-Term Effects</u>

A moderate dose of alcohol (3 drinks) depresses the inhibitory and behavioral centers of the brain. Some users may experience euphoria, a loss of inhibition, and increased self-confidence; others may become truculent and depressed. Thought processes, memory, perception, speech, and motor skills will all be impaired by a moderate dose of alcohol.
The control functions of the higher brain are exceedingly relaxed by higher doses of alcohol. Users experience highly exaggerated emotions and unpredictable mood swings. A user's thinking, judgment, perceptions, and motor functions may be critically impaired. Very high doses will induce a stupor and unconsciousness.

309

Long-Term Effects

Users who consume daily high doses of alcohol experience depression, anxiety, and permanently impaired speech, perception, and motor skills. Liver disorders such as alcoholic hepatitis and cirrhosis may develop. A chronic user of alcohol develops a physical and psychological dependence on the drug as his or her brain develops a tolerance and becomes less sensitized to alcohol's effects.

AMPHETAMINES

Code Names

speed (Benzedrine or Dexedrine), bennies, black beauties (Biphetamine), crystal (Desoxyn), pep pills, lip poppers, ice, uppers

Description

Amphetamines are central nervous system stimulants produced through chemical synthesis. Legal amphetamines manufactured by the pharmaceutical industry are white, odorless crystals or water-soluble powders. Illicit concoctions may be impure off-white or yellowish powders or crystals, or capsules and tablets in various sizes and colors. Amphetamines are swallowed, sniffed, or injected.

Short-Term Effects

Users who consume amphetamines in moderate doses up to 60 mg. experience overstimulation, restlessness, and dizziness. The user may be euphoric and can expect insomnia. Appetite may be reduced; heart rate increases. Consumption of moderate doses of amphetamines may also cause palpitations, dry mouth, headaches, increased and irregular breathing, and diarrhea. Amphetamine doses over 60 mg. produce intense exhilaration, euphoria, rapid thought pattern, and garrulousness in some users; however, other users may become depressed, paranoid, irritable, and confused. Physical manifestations of higher dosage may include excessive sweating, fever, anginal pain, and fainting. Overdoses cause coma, cerebral hemorrhage, and death.

Long-Term Effects

Long-term amphetamine abuse subjects the user to chronic sleep disruption, anxiety, lack of appetite, high blood pressure, and paranoia. Chronic abusers develop a tolerance for such effects as appetite suppression, sleep disturbance, and euphoria as they develop a physical dependence. Due to the powerful euphoria amphetamines produce, abuse potential is high. Users may inject as much as 1000 mg. every 2 or 3 hours during binges.

BARBITURATES AND RELATED DEPRESSANTS

Code Names

barbs, ludes, rainbows, 714s, downers, goofballs, blues, blue devils, yellow jackets, yellows, reds, red devils

Description

Barbiturates are sedative-hypnotic substances which are potent central nervous system depressants. They are produced by chemical synthesis. In pure form, barbiturates are white, bitter, odorless, water-soluble powders in tablets or capsules. Intravenous barbiturate forms are restricted to medical use. Secobarbital, pentobarbital, and amobarbital are common barbiturates. Other depressants include such drug groups as methaqualone (which includes Quaaludes) and benzodiazepines (which include Librium, Valium, and Xanax).

Short-Term Effects

Moderate dosages of up to 100 mg. generate tranquility, relaxation, mild euphoria, and lethargy as psychological responses for the user. But physical reactions may include impairment of motor coordination, short-term memory, and thought processes; nausea; vomiting; abdominal pain; decreased blood pressure; and lower heart rate. Doses over 200 mg. produce exaggerated levels of activity, intense and extreme emotions, impaired thinking and motor and perceptual functions, drowsiness, unconsciousness, and progressive decline in blood pressure and breathing. An overdose would depress major bodily functions and result in coma and death. Barbiturate overdose is a factor in nearly one-third of all reported drug-related deaths. There is little difference between the amount of barbiturate that produces sleep and the amount that kills.

Long-Term Effects

In the long term, barbiturate abuse causes impaired memory, judgment, and thinking; hostility, depression, or mood swings; reduced attention span; chronic fatigue; slurred speech; and impaired motor coordination. The abuse potential is very high. Tolerance to the sleep-inducing and pleasurable effects develops rapidly. Both abuse of barbiturates and withdrawal have frequently resulted in death.

CANNABIS (MARIJUANA, HASHISH)

Code Names

Mary Jane, Acapulco Gold, Colombian, grass, hemp, pot, dope, Jamaican, reefer, weed, ragweed, Thai sticks, ace, herb, tea, hash, Lebanese gold, Nepalese fingers, black Afghan

Description

Cannabis is a plant found in tropical and temperate climates. It contains a mild hallucinogenic substance called delta-9-tetra-hydrocannabinol (THC). The female plant secretes a sticky resin that covers the flowering tops and upper leaves.

Marijuana is prepared by crushing the dried flowering top and leaves into a tealike substance, which is usually rolled into a cigarette (a joint) and smoked. Hashish is prepared from the dried cannabis resin and crushed flowers, which are compressed into hard chunks or cubes and often smoked in a pipe.

Short-Term Effects

Use of a moderate dose of marijuana (one joint) produces an immediate feeling of well-being, relaxation, and emotional disinhibition. Effects of marijuana are felt within minutes, reach their peak in 10 to 30 minutes, and may linger for 2 or 3 hours. The user may also experience a distorted sense of time and distance. The user may laugh spontaneously and suffer a reduced attention span and loss of memory. There may be mild impairment of thinking and motor skills. Physically, the user may find his heart and pulse rates drop slightly, his eyes redden, and his lungs irritated. Higher doses exceeding one joint provide intensification of low-dose effects. Higher doses also cause pseudohallucinations, impaired judgment, slowed reaction time, limited motor skills, confusion of time sense, and short-term memory loss. Chronic intoxication lasting several weeks may continue after termination of use.

Long-Term Effects

In the long term, regular users of cannabis may develop a mild psychological dependence. But cannabis does not appear to cause harmful physiological effects in healthy adults who use it in moderate doses. Higher doses of cannabis, however, may cause significant psychological adjustment problems for some users. And chronic heavy smoking of cannabis increases the risk of lung cancer. The euphoric effects of cannabis are generally not as intense as those of heroin and cocaine. Abuse potential is high because cannabis is available illicitly at relatively low cost. Marijuana available today is up to 10 times more potent than that available 10 years ago.

COCAINE

Code Names

C, coke, lady, nose candy, crack, white lady, Cola, Bolivian rock, Bolivian marching powder, flake, snow, stardust, blow, Peruvian flake, mother of pearl, toot, freebase

Description

Cocaine is a powerful central nervous system stimulant of brief duration. The drug is derived from the coca bush leaf found primarily in Peru and Bolivia. Hydrochloric acid added to coca base produces a salt, cocaine hydrochloride, which is 90 to 100 percent pure cocaine. Cocaine hydrochloride is an odorless white crystalline, water-soluble powder with a bitter, numbing taste. It is usually in the form of flakes or rocks.

Crack is a very common, less expensive form of cocaine. Crack is made by mixing ordinary baking soda and cocaine that has been cut with other substances. The mixture is cooked over an open flame and dried into small rocks that resemble pieces of crumbled white soap. The rocks are smoked, usually in a glass pipe. As they are heated, they make a cracking sound; hence the name "crack."

Short-Term Effects

Moderate doses of 25 to 50 mg. produce euphoria, heightened alertness, loss of appetite, sleeplessness, elevated self-confidence, increased speed of performance, anxiety, and panic. Physical effects include increased heart and respiratory rates, constriction of blood vessels, and elevated blood pressure.

Higher doses of 100 to 300 mg. intensify the lower dosage effects. Higher doses aggravate the negative effects such as tremors, vertigo, muscular twitches, paranoia, and toxic psychosis.

Long-Term Effects

Feeling of competence and power experienced by the infrequent user surrender in the chronic user to a sense of inadequacy, impotence, depression, nervousness, excitability, agitation, paranoia, and hypersensitivity. The chronic user has pronounced mood swings, memory disturbance, and insomnia.

The powerful euphoria and multiple means of administration (nasal, oral, and intravenous) make cocaine very popular. Long-term users may consume larger doses in shorter periods of time. Eventually, their lives may be devoted exclusively to their cocaine addiction. The onset of toxic psychosis will be heralded by anxiety, restlessness, and extreme irritability: the symptoms of paranoid schizophrenia.

Cocaine is a peculiar problem in the workplace because the short-term effects enhance the ability to perform simple tasks (especially for fatigued workers) and promote self-confidence. But eventually cocaine becomes a necessary prelude to work for the addict who loses confidence in his ability to work without it. Ninety percent of users of cocaine use it at work. People who have used marijuana extensively are most at risk for cocaine addiction.

HALLUCINOGENS

Code Names

mushrooms (psilocybin), peyote (mescaline), ecstasy (M.D.A.), acid (LSD), angel dust (PCP)

Description

The various hallucinogens distort perception of time and space and create illusions and hallucinations. PCP (phencyclidine) and LSD (lysergic acid) are the most commonly used hallucinogens. Most hallucinogens are taken orally, although PCP is often smoked after it has been sprinkled on parsley, marijuana, or tobacco. LSD comes in a liquid form and most often is swallowed after being placed on a sugar cube or blotting paper.

Effects

All hallucinogens have an effect or "high" of a duration that is relatively long compared with that of other drugs. Eight hours or more is common.

PCP can create the same effects as acute mental illness. The user will undergo changes in body image, perceptual distortions evidenced as hallucinations of the eye and ear, and feelings of emptiness or nothingness. Commonly, the user will have difficulty thinking and speaking. Many users face acute psychotic episodes. LSD use frequently culminates in "bad trips"—psychological reactions including exaggerated suspicions, fears, confusion, anxiety, and loss of control. Physically, LSD increases blood pressure, heart rate, and blood sugar. Nausea, chills, flushes, irregular breathing, sweating, and trembling occur. M.D.A. has recently been linked with organic brain damage. Dependency on hallucinogens is less likely than dependency on any other commonly abused drug.

HEROIN

Code Names

dust, H, horse, Mexican brown, gum, junk, smack, China white, hombre, dope, scag

Description

Heroin is a powerful, semisynthetic narcotic analgesic produced from opium poppies harvested in Southeast and Southwest Asia and Mexico. In pure form, heroin is a fine, white, water-soluble crystalline substance. Its taste is bitter. Heroin may be snorted, smoked, or injected. Pure heroin is usually cut by sugars, starch, powdered milk, quinine, or other diluents.

Short-Term Effects

Moderate doses of 3 to 4 mg. produce mental cloudiness, euphoria, suppression of pain, and feelings of well-being. Physically, moderate doses may lower a user's body temperature as the user experiences sweating, nausea, vomiting, reduced appetite, and a relaxation of activity. Higher doses of 10 to 25 mg. intensify the psychological effects experienced with lower doses. After taking a higher dose, a user will experience decreased sensitivity and reduced ability to concentrate. His or her breathing will be slow and shallow. An overdose will produce deep sleep, stupor, coma, and death.

Long-Term Effects

Heroin used under medical supervision has not produced marked physiological or psychological deterioration. Most of the severe adverse consequences of heroin addiction are generally related to lifestyle and needle administration. The powerful dependence liability of heroin results from both its powerful euphoric and analgesic effects and its solubility. Out of all drugs of abuse, recidivism is highest among those who have tried to terminate heroin use.

INHALANTS

Code Names

solvent, rush, bolt, locker room, bullet, climax, poppers, laughing gas, whippets, buzz, bomb

Description

Inhalants include a variety of psychoactive substances which are inhaled as gases or volatile liquids. Many are readily available in most households and are inexpensive. They include paint thinner, glue, gasoline, and other products that are not considered to be drugs.

Short-Term Effects

Inhalants may cause nausea, sneezing, coughing, nose bleeds, fatigue, lack of coordination, and loss of appetite. Inhalants such as aerosol sprays may also decrease the heart and respiratory rates and impair judgment. Others may cause rapid pulse, headaches, and involuntary passing of urine and feces.

Long-Term Effects

Repeated sniffing of concentrated vapors can cause permanent nervous system damage. Long-term use can cause weight loss, fatigue, muscle weakness, hepatitis, or organic brain damage.

Appendix B

GLOSSARY OF SUBSTANCE ABUSE TERMINOLOGY

ABSTINENCE   Refrainment from using something, such as a drug, by one's own choice.

ABUSERS   People who use drugs in ways that threaten their health or impair their social or economic functioning.

ACID   Slang term for LSD (lysergic acid diethylamide).

ACTIVE PRINCIPLE   The main chemical constituent of a drug plant. Although active principles may be responsible for many of the effects of drug plants, they do not exactly reproduce those effects and in pure form have higher toxicity and potential for abuse.

ADDICTION   The point at which a person's chemical usage causes repeated harmful consequences and the person is unable to stop using the drug of choice. Medically the term implies that withdrawal will take place when the mood-changing chemical is removed from the body.

ADULT CHILDREN OF ALCOHOLICS (ACOA)   A self-help program designed for those adults who have an alcoholic parent or alcoholic parents. The program explores effects on relationships and life choices and patterns.

AFTERCARE   Continuation of the recovery process begun in treatment for the chemically dependent and his or her family. Family members may be involved in a variety of aftercare programs such as AA, Al-Anon, Alateen, growth groups, family groups, or peer groups.

AL-ANON   A fellowship of relatives and friends of alcoholics who share their experience, strength, and hope in order to solve their common problems. They believe that alcoholism is a family illness and that changed attitudes aid in recovery of the alcoholic.

ALATEEN   A fellowship of children and young persons who share their experience, strength, and hope in order to solve common problems. They believe that alcoholism is a family illness and that changed attitudes aid in recovery of the alcoholic.

ALCOHOL   A primary and continuous depressant of the central nervous system. Its effect is analogous to a general anesthetic.

ALCOHOLICS ANONYMOUS   A fellowship of men and women who share their experience, strength, and hope with each other that they may solve their common problem, and help others to recover from alcoholism. Their primary purpose is to stay sober and help other alcoholics.

ALCOHOLISM   A treatable illness brought on by harmful dependence upon alcohol, which is physically and psychologically addictive. As a disease, alcoholism is primary, chronic, progressive, and fatal.

AMPHETAMINES   Synthetic amines (uppers) that act with a pronounced stimulant effect on the central nervous system.

ANGEL DUST   Slang term for PCP (phencyclidine).

ANTIDEPRESSANTS   Pharmaceutical drugs prescribed for the treatment of persistent and severe depression. Imipramine (Tofranil) and amitriptyline (Elavil) are examples.

ANTIHISTAMINES   A large class of synthetic drugs used to relieve allergic symptoms.

APATHY   Lack of feeling, emotion, or interest in what excites most people.

BAD TRIP   An unpleasant experience on a psychoactive drug, especially a hallucinogen. This may include paranoia, panic, scary hallucinations, and depression.

BARBITURATES   Central nervous system depressants derived from barbituric acid. They have a hypnotic sedative effect.

BARBS   Barbiturates such as secobarbital.

BEHAVIORAL DISORDER   Behavior that is inappropriate and/or excessive with no implication of mental illness.

BLACKOUT   A drug-induced loss of memory which appears similar to amnesia. A person in a blackout appears to be functioning normally but will not, in fact, remember anything about what happened during that time. Blackouts can last varying lengths of time.

BUMMER   Slang term for an unpleasant experience on a psychoactive drug.

BURN-OUT   A condition of emotional and intellectual impairment that is thought to be the result of excessive use of psychoactive drugs.

CEREBRAL CORTEX The upper portion of the brain which controls intellect, abstract thoughts, and perception.

CHARACTEROLOGICAL CONFLICT The emotional distress that is created when a person's behavior is repeatedly in contradiction with his or her value system.

CHEMICAL DEPENDENCY A harmful dependence on mood-changing chemicals. Alcoholism is included in this definition.

CHRONIC Continuing indefinitely; perpetual, constant. Not curable. Alcoholism can only be arrested, not cured, so it is considered a chronic disease.

CIRRHOSIS A condition in which cells die and are replaced by scar tissue. Cirrhosis of the liver is a fatal disease, since the scar tissue cannot perform the functions of the liver.

CO-ALCOHOLIC A person close to the alcoholic who feels a responsibility for his or her condition and unwittingly aids in the progression of the disease. Co-alcoholics often manipulate the circumstances and lifestyle of alcoholics, thus removing alcoholics from responsibility for the consequences of their behavior. The co-alcoholic takes the responsibility on himself or herself.

CO-DEPENDENCY An emotional, psychological, and behavioral condition that develops as a result of an individual's prolonged exposure to, and practice of, a set of oppressive rules which prevent the open expression of feelings as well as the direct discussion of personal and interpersonal problems.

COCAINE A drug extracted from the leaves of the coca plant which grows in South America. Cocaine is a central nervous system stimulant.

COKE Slang term for cocaine.

COMPLIANCE A stage in the treatment process in which a person outwardly cooperates with the program without the accompanying internal acceptance and personal motivation. Full recovery is not possible if a person remains at this level.

COMPULSION An irresistible urge to keep repeating the same irrational behavior without the ability to stop.

CONFRONTING Telling another person how one sees him or her behaving.

CONGRUENT Allowing outside expressions and behavior to match inside feelings.

CONTINUUM OF CARE   Process by which the disease of alcoholism can be arrested. The continuum involves (1) obtaining information about the disease; (2) recognition; (3) intervention; (4) treatment; and (5) aftercare.

CONTROLLED SUBSTANCES   Plants and chemicals listed in the federal Controlled Substances Act (Pub. L. No. 91-513, Title II, 84 Stat. 1247 (1970); 21 U.S.C. §812 for Schedules of Controlled Substances), the law regulating disapproved psychoactive drugs and those approved only for medical use.

CONTROLLING   Being responsible for others (instead of to them). Needing to control others' behavior in order to feel better about one's actions to that person; needing others to act and feel in certain ways to avoid facing reality and feeling pain about it.

CRASH   To experience depression, lethargy, or sleepiness after a drug-induced high. Especially common after using stimulants.

CROSS-DEPENDENCE   Dependence on substances caused by dependence on one substance.

CROSS-TOLERANCE   Development of a tolerance for a substance as a result of tolerance for another substance.

CUT   To adulterate a drug by adding to it some substance to make it go further.

DEAL   To sell or distribute illegal drugs.

DECREASING TOLERANCE   A late stage in alcoholism when parts of the liver are no longer able to detoxify the alcohol, as cirrhosis begins to progress. Therefore, it takes less and less alcohol to bring on intoxication.

DEFENSES   Unconscious reactions which keep a person's emotions hidden from himself or herself and others. Specific defenses include: rationalization, minimizing, and feeling repression. Each defense serves to avoid the feelings a person experiences now.

DELIRIUM TREMENS (D.T.'S)   The most severe form of withdrawal from alcohol, marked by agitation, hallucinations, and other mental and physical imbalances.

DELUSION   The combination of euphoric recall, blackouts, and defense mechanisms which act to keep the alcoholic from being able to see and realize the nature, extent, and severity of his harmful dependency.

DENIAL   A symptom of addiction; inability to recognize the true nature of a problem; resistance to seeking or accepting help.

DEPRESSANTS Drugs that reduce the activity of the nervous system (alcohol, downers, and narcotics).

DETOXIFICATION Changing ethyl alcohol into chemicals not harmful to the body. It also applies to the first stage of treatment in which a person is given medical help in withdrawing from the physical effects of alcohol or other drugs.

DOPE Psychoactive drugs in general, especially illegal ones.

DOWNERS Barbiturates, minor tranquilizers, and related depressants.

DRUG ABUSE Pathological use of a prescribed or unprescribed chemical substance.

DRY DRUNK A person who is sober but still living a defensive lifestyle. Nothing is being done about the mental mismanagement. Often characterized by rigid defiance, self-hatred, and continuation of destructive patterns in social relationships.

DUI Driving Under the Influence. A drunk-driving charge under various state statutes.

DUSTER A PCP-laced joint.

DWI Driving While Intoxicated. A drunk-driving charge under various state statutes.

DYSFUNCTIONAL SYSTEM Family or group that communicates defensively within itself, reacting to one another in predictable ways. Each member is locked into a survival role, which perpetuates the system. One or more members must risk breaking the rules of the system for change to take place.

EMPLOYEE ASSISTANCE PROGRAM A worksite-based program designed to assist in the identification and resolution of productivity problems associated with employees impaired by personal concerns including, but not limited to: health, marital, family, financial, alcohol, drug, legal, emotional, stress, or other personal concerns that may adversely affect employee job performance.

ENABLER Any person who inadvertently behaves in a way that makes the alcoholic more sick.

ENABLING Allowing irresponsible and destructive behavior patterns to continue by taking responsibility for others, not allowing them to face the consequences of their own actions.

EUPHORIA A feeling of great happiness or well-being.

EUPHORIC RECALL   The distorted perception of reality due to the chemical's effect on the central nervous system. The distortion causes the person to recall the feelings of intoxication but not his or her behavior while intoxicated.

FAMILY DISEASE   Chemical dependency is a family disease because the family is unable to get "separatedness" from the chemical problem. In its communication within itself as well as in its response to the outside world, the entire family revolves around the chemically dependent member, whose life in turn revolves around a chemical.

FIX   Slang term for a dose of a mood-altering drug, especially an intravenous dose of an opiate.

FLASHBACK   A recurrence of symptoms associated with LSD or other hallucinogens some time after the actual drug experience.

FREEBASE   A smokable form of cocaine.

GROUP THERAPY   A forum in which people with common needs get together to discover themselves as feeling persons and to find alternative ways of dealing with life's problems.

HALFWAY HOUSE   Residence for those who need daily support and confrontation as they restructure their lives as chemically free members of society.

HALLUCINATION   The perception of something that is not there, such as seeing pink elephants or hearing voices that other people cannot hear. Can be a symptom of physical or mental illness, or the result of taking some kinds of psychoactive drugs.

HALLUCINOGENS   Drugs that stimulate the nervous system and produce varied changes in perception and mood.

HARMFUL DEPENDENCE   The point in the progression of the disease where the individual experiences growing preoccupation with drug usage, increasing tolerance to the effect of the drug, a lifestyle that is changing to accommodate the increased usage, and repeated harmful consequences resulting from drug use.

HASH   Slang term for hashish.

HASH OIL   A dark, syrupy liquid obtained by extracting the resin of marijuana with solvents and concentrating it.

HASHISH   The concentrated resin of the marijuana plant.

HEROIN   A semisynthetic derivative of morphine originally used as an analgesic and cough depressant. In harmful doses it induces euphoria; tends to make the user think he or she is removed from reality, tension, and pressures.

HIGH   An altered state of consciousness, marked by euphoria, feelings of lightness, self-transcendence, and energy.

IMPAIR   To weaken, make worse, lessen in power, or affect in an injurious manner.

INTERVENTION   Carefully planned meeting in which those closest to a chemically dependent person, having recognized signs of the disease, talk with the person about the harmful effects of the person's behavior upon his or her welfare and encourage the person to seek help.

INTRAMUSCULAR   Within a muscle, such as the injection of a drug into the muscle of an arm or leg.

INTRAVENOUS   Within a vein, such as the injection of a drug directly into the bloodstream.

JOINT   A marijuana cigarette.

JUNK   Slang term for narcotics.

JUNKIE   A heroin addict.

LETTING GO   Realizing that a situation or another person's behavior is out of one's control. Giving up the fight to gain control.

LEVELING   Telling another person how one feels.

LIMBUS   The middle part of the brain which controls emotions. It is affected by mood-changing (psychoactive) drugs.

LIVER HEPATITIS   A condition in which the liver cells enlarge in order to process large amounts of alcohol. It is reversible if drinking ceases completely. It is a dangerous condition.

LOCKED IN   Being unable to stop reacting to others, using defenses compulsively, and manipulating compulsively.

LOOK-ALIKE DRUGS   Tablets and capsules made to resemble pharmaceutical stimulants and depressants.

LUDES   Tablets of methaqualone (Quaalude).

MAGIC MUSHROOM   Mushroom that contains the natural hallucinogen psilocybin.

NARCOTICS   A class of depressant drugs derived from opium or related chemically to compounds in opium. Regular use leads to addiction.

NURTURING SYSTEM   Family or group whose members have high self-worth, communicate openly and honestly, and share excitement in spontaneous interaction with one another and the outside world.

OBSESSION   Persistent thought or desire to do something or have something.

OTC   Over-the-Counter, referring to drugs sold legally without prescription.

POLYDRUG USE   The consumption of more than one drug at the same time.

POP   To swallow a drug in pill form.

POT   Slang term for marijuana.

POTENCY   The measure of relative strength of similar drugs.

PRIMARY DISEASE   A disease that is not just a symptom of some underlying disorder. Chemical dependency is an example of a primary disease.

PSYCHEDELICS   Synonym for hallucinogens.

PSYCHOACTIVE DRUGS   Drugs that affect the mind, especially mood, thought, or perception.

REACTION TIME   The time interval between the application of a stimulus and the detection of a response.

RECOVERY   The process that leads to a change of attitudes and behavior and that makes it possible to begin a new and positive way of life, lived one day at a time.

RECREATIONAL DRUGS   Any drugs used nonmedically for enjoyment or entertainment.

REFLEX   A simple nervous circuit. For example, a tendon reflex is initiated by striking a tendon; this stimulus travels to the spinal cord along a single nerve and quickly produces a response in another nerve that causes a contraction in the muscle.

REHABILITATE   To restore to a condition of health and useful and constructive activity.

RELAPSE   A behavior pattern whereby the symptoms of the disease (alcoholism, co-dependency, etc.) become reactivated. To use or repeat addictive behaviors, with or without the use of chemicals.

RUSH   A sudden, dramatic change in consciousness and body sensation resulting from taking certain psychoactive drugs by inhalation or injection.

SLEEPING PILLS   Barbiturates and related sedative-hypnotics.

SNIFF   To inhale the fumes of organic solvents to produce changes in consciousness.

SNORT   To inhale a powdered drug.

SOBRIETY   A chemical free life.

SPEED   Stimulants, especially amphetamines.

SPEEDBALL   A combination of a stimulant and depressant, especially cocaine and heroin, intended for intravenous use.

STEROIDS   A large family of pharmaceutical drugs related to the adrenal hormone cortisone.

STIMULANTS   Drugs that increase the activity of the nervous system, causing wakefulness.

STONED   Intoxicated on a psychoactive drug.

STREET DRUGS   Psychoactive drugs manufactured and sold illegally.

SURVIVAL ROLES   Behavior adopted by family members to cover feelings in an attempt to maintain equilibrium in a dysfunctional system.

TRAFFICKING   In drug law, the distribution, sale, exchange, or giving away of significant amounts of prohibited substances.

TREATMENT   Program in which the chemically dependent person and his or her family begin the process of recovery from the disease. Each member receives information about the disease and recognizes his or her participation in the disease by examining past and present behavior. The family then works together to develop a nurturing system.

TUNNEL VISION   A narrow or one-sided attitude. A person with tunnel vision is unable or unwilling to broaden his or her perspective.

UPPERS   Stimulants.

USERS   People who use psychoactive drugs in a nonabusive way (as opposed to abusers).

WHOLENESS   A feeling of freedom to be oneself. Having high self-worth, taking responsibility for oneself, and letting others do the same. A process which begins inside and involves recognizing and developing one's physical, mental, social, emotional, spiritual, and will powers.

WINDOWPANE   Slang term for LSD in the form of tiny, transparent gelatin chips.

WITHDRAWAL   Symptoms that appear during the process of stopping the use of a drug that has been taken regularly.

Appendix C

MODEL POLICY, PROCEDURE, AND PROGRAM

Manufacturing/Service Company

MODEL SUBSTANCE ABUSE PROGRAM
Substance Abuse Policy

As a part of (Company's) commitment to safeguarding the health of its employees, to providing a safe place for its employees to work, and to supplying its customers with the highest quality products and service possible, this policy establishes the Company's position on the use or abuse of alcohol, drugs, or other controlled substances by its employees. Because substance abuse, either while at work or away from work, can seriously endanger the safety of employees and render it impossible to supply top-quality products and service, the (Company) has established this program to detect users and remove abusers of alcohol, drugs, or other controlled substances. (Company) is committed to preventing the use and/or presence of these substances in the workplace. It is also the policy of (Company) to provide as an employee benefit the (Company) Employee Assistance Program in order to deal with substance abuse and other problems that the Company's employees and their families may encounter.

The intent of this policy is:

(1) To provide clear guidelines and consistent procedures for handling incidents of employees' use of alcohol, drugs, or controlled substances that affect job performance, and to make every effort to institute and maintain a drug free workplace.

(2) To ensure that employees conform to all state and federal regulations regarding alcohol, drugs, or controlled substances.

(3) To provide substance abuse prevention education for all employees and supervisory training regarding problem recognition and the implementation of this policy.

(4) To offer assistance to employees and their family members in resolving problems which affect job performance.

The essential parts of this program are as follows:

(1) (Company) prohibits the unlawful manufacture, distribution, dispensation, presence, or use of alcohol, drugs, or other controlled substances on its property or worksites. Employees violating this prohibition will be referred to the (Company) EAP, or disciplined up to and including termination.

(2) (Company) will present a Drug Free Awareness Education Program for all supervisors and employees on a periodic basis.

(3) (Company) will utilize drug testing to help administer this policy. The following types of testing will be used:

 a. All applicants will be tested.

 b. Employees will be tested for cause.

 c. Eligible employees will be tested as part of annual or biennial physical examinations.

 d. Employees who occupy sensitive positions from a safety and health or security standpoint, including all transportation positions, will either be randomly tested, or tested on at least an annual basis.

 e. Employees will be tested where required by a customer's program or by contract with a federal or state agency.

 f. Employees will be tested following accidents where required by law or under this policy.

 g. Employees will be tested when returning from a lengthy absence from duty.

 h. Employees will be tested pursuant to (Company's) Employee Assistance Program.

(4) This policy applies to all applicants and employees of (Company).

(5) The (Company) Employee Assistance Program (EAP) is available to all employees and their families for the purpose of dealing with alcohol or drug problems before these problems become serious enough to affect job performance or become life-threatening.

(6) On projects covered by the Drug Free Workplace Act or other federal or state contracts, laws, or regulations, all employees will be given a copy of this policy, be required to notify the Company of any conviction for violation of a criminal drug statute in the workplace within five days, and acknowledge receipt of this policy by signing the Employee Acknowledgement Form.

Substance Abuse Procedures

A. Drug Free Awareness Education Program

 1. All employees are to be informed of (Company's) Substance Abuse Program, and be made aware of its contents.

2. In order to protect the safety and health of its employees, the Company will present a Drug Free Awareness Education Program to all supervisors and employees on a periodic basis. The education program will consist of materials presented over at least 60 minutes of time concerning the dangers of drug abuse in the workplace, the (Company's) policy for a drug free workplace, available counseling and treatment through the Company's EAP, and the penalties for violating the Company's Substance Abuse Program. Company officials will obtain or develop quality materials in order to continue to educate employees on the symptoms of, the problems caused by, and the developments related to, alcohol, drugs or other controlled substances, and the promotion of a healthy lifestyle.

3. Management and supervisory personnel will also receive training on at least an annual basis regarding the symptoms of alcohol and drug abuse. Their training will include, but not be limited to, the following:

   a. Recognition/observation;
   b. Documentation;
   c. Confrontation/intervention;
   d. Referral; and
   e. Reintegration procedures.

B. Explanation of Terms—Legal Drugs/Illegal Drugs/Controlled Substances

   1. Legal Drugs

   Legal drugs include alcohol, medications prescribed by a physician, and over-the-counter medications. (Company) prohibits the use or abuse of such drugs to the extent that job performance or fitness for duty is adversely affected. Employees shall notify their supervisor when taking prescribed medication. Upon request, the employee shall furnish the Company with the physician's statement regarding the possible/probable side effects of the medication.

   2. Illegal Drugs

   Illegal drugs include those controlled substances under federal or state law which are not authorized for sale, possession, or use and legal drugs which are obtained or distributed illegally. The manufacture, use, possession, sale, purchase, or transfer of illegal drugs by an employee is prohibited. Arriving on Company property or jobsites while under the influence of an illegal drug is prohibited.

C. Testing of Applicants

   1. All applicants will be informed of (Company's) Substance Abuse Program.

2. All applicants will be drug tested as a part of the application process.
3. Applicants will be advised of the testing requirements in detail by an authorized (Company) official prior to an offer of hire. The Substance Abuse Program will be explained to all applicants, and applicants must complete, sign, and date a Chemical Screening Consent and Release Form and their signature must be witnessed and dated. An application will not be processed further unless the applicant submits to the testing procedure.
4. Applicants will be furnished a test kit by the company physician, official, or designated laboratory who is responsible for assuring the specimen is properly collected and transmitted to the testing company in accordance with directions on the testing kit and the proper chain of custody. If the physician, official, or lab personnel has a reasonable suspicion that the specimen has been tampered with by the applicant, the applicant should not be considered any further for employment and should be so advised.
5. The applicant's ability to meet (Company) medical standards will be transmitted directly to the Company President or Designated Official who will keep the results strictly confidential. If an applicant's test is positive, he will not be considered for employment at that time and will be so informed that he has failed to meet Company medical standards. The applicant will be offered referral to professional evaluation at the applicant's own expense. (See Applicant Referral Form.)

D. Testing of Employees—Selection Procedures
1. For-Cause Testing—Current employees may be asked to submit to a test if cause exists to indicate that their health or ability to perform work may be impaired. Factors which could establish cause include, but are not limited to:
   a. Sudden changes in work performance;
   b. Repeated failure to follow instructions or operating procedures;
   c. Violation of Company safety policies;
   d. Involvement in an accident, or near-accident;
   e. Discovery or presence of substances in an employee's possession or near the employee's workplace;
   f. Odor of alcohol and/or residual odor peculiar to some chemical or controlled substances;
   g. Unexplained and/or frequent absenteeism;
   h. Personality changes or disorientation; and
   i. Arrest or conviction for violation of a criminal drug statute.
   If the Company President or other authorized Company official believes cause exists, or has a reasonable suspicion that an employee may be impaired or using substances, these findings and observations will be documented on the Substance Abuse Investi-

gation Form. Upon review and approval by the Company President, or Designated Official, the employee will be asked to consent to a test(s) and sign a Chemical Screening Consent and Release Form.

2. Annual or Biennial Testing—Drug testing will be performed on eligible employees as part of annual physical examinations or biennial physical examinations where the examinations are required by law, regulation, or Company policy.

3. Sensitive-Position Testing—All employees whose work is classified as "sensitive" from a safety and health or security standpoint either by company officials, by the requirements of a federal or state contract, or by federal or state law, will be randomly tested, or tested on at least an annual basis. The random testing procedures will be put into effect on a nondiscriminatory basis by use of randomly selected social security numbers, or alternative procedures which will be explained to all affected employees. Drug testing of employees in sensitive positions is mandatory and a condition of either future or continued employment. Sensitive positions as determined by law usually include employees who have access to classified information, employees in positions that involve National Security, health, or safety, or functions that require a high degree of trust and confidence. All transportation positions will be subject to this requirement. These positions also include those requiring the operation of Company vehicles, machinery, or equipment, or the handling of hazardous materials, the mishandling of which may place fellow employees or the general public at risk of serious injury, or the nature of which would create a security risk in the workplace. Employees in sensitive positions will be notified of their status and the requirement of drug testing.

4. Customer Substance Abuse Program Testing—All employees who have access to customer facilities who have contractor or vendor substance abuse programs will be requested to submit to drug testing in compliance with those customer programs. Whenever possible the drug testing and certification for customer substance abuse programs will be coordinated with the Company's other drug testing provisions.

5. Post-Accident Testing—All employees involved in reportable accidents will be drug tested for the use of controlled substances as soon as possible after the reportable accident, where the testing is required by law. Any employee who is seriously injured and cannot provide a specimen at the time of the accident shall provide the necessary authorization for obtaining hospital records and other documents that would indicate whether there were any controlled substances in the employee's system.

6. Return to Service/Post-Rehabilitation Testing—Employees who return to service after an extended period of time away from employment with the Company (usually six months or greater) will be required to submit to drug testing. Additionally, employees who have been referred to rehabilitation through the Company EAP will be tested before they return to the job.

7. Other Testing Programs—Employees may be required to submit to drug testing when required by federal or state law, regulation, or by contractual obligation, not otherwise anticipated by the provisions of this policy. In the event that other drug testing is required, every effort will be made to coordinate new testing requirements with the Company's other drug testing provisions.

E. Testing of Employees—Testing and Post-Test Procedures

1. All testing will be done by a lab chosen by the Company President. The Company will determine the controlled substances for which testing will be performed.

2. If an initial drug test is positive, a confirmation test will be performed on the same specimen using Gas Chromatography/Mass Spectrometry (GC/MS).

3. The Company may utilize breathalyzers or other testing procedures to detect alcohol use or possible impairment of employees. Positive breathalyzer results should be confirmed by a blood test at a local hospital or medical facility if possible. If alcohol use or possible impairment is suspected, an employee should be treated in the same fashion as other for-cause investigations, including use of the Substance Abuse Investigation Form and the Chemical Screening Consent and Release Form.

4. Once selected for a drug test under this policy, an employee will be required to sign a Chemical Screening Consent and Release Form. If the employee refuses to sign the Chemical Screening Consent and Release Form when knowingly able, he or she will be either referred to the (Company) EAP or terminated, depending on the circumstances.

5. The procedure for collecting and testing the specimens is the same as for applicants. An authorized Company official will explain to the employee the testing procedures and the Company's Substance Abuse Program.

6. All results are to be kept confidential. The employee will be informed of the results by the Company President or Designated Official. Employees with negative test results may return to work. A confirmed positive test will result in referral of the employee to the Company's EAP for assessment, which may include suitable medical treatment and/or rehabilitation.

7. Alternatively, employees with a confirmed positive test result may, at their option and expense, have a second confirmation test made on the same specimen. An employee will not be allowed to submit another specimen for testing.

8. If an employee refuses to seek the assistance of the (Company's) EAP after testing positive and being informed of Company policy, he or she may be terminated for violation of Company policy and failing to meet Company medical standards, or the employee may be given the opportunity to resign.

9. If an employee agrees to enter the (Company's) EAP, a Company official will stay in contact with the employee's physician or counselor during the treatment to assure that the employee is in compliance with the prescribed treatment. The employee will be placed on medical leave during his or her absence. Once the Company has been informed in writing by the physician or counselor that the employee is again suitable for employment, before the employee may be reinstated, the employee must sign the Surveillance Agreement Form and agree to random drug testing for a period of one year.

10. After signing the Surveillance Agreement Form and before returning to work, the employee must test negative on the drug test.

11. An employee awaiting pending test results may be placed on probationary status, and may be sent home without pay during the time required for a specimen to be evaluated.

F. Searches

1. At the request of the Company President, based upon suspicion or evidence of sale, possession, or use of controlled substances, an employee shall be required to:

   a. Submit to the search of their person and/or any personal article brought upon Company premises, Company worksite, or while on Company business.

   b. Submit to seizure of any controlled substance found in their possession. Suspected illegal substances will be turned over to appropriate law enforcement authorities. Employees will be required to furnish the company with a physician's name and/or prescription for confirmation of the prescription of a legal substance found in the employee's possession.

   c. Submission to a personal search or search of personal articles as used above shall include the search of any vehicle brought upon Company premises, worksites, or used on Company business. A personal search also includes a search of items within the employee's work area.

   d. Failure to submit to a search will result in termination.

G. Disciplinary Action

1. Any employee engaging in the use of alcohol while on Company property, Company worksite, or while on Company business or who reports for duty under the effects of alcohol will be removed from the workplace, required to undergo testing, referred to the EAP, or disciplined up to and including termination;

2. Any employee engaged in the use, possession, purchase, sale, or transfer of any illegal drug while on Company property, worksites, or while on Company business will be removed from the workplace, required to undergo testing, referred to the EAP, or disciplined up to and including termination and may be subject to criminal investigation and/or prosecution.

3. If an employee is arrested or convicted for driving under the influence or for violation of a criminal drug statute, the Company President or Designated Official will thoroughly investigate all of the circumstances, and Company officials may utilize the drug testing procedure if cause is established by the investigation. After the investigation has been completed the Company President will determine the best course of action to be undertaken for the benefit of the Company and the individual. At a minimum the individual will be removed from the worksite, required to seek counseling in the Company EAP, and may be disciplined up to and including termination depending on the circumstances.

4. If an employee is convicted for violation of a criminal drug statute in the workplace, the employee must notify the Company within five days of the conviction. The Company in turn will notify the contracting agency of the employee's conviction for violation of a criminal drug statute in the workplace within ten days. Employees convicted of violating criminal drug statutes in the workplace will be removed from the workplace, referred to the EAP, or disciplined up to and including termination.

H. Employee Assistance Program

1. The (Company) recognizes alcoholism, drug abuse, and psychological adjustment problems as treatable conditions. Employees are encouraged to voluntarily seek assistance prior to there being cause for disciplinary action. Employees having such problems will be accommodated by the granting of leaves of absence. The purpose of this program is to assist all employees whose work performance or behavior is being adversely affected by certain non-work-related problems. It is in the best interest of both the employee and the Company that referral for professional assistance be voluntary, and in lieu of disciplinary action.

2. Employee Assistance Programs (EAPs) are primarily designed to help employees and their families with any problem which is related to deteriorating job performance of the employee. Examples of some problems include not only substance abuse, but legal, financial, or personal problems, psychological or psychiatric disorders, and marital/family problems. The problem may not be job related but will eventually affect job performance. The intent of this aspect of the policy is to rehabilitate the employee, not just to take punitive action against the employee.

3. The EAP will provide education, encouragement, and assistance as well as referral services for assessment and rehabilitation. The EAP may also be able to assist the employee in seeking rehabilitative services through medical insurance.

4. Voluntary Referral—Employees may avail themselves of the EAP services at any time they feel they need to seek help with a problem which is causing or may cause their job performance to decline. The employee may contact the Designated Official within the Company or contact an outside source directly for an assessment.

5. Management Referral—This type of referral is based on observation and documentation of deteriorating job performance by supervisory personnel or by suspected or actual behavior as set forth in this policy. Referrals may consist of assessment through the EAP service and/or a medical assessment including drug testing. An employee will be asked to consent to referral and sign the Employee Assistance Program Referral Agreement.

6. Strict confidentiality shall be maintained during any phase of intervention, EAP services, assessment, testing, rehabilitative process, and during the follow-up procedure. This shall apply to both voluntary referrals and management referrals.

7. Acceptance of EAP services, including treatment and/or counseling, shall necessitate management to follow up with the EAP regarding the employee's progress and/or completion of treatment and any aftercare procedure. All details are strictly confidential and management shall only be concerned with the satisfactory completion of each phase of rehabilitation. All decisions regarding counseling and/or treatment shall be made by a joint decision of management and the EAP.

8. Medical benefits are provided in accordance with the Company's health insurance plan. The Company's medical coverage will cover certain expenses incurred during the treatment for alcoholism or other drug addictions. Coverage may vary depending upon: type of policy, policy limits, treatment type, and whether treatment is rendered as inpatient or outpatient. Coverage may or may not apply to outside counseling services. For additional information or clarification of benefits, employees should contact their Personnel Department. All other costs of treatment for rehabilitation will be the responsibility of the employee.

9. Treatment for alcoholism and other drug addictions is regarded as any other illness or disability. If eligible, employees may apply for these benefits as conditioned by their group coverage.

10. Any employee who exhibits chronic behavioral problems should be viewed as one who may possibly be in need of this program. Particularly where substance abuse is suspected, or perceived to be a likely cause of performance deficiency, the employee should be advised to seek counseling with the (Company's) EAP.

11. If an employee enters the (Company's) EAP, arrangements will be made by the Company President or Designated Official to accommodate or rearrange the work schedule of the affected employee.

12. If an employee refuses to cooperate with the counselors of the (Company's) EAP after having been referred to the program because of testing positive, he or she may be terminated for violation of Company policy and failing to meet Company medical standards, or the employee may be given the opportunity to resign.

13. If an employee has been referred to the (Company's) EAP due to testing positive, and in the opinion of the Program counselor the employee is able to continue working while undergoing therapy, the employee must sign the Surveillance Agreement Form and agree to random drug testing during the period of counseling in the program and for a period of one year. If the employee tests positive during the year, he or she will be terminated.

14. Upon the completion of rehabilitation, the EAP counselor will certify to the Company President or the Designated Official that the employee may return to work. The employee must then test negative on the drug test and sign the Surveillance Agreement Form agreeing to random testing for a period of one year. If the employee tests positive during that year, he or she will be terminated. However, upon successful completion of all tests during the one-year period, all records of the employee's substance abuse problem will be removed from the employee's personnel records.

I. Miscellaneous Matters

1. This Substance Abuse Program policy primarily governs Company actions in the area of alcohol, drugs, or other controlled substances. Other Company policies may be applicable in this area to the extent they do not conflict with this policy.

2. In any of the selection or testing situations described in this policy, if prescription drugs are detected and the applicant or employee is able to prove medical or professional authorization for the prescription, the Company reserves the right to contact the individual's physician or professional, or the Company officials may send the individual to the Company physician for verification and review of the situation.

3. No part of this policy, nor any of the procedures thereunder, is intended to affect the Company's right to manage its workplace, to discipline its employees, or guarantee employment, continued employment, or terms or conditions of employment. The Substance Abuse Program in no way creates an obligation or contract of employment. The Company reserves the right to alter or amend the program at any time at its sole discretion.

4. If any part of this policy is determined to be void or unenforceable under state or federal law, the remainder of the policy, to the extent possible, will remain in full force and effect.

Manufacturing/Service Company

Model Substance Abuse Program

CHEMICAL SCREENING CONSENT AND RELEASE FORM

I, _____, hereby acknowledge that I have been informed of the Company's Substance Abuse Program and agree to be bound by this program thereby for purposes of applying for, accepting, or continuing employment with the Company. I also hereby state that I am not a user of controlled substances except as listed below under medical supervision.

I understand and consent freely and voluntarily to the Company's request for a urine or other specimen or sample. I hereby release and hold harmless the Company, the laboratory, their employees, agents, and contractors from any liability arising from this request to furnish this or any specimen or sample, the testing of the specimen or sample, and any decisions made concerning my application for employment or my continued employment, based upon the results of the tests. I consent to allow any Company employee, designated physician, laboratory, hospital, or medical professional to perform appropriate chemical tests for the presence of alcohol, drugs, or other controlled substances. I give my permission to any Company employee, designated physician, laboratory, hospital, or medical professional to release the results of these tests to the Company, and I release any such designated institution or person from any liability whatsoever arising from the release of this information.

I have taken within the past 30 days or am presently taking the following medications:

Name of Drug	Condition for Which Taken	Prescribing Physician
_____	_____	_____
_____	_____	_____
_____	_____	_____
_____	_____	_____

I hereby consent to allow (Company) or its designated representative to verify and/or confirm the above information with the prescribing physician listed above.

I certify that I have been furnished Test Kit No. ___ and that the bottle in that kit was personally given by me to the company physician or laboratory personnel and contained a specimen of my urine.

_____   _____   _____
President or   Applicant/Employee Signature   Date
Designated Official
(Company)

Manufacturing/Service Company

Model Substance Abuse Program

REFERRAL NOTICE

You have indicated on your Chemical Screening Consent and Release Form that you are not a user of any controlled substances. However, our screening test has revealed the presence of a controlled substance.

As a result, you will not be considered for employment at this time. However, you may elect to receive professional evaluation and/or to enter a rehabilitation program (at your own expense) at a facility approved by the Company. After successful completion, you may reapply for a position with our Company.

President or Designated Official   Date
(Company)

I acknowledge receipt of this notice.

Applicant's Signature   Date

Manufacturing/Service Company

Model Substance Abuse Program

EMPLOYEE ACKNOWLEDGMENT FORM

I, _____, hereby acknowledge that the (Company's) Substance Abuse Program has been reviewed and explained to me, and that I have received a copy of the Company's substance abuse policy.

I further acknowledge the following:

1. That I have been notified that the unlawful manufacture, distribution, dispensation, possession, or use of alcohol, drugs, or other controlled substances is prohibited in the Company's workplace, and that violations of these prohibitions will subject me to referral to the Company's EAP or termination;

2. That the Company has presented its Drug Free Awareness Education Program to me concerning the dangers of drug abuse in the workplace, and the availability of drug counseling, rehabilitation, and the Company's EAP;

3. That as a condition of continued employment, I will abide by the Company's Substance Abuse Program, and if convicted of a violation of a criminal drug statute in the workplace, I will notify the Company within five days of the conviction.

I understand and agree to the above terms and conditions of employment. I understand that the above in no way creates an obligation or contract of employment and that I, as well as the Company, have the right to end the employment relationship at any time.

Employee Name _____
              (Please Print)

Social Security # _____

Date _____

_____   _____
Employee Signature   Company Witness

Manufacturing/Service Company

Model Substance Abuse Program

SUBSTANCE ABUSE INVESTIGATION FORM

I, _____, have observed the following condition(s) affecting the work of _____, which give rise to suspicion of substance abuse, and request an investigation of same:

Condition(s) observed: _____

_____

_____

_____

Date: _____   _____
                              Supervisor

Cause exists for medical and/or drug tests of this employee.

Date: _____   _____
                              President or Designated Official
                              (Company)

Manufacturing/Service Company

Model Substance Abuse Program

EMPLOYEE ASSISTANCE PROGRAM REFERRAL AGREEMENT

I acknowledge my identification as a user of alcohol, drugs, or other controlled substances. I recognize my obligation to meet the medical standards of the (Company) to maintain my eligibility for employment. Therefore, I agree to accept referral to the (Company) Employee Assistance Program in order to maintain abstinence from any controlled substance.

Further, I agree and give my permission to _____, or its designated representative as the EAP counselor, to release to and inform the President or Designated Official of the (Company) of the status of my rehabilitation, my completion of the program, or my abandonment of the prescribed treatment.

I further understand that my abandonment of the prescribed EAP treatment program prior to completion of the program as determined by the EAP counselor, may result in the termination of my employment for violation of Company policy and failure to meet Company medical standards.

President or Designated Official (Company)	Employee Signature	Date

Manufacturing/Service Company

Model Substance Abuse Program

SURVEILLANCE AGREEMENT

I acknowledge that the (Company's) Substance Abuse Prevention Program has been explained to me and that I understand that policy and program. I further acknowledge that the Company policy prohibits the presence, use, sale, or distribution of alcohol, drugs, or other controlled substances in the workplace, and that violations of this policy may lead to discipline up to and including termination.

I recognize my obligation to meet the medical standards of (Company) to maintain my eligibility for employment. Therefore, I agree to adhere to Company policy and maintain abstinence from all controlled substances and any controlled agent that may affect my work performance unless medically prescribed.

Check Appropriate Line:

_____ Employee—Safety Sensitive Position

I agree, when requested by Company officials, to submit to unannounced random drug surveillance tests at any time. I understand that a positive test result shall be cause for referral to the (Company) Employee Assistance Program or other disciplinary actions which may be taken in accordance with Company policy.

_____ Employee—Post-Rehabilitation

I agree, when requested by Company officials, to submit to an unannounced random drug surveillance test at any time for a period of at least one year from _____ through _____. I understand that a positive test result shall be cause for immediate discharge from my employment for failing to meet Company medical standards.

I understand that refusal or failure to submit to a random drug surveillance test shall be cause for immediate discharge from my employment for failing to meet Company medical standards. I understand and agree to the above terms and conditions of employment. I also understand that the above does not in any way create a contract for employment.

Employee _____
(Please Print)

SSN _____

_____
President or Designated Official
(Company)

_____
Employee Signature   Location

Date _____

Appendix D

SUBSTANCE ABUSE POLICIES

Example 1: Large Manufacturing Company (LMC)

SUBSTANCE ABUSE PROGRAM

As a part of the LMC's commitment to safeguarding the health of its employees, to providing a safe place for its employees to work, and to supplying its customers with the highest quality products and service possible, this policy establishes the Company's position on the use or abuse of alcohol, drugs, and other psychoactive substances by its employees. Because substance abuse, whether while at work or otherwise, can seriously endanger the safety of employees and render it impossible to supply top quality products and service, the Company has established this program to detect users and remove abusers of alcohol, drugs, or other psychoactive substances. The LMC is committed to preventing the use and/or presence of these substances in the workplace. It is also the policy of the LMC to provide as an employee benefit the LMC Employee Assistance Program in order to deal with substance abuse and other problems that the company's employees and their families may encounter. The essential parts of this program are as follows:

(1) The company prohibits the presence or use of alcohol, drugs, or other psychoactive substances on its property;

(2) The Company will present a substance abuse education program for all employees on a periodic basis;

(3) Applicants for full-time employment will be screened and tested to detect illegal substance use;

(4) All employees will be screened and tested on a one-time basis upon implementation of this policy;

(5) Drug screening test(s) will be performed on all employees on an annual basis;

(6) Where cause exists to believe that an employee is impaired or under the influence of these substances, a confidential investigation, including drug screening, will be undertaken to detect sub-

stance abuse. If substances are detected, appropriate referral for professional evaluation in the LMC EAP, or discipline, will be implemented;

(7) Where a customer requires drug screening for the LMC's employees with regular access to their premises, these employees will be tested and recertified in compliance with the customer's program on a random basis once each year.

Example 2: Large Service Company (LSC)

The LSC is committed to providing a safe, productive work environment for its employees and to providing safe, quality products and services for our customers and the public. To meet this commitment, the company has adopted this policy on alcohol and drugs.

The company recognizes the dangers of alcohol and drug abuse and desires to help its employees avoid such dangers. The company will disseminate educational materials about alcohol and drugs and the effects of these substances. The company will also sponsor, from time to time, lectures and seminars on selected substance abuse topics. Coordinators will be available throughout LSC's North American Operations to answer individual questions. A training program will be implemented for managers and supervisors to increase their awareness of substance abuse problems in the work place and to ensure the effective enforcement of this policy.

LSC employees are prohibited from the illegal use, possession, sale, purchase, distribution, or transportation of drugs, and the unauthorized use, possession, or transportation of alcohol on company premises, at company work sites, or on company time. Employees are prohibited from reporting to work or being at work while unable to perform their jobs as safely and efficiently as possible because of alcohol or drug use.

The company requires employees to report to work and remain in a condition satisfactory to perform their duties safely and effectively while at work. To achieve this objective, the company will enforce this policy through an alcohol and drug testing program.

All applicants for employment are required to take and pass a drug test, except for field hourly applicants currently working in this industry and employees transferring from other LSC operations. Active employees may be required to take alcohol or drug tests following a medical evaluation when a reasonable, objective basis exists to believe that the employees may be impaired in their job performance due to substance abuse.

LSC employees believed to have substance abuse problems will be referred to, and may participate in, the Employee Assistance Program. The program is designed to help employees suffering from alcohol or drug abuse problems to rehabilitate themselves and return to their jobs. Participation in the EAP does not exempt an employee from disciplinary action.

Any employee who refuses to comply with this policy or who tests positive for alcohol or drugs may be subject to disciplinary action, up to and including discharge.

This policy applies to all LSC employees at all facilities, locations, and work sites in the United States. The Personnel Department will maintain detailed procedures for the implementation and administration of this policy. The support and cooperation of each LSC employee is essential to our success in achieving our goal of a safe, productive work environment.

Example 3: Small City Government (SCG)

ALCOHOL AND CONTROLLED SUBSTANCE POLICY

It is recognized that the use and abuse of alcohol and controlled substances is one of the greatest health problems in the United States, one that touches every community and that is epidemic in scope.

The use of controlled substances at any time by any SCG employee constitutes a direct threat to the lives and property of citizens and the public health, safety, and welfare of all persons in the city and creates a situation fraught with serious consequences to the general public at large. Additionally, the use of alcohol by an SCG employee in a manner that affects his or her job performance or brings discredit upon the city constitutes a similar threat to the public. Accordingly, if an employee's personal habits or health problems affect his or her job performance, good management compels the SCG to become involved with these problems and the legitimate interest of the SCG in becoming so involved must include a program designed to ensure that SCG employees do not engage in drug abuse on or off the job or in alcohol abuse in a manner that affects their job performance or brings discredit upon the city.

Recognizing the problem of alcohol and controlled substance abuse and its potential danger is an important part of the solution to the problem. It then becomes incumbent upon the SCG, in the exercise of its duty and responsibility to safeguard and protect the safety, health, peace, security, good order, comfort, convenience, morals, and general welfare to not only identify the problem, but to undertake a solution of and to defeat the problem. In this regard, the SCG has developed and does hereby propose a comprehensive alcohol and controlled substance policy and in so doing, recognizes that while the implementation of policy may be costly, the program will be more than cost-effective if the eradication of alcohol and controlled substance abuse among SCG employees can be accomplished.

Therefore, in furtherance of the foregoing and to ensure that all of its employees are subject to and receive the benefit of this policy, and in its continuing desire to protect the person and property of its citizens, the general public, and for the protection of the fellow employees of each employee of the City and the property of the City, the policy is hereby adopted and implemented.

Example 4: Large Utility Company (LUC)
I. Drugs
  Employees shall not be under the influence of any substance, legal or illegal, which adversely affects their ability to perform their duties in any way.

  The illegal use, possession, distribution, or sale of drugs (including marijuana) on LUC property or on LUC business will result in termination. The illegal off-duty use, possession, distribution, or sale of drugs (including marijuana) which adversely affects the LUC or its employees will result in termination. No one will report or return to work under the influence of any illegal drugs. Any employee reporting to work or returning to work under the influence of any illegal drugs will be terminated.

  The abuse of legal or prescription drugs that adversely affects an employee's ability to perform his or her duties in any way will result in the employee's immediate removal from LUC property, and the employee will be subject to discipline up to and including termination of employment.

  Remember:

  Illegal involvement with drugs on LUC property or on LUC business will result in termination.

  Illegal involvement with drugs off duty will result in termination when it adversely affects LUC or its employees.

  All employees are responsible for preventing and reporting actions that threaten harm to the company or to their fellow employees. Employees are expected to use good judgment and common sense in exercising this responsibility.

  Employees in certain positions, such as security personnel and supervisors, are responsible for enforcing company policies. Illegal use of drugs by such employees whether on or off duty in itself impairs their ability to enforce these company policies. Therefore, any illegal involvement with drugs by these employees will result in termination.

  For employees required to have unescorted access to nuclear stations, the illegal involvement with drugs on duty or off duty will result in termination.

  The abuse of legal or prescription drugs within the protected area of a nuclear power station will result in immediate revocation of access to vital areas, and the employee will be subject to discipline up to and including termination.
II. Alcoholic Beverages
  No employee will use alcoholic beverages on the job. No employee will report to work or return to work while under the influence of alcoholic beverages. Employees in violation of this policy will be removed from LUC property and will be subject to discipline up to and including termination of employment.

Appendix E

SUBSTANCE ABUSE PROCEDURES

Employer Summary Statements

Example 1: Large Manufacturing Company
    The essential parts of this process are as follows:
(1) The company prohibits the presence or use of alcohol, drugs, or other psychoactive substances on its property;
(2) The company will present a substance abuse education program for all associates on a periodic basis;
(3) Applicants will be screened and tested to detect illegal substance use;
(4) New associates will be subject to surveillance testing during their first year of employment;
(5) Drug screening test(s) will be performed on eligible associates as part of annual, or periodic recurring, physical examinations where the examinations are required or routinely performed;
(6) Where cause exists to believe that an associate is impaired or under the influence of these substances, a confidential investigation, including drug screening, will be undertaken to detect substance abuse. If substances are detected, appropriate referral for professional evaluation, or discipline, will be implemented;
(7) All outside contractors will be required by contract or purchase order to certify the drug free condition of their employees before these employees are allowed on company property.
    In addition to applicants, all associates are covered by and considered part of this process, whether management, production, or administrative associates.

Example 2: Small City Government (SCG)
    The essential parts of this program are as follows:
A. The SCG prohibits the presence or use of alcohol or drugs on SCG property or premises, in SCG vehicles, or while the SCG employee is on the job.

B.   Applicants for employment will be screened and tested to detect illegal substance abuse.
C.   The SCG recognizes that certain sensitive positions are critical to the public welfare from a health and safety point of view. As a result, all current SCG employees in sensitive positions from a health and safety standpoint will submit to a drug screening program as part of their annual medical examination. Each department will be analyzed periodically to determine the departments or positions which will be tested.
D.   Where cause exists to believe that an SCG employee is impaired or under the influence of drugs or alcohol, a confidential investigation, including drug or alcohol screening, will be undertaken to detect substance abuse.
E.   In any situation where substances are detected, City employees will be referred to the SCG Employee Assistance Program for professional evaluation and/or treatment, or discipline will be implemented when necessary.
F.   All applicants and employees of the SCG are covered by this Substance Abuse Prevention Program.
G.   The SCG Human Resources Director will develop and present a Substance Abuse Education Program and make it available to all SCG employees. The Human Resources Director shall utilize any SCG personnel or assets at his or her disposal and/or any outside experts or consultants that may be deemed appropriate.

Continuing Education

Example 1: Large Manufacturing Company
   In order to protect the safety and health of its associates, the company will present a Substance Abuse Education Program to all associates on a periodic basis. Company officials will obtain or develop quality materials in order to continue to educate associates on the problems caused by, and the developments related to, alcohol, drugs, or other psychoactive substances.

Example 2: Federal Personnel Manual
   The Federal Personnel Manual is issued by the Office of Personnel Management. It provides guidance in implementing federal personnel policies and regulations for all federal employees.
Training and Education
A.   Supervisory Training. Employee counselors will conduct or otherwise provide training sessions for agency supervisors on the handling of problems of substance abuse. Appropriate topics include:
   (1)   Drug awareness and symptoms of drug use.
   (2)   Recommended methods for dealing with the suspected or identified drug user.

(3)   Supervisory responsibilities under E.O. 12564.
(4)   Confrontation and referral techniques.
(5)   Explanation of the (agency) employee assistance program and its relationship with the (agency) drug testing program.
(6)   General principles of rehabilitation including techniques for supervisors to assist employees in returning to the work site, given specific (agency) needs and requirements.
(7)   Personnel management issues (e.g., relationship of this program to performance appraisal and disciplinary programs; leave usage; and supervisory notes and documentation).

B.   Employee education. The Employee Assistance Coordinator will ensure that employee seminars on topics dealing with drug use are provided periodically. Managers and supervisors shall encourage employee attendance at these seminars and provide other appropriate support. On a continuing basis, educational materials and information on drug abuse will be available to individual employees.

Example 3: National Drug Policy Board

The National Drug Policy Board was the predecessor to the Office of National Drug Policy, a federal agency in the Executive branch.

Objectives—The EAP Administrator shall offer drug education to all (Agency) employees. Drug education should include education and training to all levels of the (Agency) on:
1.   Types and effects of drugs;
2.   Symptoms of drug use, and the effects on performance and conduct;
3.   The relationship of the EAP to the drug testing program; and
4.   Other relevant treatment, rehabilitation, and confidentiality issues.

Means of Education Drug education activities may include:
1.   Distribution of written materials;
2.   Videotapes;
3.   Lunchtime employee forums; and
4.   Employee drug awareness days.

Example 4: Large Construction Company

A.   Drug Free Awareness Education Program
1.   All employees are to be informed of (company's) Substance Abuse Program, and be made aware of its contents.
2.   In order to protect the safety and health of its employees, the company will present a Drug Free Awareness Education Program to all supervisors and employees on a periodic basis. The education program will consist of materials presented over at least 60 minutes of time concerning the dangers of drug abuse on the work site, the (company's) policy for a drug free work site, available counseling and treatment through the company's EAP, and the penalties for violating the company's Substance Abuse

Program. Company officials will obtain or develop quality materials in order to continue to educate employees on the symptoms
of, the problems caused by, and the developments related to,
alcohol, drugs, or other controlled substances, and the promotion
of a healthy lifestyle.

3. Management and supervisory personnel will also receive training
    on at least an annual basis regarding the symptoms of alcohol and
    drug abuse. Their training will include, but not be limited to, the
    following:
    a. Recognition/observation;
    b. Documentation;
    c. Confrontation/intervention;
    d. Referral; and
    e. Reintegration procedures.

Scope and Application

Example 1: Small Manufacturing Company (SMC)
This policy covers all domestic employees of the SMC, including
salaried, hourly, permanent, and temporary employees, if they are put on
the company's payroll.

Example 2: Small Government Utility (SGU)
A. All employees holding sensitive positions from a public health and
    safety viewpoint will be tested on a one-time basis in August of 1988.
B. All other SGU employees will be encouraged to participate volun-
    tarily in the Substance Abuse Prevention Program. Each member of
    the Board of Directors has agreed to participate voluntarily in the
    program. Participation by employees not in sensitive positions is
    entirely voluntary and no adverse consequences will occur for failure
    to participate.
C. Applicants for employment will be tested to detect illegal substance
    abuse.
D. All SGU employees holding sensitive positions from a public health
    and safety viewpoint will be tested for illegal substance use during
    their annual physical.

Definition of Substance Abuse

Example 1: Midsized Manufacturing Company
Substance abuse is defined as (1) reporting to work or working while
under the influence of or impaired by alcohol or any other drug, (2) chemical dependency on alcohol or other drugs where job performance or safety
of employees is adversely affected, or (3) the use of illegal drugs. The term
"illegal drugs" as used in this policy includes, but is not limited to,

marijuana, cocaine, heroin, and similar drugs whose possession and use are prohibited under state or federal law in this country, as well as prescription drugs unless validly prescribed by an employee's physician. So called "designer drugs," "look alikes," synthetic drugs, and similar substances are also considered illegal drugs for purposes of this policy, even if they are not specifically prohibited by state or federal law. This policy is also designed to cover other substances which may be abused, whether available legally over-the-counter (such as cough syrup or drugs obtained with a valid prescription), or never intended for human consumption (such as glue).

Example 2: National Drug Policy Board
Illegal Drugs means a controlled substance included in Schedule I or II, as defined by Section 802(6) of Title 21 of the United States Code, the possession of which is unlawful under chapter 13 of that Title. The term "illegal drugs" does not mean the use of a controlled substance pursuant to a valid prescription or other uses authorized by law.

Example 3: Large Service Company
Drug abuse is the use of a drug for other than medicinal reasons which results in impaired physical, mental, emotional, or social well-being of the user.

Drug misuse is the inappropriate use of prescription or over-the-counter drugs, with similar results.

Example 4: Small City Government
Definitions
1. Controlled or illegal substance shall mean controlled substances as that term is now or hereafter defined by Section 16-13-21 of the Official Code of Georgia Annotated.
2. Alcohol or alcoholic beverage as used herein shall mean alcoholic beverages as that term is now or hereafter defined by Section 3-1-2 of the Official Code of Georgia Annotated.
3. Psychoactive substance or substances as used in this policy shall mean and include controlled and illegal substances, drugs, and alcohol, ingestion of which impairs a person's physical or mental faculties, thereby adversely affecting his or her ability to perform job duties.
4. Drugs shall mean and include controlled substances, illegal substances, and alcohol as herein defined. The term "drugs or alcohol" may be used in this policy for the sake of clarity although it is understood that alcohol is a drug.
7. Prescription or nonprescription medication shall include any medication given under the prescription of physician or any medication purchased over the counter that could hinder an employee's ability to reasonably and safely complete his assigned task or employment function.

Testing of Applicants

Example 1: Large Manufacturing Company (LMC)
1. All applicants will be advised of LMC's Substance Abuse Prevention Process.
2. All applicants will be tested as a part of the application process.
3. Applicants will be advised of the testing requirements in detail by the personnel or employment manager prior to an offer of hire or referral to the nurse for a physical.

Example 2: Midsized Manufacturing Company
A.   Applicant Drug Testing
        All applicants will be required to undergo a drug screening test as part of their routine pre-employment processing. Employees who have been on layoffs of six months or less, and who have been previously tested, will not be retested.
B.   Employment Policy
        Employment will be denied when the results of the applicant's drug screening test are positive for illegal drugs, or prescription drugs (such as barbiturates, amphetamines, opiates, etc.) unless the applicant has a current prescription and a valid medical reason for the use of such drugs.

Example 3: National Drug Policy Board
Procedures
        The Drug Program Coordinator (DPC) shall direct applicants to an appropriate collection facility. The drug test must be undertaken as soon after notification as possible, and no later than 48 hours from notice to the applicant. Where appropriate, applicants may be reimbursed for reasonable travel expenses.
        Applicants will be advised of the opportunity to submit medical documentation that may support a legitimate use for a specific drug and that such information will be reviewed only by the Medical Review Officer to determine whether the individual is licitly using an otherwise illegal drug.

Example 4: Small Government Utility (SGU)
A.   Testing of Applicants for Employment
        1.   All applicants will be advised of SGU's Substance Abuse Prevention Program.
        2.   All applicants will be tested as a part of the application process.
        3.   Applicants will be advised of the testing requirements in detail by the appropriate SGU employee prior to an offer of hire or referral to the pre-employment medical examination. Signs advising applicants of the SGU's applicant testing policy will be posted at SGU hiring offices. The Substance Abuse Prevention Program will be explained to all applicants, and applicants must complete,

sign, and date the Chemical Screening Consent Form, and their signature must be witnessed and dated. The application will not be completed or processed further unless the applicant submits to the testing procedures.

Notice/Posting

Example 1: Midsized Manufacturing Company
Posting
 The following poster will be displayed where it may be easily seen by employees and persons seeking employment:
 APPLICANTS FOR EMPLOYMENT WILL BE REQUIRED TO UNDERGO A DRUG SCREENING TEST BEFORE CONSIDERATION FOR EMPLOYMENT.

Example 2: Small Government Utility (SGU)
 Signs advising applicants of the SGU's applicant testing policy will be posted at SGU hiring offices.

Example 3: National Drug Policy Board
Vacancy Announcements
 Every vacancy announcement for positions designated for applicant testing shall state:
 All applicants tentatively selected for this position will be required to submit to urinalysis to screen for illegal drug use prior to appointment.
 In addition, each applicant will be notified that appointment to the position will be contingent upon a negative drug test result. Failure of the vacancy announcement to contain this statement notice will not preclude applicant testing if advance written notice is provided applicants in some other manner.

Application Form/Medical History Questionnaire

Example 1: Large Manufacturing Company
Testing of Applicants
 The Substance Abuse Prevention Process will be explained to all applicants, and applicants must complete, sign, and date the Medical History Questionnaire, and their signature must be witnessed and dated. An application will not be complete or processed further unless the applicant submits to the testing procedure.

Example 2: Midsized Manufacturing Company (MMC)
 The employment application form should include the following language:
 Employment with MMC is contingent upon the successful completion of a drug screening test. Successful completion of the test is no guarantee of employment or job availability.

Example 3: Large Service Company (LSC)
APPLICANT SUBSTANCE ABUSE SCREENING PROGRAM
This is to inform you that LSC has a Substance Abuse Policy and an Applicant Substance Abuse Screening Program. As an applicant you are requested to sign the attached "Applicant Consent" form for substance abuse testing.

Failure to sign the "Consent Form" will result in no further processing of your application for employment.

Manager, Employee Relations, LSC

Example 4: Federal Personnel Manual
Applicant Testing. The head of each Executive agency is authorized, but not required, to test any applicant for illegal drug use. Agency heads who choose to test applicants for illegal drug use have a variety of options. For example, depending on the mission of the agency, an agency may wish to test all applicants for employment. On the other hand, an agency may determine that it will limit applicant testing to applicants for testing designated positions. Where an applicant must submit to a physical examination as a condition of employment, an agency may wish to require a drug test as part of the physical examination procedures.

(1) Agencies should include notice of drug testing on vacancy announcements for those positions where drug testing is required. A sample notice provision for vacancy announcements or other information about the position would read as follows: "All applicants for this position will be required to submit to a urinalysis for illegal drug use prior to appointment in the Federal service."

Consent and Release

Example 1: Large Manufacturing Company (LMC)
I understand that LMC has a Substance Abuse Prevention Process. The details of this process have been explained to me. I consent freely and voluntarily to the company's request for a urine or other specimen or sample. I hereby release the company, the laboratory, their employees, agents, and contractors from any liability whatsoever arising from this request to furnish this urine or other specimen or sample, the testing of the specimen or sample, and any decisions made concerning my application for employment, or continued employment, based upon the results of the tests. I consent to allow LMC and a company-approved laboratory, to perform appropriate chemical tests for the presence of drugs or other psychoactive substances. I give my permission to the laboratory to release the results of these tests to LMC. I understand that if accepted for employment by LMC I agree, as a condition of my employment, that I will

adhere to the company's Substance Abuse Prevention Process including surveillance testing during the first year of my employment. I have been furnished Test Kit No. _____.

_____	_____	_____
Company	Applicant/Employee	Date
Official	Signature	

Example 2: Midsized Manufacturing Company (MMC)
Release
    Prior to the drug screening test, the applicant must sign a Release of Liability. Failure to sign the release or cooperate in the test procedure as requested will be considered as a withdrawal of the individual's application for employment.

RELEASE OF LIABILITY

    I understand that in accordance with MMC's policy of providing and maintaining a safe and healthful working environment for all employees, that I will voluntarily submit to a drug or alcohol screen test.

    I hereby authorize the release of the results of the test to management of the company and its designated medical representative.

    I release the company, its employees, management, and its designated medical representatives from any and all claims or causes of action resulting from this test and any decisions resulting therefrom.

_____
Printed Name

_____
Signature
Date: _____

_____
Witness
Date: _____

Example 3: Small Service Company
    CHEMICAL SCREENING CONSENT AND RELEASE FORM
    I, _____, hereby acknowledge that I have been informed of the Company's Substance Abuse Program and agree to be bound by this program thereby for purposes of applying for and, if offered, accepting employment with the company.

    Specifically, I understand and consent freely and voluntarily to the company's request for a urine or other specimen or sample. I hereby release and hold harmless the company, the laboratory, their employees, agents, and contractors from any liability arising from this request to furnish this or any specimen or sample, the testing of the specimen or sample, and any decisions made concerning my application for employment or, if offered, my continued employment, based upon the results of the tests. I consent to allow any company employee, designated physician, laboratory, hospital, or medical professional to perform appropriate chemical tests for the presence of drugs or other psychoactive substances. I give my permission to any company employee, designated physician, laboratory, hospital, or medical professional to release the results of these tests to the company, and I release any such designated institution or person from liability arising from the release of this information.

I have taken within the past 30 days or am presently taking the following medications:

Name of Drug	Condition for Which Taken	Prescribing Physician
_____	_____	_____
_____	_____	_____
_____	_____	_____
_____	_____	_____

I hereby consent to all the company approved laboratory or its designated representative to verify and/or confirm the above information with the prescribing physician listed above.

The specimen bottle was personally given by me to the company approved laboratory and contained a specimen of my urine.

Company Official	Applicant/Employee Signature	Date

Example 4: Large Service Company (LSC)
EMPLOYMENT APPLICANT ACKNOWLEDGMENT, RELEASE, AND CONSENT

I have read and understand the LSC Substance Detection Policy and agree to be bound thereby for purposes of applying for and, if offered, accepting employment at LSC.

Specifically, I understand and agree to undergo substance (drug and alcohol) screening of my blood, urine, breath, saliva, or otherwise for purposes of assuming employment. I further understand and agree that once employed, upon reasonable suspicion, or if I am involved in an accident or safety incident where there is reasonable suspicion, I will be subject to further substance screening or face disciplinary consequences, up to and including loss of employment. I hereby authorize any company employee, designated physician, laboratory, hospital, or medical professional to conduct such screening and provide the results thereof to the company, and I release any such designated institution or person from liability therefor.

I also understand and agree that once employed, certain areas such as my work area, desk, files, any company motor vehicle, my personal car, lunch box, wallet or purse, and outer clothing may be subject to search, without cause or on suspicion of substance possession, depending upon the circumstances as set forth in the policy.

_____   _____
Date   Applicant

Example 5: Large Private Utility (LPU)
EMPLOYEE CONSENT FOR DRUG ANALYSIS
I, _____, Employee No. _____, do hereby give my consent to LPU and (name of Toxicological Service Co.) to perform appropriate tests or examinations on me for drugs. I further give my permission to LPU and (name of Toxicological Service Co.) to release the results of the tests or examinations to my employer.

I have taken or am taking the following medications within the past 30 days:

Name of Drug	Condition for Which Taken	Prescribing Physician/ Over-the-Counter
_____	_____	_____
_____	_____	_____
_____	_____	_____
_____	_____	_____

Specimen No. V. _____

_____   _____   _____
Signature of employee   Date   Witness

_____
Employer

Example 6: Large Manufacturing Company
SUBSTANCE ABUSE SCREENING TEST
EMPLOYEE CONSENT
I, _____, understand and agree that the test I am about to receive includes a
( )   Blood test for substance abuse or chemical dependency.
( )   Urine test for substance abuse or chemical dependency.
I understand that if I decline to sign this consent and thereby decline to take the test, the Employee Relations Department will be so notified.

If the test is confirmed as positive the results will be reported to the Employee Relations Department. An exception will be made for the use of legally prescribed medications taken under the directions of a physician.

I have taken the following drugs or substances within the last 96 hours:

Identify Name and Amount

(   ) Sleeping Pills   _____
(   ) Diet Pills   _____
(   ) Pain Relief Pills   _____
(   ) Cold Tablets   _____
(   ) Anti-Malaria Drugs   _____
(   ) Any Other Medication   _____
       or Substance   _____
I hereby (   ) consent
       (   ) refuse to consent
to the test(s) for substance abuse.

Signed: _____

Date: _____

Witness: _____

Contingent Employment

Example 1: Midsized Manufacturing Company
APPLICANTS
    Acceptance for employment is contingent upon a determination that an applicant has successfully completed a drug screening test. No one shall be permitted to begin work until the results of the test have been obtained.

Example 2: Large Manufacturing Company
Testing of Applicants
    The applicant's ability to meet company medical standards will be transmitted directly to the personnel manager. The personnel manager will keep the results strictly confidential. If an applicant's test is positive, he will not be considered for employment at that time and will be so informed that he has failed to meet company medical standards. The applicant will be offered referral to professional evaluation at the applicant's own expense.

Example 3: National Drug Policy Board
Vacancy Announcements
    Every vacancy announcement for positions designated for applicant testing shall state:
    All applicants tentatively selected for this position will be required to submit to urinalysis to screen for illegal drug use prior to appointment.

In addition, each applicant will be notified that appointment to the position will be contingent upon a negative drug test result. Failure of the vacancy announcement to contain this statement notice will not preclude applicant testing if advance written notice is provided applicants in some other manner.

Consequences

The (Agency) will decline to extend a final offer of employment to any applicant with a verified positive test result, and such applicant may not reapply to the (Agency) for a period of six months. The Personnel Officer working on the applicant's certificate shall be directed to object to the applicant on the basis of failure to pass the physical, a lack of personal characteristics necessary to relate to public employment, or failure to support the goals of the (Agency). The (Agency) shall inform such applicant that a confirmed presence of drug in the applicant's urine precludes the (Agency) from hiring the applicant.

Notification of Results

Example: Midsized Manufacturing Company

Communication of Test Results

1. Confidentiality—The laboratory should be instructed to provide the results of any drug screening test to a designated company official only. The number of personnel who are informed of the results shall be limited to those with a valid need to know.
2. Negative Test Results—In the event the drug screen test results are negative, the applicant may be offered a position. If it is accepted, the results of the test will be maintained in the employee's medical records file.
3. Positive Test Results—In the event a drug screening test is positive, the following procedures should be followed:
    (a) The applicant shall be informed that he or she is not medically acceptable for work. If the applicant requests additional information, the specific test results may be discussed with the applicant, but where possible such a discussion should be conducted by the designated company official who received the results of the test. If the telephone is used, great care should be exercised to ensure the correct identity of the applicant. The applicant should be asked to provide an explanation, and whether a second confirmation of the results of the drug screening test is desired.
    (b) Because of the sensitive nature of drug and/or alcohol screening tests, extreme caution should be exercised to avoid making any statements concerning a medical examination or applicant's drug screening results to other members of management, even to friends and members of an employee's family or to any other person.

Confidentiality

Example 1: Midsized Manufacturing Company

All information involving medical examinations, counseling, rehabilitation, or treatment of an individual employee or applicant shall be treated as confidential medical information. All such information will be accessible only to those Company officials and designated medical or professional persons with a valid need to know. It will not be provided to any other party without the written consent of the employee except pursuant to administrative or legal procedure or process.

Example 2: National Drug Policy Board

The laboratory may disclose confirmed laboratory test results only to the Medical Review Officer. Any positive result which the Medical Review Officer justified by licit and appropriate medical or scientific documentation to account for the result as other than the intentional ingestion of an illegal drug will be treated as a negative test result and may not be released for purposes of identifying illegal drug use. Test results will be protected under the provisions of the Privacy Act, 5 U.S.C. §552a, *et seq.*, and Section 503(e) of the Act, and may not be released in violation of either Act. The Medical Review Officer may maintain only those records necessary for compliance with this order. Any records of the Medical Review Officer, including drug test results, may be released to any management official for purposes of auditing the activities of the Medical Review Officer, except that the disclosure of the results of any audit may not include personal identifying information on any employee.

In order to comply with Section 503(e) of the Act, the results of a drug test of an (Agency) employee may not be disclosed without the prior written consent of such employee, unless the disclosure would be—

1. To the Medical Review Officer;
2. To the Administrator in the EAP in which the employee is receiving counseling or treatment or is otherwise participating;
3. To any supervisory or management official within the (Agency) having authority to take adverse personnel action against such employee; or
4. Pursuant to the order of the court of competent jurisdiction or where required by the United States Government to defend against any challenge against any adverse personnel action.

For purposes of this section, "management official" includes any management or government official whose duties necessitate review of the test results in order to process adverse personnel action against the employee. In addition, test results with all identifying information removed shall also be made available to (Agency) personnel, including the DPC, for data collection and other activities necessary to comply with Section 503(f) of the Act.

Opportunity to Contest Results

Example 1: Midsized Manufacturing Company
    If the applicant requests a second confirmation test, it shall be done on the original sample using gas chromatography/mass spectrometry (GC/MS) or equivalent, and shall be done at the applicant's expense. The cost of the test (as determined by the laboratory) shall be paid before retesting is done.

  (b)   If the results of the reconfirmation test are negative, the applicants will be reimbursed the cost of the additional test and the results of the initial positive test will not be used to deny employment.

  (c)   If no reconfirmation test is requested, or, if the reconfirmation test is again positive, and a satisfactory explanation is still not provided, the applicant will again be informed of the results of the drug screening test and denied employment. Upon adequate proof of successful completion of a rehabilitation program, or after a six-month waiting period, the applicant may reapply for employment with the company.

Example 2: Large Service Company
    Applicants initially testing positive should be contacted, given the opportunity to explain the positive result, and depending on the response should consider an opportunity for retest assuming test completion within a 24-hour time frame.

Example 3: Small Government Utility
General
    If a specimen is confirmed positive, the applicant will be informed of the results by the General Manager or his designee. If an applicant disagrees with the test result, he may have an opportunity to contest the results if the applicant requests within 10 days of being notified of the results that an approved, federally licensed laboratory retest the original specimen at the applicant's own expense. One retest of the original specimen will be allowed under this procedure.

Example 4: National Drug Policy Board
                Opportunity to Justify a Positive Test Result
    When a confirmed positive result has been returned by the laboratory, the Medical Review Officer shall perform the duties set forth in the HHS Guidelines. For example, the Medical Review Officer may choose to conduct employee medical interviews, review employee medical history, or review any other relevant biomedical factors. The Medical Review Officer must review all medical records made available by the tested

employee when a confirmed positive test could have resulted from legally prescribed medication. Evidence to justify a positive result may include, but is not limited to:

1. A valid prescription; or
2. A verification from the individual's physician verifying a valid prescription.

Individuals are not entitled, however, to present evidence to the Medical Review Officer in a trial-type administrative proceeding, although the Medical Review Officer has the discretion to accept evidence in any manner the Medical Review Officer deems most efficient or necessary.

If the Medical Review Officer determines there is no justification for the positive result, such result will then be considered a verified positive test result. The Medical Review Officer shall immediately contact the EAP Administrator upon obtaining a verified positive test result.

Referral Options

Example 1: Large Manufacturing Company
Substance Abuse Prevention Process
REFERRAL NOTICE

You have indicated on your Medical History Questionnaire that you are not a user of any psychoactive substances. However, our screening test has revealed the presence of a psychoactive substance.

As a result, you will not be considered for employment at this time. However, you may elect to receive professional evaluation and/or to enter a rehabilitation program (at your own expense) at a facility approved by the company. After successful completion, you may reapply for a position with our company.

_____   _____
Company Official   Date

    I acknowledge receipt of this notice.

_____   _____
Applicant's Signature   Date

Example 2: Small City Government (SCG)

    If an applicant's test is positive, he or she will not be considered for employment at that time and will be so informed that he or she has failed to meet SCG medical standards. The applicant will be offered referral to professional evaluation at the applicant's own expense (Applicant Referral Notice Form).

APPLICANT REFERRAL FORM

You have indicated on your Medical History Questionnaire that you are not a user of any controlled substances. However, our screening test has revealed the presence of a controlled substance.

As a result, you will not be considered for employment at this time. However, you may elect to receive professional evaluation and/or to enter a rehabilitation program (at your own expense) at a facility approved by the SCG. After successful completion, you may reapply for a position with the SCG.

_____   _____
City Official   Date

I acknowledge receipt of this letter.

_____   _____
Applicant's Signature   Date

Employee Testing

Mandatory, Across-the-Board Testing

Example 1: Small Construction Company (SCC)

NOTICE TO EMPLOYEES

SCC now has a Substance Abuse Prevention Policy to protect you and our customers from the problems associated with substance abuse by employees. As a part of this policy, all employees will be required to participate in a chemical screening test for drugs on Wednesday, July 13, 1988.

Any questions should be directed to the general manager.

Date: July 7, 1988   _____
                                                                   General Manager

Example 2: Small Service Company (SSC)

NOTICE TO ALL EMPLOYEES

As part of SSC's continuing commitment to providing a safe workplace for all of its employees and to supplying its customers with the highest quality products and service possible, SSC has established a Substance Abuse Program including a Company Employee Assistance Program.

In the next few weeks, the SSC will present an education program for the employees to introduce and explain this important program to you. An important feature of the Substance Abuse Program is that all SSC employees will be tested for the presence of illegal substances. The testing procedures will be explained to you during the education program.

If you have any questions regarding any part of this program, please contact the personnel office or your supervisor.

Annual Physical, Biennial, or Fitness for Duty Testing

Example 1: Large Manufacturing Company

Testing of Associates—Selection Procedures

Drug screening test(s) will be performed on eligible associates as part of annual physical examinations, or periodic recurring physical examinations, where the examinations are required by law, regulation, or company policy, or are routinely performed pursuant to company or location policy. As a part of the physical examination process, the associate will be asked to consent to a test(s) and sign the Associate Chemical Screening form.

Example 2: Small City Government (SCG)
City Employees—Annual Medical Examination
    Annual medical examinations or physical examinations will be conducted for all positions considered sensitive from a health and safety standpoint and which may directly affect public safety or employee safety. These annual examinations will include drug screening tests and will be scheduled the month before, the month of, or the month following the SCG employee's birthday.
    All SCG departments will be analyzed periodically from a health and safety standpoint to determine which positions in these departments are particularly sensitive. A determination has been made that this portion of the policy will initially apply to, but not be limited to, certain officers and employees of the police department and fire department including sworn police officers, police dispatchers, certified firefighters, and fire dispatchers.

Example 3: Large County Government
Law Enforcement (Sheriff's Department) Annual Physical
    All current law enforcement, Sheriff employees, will be required to submit to an annual physical by the county physician on their anniversary date (date of hire). As a part of the annual physical, the employee will be subject to substance testing. Failure to pass medical standards will result in punitive action.

Example 4: Large Service Company (LSC)
Fitness for Duty Physicals, Medical Examinations, and Testing
    LSC also reserves the right, at its discretion, to require employees or other persons to submit to medical or physical examinations or tests at any time as a condition of continued employment, including but not necessarily limited to, urine drug test (screens), blood and plasma test or other examinations to determine the use of any illegal or unauthorized drugs or substances prohibited in this policy or to prove the employee's fitness for duty.

Example 5: Small Service Company
    Drug screening test(s) will be performed on all employees on an annual basis. As a part of the annual testing program, employees will be asked to consent to a test(s) and sign the Chemical Screening Consent Form.

Example 6: Small Government Utility (SGU)
    Annual medical examinations or physical examinations will be conducted for all SGU employees. These annual examinations will include drug screening tests and will be scheduled the month before, the month of, or the month following the employee's birthday.

Probationary Testing

Example: Large Manufacturing Company (LMC)
Testing of Associates—Selection Procedures
    New associates will be subject to surveillance testing during their first year of employment. Every effort will be made by LMC to select associates for the surveillance testing at reasonable and convenient times during the

applicable period, and selection will be made for the test based on a method determined by the Corporate Director of Personnel. Once notified of his or her selection for the surveillance test, the associate will be asked to consent to a test(s) and sign an Associate Chemical Screening Form.

"Safety-Sensitive Position" Testing

Example 1: Midsized Manufacturing Company (MMC)
Safety Sensitive Areas

(a) MMC may, at its discretion, test employees in safety-sensitive positions at any time. Safety-sensitive jobs are those positions which involve a high degree of risk of significant personal injury or property damage in the event of an accident.

(b) A determination should be made by the Vice President concerning which jobs, if any, should be classified as safety sensitive.

(c) A list of safety-sensitive jobs should be prepared and submitted to the Vice President for review.

(d) After approval by the Vice President, a confidential written notice should be given to all employees currently holding those positions. The notice should specify that their jobs have been determined to be safety sensitive and that their continued employment in that position is contingent upon their agreement to permit unscheduled drug or alcohol screening tests when requested to do so. The employees will not be required to sign releases until a request to take a test is made.

Example 2: National Drug Policy Board
Sensitive Employees in Testing Designated Positions

The Executive Order requires random testing for employees in sensitive positions that have been designated as testing designated positions. As further specified in Appendix A, the (Agency head) has determined that these positions are testing designated positions that will be randomly tested. Accompanying the list of testing designated positions are the criteria and procedures used in designating such positions, pursuant to the Act including the justification for such criteria and procedure.

Example 3: Small City Government (SCG)

SCG recognizes that certain sensitive positions are critical to the public welfare from a health and safety point of view. As a result, all current SCG employees in sensitive positions from a health and safety standpoint will submit to a drug screening program as part of their annual medical examination. Each department will be analyzed periodically to determine the departments or positions which will be tested.

"For-Cause" Testing

Example 1: Large Manufacturing Company
Testing of Associates—Selection Procedures

Current associates may be asked to submit to a test if cause exists to indicate that their health or ability to perform work may be impaired. Factors which could establish cause include, but are not limited to:

a. Sudden changes in work performance;
b. Repeated failure to follow instructions or operating procedures;
c. Accidents or violation of company safety policies;
d. Discovery or presence of substances in an associate's possession or near the associate's workplace;
e. Odor of alcohol and/or residual odor peculiar to some chemical psychoactive substances;
f. Unexplained and/or frequent absenteeism; or
g. Personality changes or disorientation.

If a manager believes cause exists, or has a reasonable suspicion that an associate may be impaired or using substances, he should report his findings and observations to the personnel manager. Factors which substantiate cause should be documented on the Substance Abuse Investigation Form. Upon approval by the personnel manager, the location manager, and a corporate personnel representative, the associate will be asked to consent to a test(s) and sign an Associate Chemical Screening Consent form.

Substance Abuse Prevention Process
SUBSTANCE ABUSE INVESTIGATION FORM
I have observed the following condition(s) affecting the work of _____ which give rise to suspicion of substance abuse, and request an investigation of same:

Condition(s) observed: _____

_____

_____

_____

Date: _____   _____
                                 Supervisor

Cause exists for medical and/or drug tests of this associate.

Date: _____   _____
                                 Personnel Manager

Date: _____   _____
                                 Location Manager

Example 2: Midsized Manufacturing Company
REASONABLE CAUSE FORM
This form is to be used to document the reasons for requesting that an employee be asked to submit to a medical evaluation or drug or alcohol screen test. All questions which apply should be answered. Additional pages, if necessary, should be attached along with any other relevant documents.

Employee's Name _____

Facility _____Shift _____

A. Was There an Incident? Yes _____No _____

    1. Description of event _____

        _____

    2. Time and date _____

    3. Extent of injury to persons or property _____

        _____

    4. Employee's actions _____

        _____

B.   Is the Employee in a Safety-Sensitive Position?
    Yes _____ No _____

C.   Observation of Employee (Date: _____ Time: _____):
    1. WALKING
        • Falling   • Holding On   • Staggering
        • Stumbling   • Swaying   • Unsteady
        • Unable to Walk
    2. STANDING
        • Feet wide apart   • Rigid   • Swaying
        • Sagging at knees   • Staggering
        • Unable to stand
    3. SPEECH
        • Mute   • Incoherent   • Rambling
        • Shouting   • Silent   • Slobbering
        • Slow   • Slurred   • Whispering
    4. DEMEANOR
        • Calm   • Cooperative   • Crying
        • Fighting   • Polite   • Sarcastic
        • Silent   • Sleepy   • Talkative
        • Excited
    5. ACTIONS
        • Calm   • Drowsy   • Erratic   • Hostile
        • Fighting   • Hyperactive   • Profanity
        • Resisting communications   • Threatening
    6. EYES
        • Bloodshot   • Closed   • Dilated
        • Droopy   • Glassy   • Watery
    7. FACE
        • Flushed   • Pale   • Sweaty
    8. APPEARANCE/CLOTHING
        • Bodily excrement stains on clothing
        • Unruly   • Having odor   • Messy
        • Neat   • Dirty   • Partially dressed
    9. BREATH

- Alcoholic odor • Faint alcoholic odor
- No alcoholic odor • Marijuana odor
- Faint marijuana odor • No marijuana odor
10. MOVEMENTS
   - Fumbling • Hyperactive • Jerky
   - Nervous • Normal • Slow
11. EATING/CHEWING
   - Candy • Gum • Mints • Nothing
   - Other _____

D. History
   1. To your knowledge, has the employee previously signed a Last Chance Agreement? Yes _____ No _____ Don't Know _____

   2. If yes, when? _____

E. Attendance
   1. Number of Mondays or Fridays missed in the last two months
   2. Total absences in last two months _____
   3. Times tardy in last two months _____
   4. Times employee left early in last two months _____

F. Performance Level
   1. Has there been a recent change in the employee's level of performance? Yes _____ No _____
   2. If yes, describe _____
   _____

G. Other Observations _____
   _____
   _____

H. Other Factors_____
   _____
   _____

I. Other Witnesses_____
   _____
   _____

_____   _____
Signature   (Date)

_____
Printed Name

                              Approved: _____
                              Approved: _____

Example 3: National Drug Policy Board
Grounds
    Reasonable suspicion testing may be based upon, among other things:
1. Observable phenomena, such as direct observation of drug use or possession and/or other physical symptoms of being under the influence of a drug;
2. A pattern of abnormal conduct or erratic behavior;
3. Arrest or conviction for a drug-related offense, or the identification of an employee as the focus of a criminal investigation into illegal drug possession, use, or trafficking;
4. Information provided either by reliable and credible sources or independently corroborated; or
5. Newly discovered evidence that the employee has tampered with a previous drug test.

Although reasonable suspicion testing does not require certainty, mere "hunches" are not sufficient to meet this standard.

Example 4: Small Government Utility (SGU)
SGU Employees—For-Cause Testing
1. An SGU employee may be asked to submit to a drug screening test if cause or a reasonable suspicion exists to indicate that his or her health or ability to perform work may be impaired by drug use. Factors that could establish reasonable suspicion include, but are not limited to:
    a. Sudden changes in work performance;
    b. Failure to follow instructions or procedures;
    c. Violation of safety policies and other rules and regulations;
    d. Involvement in an accident or near-accident in which safety precautions were violated and/or unusually careless acts were performed;
    e. Discovery or presence of substances in an employee's possession, vehicle, or near the individual's workplace;
    f. Odor of alcohol and/or residual odor peculiar to some drug or chemical substance;
    g. Appearance that the employee is "unfit for duty";
    h. Unexplained and/or frequent absenteeism or tardiness;
    i. Personality changes, unusual appearance, or disorientation; or
    j. Arrest for drug-related activity.
2. If a supervisor believes cause exists, he should report the findings and observations to the department head or his designee. The department head will then convey this information to the General Manager. Factors that substantiate cause should be documented on the Employee Substance Abuse Investigation Form. Upon approval by the department head or his or her designee and the General Manager, the employee will be asked to consent to substance abuse testing.
3. If the employee refuses to consent to testing, he or she will be either referred to the Employee Assistance Program or disciplined up to and including discharge, depending upon the circumstances.

4. The procedure for collecting and testing the specimens is the same as described earlier in this policy in Section IV(A)(4). The General Manager or his or her designee shall again explain to the employee the testing procedures and SGU's Substance Abuse Prevention Program.

Post-Accident Testing

Example 1: Federal Personnel Manual
Specific Condition Testing
    The head of each agency is also authorized by the agency to perform drug testing regarding an accident or unsafe practice.

Example 2: National Drug Policy Board
Accident or Unsafe Practice Testing
    The (Agency) is committed to providing a safe and secure work environment. Employees involved in on-the-job accidents or who engage in unsafe on-duty job-related activities that pose a danger to others or the overall operation of the (Agency) may be subject to testing. Based on the circumstances of the accident or unsafe act, the (operating unit head) may initiate testing when:
    (State criteria here.)
    (Consider the following example of appropriate criteria:)
    (Based on the circumstances of the accident or unsafe act, testing may be initiated when the accident or unsafe practice results in—
    1. A death or personal injury requiring immediate hospitalization, or
    2. Damage to government or private property in excess of $_____.)

Example 3: Large County Government (LCG)
    Current employees may be asked to submit to a test where cause exists to indicate that the LCG's drug and alcohol policy has been violated. Factors which could establish cause include, but are not limited to, Vehicle accidents.

Contractor Testing

Example 1: Large Service Company (LSC)
    On-site vendors and contractors whose employees have significant potential impact on the safety of the workplace should be required to have a compatible testing program as appropriate.
    Contract employees and vendors will be held to the same standards as LSC employees when performing services for the company on company property. Discipline will be left to the contractor or vendor. Any abuses you observe on the part of contract or vendor employees should be immediately reported to your supervisor.

Example 2: Small Construction Company (SCC)
Customer Substance Abuse Program Testing—All employees who have access to customer facilities that have contractor or vendor substance abuse programs will be requested to submit to drug testing in compliance with those customer programs. Whenever possible the drug testing and certification for customer substance abuse programs will be coordinated with the SCC's other drug testing provisions.

Example 3: Large Manufacturing Company (LMC)
E. Miscellaneous Matters
   5. All outside contractors of LMC will certify in writing to LMC that the contractor's employees having access to LMC property have been tested or screened for drugs or other psychoactive substances within the last twelve (12) months, and that the contractor's employees have tested negative for drugs or other psychoactive substances. All contracts, purchase orders, or agreements with contractors of LMC will be amended or written to include language of such contractor's certification regarding its employees' drug free condition.

Example 4: Department of Defense
23.7501 Policy
   It is the policy of the Department of Defense that defense contractors shall maintain a program for achieving a drug free work force.

Example 5: Small Service Company
Customer Substance Abuse Program
   All employees who have access to customer facilities who have contractor or vendor Substance Abuse Programs will be requested to submit to drug screening test(s) in compliance with those Customer Programs. Whenever possible the drug screening testing and certification for customer substance abuse programs will be coordinated with the company's Annual Drug Screening Program.

Random Testing

Example 1: Federal Personnel Manual
AGENCY DRUG TESTING PROGRAMS
A. Random and Comprehensive Testing in Sensitive Positions—The head of each Executive agency shall establish a program to test for the use of illegal drugs by employees in sensitive positions.
   (1) For purposes of this program, the term "employee(s) in a sensitive position" refers to:

    i. An employee in a position that an agency head designates Special Sensitive, Critical-Sensitive, or Noncritical-Sensitive under Chapter 731 of the Federal Personnel Manual or an employee in a position that an agency head designates as sensitive in accordance with Executive Order No. 10450, as amended;

   ii. An employee who has been granted access to classified information or may be granted access to classified information pursuant to a determination of trustworthiness by an agency head under Section 4 of Executive Order No. 12356;

  iii. Individuals serving under Presidential appointments;

  iv. Law enforcement officers as defined in 5 U.S.C. 8321(20); and

   v. Other positions that the agency head determines involve law enforcement, national security, the protection of life and property, public health or safety, or other functions requiring a high degree of trust and confidence.

(2) The head of each agency has discretion to determine which sensitive positions for which random testing is authorized should be subject to such testing. This determination should be based on the nature of the agency's mission, its employees' duties, the efficient use of agency resources, and the danger that could result from the failure of an employee to discharge his or her duties adequately. Thus, who will actually be tested is a function of a two-step analysis by the agency head.

(3) When selecting testing designated positions, agencies should ensure that the selection process does not result in arbitrary, capricious, or discriminatory selections. Agencies must be able to justify their selection of testing designated positions as a neutral application of the selection criteria set forth above. Agencies are absolutely prohibited from selecting positions for drug testing on the basis of a desire to test particular individual employees.

(4) Individuals in testing designated positions may be selected for random testing in a variety of ways. For example, their names or social security numbers may be selected randomly by computer, they may be selected according to their birth dates, or they may be selected by the first letter in their surnames.

(5) Random testing contemplates unscheduled testing and random sampling of the employees within the group of testing designated positions. As an alternative to random testing, the head of an agency may, at his or her discretion, designate that all employees in testing designated positions shall be tested.

Example 2: National Drug Policy Board
Position Titles Designated for Random Drug Testing
The position titles designated for random drug testing are listed in Appendix A, along with the criteria and procedures applied in designating such positions for drug testing including the justification for such criteria and procedures.
Sensitive Employees in Testing Designated Positions
The Executive Order requires random testing for employees in sensitive positions that have been designated as testing designated positions. As further specified in Appendix A, the (Agency head) has determined that these positions are testing designated positions that will be randomly tested. Accompanying the list of testing designated positions are the criteria and procedures used in designating such positions, pursuant to the Act, including the justification for such criteria and procedure.
Determining the Testing Designated Position
Among the factors the (agency head) has considered in determining a testing designated position are the extent to which the (Agency)—
1. Considers its mission inconsistent with illegal drug use;
2. Is engaged in law enforcement;
3. Must foster public trust by preserving employee reputation for integrity, honesty, and responsibility;
4. Has national security responsibilities;
5. Has drug interdiction responsibilities; or
The extent to which the position considered—
1. Authorizes employees to carry firearms;
2. Gives employees access to sensitive information;
3. Authorizes employees to engage in law enforcement;
4. Requires employees, as a condition of employment, to obtain a security clearance;
5. Requires employees to engage in activities affecting public health or safety.
These positions are characterized by critical safety or security responsibilities as related to the mission of the (Agency). The job functions associated with these positions directly and immediately relate to public health and safety, the protection of life and property, law enforcement, or national security. These positions are identified for random testing because they require the highest degree of trust and confidence. The Secretary reserves the right to add or delete positions determined to be testing designated positions pursuant to the criteria established in the Executive Order and this plan.
Implementing Random Testing
In implementing the program of random testing the Drug Program Coordinator shall—
1. Ensure that the means of random selection remains confidential; and

2. Evaluate periodically whether the numbers of employees tested and the frequency with which those tests will be administered satisfy the (Agency's) duty to achieve a drug free work force.

The number of sensitive employees occupying testing designated positions and the frequency with which random tests will be administered are specified in Appendix A.

Notification of Selection

An individual selected for random testing, and the individual's first-line supervisor, shall be notified the same day the test is scheduled, preferably within two hours of the scheduled testing. The supervisor shall explain to the employee that the employee is under no suspicion of taking drugs and that the employee's name was selected randomly.

Deferral of Testing

An employee selected for random drug testing may obtain a deferral of testing if the employee's first-line and second-line supervisors concur that a compelling need necessitates a deferral on the grounds that the employee is:

1. In a leave status (sick, annual, administrative, or leave without pay);

2. In official travel status away from the test site or is about to embark on official travel scheduled prior to testing notification.

An employee whose random drug test is deferred will be subject to an unannounced test within the following 60 days.

Example 3: Large Manufacturing Company

RANDOM TESTING

This type of testing is characterized by randomly selecting employees for drug and alcohol testing on an unannounced basis in "critical" jobs. Testing on an across-the-site basis should be considered only under unusual circumstances since significant legal risks and employee relations negatives can be encountered. Frequency and selection of employees should be designed not to discriminate against any individual or group in the testing population. Random testing, however, does not require that all employees be tested over time.

Recommendation

Random testing for drugs and alcohol should be considered for narrowly defined critical jobs at an unannounced frequency. Critical jobs include only those jobs that may directly have a substantial impact on the safety of the workplace, community, or environment.

Background Information

• This type of testing provides the largest employee population sample on a continuing basis.

• Targeted to critical jobs, random testing can be an effective deterrent to the use of controlled substances.

• Employees will not likely have time to mask or hide drug use since tests will not be announced.

- Since the selection process impacts more heavily on entire segments of jobs in the employee work force, it has the potential to create the most significant negative employee relations impact.
- Random testing is a less clearly defensible system given existing legal standards. Testing truly critical jobs only is a more defensible position than random testing of the entire employee population.
- Using an off-site testing laboratory, there is a 48–72 hour lag time between test and determination.
- Careful consideration should be given to the employee relations impact of random testing since this employee testing is initiated without any indication of performance problems.

Guidelines
- All applicable general testing guidelines apply to random testing.
- Employees with a confirmed positive test should be first considered by management for appropriate counseling, rehabilitation programs, follow-up testing, reassignment, or other appropriate action. Disciplinary action should normally be contemplated only after other actions to rehabilitate the employee have been carefully considered and found inappropriate.
- Sites should carefully design and monitor random testing programs to minimize potentially negative employee reactions.
- The Employee Relations Department and legal counsel should be consulted prior to establishing a random sampling plan.

Example 4: Small City Government
POLICY
    The City recognizes that certain sensitive positions are critical to the public welfare and fellow employees from a health and safety point of view. As a result, all current SCG employees in sensitive positions from a health and safety standpoint will submit to a random drug screening program. Each department will be analyzed periodically to determine the departments or positions which will be tested.
PROCEDURE
SCG Employees—Random Testing
    1. Random testing will be conducted for all positions considered sensitive from a health and safety standpoint and which may directly affect public safety or employee safety.
    2. Random testing will be scheduled each month in each SCG department which includes positions subject to random testing. The random selection procedure will be administered by the Human Resources Director. The method of random selection will be to select approximately one-twelfth ($\frac{1}{12}$) of the affected employees in each department using a random number table keyed to the social security number of each affected employee. Each affected employee in a department will have an equal chance of being tested each month.

Notice and Employee Acknowledgment

Example 1: Midsized Manufacturing Company (MMC)
NOTIFICATION TO EMPLOYEES
A summary of the MMC's Substance Abuse Program shall be distributed to all employees.

Example 2: Federal Personnel Manual
(Agency Name)
ACKNOWLEDGMENT OF NOTICE TO EMPLOYEES
WHOSE POSITION IS DESIGNATED SENSITIVE FOR DRUG
TESTING PURPOSES
I acknowledge receiving notice of the establishment of (agency name's) employee drug testing program. I understand that I may be selected for screening by urinalysis testing for the presence of controlled substances. I understand that a confirmed positive result of that testing or refusal to submit to testing may result in disciplinary action up to and including dismissal from the Federal service.

I have read the notice announcing the establishment of an employee drug testing program.

_____

Printed or Typed Name

_____

Signature of Employee

_____

Date

Example 3: Large Manufacturing Company
EMPLOYEE COVERAGE FORM
I, _____, have read and understand the policies and procedures in the site substance abuse programs.

I understand that the use, possession, sale, or distribution of alcohol, drugs, or controlled substances in the workplace is strictly prohibited. I also understand that the presence of such substances in my system during work hours places unacceptable risks and burdens on the safe and efficient operation of this site and, consequently, is strictly forbidden.

I also understand, in connection with this site's substance abuse program, that I am subject to testing for the presence of drugs (and alcohol) in my system and that my person, my personal effects, and my vehicle are subject to inspection for contraband, including drugs or alcohol, while on LMC property.

I further understand that site medical personnel are available for counseling regarding substance abuse, including possible referral to LMC-approved rehabilitation programs.

I fully understand that my cooperation with, and adherence to, the site's policies and procedures regarding substance abuse are conditions of my continued employment and that, if I violate, am insubordinate, or refuse to cooperate with any of these policies and procedures, I am subject to discipline, up to and including discharge.

_____

Signature

Example 4: Large Private Utility (LPU)
CHEMICAL ABUSE POLICY REQUIREMENTS
ACKNOWLEDGMENT

My signature on this form indicates that I have received a copy of "Chemical Substance Abuse," and "Chemical Substance Abuse Screening Program." I understand that I am responsible for knowing the contents of these policies and familiarizing myself with any future revisions.

I further understand that compliance with the drug screening program outlined in these policies is a condition of employment and/or unescorted access privileges. This includes, but is not limited to, random screening and specific testing participation in the event my fitness for duty is reevaluated.

I also understand that as a condition of employment, my vehicles, person, and personal lunch boxes, packages or bundles within the LPU property boundary may be searched. In addition, LPU property such as desks, file cabinets, lockers, or equipment may be searched without my consent. I understand that refusing a search subjects me to disciplinary action, including discharge and/or withdrawal of unescorted access privileges. Further, my acceptance of employment with LPU, its contractors, subcontractors, or others conducting work for LPU or its partners on LPU property constitutes consent for such searches. I also understand that narcotics or other forms of drugs or intoxicants are strictly forbidden on LPU property.

_____   _____   _____
Signature   Date   Supervisor/Witness

_____   _____
Company   Work Location/Group

SAMPLE GATE NOTICE

To preserve the safety of this workplace, the use, possession, sale, distribution, or presence of alcohol, drugs, or other controlled substances for nonmedical reasons in the workplace is prohibited.

Entry into company property is deemed consent to our inspection of person, vehicle, or personal effects. If you do not consent to inspection, please do not enter or remain on the property.

Voluntary Referral and Management Referral

Example 1: Small Government Utility (SGU)
Voluntary Referral
1. SGU employees experiencing problems with alcohol or other drugs are urged to seek assistance voluntarily through the Employee Assistance Program to resolve such problems before they become serious enough to require management referral or disciplinary action. The Employee Assistance Program counselors may be contacted directly.
2. If a supervisor has reason to believe that an employee has a problem for which rehabilitation is appropriate, the supervisor should inform the General Manager and remind the employee of this program, offering to arrange an appointment if the employee wishes through the Personnel Department.
3. Dependents of employees may voluntarily seek counseling and information on an entirely confidential basis by contacting the Employee Assistance Program counselor directly.

Management Referral
1. Employees whose job performance has deteriorated due to unknown factors may be referred by management to the Employee Assistance Program for evaluation of their performance problems.
2. Participation in the Employee Assistance Program is voluntary.
3. Any employee who exhibits chronic behavioral problems should be viewed as one who may possibly be in need of this program. The supervisor should confer with the General Manager and discuss whether to encourage the employee voluntarily to accept referral to the program, particularly when substance abuse is perceived to be a likely cause of a performance deficiency. The supervisor should refer to SGU's Substance Abuse Prevention Program and carefully follow its procedures when substance abuse is suspected.

Example 2: Federal Personnel Manual
B. Voluntary referrals, or self-referrals, are to be encouraged throughout EAP materials.
C. In the case of a management referral as a result of a positive drug screen, the employee assistance staff will interview and/or consult with supervisors and management officials, as requested, and provide them with guidance on how to refer the drug abusing employee to the assistance program. Once the referral is made, and the employee agrees to the appointment with the counselor, the counselor will require the employee to sign a consent for release of information to the supervisor before assistance will be provided. This consent will cover the release of information pertaining to the employee's compliance with the agreed upon treatment plan and the employee's progress during and at the end of treatment. Upon obtaining the signed con-

sent, the counselor will assess the problem(s), review the employee's health insurance coverage, and refer the individual to an appropriate treatment resource in the community. The counselor will monitor the employee's treatment and keep the supervisor advised as to the progress being made. The counselor will periodically follow up with the employee and his or her supervisor after any treatment which occurs and offer support and assistance as needed.

Example 3: Large Railroad Company (LRC)

VOLUNTARY REFERRALS

Although considered to be volunteers for the purpose of classification by the EAP Counselor, employees from this group invariably enter the program as a result of a crisis in their life.

The decision to address serious problems such as alcoholism or drug abuse is usually precipitated by crises such as a D.W.I. arrest, possession of illegal drugs, threat of divorce, financial trouble, or one of many other issues which accompany substance abuse.

Mandatory Referral

Based on these facts, the most effective method of motivating an individual is to create a crisis or allow the person to face the consequence of his or her behavior. This can be accomplished in a variety of ways. The most effective crisis intervention, for our consideration, is the supervisor referral which is based on declining job performance.

Voluntary Referral

There are, of course, those isolated individuals who become aware of the severity of their problem and seek help from the EAP Counselor on his or her own initiative.

Volunteers who enter the program can expect all the services provided by the EAP Counselor to be on a confidential basis. The laws concerning confidentiality are very precise. They state an individual is entitled to protection under the Bill of Rights, which guarantees privacy of all persons and their papers. The only information a supervisor or any other person will receive is information which the employee specifically agrees to release and only then with a signed consent form.

These employees are returned to the workplace as soon as they are ready to resume work activities. In these cases, the counselor can report the employee back to work without a physical examination. This is made possible by a Ready to Return to Work Agreement with the Chief Medical Officer who will confirm the medical qualification at a later date.

Supervisor Referrals

The LRC's Employee Assistance Program is designed to help employees whose job performance has deteriorated to unsatisfactory levels and to get them the professional help that will make them productive again. Job performance problems such as absenteeism, increased frequency of on-the-job accidents, or frequent disciplinary actions and reduced productivity are often caused by personal problems. The employee may be experiencing problems with alcohol, drugs, due to emotional or financial stress, or relocation difficulties, etc.

The supervisor's role is to identify and document the <u>Job Performance Problem</u> when the employee's <u>personal</u> problems become critical enough to affect his or her ability to perform at an acceptable level. LRC supervisors are well trained to establish levels of work performance and to recognize changes in productivity. It is these sometime subtle changes that the supervisor should look for and <u>not</u> attempt to determine what the personal problem is or try to do behavior counseling. The EAP counselor will provide this service and relieve the supervisor of the burden of trying to solve such problems.

The Employee Assistance Program is available as an additional resource to be utilized by supervisors. If used properly the EAP will free the supervisor to manage and motivate <u>all</u> his or her people rather than attempt to counsel a few problem employees.

Example 4: National Drug Policy Board
F. Voluntary Referral

Under Executive Order 12564, the (Agency) is required to initiate action to discipline any employee found to use illegal drugs in every circumstance except one. If an employee (1) voluntarily admits his or her drug use; (2) completes counseling or an EAP; and (3) thereafter refrains from drug use, such discipline "is not required."

(If you do not wish to create an absolute bar to discipline for individuals who voluntarily come forward, insert the following language:)

The decision whether to discipline a voluntary referral will be made by the agency head on a case by case basis depending upon the facts and circumstances. Although an absolute bar to discipline cannot be provided for certain positions because of their extreme sensitivity, the Agency, in determining whether to discipline, shall consider that the employee has come forward voluntarily.

(If you wish to create an absolute bar to discipline for individuals who voluntarily come forward, insert the following language:)

Because the Order permits an agency to create a "safe harbor" for an employee who meets all three of these conditions, the (Agency) has decided to create such a "safe harbor" and will not initiate disciplinary action against employees who meet all three of these conditions:

a. Voluntarily identifies him/herself as a user of illegal drugs prior to being identified through other means;
b. Obtains counseling or rehabilitation through an Employee Assistance Program; and
c. Thereafter refrains from using illegal drugs.

This self-referral option allows any employee to step forward and identify him/herself as an illegal drug user for the purpose of entering a drug treatment program under the EAP. In stepping forward, and consistent with Section XIIB, an employee may volunteer for a drug test as a means of identification. Although this self-identification test may yield a verified positive test result, such result shall merely constitute an identification for purposes of this Section.

Since the key to this provision's rehabilitative effectiveness is an employee's willingness to admit his or her problem, this provision will not be available to an employee who is asked to provide a urine sample when required, or who is found to have used illegal drugs and who thereafter requests protection under this provision.

Investigations

Example 1: Small Government Utility

If a supervisor believes cause exists, he should report the findings and observations to the department head or his designee. The department head will then convey this information to the General Manager. Factors which substantiate cause should be documented on the Employee Substance Abuse Investigation Form. Upon approval by the department head or his designee and the General Manager, the employee will be asked to consent to substance abuse testing.

SUBSTANCE ABUSE INVESTIGATION FORM

I have observed the following condition(s) affecting the work of _____, which give rise to suspicion of substance abuse, and request an investigation of same:

Condition(s) observed: _____

_____
_____
_____
_____

Date: _____   _____
                                     Department Head

Cause exists for medical and/or drug tests of this employee.

Date: _____   _____
                                     General Manager

Example 2: National Drug Policy Board
Procedures

If an employee is suspected of using illegal drugs, the appropriate supervisor will gather all information, facts, and circumstances leading to and supporting this suspicion. (Agencies should insert a higher level approval requirement that is consistent with their organization structure. In some agencies, this may be the next level supervisor above the supervisor making the finding that a reasonable suspicion of illegal drug use exists. In other agencies, it may be more appropriate to have the Assistant Secretary of Administration approve reasonable suspicion testing.)

When reasonable suspicion has been established, the appropriate supervisor will promptly detail, for the record and in writing, the circumstances which formed the basis to warrant the testing. A written report will be prepared to include, at a minimum, the appropriate dates and times of reported drug-related incidents, reliable/credible sources of information, rationale leading to the test, findings of the test, and the action taken.

Alcohol Testing

Example 1: Large Manufacturing Company

Testing on a random or for-cause basis using a breathalyzer can be used as an assist to management investigating an unusual incident, behavior, or a deviation from performance standards. Supervisory judgment of ability to perform the job should dictate action taken. The test should be used to assist management in determining the incident cause. Random testing for alcohol should be considered for narrowly defined critical jobs only.

Recommendation

Traditional practice relying on supervisor judgment may be sufficient for most sites. Sites may consider using a breathalyzer to assist in evaluating performance deviations, incidents, or unusual behavior. Random testing should be considered for narrowly defined critical jobs. Assistance from the Employee Relations Department and legal counsel is recommended in designing a site random testing program.

Background Information

- Test will give positive indication of alcohol in the body.
- Test results are available instantaneously.
- Testing procedure is relatively simple and reasonably accurate.
- Alcohol will be detectable for only a few hours after ingestion; therefore, the testing time is a significant factor.

Example 2: Large Manufacturing Company

Miscellaneous Matters

Company facilities will utilize breathalyzers or other testing procedures to detect alcohol use or possible impairment of associates. If alcohol use or possible impairment is suspected, an associate should be treated in the same fashion as others in a for-cause investigation, including use of the Substance Abuse Investigation Form and the Associate Chemical Screening Form.

Transportation of Impaired Employees

Example 1: Large Service Company
Following the alcohol and/or drug test, make arrangements for the employee to be taken home. Do not allow the employee to go home alone. Employment status and return to work determination will be made following the medical review of the laboratory analysis of the specimen. This usually takes 24–72 hours.

Example 2: Midsized Manufacturing Company (MMC)
If the Company believes that an employee may be impaired by drugs or alcohol and appears to be unable to drive safely, arrangements shall be made for transportation provided by the MMC. If the employee refuses to accept transportation provided or arranged by MMC, and insists upon driving, he or she should be strongly discouraged from doing so, but not forcibly restrained. If appropriate, MMC may take disciplinary action, up to and including termination of employment, against the employee who still insists upon operating a motor vehicle. Finally, the employee should be advised that MMC will notify local law enforcement authorities if the employee still attempts to drive. If the employee does attempt to drive, the police shall be notified immediately, and all actions taken to persuade the employee not to drive shall be documented.

Collection and Testing Procedures: Collection Personnel and Test Kits

Example 1: Large Manufacturing Company (LMC)
Testing of Applicants and Associates
Applicants or associates will be furnished a test kit by the nurse, or other responsible associate, who is responsible for assuring the specimen is properly collected and transmitted to the testing company in accordance with directions on the testing kit and the proper chain of custody. If the LMC associate has a reasonable suspicion that the specimen has been tampered with by the applicant, the applicant should not be considered any further for employment and should be so advised.

Example 2: Large County Government
(5)   While at the county physician's office, applicants will be furnished a test kit by the nurse who is responsible for assuring the specimen is properly collected and transmitted to the testing company in accordance with directions on the testing kit and the proper chain of custody.

Example 3: Small Manufacturing Company
1.   The urine collection will be coordinated by the occupational health nurse at this time during the scheduled preplacement examination.

Accuracy Safeguards (Observable Voids, Temperature/pH, Toilet Bluing)

<u>Example</u>: Department of Transportation

(f) <u>Integrity and identity of specimen.</u> Employers shall take precautions to ensure that a urine specimen not be adulterated or diluted during the collection procedure and that information on the urine bottle and on the urine custody and control form can identify the individual from whom the specimen was collected. The following minimum precautions shall be taken to ensure that unadulterated specimens are obtained and correctly identified:

(1) To deter the dilution of specimens at the collection site, toilet bluing agents shall be placed in toilet tanks wherever possible, so the reservoir of water in the toilet bowl always remains blue. Where practicable, there shall be no other source of water (e.g., no shower or sink) in the enclosure where urination occurs. If there is another source of water in the enclosure, it shall be effectively secured or monitored to ensure it is not used (undetected) as a source for diluting the specimen.

(2) When an individual arrives at the collection site, the collection site person shall ensure that the individual is positively identified as the employee selected for testing (e.g., through presentation of photo identification or identification by the employer's representative). If the individial's identity cannot be established, the collection site person shall not proceed with the collection.

(3) If the individual fails to arrive at the assigned time, the collection site person shall contact the appropriate authority to obtain guidance on the action to be taken.

(4) The collection site person shall ask the individual to remove any unnecessary outer garments such as a coat or jacket that might conceal items or substances that could be used to tamper with or adulterate the individual's urine specimen. The collection site person shall ensure that all personal belongings such as a purse or briefcase remain with the outer garments. The individual may retain his or her wallet.

(5) The individual shall be instructed to wash and dry his or her hands prior to urination.

(6) After washing hands, the individual shall remain in the presence of the collection site person and shall not have access to any water fountain, faucet, soap dispenser, cleaning agent, or any other materials which could be used to adulterate the specimen.

(7) The individual may provide his or her specimen in the privacy of a stall or otherwise partitioned area that allows for individual privacy.

(8)   The collection site person shall note any unusual behavior or appearance on the urine custody and control form.

(9)   In the exceptional event that an employer-designated collection site is not accessible and there is an immediate requirement for specimen collection (e.g., an accident investigation), a public restroom may be used according to the following procedures: A collection site person of the same gender as the individual shall accompany the individual into the public restroom which shall be made secure during the collection procedure. If possible, a toilet bluing agent shall be placed in the bowl and any accessible toilet tank. The collection site person shall remain in the restroom, but outside the stall, until the specimen is collected. If no bluing agent is available to deter specimen dilution, the collection site person shall instruct the individual not to flush the toilet until the specimen is delivered to the collection site person. After the collection site person has possession of the specimen, the individual will be instructed to flush the toilet and to participate with the collection site person in completing the chain of custody procedures.

(10) Upon receiving the specimen from the individual, the collection site person shall determine that it contains at least 60 milliliters of urine. If there is less than 60 milliliters of urine in the container, additional urine shall be collected in a separate container to reach a total of 60 milliliters. (The temperature of the partial specimen in each separate container shall be measured in accordance with paragraph (f)(12) of this section, and the partial specimens shall be combined in one container.) The individual may be given a reasonable amount of liquid to drink for this purpose (e.g., a glass of water). If the individual fails for any reason to provide 60 milliliters of urine, the collection site person shall contact the appropriate authority to obtain guidance on the action to be taken.

(11) After the specimen has been provided and submitted to the collection site person, the individual shall be allowed to wash his or her hands.

(12) Immediately after the specimen is collected, the collection site person shall measure the temperature of the specimen. The temperature measuring device used must accurately reflect the temperature of the specimen and not contaminate the specimen. The time from urination to temperature measure is critical and in no case shall exceed 4 minutes.

(13) If the temperature of a specimen is outside the range of 32.5°–37.7° C/ 90.5°–99.8° F, that is a reason to believe that the individual may have altered or substituted the specimen, and another specimen shall be collected under direct observation of

a same-gender collection site person and both specimens shall be forwarded to the laboratory for testing. An individual may volunteer to have his or her oral temperture taken to provide evidence to counter the reason to believe the individual may have altered or substituted the specimen caused by the specimen's temperature falling outside the prescribed range.

(14) Immediately after the specimen is collected, the collection site person shall also inspect the specimen to determine its color and look for any signs of contaminants. Any unusual findings shall be noted on the urine custody and control form.

((15) and (16) omitted.)

(17) Both the individual being tested and the collection site person shall keep the specimen in view at all times prior to its being sealed and labeled. As provided below, the specimen shall be sealed (by placement of a tamperproof seal over the bottle cap and down the sides of the bottle) and labeled in the presence of the employee. If the specimen is transferred to a second bottle, the collection site person shall request the individual to observe the transfer of the specimen and the placement of the tamperproof seal over the bottle cap and down the sides of the bottle.

(18) The collection site person and the individual shall be present at the same time during procedures outlined in paragraphs (f)(19)–(f)(22) of this section.

(19) The collection site person shall place securely on the bottle an identification label which contains the date, the individual's specimen number, and any other identifying information provided or required by the employer. If separate from the label, the tamperproof seal shall also be applied.

(20) The individual shall initial the identification label on the specimen bottle for the purpose of certifying that it is the specimen collected from him or her.

(21) The collection site person shall enter on the urine custody and control form all information identifying the specimen. The collection site person shall sign the urine custody and control form certifying that the collection was accomplished according to the instructions provided.

Dealing With Tampering

Example 1: Federal Personnel Manual

Agencies should provide guidance on the circumstances when observation may be required. Generally, an employee or applicant may be required to provide a sample under observation if there is reason to believe that the employee or applicant may alter or substitute the urine specimen. For example, employers may wish to require observation when facts and circumstances suggest that the person to be tested (a) is an illegal drug user; (b) is under the influence of drugs at the time of the test; (c) has previously been confirmed by the agency to be an illegal drug user; (d) is seen to have equipment or implements used to tamper with urine samples; (e) has recently been determined to have tampered with a sample.

Example 2: Midsized Manufacturing Company
Conduct of and Handling of Test Results

Applicants

If a urine sample is obviously not authentic (such as when an applicant substitutes cold tap water for urine), the applicant shall be immediately informed that the sample is not acceptable and that the applicant will no longer be considered for employment. The applicant may reapply after a six (6) month period.

Employees

Adulterated or unreadable samples, or samples which are clearly not authentic, shall be considered as evidence of an employee's failure to cooperate with Company policy. The employee will be questioned concerning the adulterated sample according to Company policy. If a satisfactory explanation is not provided, the employee is subject to disciplinary action up to and including termination of employment. If a satisfactory explanation is provided, a new drug screen test may be performed.

Split Samples

Example: Department of Transportation (DOT)

Under § 40.21(c), an employer may test the sample obtained under a DOT drug rule only for the drugs required or specifically authorized to be tested under the DOT drug rule. That is, an employer must test the sample for the five major drugs listed in each DOT drug regulation. If the DOT agency involved authorizes testing for Drug X under § 40.21(b), the employer may also test the sample for that drug. If the employer wants to test, in addition, for Drug Y, the employer must obtain a second sample from the employee. The obtaining of this second sample is not under the authority of the DOT regulation. The employer must base its request for the second sample on whatever other legal authority is available, since the employer cannot rely on the DOT regulation as the basis for the request.

Chain of Custody

Example 1: Small Manufacturing Company
1. In the presence of the person giving the specimen, the specimen container shall be sealed with evidence tape.
2. The time and date and signature of the occupational health nurse will be entered on the Chain of Custody form.

3. In the presence of the person giving the specimen the sealed specimen shall then be placed in the plastic chain of custody zip lock bag and it shall also be sealed with evidence tape.

4. The occupational health nurse will ensure that appropriate chain of custody documentation is completed at the plant and by the courier receiving the specimen for the laboratory.

5. The courier will transport the specimens to the independent lab for confirmation.

Example 2: Department of Defense Directive 1010.1
            Effective June 1, 1985

General

1. Chain of custody procedures are designed to ensure accuracy in referral of service members for counseling and rehabilitation programs, and to ensure that commanders are provided with an accurate assessment of the military fitness of the command. Such procedures also ensure that any use of urinalysis results in other proceedings will be based upon reliable procedures. This enclosure establishes minimum requirements for chain of custody procedures, which may be supplemented by each Military Department.

2. The individual directing that a urine test be conducted shall identify, as appropriate, the service member, work group, unit (or part thereof) to be tested. A responsible individual, such as the alcohol and drug coordinator or the base or unit urine test program monitor, shall be assigned to coordinate urine collection.

Example 3: Department of Transportation

§ 40.29 Laboratory analysis procedures.

(a) Security and chain of custody.

(1) Drug testing laboratories shall be secure at all times. They shall have in place sufficient security measures to control access to the premises and to ensure that no unauthorized personnel handle specimens or gain access to the laboratory processes or to areas where records are stored. Access to these secured areas shall be limited to specifically authorized individuals whose authorization is documented. With the exception of personnel authorized to conduct inspections on behalf of Federal agencies for which the laboratory is engaged in urine testing or on behalf of DHHS, all authorized visitors and maintenance and service personnel shall be escorted at all times. Documentation of individuals accessing these areas, dates, and time of entry and purpose of entry must be maintained.

(2) Laboratories shall use chain of custody procedures to maintain control and accountability of specimens from receipt through completion of testing, reporting of results, during storage, and continuing until final disposition of specimens.

The date and purpose shall be documented on an appropriate chain of custody form each time a specimen is handled or transferred, and every individual in the chain shall be identified. Accordingly, authorized technicians shall be responsible for each urine specimen or aliquot in their possession and shall sign and complete chain of custody forms for those specimens or aliquots as they are received.

Lab Selection

Example 1:   Large Manufacturing Company
Miscellaneous Matters
1.   All testing will be done by a lab chosen by the Corporate Director of Personnel.

Example 2:   Small City Government
Testing Procedures—General Matters
1.   All testing will be done by a lab chosen by the Mayor and City Council in consultation with the City Manager and Human Resources Director.

Example 3:   Large Construction Company
   Human Resources is responsible for the day-to-day administration of this policy and to assist supervisors in any disciplinary action arising from the implementation of this policy. This includes, but is not limited to, the scheduling of screening for applicants and employees and the coordination with the contracted toxicological service.

Confirmation Techniques

Example 1:   Large Manufacturing Company
Miscellaneous Matters
   If an initial screening test is positive, a confirmation test will be performed on the same specimen, unless the applicant or associate admits to using drugs or other psychoactive substances, whereupon the admission will be considered a confirmation.

Example 2:   Department of Transportation
Confirmatory test
   A second analytical procedure is to identify the presence of a specific drug or metabolite which is independent of the initial test and which uses a different technique and chemical principle from that of the initial test in order to ensure reliability and accuracy. (At this time gas chromatography/mass spectrometry (GC/MS) is the only authorized confirmation method for cocaine, marijuana, opiates, amphetamines, and phencyclidine.)

Example 3:   Large Manufacturing Company
Testing
   Confirmatory tests should use gas chromatography/mass spectrometry or high-pressure liquid chromatography or equivalent techniques that can positively identify compounds.

Drugs to be Tested

Example 1: Small Manufacturing Company
Miscellaneous Matters
    The company will determine the psychoactive substances for which testing will be performed.

Example 2:   Large Manufacturing Company
    Medical Division has established a recommended list of drugs to be tested for and selected appropriate screening and confirmatory tests for each substance. Local patterns of drug abuse may prompt site management to test for additional substances.

Example 3:   Department of Defense
Drugs Tested
    The ASD(HA) periodically shall issue a list of drugs for which the drug testing laboratories may report results. Each Military Department may determine which of the drugs on the list will be tested in the laboratories for which it is responsible.

Notification of Results/Confidentiality

Example: Midsized Manufacturing Company (MMC)
Conduct of and Handling of Test Results and Referral for Counseling or Rehabilitation
1.   Procedures established by MMC's designated testing laboratory shall be followed for the collection of sample body fluids.
2.   The laboratory should be instructed to communicate the results of any tests to a designated MMC official only.
3.   Negative results should, in turn, be communicated orally but confidentially to the employee by a member of management. If an employee has been suspended pending the results of the examination, the employee may, if appropriate, be reinstated with back pay.
4.   Positive test results (positive drug test results must be confirmed by the laboratory using GC/MS) will be handled as follows:
    (a)   The employee should be met with in private by a representative of management and one other member of management. In extreme cases, security personnel may attend as well.
    (b)   The results of the medical examination or drug or alcohol screening test should be given to the employee and the employee should be requested to provide an explanation.
    (c)   If the results were positive tests for drugs, the employee should be asked if he or she desires an additional confirming drug test on the original sample, at the employee's expense. If an employee

    desires such a reconfirmation test and pays for it, no further action should be taken until the results have been obtained. If the employee has already been suspended, the suspension shall continue pending the results of the reconfirmation test.

(d) If a satisfactory explanation is not provided, the employee may be disciplined or referred for appropriate counseling and rehabilitation, as MMC determines.

(e) If the employee refuses referral for counseling or rehabilitation, he or she will be suspended pending final action or termination.

(f) If the employee agrees to referral for counseling or rehabilitation, the employee shall sign the Last Chance Assistance Agreement.

(g) A confidential written memorandum of the discussion with the employee should be prepared.

(h) Upon request, an employee shall be allowed access to the results of any drug or alcohol test conducted pursuant to this program. The employee is entitled to a copy of the results.

Opportunity to Contest Results

Example 1:   Small City Government (SCG)

    If a specimen is confirmed positive, the employee will be informed of the results by the Human Resources Director or his designee. If an employee disagrees with the test result, he or she may have an opportunity to contest the results if the employee requests within 30 days of being notified of the results that an SCG-approved, federally licensed laboratory retest the original specimen at the employee's own expense. One retest of the original specimen will be allowed under this procedure.

Example 2:   National Drug Policy Board

    When a confirmed positive result has been returned by the laboratory, the Medical Review Officer shall perform the duties set forth in the HHS Guidelines. For example, the Medical Review Officer may choose to conduct employee medical interviews, review employee medical history, or review any other relevant biomedical factors. The Medical Review Officer must review all medical records made available by the tested employee when a confirmed positive test could have resulted from legally prescribed medication. Evidence to justify a positive result may include, but is not limited to:

1. A valid prescription; or
2. A verification from the individual's physician verifying a valid prescription.

    Individuals are not entitled, however, to present evidence to the Medical Review Officer in a trial-type administrative proceeding, although the Medical Review Officer has the discretion to accept evidence in any manner the Medical Review Officer deems most efficient or necessary.

If the Medical Review Officer determines there is no justification for the positive result, such result will then be considered a verified positive test result. The Medical Review Officer shall immediately contact the EAP Administrator upon obtaining a verified positive test result.

Rehabilitation Options/Time Off for Rehabilitation and Counseling

Example 1: Midsized Manufacturing Company
Work time lost for counseling/rehabilitation will be paid according to eligibility for sick days, applicable short-term disability benefits, and eligible vacation pay.

Example 2: Small Service Company (SSC)
Employees who enroll in the SSC's EAP may be granted a leave of absence so he or she may maintain continuous employment and other benefits applicable to those employed by the company.

Example 3: Small Government Utility
Employees who enroll in the Employee Assistance Program may be granted a medical leave of absence so they may maintain continuous service and other applicable benefits.

Example 4: National Drug Policy Board
Employees shall be allowed up to one hour (or more as necessitated by travel time) of excused absence for each counseling session, up to a maximum of (Agency must state limit here), during the assessment/referral phase of rehabilitation. Absences during duty hours for rehabilitation or treatment must be charged to the appropriate leave category in accordance with law and leave regulations.

Medical Benefits for Counseling/Rehabilitation

Example 1: Midsized Manufacturing Company
Benefits are available under the medical insurance plan, depending on the medical diagnosis.

Example 2: Small Government Utility (SGU)
Medical benefits are provided in accordance with the SGU health insurance plan. Other costs of treatment or rehabilitation will be the responsibility of the employee.

Example 3: Small Service Company (SSC)
Medical benefits are provided in accordance with SSC's health insurance plan. All other costs of treatment for rehabilitation will be the responsibility of the employee.

Post-Rehabilitation Agreements

Example 1: Large Manufacturing Company (LMC)
Testing of Associates—Testing Procedures
    If an associate agrees to seek professional evaluation, the personnel manager should stay in contact with the associate's physician or counselor during the treatment to assure that the associate is in compliance with the prescribed treatment. The associate will be placed on medical leave during his absence. Once LMC has been informed that the associate is again suitable for employment, before the associate may be reinstated, the associate must sign the Surveillance Agreement Form and agree to random drug screening for a period of one year.

Example 2: Midsized Manufacturing Company (MMC)
Effect of a Positive Test After Referral
    After an employee has been referred for counseling or rehabilitation under MMC's Substance Abuse Program, a condition of continued employment is that the employee promise to remain drug- or alcohol-free. If such an employee is again requested to take a drug or alcohol screening test, and the results are positive, that employee will be discharged.

LAST CHANCE ASSISTANCE AGREEMENT

1. I promise to fully cooperate and participate in MMC's counseling/rehabilitation program in accordance with instructions and requirements of program administrators. I understand that my leave to continue in a counseling or rehabilitation program may be reviewed on a weekly basis.
2. I authorize counseling or rehabilitation representatives to confer with MMC officials regarding my attendance, progress, and suitability for continued employment or return to active employment, as the case may be, including the disclosure of medical/psychiatric evaluations of me.
3. I understand that, upon my continued active employment or return to active employment, I must meet all established standards of conduct and job performance required of any other employee, and that I will be subject to the same disciplinary procedure.
4. I understand and agree that I will willingly submit to unscheduled drug and/or alcohol testing at any time, and that my failure to take such a test as requested, or to have a positive test result, will be cause for my termination of employment. I agree that unscheduled testing may be required of me for up to twelve months following the date of this agreement.
5. I understand and agree that my future employment depends upon my remaining free of drugs and/or free of alcohol abuse for the entire duration of my continued employment, and that this "LAST

CHANCE" opportunity afforded me by MMC is conditioned accordingly. Such conditions, including those above, are recognized to be in addition to MMC's right to alter my employment relationship with it at will, and for reasons not set forth above.

Employee
Date: _____

APPROVED:

_____

_____

Title
Date: _____

Employee Failure to Cooperate

Example 1: Midsized Manufacturing Company (MMC)
Employee compliance with MMC's program is a condition of employment. Failure or refusal of any employee to fully cooperate and participate in the program, sign any required document, or submit to a drug or alcohol test will be grounds for termination of employment, unless a compelling, satisfactory reason is provided. Employees who continue employment while undergoing counseling or rehabilitation will be required to meet all established standards of conduct and job performance. Employees who have been referred for counseling or rehabilitation under this policy shall be required to fully cooperate and participate in their rehabilitation. This may include the requirement for regular attendance at Alcoholics Anonymous or similar therapy sessions. Employees may be required to undergo drug or alcohol screening tests at any time during the course of their counseling or rehabilitation for a period up to one year. If MMC determines that an employee has failed to cooperate under the terms of the company's policy, the employee should be suspended without pay, pending further investigation and final decision or disciplinary action.

Example 2: Small Service Company (SSC)
If an employee refuses to seek the assistance of SSC's EAP after testing positive and being informed of SSC policy, he or she may be terminated for violation of SSC policy and failing to follow SSC medical standards, or the employee may be given the opportunity to resign.

Example 3: National Drug Policy Board
Failure to Appear for Testing
Failure to appear for testing without a deferral will be considered refusal to participate in testing, and will subject an employee to the range of disciplinary actions, including dismissal, and an applicant to the can-

cellation of an offer of employment. If an individual fails to appear at the collection site at the assigned time, the collector shall contact the DPC to obtain guidance on action to be taken.

Example 4: Small City Government

If the employee refuses to sign the consent form while knowingly able, he will be either referred to the Employee Assistance Program or disciplined up to and including discharge, depending upon the circumstances.

Example 5: Small Government Utility (SGU)

If, during the one-year surveillance agreement period, the employee tests positive on a drug test, he or she will be terminated for violation of SGU policy and failing to meet SGU medical standards.

Disciplinary Options

Example 1: Large Manufacturing Company (LMC)

This Substance Abuse Prevention Process policy primarily governs LMC actions in the area of alcohol, drugs, or other psychoactive substances. Other LMC policies may be applicable in this area to the extent they do not conflict with this policy.

Example 2: Small City Government (SCG)

In any situation where SCG's Substance Abuse Prevention Program conflicts with other SCG personnel policies, the Substance Abuse Prevention Program will prevail.

Management Communications With EAP/Rehabilitation Counselor

Example 1: Large County Government

If an employee agrees to seek professional evaluation, cooperation with the program will be a condition of continued employment. The Personnel Director should stay in contact with the employee's physician or counselor during the treatment to assure that the employee is in compliance with the prescribed treatment. The employee may be placed on sick leave pursuant to County Policy and Procedures, Chapter IX, Leave of Absence, during his or her absence up to a period of 60 calendar days or for the duration of that employee's leave accrual, whichever is longer. Once the county has been informed that the employee is suitable to return to his or her position, the employee, prior to reinstatement, must sign the Surveillance Agreement Form, and agree to drug screening testing for a period of one (1) year, for probable cause.

Example 2: Federal Personnel Manual

CONSENT FOR RELEASE OF PATIENT INFORMATION
DURING OR AFTER TREATMENT OR REHABILITATION

I, _____, hereby consent to the disclosure of
(Employee/Patient Name)

information concerning my progress in terminating illegal drug use. I authorize the _____to disclose that infor-
(Treatment/Rehabilitation Facility)
mation to _____, director of the Employee Assistance
(Name)
Program at _____ and to
(Name of Agency)
_____, my supervisor and to the agency Medical
(Name of Supervisor)
Review Official for drug use monitoring under Executive Order 12564, which provides for a drug free Federal workplace.

I understand that this consent is subject to revocation at any time, except to the extent that action has been taken in reliance thereon, and that it will expire without express revocation upon _____.
(Date, Event, Condition)

This consent to disclose the above-described treatment records was freely given, without reservation, for the purpose set out above.

_____
(Signature of Employee/Patient)

_____
(Date on which consent is signed)

CLAUSE FOR USE IF EMPLOYEE IS A MINOR OR LEGALLY INCOMPETENT

I, _____, the [parent/legal guardian or personal legal
(Name)
representative] of the above-named employee/patient, hereby consent to the aforementioned release of information on his/her behalf.

_____
(Signature)

_____
(Date)

POST-REHABILITATION SURVEILLANCE AGREEMENT

I acknowledge my identification as a user of psychoactive agents. I recognize my obligation to meet the medical standards of MMC to maintain my eligibility for employment. Therefore, I agree to maintain abstinence from any psychoactive agent unless medically prescribed. Further, I agree, when requested by MMC officials, to submit to random drug surveillance tests for a period of at least one year from _____ through _____.

I understand that refusal or failure to submit to a drug surveillance test or a positive finding on that test shall be cause for immediate discharge from my employment for failing to meet MMC medical standards.

I understand and agree to the above terms and conditions of employment.

Associate _____

SSN _____

_____
Associate Signature

_____
Company Official

Date _____

Effect on Personnel Records

Example 1: National Drug Policy Board
Confidentiality of Records in General
 All drug testing information specifically relating to individuals is confidential and should be treated as such by anyone authorized to review or compile program records. In order to efficiently implement this order and to make information readily retrievable, the DPC shall maintain all records relating to reasonable suspicion testing, suspicion of tampering evidence, and any other authorized documentation necessary to implement this order.

 All records and information of the personnel actions taken on employees with verified positive test results should be forwarded to the (Labor Management Relations Section). Such shall remain confidential, locked in a combination safe, with only authorized individuals who have a "need to know" having access to them.

Example 2: National Drug Policy Board
Maintenance of Records
 The (Agency) shall establish or amend a recordkeeping system to maintain the records of the (Agency's) Drug Free Workplace Program consistent with the (Agency's) Private Act System of Records and with all applicable federal laws, rules, and regulations regarding confidentiality of records including the Privacy Act 5 U.S.C. § 552a. If necessary, records may be maintained as required by subsequent administrative or judicial proceedings, or at the discretion of the (Agency head).

Aftercare Follow-Up

Example: Small Service Company (SSC)
 For two years after successful completion of rehabilitation and return to work, the employee will have periodic, confidential meetings with SSC's EAP representative so that the employee's aftercare program can be assessed and evaluated. The EAP representative will discuss the matter with the company president if a problem exists and appropriate action will

be taken according to SSC policy. After the two-year time period, so long as the employee has maintained compliance with the program, all records and references to the employee's substance abuse problem will be deleted from the records.

Medical Authorization Review—Prescription Drugs

Example: Large Manufacturing Company (LMC)
Miscellaneous Matters
    In any of the selection or testing situations described in this policy, if prescription drugs are detected and the applicant or associate is able to prove medical or professional authorization for the prescription, LMC reserves the right to contact the individual's physician or professional, or LMC officials may send the individual to the company physician for verification and review of the situation. The appropriate consent form to be utilized will be the Associate Chemical Screening Consent Form.

Use of Employer Vehicles

Example: Midsized Manufacturing Company (MMC)
Special Provisions for Employees Who Operate Company-Owned or Leased Vehicles, or Who Operate Personal Vehicles on Company Business
    Substance abuse by employees who operate company-owned or leased (including short-term car rental) vehicles or their own vehicles on MMC business can create a very serious risk for both themselves and members of the public, and behavior off-the-job can have an influence upon behavior on-the-job. Therefore, the following rules and disciplinary action shall apply to those employees:

(a) Employees who operate company-owned or leased vehicles (including short-term car rental) shall be subject to disciplinary action up to and including termination of employment for a conviction for driving that vehicle while under the influence of alcohol or drugs. This provision applies regardless of whether the vehicle is being operated for personal or business use.

(b) Employees who operate their own personal vehicles on MMC business shall be subject to disciplinary action up to and including termination of employment for a conviction for driving while under the influence of alcohol or drugs when the employees are operating those vehicles on MMC business. (For purposes of this paragraph, "operating on MMC business" shall mean that the employees would be entitled to reimbursement by MMC for that specific trip.)

(c) Employees who must operate a vehicle as an integral part of their jobs, such as MMC truck drivers, are subject to disciplinary action for a conviction for driving under the influence of alcohol or drugs even if such offense occurred in the employees' own personal vehicles and not while on MMC business. The first conviction shall be subject to disciplinary action up to and including termination of employment; a second conviction in a 12-month period will result in termination of employment.

(d) Any employees who are covered under the above provisions shall report to their supervisor any citation alleging that they were driving under the influence of alcohol or drugs regardless of whether the offense may have occurred in the employees' vehicles, MMC-owned or leased vehicles, on personal business, or on MMC business. Failure to report such citations may result in disciplinary action up to and including termination of employment. The report must be made within five days of the citations unless the employees are unable to make such reports due to extenuating circumstances.

Employer Entertainment Functions

Example 1: Small Construction Company
There may be occasional social or customer functions where alcohol may be served, but these will be highly restricted and approved in advance by the General Manager.

Example 2: Large Service Company
Local management at each location will determine the appropriateness of serving alcoholic beverages at company-sponsored functions.

Searches

Example 1: Large Manufacturing Company (LMC)
Miscellaneous Matters
LMC reserves the right to search all vehicles, containers, lockers, or other items on LMC property in furtherance of this policy. Individuals may be requested to display personal property for visual inspection upon company request. Failure to consent to search or display for visual inspection will be grounds for termination of associates, or reason for denial of access to LMC premises by any others.

Example 2: Large Construction Company
Searches of department property, lockers, or personal property brought onto company property may be made on a regular or random basis to determine the presence of alcohol and illegal drugs. Personnel who refuse such searches will be terminated.

Example 3: Large Manufacturing Company
 Search policies should be communicated to employees as a condition of employment prior to implementation of any search procedure. Employees should understand they are subject to searches of personal or company property while on site property.
 Employees who refuse to cooperate during a search should not be detained but should understand that searches are a condition of employment and failure to comply can result in disciplinary action up to and including discharge.
 Search procedures should be a carefully thought-out balance between individual rights and legitimate business concerns. Legal counsel and Employee Relations assistance is recommended to ensure lawfulness of search procedures as well as to minimize the impact on employee relations.
 Random searches should be designed in a manner not to discriminate against any class of employees (e.g., race, sex) and should not exclude office workers and the exempt work force.
 Sites should consider establishment of work rules banning employee possession of contraband including drugs, alcohol, unauthorized company property, and other items not authorized on sites.
 Contraband confiscated in the search process should be tightly controlled. Consult legal counsel regarding procedures for handling and control of such material.
 Privacy guidelines apply to searches. Sites should consider privacy guidelines in development of search programs.
 Site use of trained detection animals to search LMC premises on a random basis should be preceded by a well-conceived communication program and sensitivity to employee relations concerns.
 Sites considering random searches other than gate or routine in-plant searches should seek guidance from legal counsel.

Example 4: Midsized Manufacturing Company (MMC)
1. Normal industrial search practices as a part of a general security program, such as locker inspections and gate inspections, are not affected by this policy and may be continued or implemented as provided by such policies.
2. Special Drug Searches
 Where there is reason to believe that a specific employee or group of employees may be in possession of drugs that are prohibited under MMC's policy, the employee or employees may be required, as a condition of employment, to submit to a reasonable search of their clothing, personal lockers, purses, lunch boxes, or other containers, desks, or personal vehicles while on MMC property. Searches shall not be conducted unless approved by the facility manager with the concurrence of the vice president.
3. Procedure for Searches
 (a) Searches shall be conducted under the direct supervision of a member of management with a second member of management present as a witness.

(b)   Searches of personal effects and clothing shall be conducted by persons of the same gender as the person being searched.

(c)   The employee shall be asked to consent to any search, asked to cooperate, and told that submission is a condition of employment. Failure to cooperate will result in immediate suspension without pay and may result in the employee's discharge.

(d)   The search should not involve the "touching" of the employee in any way.

(e)   Any suspected contraband should be taken and sealed in a container with the employee's name, date, and a general description. Management shall not make any determination or statement that the substance is an illegal drug. A receipt should be given for any property seized. A proper chain of custody should be maintained.

(f)   Seized property should be locked in a cabinet under the exclusive control of a designated member of management.

(g)   The local law enforcement agency(ies) shall be notified for purposes of identification and analysis of any seized property and for further investigation.

(h)   If the seized property is found not to be violative of MMC policy, it shall be returned to the employee.

Criminal Charges

Example 1: Large Manufacturing Company (LMC)
Miscellaneous Matters

7.   If an associate is arrested or convicted for drug-related crimes, LMC will thoroughly investigate all of the circumstances, and LMC officials may utilize the drug testing procedure if cause is established by the investigation. In most cases, an arrest for drug-related crime constitutes cause under this policy. Generally speaking, the following procedures will apply:

   a.   If arrested an associate will be suspended, without pay;

   b.   If convicted an associate will be terminated;

   c.   If an associate has been arrested and the case dismissed, LMC management will make a determination as to whether to authorize the associate's return to work based on its investigation of the circumstances. If the associate is authorized to return to work, since safety for the individual and other associates is one of the primary reasons for this process, the associate must agree to surveillance testing for one year, and sign the Surveillance Agreement before the associate will be allowed to return to work.

Example 2: Small City Government (SCG)
    If an SCG employee is arrested or convicted for drug-related crimes, SCG will thoroughly investigate all of the circumstances, and SCG officials may utilize the drug testing procedure if cause is established by the investigation. In most cases, an arrest for drug-related crime constitutes cause under this policy. Generally speaking, the following procedures will apply:

    a. If arrested, an employee will be suspended with pay until SCG completes its investigation whereupon the employee will either be referred to the Employee Assistance Program and/or disciplined up to and including discharge, depending on the circumstances;

    b. If convicted, an employee will either be referred to the Employee Assistance Program and/or disciplined up to and including discharge, depending on the circumstances;

    c. If an employee has been arrested and the case dismissed, the employee may either be referred to the EAP and/or disciplined up to and including discharge, depending on the circumstances.

Employment-at-Will Statement

Example 1: Midsized Manufacturing Company (MMC)
    No part of this policy, nor any of the procedures thereunder, is intended to affect MMC's right to manage its workplace, to discipline its employees, or guarantee employment, continued employment, or terms or conditions of employment.

Example 2: Large Manufacturing Company (LMC)
    Because of the seriousness of such situations, LMC completely reserves the right to alter or change its policy or decisions on a given situation depending upon its investigation and the totality of the circumstances.

Severability

Example 1: Midsized Manufacturing Company
    If any part of this policy is determined to be void or unenforceable under state or federal law, the remainder of the policy, to the extent possible, will remain in full force and effect.

Example 2: Small City Government
    If any of the provisions of the Substance Abuse Prevention Program shall be held unconstitutional or otherwise invalid by any court of competent jurisdiction, the decision of such court shall not affect or impair any of the remaining provisions.

Appendix F

SUBSTANCE ABUSE PROGRAMS

Disciplinary Program

Example: Midsized Construction Company (MCC)

No employee or person search, urine drug screen, or inspection will be conducted without written consent. However, any MCC employee who refuses to submit to a search or inspection, urine drug screen, or blood and plasma sampling, or is found in possession, use, or transportation of any illegal substances, contraband, or any of the above-mentioned drugs and unauthorized items will be subject to disciplinary action up to and including discharge from employment. Preliminary findings of a policy violation may require that the employee be suspended pending the results of a company investigation. If the company investigation concludes that the employee has used drugs or the employee tests positive on the drug test, the employee will be discharged.

Employee Assistance Programs

Philosophy and Recognition

Example 1: National Drug Policy Board

The (Agency) EAP plays an important role in preventing and resolving employee drug use by: demonstrating the (Agency's) commitment to eliminating illegal drug use; providing employees an opportunity, with appropriate assistance, to discontinue their drug use; providing educational materials to supervisors and employees on drug use issues; assisting supervisors in confronting employees who have performance and/or conduct problems and making referrals to appropriate treatment and rehabilitative facilities; and follow-up with individuals during the rehabilitation period to track their progress and encourage successful completion of the program.

Example 2: Federal Personnel Manual

EAP Role. Employee Assistance Programs play an important role in identifying and resolving employee substance abuse by demonstrating the agency's commitment to eliminating illegal drug use; providing employees an opportunity, with appropriate assistance, to discontinue their drug abuse; providing educational materials to managers, supervisors, and employees on drug abuse issues; assisting supervisors in confronting employees who have performance and/or conduct problems which may be based in substance abuse; assessing employee-client problems and making referrals to appropriate treatment and rehabilitation facilities; and following up with individuals during the rehabilitation period to track their progress and encourage successful completion of the program.

Example 3: Large Construction Company (LCC)

LCC recognizes alcoholism, drug abuse, and psychological adjustment problems as treatable conditions. Employees are encouraged to voluntarily seek assistance prior to there being cause for disciplinary action. Employees having such problems will be accommodated by the granting of leaves of absence. The purpose of this program is to assist all employees whose work performance or behavior is being adversely affected by certain non-work-related problems. It is in the best interests of both the employee and LCC that referral for professional assistance be voluntary, and in lieu of disciplinary action.

Purpose and Function

Example 1: Large Service Company (LSC)

The EAP is a confidential counseling program designed to assist you and members of your family with personal problems, such as family or marital difficulties, problems with alcohol or drugs, emotional illness, or financial or legal worries. EAP Coordinators will help employees with personal problems by offering advice and providing referrals to outside rehabilitative services or agencies.

LSC's support for the EAP arises from the concern the corporation has for all LSC employees. Most everyone faces a number of crises where advice from an outside, professional counselor can be very helpful. Your Site Management strongly urges employees to seek assistance from the EAP before drug and/or alcohol problems interfere with work performance and disciplinary action must be used.

Example 2: Large Construction Company

Employee Assistance Programs (EAPs) are primarily designed to help employees and their families with any problem which is (or may result in) deteriorating job performance of the employee. Examples of some problems include not only substance abuse, but legal, financial, or personal problems, psychological or psychiatric disorders, and marital/family problems. The problem may not be job-related but will eventually affect job performance. The intent of this aspect of the policy is to rehabilitate the employee, not just to take punitive action against the employee.

Coverage of EAP

Example 1: Small Service Company (SSC)
SSC recognizes alcoholism, drug abuse, and psychological adjustment problems as treatable conditions. The SSC Employee Assistance Program is designed to assist employees whose work performance or behavior is being adversely affected by certain non-work-related problems. The SSC EAP also covers the employee's immediate family.

Example 2: Large Service Company
You or a dependent who would like confidential assistance should call the EAP Coordinator.

Example 3: Midsized Manufacturing Company
Family members of employees may voluntarily seek counseling and information on an entirely confidential basis by contacting the Employee Assistance Program counselor directly.

Nondiscrimination Provision

Example 1: Small Service Company (SSC)
No employee will have job security or promotional opportunities jeopardized by request for counseling or referral to SSC's EAP.

Example 2: Small Government Utility
Participation in the Employee Assistance Program for an alcohol or drug problem will in no way jeopardize an employee's job. In fact, successful treatment will be viewed positively.

Reference to EAP Provider

Example 1: Large Automobile Dealer
Employees experiencing problems with alcohol or other drugs are urged to seek assistance voluntarily through the Employee Assistance Program to resolve such problems before they become serious enough to require management referral or disciplinary action. The Employee Assistance Program counselors may be contacted by phone.

Example 2: Large Service Company
The EAP Coordinator will provide the necessary assistance during a telephone call or, if necessary, arrange to see you and/or a dependent for further confidential consultation. In some instances, the EAP Coordinator

may need to talk with you. If you would prefer to talk only to an outside counselor, the EAP Coordinator can arrange an initial appointment with an outside counseling service at the employee's request.

Educational Program Component

Example 1: Large Construction Company (LCC)
The EAP will provide education, encouragement, and assistance as well as referral services for assessment and rehabilitation. The EAP may also be able to assist the employee in seeking rehabilitative services through medical insurance.

In order to protect the safety and health of its employees, LCC will present a Drug Free Awareness Education Program to all supervisors and employees on a periodic basis. The education program will consist of materials presented over at least 60 minutes of time concerning the dangers of drug abuse in the worksite, the (company's) policy for a drug free worksite, available counseling and treatment through LCC's EAP, and the penalties for violating LCC's Substance Abuse Program. LCC officials will obtain or develop quality materials in order to continue to educate employees on the symptoms of, the problems caused by, and the developments related to, alcohol, drugs, or other controlled substances, and the promotion of a healthy lifestyle.

Voluntary Referral

Example 1: Small Government Utility (SGU)
1. SGU employees experiencing problems with alcohol or other drugs are urged to seek assistance voluntarily through the Employee Assistance Program to resolve such problems before they become serious enough to require management referral or disciplinary action. The Employee Assistance Program counselors may be contacted directly.
2. If a supervisor has reason to believe that an employee has a problem for which rehabilitation is appropriate, the supervisor should inform the General Manager and remind the employee of this program, offering to arrange an appointment if the employee wishes through the Personnel Department.
3. Dependents of employees may voluntarily seek counseling and information on an entirely confidential basis by contacting the Employee Assistance Program counselor directly.

Example 2: Large Service Company
Self-Referral—This occurs when you or one of your dependents voluntarily seeks assistance to solve a personal problem. Below are guidelines on how to obtain assistance from the EAP on a self-referral basis:
1. You or a dependent who would like confidential assistance should call the EAP Coordinator.

2. The EAP Coordinator will provide the necessary assistance during a telephone call or, if necessary, arrange to see you and/or a dependent for further confidential consultation. In some instances, the EAP Coordinator may need to talk with you to:

A. Determine the nature of the problem.

B. Determine the best community resource to help solve the problem.

C. Arrange for an initial appointment with a counselor at the service.

If you would prefer to talk only to an outside counselor, the EAP Coordinator can arrange an initial appointment with an outside counseling service at the employee's request.

All communication between you (or one of your dependents) and the EAP Coordinator/Consulting EAP Counselor will be confidential.

Example 3: Large Construction Company (LCC)

Employees may avail themselves of the EAP services at any time they feel they need to seek help with a problem which is causing or may cause their job performance to decline. The employee may contact the Designated Official within LCC or contact an outside source directly for an assessment.

Management Referral

Example 1: Small Government Utility (SGU)

1. Employees whose job performance has deteriorated due to unknown factors may be referred by management to the Employee Assistance Program for evaluation of their performance problems.

2. Participation in the Employee Assistance Program is voluntary.

3. Any employee who exhibits chronic behavioral problems should be viewed as one who may possibly be in need of this program. The supervisor should confer with the General Manager and discuss whether to encourage the employee to voluntarily accept referral to the program, particularly when substance abuse is perceived to be a likely cause of a performance deficiency. The supervisor should refer to SGU's Substance Abuse Prevention Program and carefully follow its procedures when substance abuse is suspected.

Example 2: Large Construction Company (LCC)

This type of referral is based on observation and documentation of deteriorating job performance by supervisory personnel or by suspected or actual behavior as set forth in this policy. Referrals may consist of assessment through the EAP service and/or a medical assessment including drug testing. An employee will be asked to consent to referral and sign the Employee Assistance Program Referral Agreement.

Confidentiality

Example 1: Small Service Company (SSC)
The employee who enters SSC's EAP should be informed that any information concerning counseling under this program will be confidential, and limited to those persons who have a need to be informed.

Example 2: Large Construction Company
Strict confidentiality shall be maintained during any phase of intervention, EAP services, assessment, testing, the rehabilitative process, and during the follow-up procedure. This shall apply to both voluntary referrals and management referrals.

Medical Records

Example 1: Small Service Company
The confidential nature of medical records of employees' problems will be preserved in the same manner as all other medical records.

Example 2: Midsized Manufacturing Company (MMC)
All information involving medical examinations, counseling, rehabilitation, or treatment of an individual employee or applicant shall be treated as confidential medical information. All such information will be accessible only to those MMC officials and designated medical or professional persons with a valid need to know. It will not be provided to any other party without the written consent of the employee except pursuant to administrative or legal procedure or process.

Relationship to Discipline

Example 1: Large Automobile Dealer
Participation in the Employee Assistance Program for an alcohol or drug problem will in no way jeopardize an employee's job. In fact, successful treatment will be viewed positively. However, participation will not:
a. Prevent normal disciplinary action for violations which may have already occurred, or
b. Relieve an employee of the responsibility to perform assigned duties in a safe and efficient manner.

Example 2: Large Construction Company (LCC)
No part of this policy, nor any of the procedures thereunder, is intended to affect LCC's right to manage its workplace, to discipline its employees, or guarantee employment. The Substance Abuse Program in no way creates an obligation or contract of employment. LCC reserves the right to alter or amend the program at any time in its sole discretion.

Relationship to Substance Abuse Program/Drug Testing

Example 1: Small Government Utility (SGU)

In other situations, such as have been described in the Substance Abuse Prevention Program, where substances have been detected and the employee has tested positive on the drug screening test, the employee may be referred to the Employee Assistance Program for professional evaluation and/or treatment under the guidelines of the program. If an employee refuses referral to the Employee Assistance Program after testing positive and being informed of SGU's policy, he or she may be terminated for violation of SGU policy and failing to meet SGU medical standards.

Example 2: Large Construction Company (LCC)

A confirmed positive test will result in referral of the employee to LCC's EAP for assessment which may include suitable medical treatment and/or rehabilitation. If an employee refuses to seek assistance of the company's EAP after testing positive and being informed of LCC's policy, he or she may be terminated for violation of that policy and failing to meet LCC medical standards, or the employee may be given the opportunity to resign.

Management Follow-Up Condition

Example 1: Small Service Company (SSC)

If an employee is enrolled in the program due to testing positive for drugs or alcohol, SSC's Designated Official will regularly confer with the counselor exchanging information on the employee's progress.

Example 2: Small Government Utility

If an employee agrees to seek referral to the Employee Assistance Program due to testing positive for alcohol, illegal drugs, or a psychoactive substance, the General Manager or his designee will stay in contact with the individual's physician or counselor associated with the Employee Assistance Program during the treatment to assure that the individual is in compliance with the prescribed treatment.

Example 3: Large Construction Company

Acceptance of EAP services, including treatment and/or counseling, shall necessitate management to follow up with the EAP regarding the employee's progress and/or completion of treatment and any aftercare procedure. All details are strictly confidential and management shall only be concerned with the satisfactory completion of each phase of rehabilitation. All decisions regarding counseling and/or treatment shall be made by a joint decision of management and the EAP.

Medical/Disability Benefits

Example 1: Small Government Utility (SGU)

Medical benefits are provided in accordance with SGU health insurance plan. Other costs of treatment or rehabilitation will be the responsibility of the employee.

Example 2: Large Construction Company (LCC)
Medical benefits are provided in accordance with LCC's health insurance plan. LCC's medical coverage will cover certain expenses incurred during the treatment for alcoholism or other drug addictions. Coverage may vary depending upon: type of policy, policy limits, treatment type, and whether treatment is rendered as inpatient or outpatient. Coverage may or may not apply to outside counseling services. For additional information or clarification of benefits, employees should contact their Personnel Department. All other costs of treatment for rehabilitation will be the responsibility of the employee.

Treatment for alcoholism and other drug addictions is regarded as any other illness or disability. If eligible, employees may apply for these benefits as conditioned by their group coverage.

Medical Leave/Work Scheduling Policy

Example 1: Midsized Law Firm (MLF)
Employees who enroll in MLF's EAP may be granted a leave of absence so they may maintain continuous employment and other benefits applicable to those employed by MLF. Requests for time off for the purpose of participating in MLF's EAP or approved private treatment and rehabilitation programs will be given favorable consideration. If an employee enters MLF's EAP, arrangements will be made within MLF by the Designated or Managing Partner to accommodate or rearrange the work schedule of the affected employee.

Example 2: Large Construction Company (LCC)
If an employee enters LCC's EAP, arrangements will be made by the LCC President or Designated Official to accommodate or rearrange the work schedule of the affected employee.

Cooperation With Counselors

Example 1: Midsized Law Firm (MLF)
If an employee refuses to cooperate with the counselors of MLF's EAP after having been referred to the program because of testing positive, he or she may be terminated for violation of Firm policy and failing to meet MLF medical standards, or the employee may be given the opportunity to resign.

Example 2: Small Government Utility (SGU)
If an employee abandons the prescribed treatment of the Employee Assistance Program, he or she may be terminated for violation of SGU policy and failing to meet SGU medical standards.

Example 3: Large Construction Company (LCC)
    If an employee refuses to cooperate with the counselors of LCC's EAP after having been referred to the program because of testing positive, he or she may be terminated for violation of LCC policy and failing to meet LCC medical standards, or the employee may be given the opportunity to resign.

Return to Work Procedures

Example 1: Small Government Utility (SGU)
    Once the General Manager has been informed in writing by the Employee Assistance Program counselor that the employee is again suitable for employment, the individual must sign the Employee Surveillance Agreement Form and agree to surveillance screening for a period of one (1) year, before the employee may be reinstated. If, during the one-year surveillance agreement period, the employee tests positive on a drug test, he will be terminated for violation of SGU policy and failing to meet SGU medical standards. However, successful completion of the one-year surveillance agreement period will mean that the surveillance agreement form and other testing file materials will be removed from the individual's records.

Example 2: Large Construction Company (LCC)
    If an employee has been referred to LCC's EAP due to testing positive, and in the opinion of the Program counselor the employee is able to continue working while undergoing therapy, the employee must sign the Surveillance Agreement Form and agree to random drug testing during the period of counseling in the program and for a period of one year. If the employee tests positive during the year, he or she will be terminated. Upon the completion of rehabilitation, the EAP counselor will certify to the LCC President or the Designated Official that the employee may return to work. The employee must then test negative on the drug test and sign the Surveillance Agreement Form agreeing to random testing for a period of one year. If the employee tests positive during that year, he or she will be terminated. However, upon successful completion of all tests during the one-year period, all records of the employee's substance abuse problem will be removed from the employee's personnel records.

Aftercare/Follow-Up

Example: Large Manufacturing Company (LMC)
    The EAP Coordinator will periodically interview participants in the EAP to either assure compliance with the rehabilitation program or to assess the efficacy of the individual's treatment regimen. During the first year after management referral into the EAP, the employee will be subject to surveillance testing and quarterly evaluations by the EAP Coordinator.

After the first year and for the following 18 months, the EAP Coordinator will counsel with the individual at least every six months in order to assess the individual's aftercare program. The EAP Coordinator will keep statistics as to the success of the EAP program based on numbers of individuals, without identifying any individual. The EAP Coordinator will submit a report of activities including utilization of the EAP and significant activities to the President of LMC each six months from the beginning of the program.

Rehabilitation Referral Programs

Example 1: Small Construction Company (SCC)

A positive test will result in referral of the employee to professional evaluation, which may include suitable medical treatment and/or rehabilitation.

If an employee refuses to seek professional evaluation after testing positive and being informed of SCC policy, he or she may be terminated for violation of SCC policy and failing to meet SCC medical standards, or the employee may be given the opportunity to resign.

If an employee agrees to seek professional evaluation, the personnel manager should stay in contact with the employee's physician or counselor during the treatment to assure that the employee is in compliance with the prescribed treatment. The employee will be placed on medical leave during his absence for full-time rehabilitation. Employees not requiring full-time rehabilitation may be temporarily assigned other work at the discretion of the General Manager and after signing a Temporary Work Assignment Agreement. Once the company has been informed that the employee is again suitable for employment, before the employee may be reinstated, the employee must sign the Surveillance Agreement Form and agree to random drug testing for a period of one year.

After signing the Surveillance Agreement Form and before returning to work, the employee must test negative on a subsequent drug test.

Example 2: Large Service Company (LSC)

If an employee tests positive under LSC's Substance Abuse Program, the employee will be referred to the drug and alcohol rehabilitation program for outpatient or inpatient rehabilitation in accordance with LSC's medical and health insurance benefit program. Successful completion of the rehabilitation program is required before the employee is allowed to return to the job.

Appendix G

FEDERAL CONTROLLED SUBSTANCES ACT
SCHEDULES OF CONTROLLED SUBSTANCES
(21 U.S.C. §812)

SCHEDULE	COMMON EXAMPLES	LISTED SUBSTANCES
I	Heroin Mescaline LSD Peyote Marijuana	(1) Unless specifically excepted or unless listed in another schedule, any of the following opiates, including their insomers, esters, ethers, salts, and salts of isomers, esters, and ethers, whenever the existence of such isomers, esters, ethers, and salts is possible within the specific chemical designation: Acetylmethadol, Allylprodine, Alphacetylmathadol, Alphameprodine, Alphamethadol, Benzethidine, Betacetylmethadol, Betameprodine, Betamethadol, Betaprodine, Clonitazene, Dextromoramide, Dextrorphan, Diampromide, Diethylthiambutene, Dimenoxadol, Dimepheptanol, Dimethylthiambutene, Dioxaphetyl butyrate, Dipipanone, Ethylmethylthiambutene, Etonitazene, Etoxeridine, Furethidine, Hydroxypethidine, Ketobemidone, Levomoramide, Levophenacylmorphan, Morpheridine, Noracymethadol, Norlevorphanol,

SCHEDULE	COMMON EXAMPLES	LISTED SUBSTANCES
		Normethadone, Norpipanone, Phenadoxone, Phenampromide, Phenomorphan, Phenoperidine, Piritramide, Proheptazine, Properidine, Racemoramide, and Trimeperidine.
		(2) Unless specifically excepted or unless listed in another schedule, any of the following opium derivatives, their salts, isomers, and salts of isomers whenever the existence of such salts, isomers, and salts of isomers is possible within the specific chemical designation:
		Acetorphine, Acetyldihydrocodeine, Benzylmorphine, Codeine methylbromide, Codeine-N-Oxide, Cyprenorphine, Desomorphine, Dihydromorphine, Etorphine, Heroin, Hydromorphinol, Methyldesorphine, Methylhydromorphine, Morphine methylbromide, Morphine methylsulfonate, Morphine-N-Oxide, Myrophine, Nicocodeine, Nicomorphine, Normorphine, Pholcodeine, and Thebacon.
		(3) Unless specifically excepted or unless listed in another schedule, any material, compound, mixture, or preparation, which contains any quantity of the following hallucinogenic substances, or which contains any of their salts, isomers, and salts of isomers whenever the existence of such salts, isomers, and salts of isomers is possible within the specific chemical designation:
		3,4-methylenedioxy amphetamine, 5-methoxy-3,4-methylenedioxy amphetamine, 3,4,5-trimethoxy amphetamine, Bufotenine, Diethyltryptamine, Di-

SCHEDULE	COMMON EXAMPLES	LISTED SUBSTANCES
I (contd.)		methyltryptamine, 4-methyl-2,5-dimethoxyamphetamine, Ibogaine, Lysergic acid diethylamide, Marihuana, Mescaline, Peyote, N-ethyl-3-piperidyl benzilate, N-methyl-3-piperidyl benzilate, Psilocybin, and Tetrahydrocannabinols.
II	Methadone PCP Quaalude Cocaine	(1) Unless specifically excepted or unless listed in another schedule, any of the following substances whether produced directly or indirectly by extraction from substances of vegetable origin, or independently by means of chemical synthesis, or by a combination of extraction and chemical synthesis: (a) Opium and opiate, and any salt, compound, derivative, or preparation of opium or opiate. (b) Any salt, compound, derivative, or preparation thereof which is chemically equivalent or identical with any of the substances referred to in clause (a), except that these substance shall not include the isoquinoline alkaloids of opium. (c) Opium poppy and poppy straw. (d) Coca leaves and any salt, compound, derivative, or preparation of coca leaves, and any salt, compound, derivative, or preparation thereof which is chemically equivalent or identical with any of these substances, except that the substances shall not include decocainized leaves or extraction of coca leaves, which extractions do not contain cocaine or ecgonine. (2) Unless specifically excepted or

SCHEDULE	COMMON EXAMPLES	LISTED SUBSTANCES
		unless listed in another schedule, any of the following opiates, including their isomers, esters, ethers, salts, and salts of isomers, esters and ethers, whenever the existence of such isomers, esters, ethers, and salts is possible within the specific chemical designation: Alphaprodine; Anileridine; Bezitramide; Dihydrocodeine; Diphenoxylate; Fentanyl; Isomethadone; Levomethorphan; Levorphanol; Metazocine; Methadone; Methadone-Intermediate, 4-cyano-2-dimethylamino-4, 4-diphenyl butane; Moramide-Intermediate, 2-methyl-3-morpholino-1, 1-diphenylpropane-carboxylic acid; Pethidine; Pethidine-Intermediate-A, 4-cyano-1-methyl-4-phenyl-piperidine; Pethidine-Intermediate-B, ethyl-4-phenyl-piperidine-4-carboxylate; Pethidine-Intermediate-C, 1-methyl-4-phenylpiperidine 4-carboxylic acid; Phenazocine; Piminodine; Racemethorphan; and Racemorphan. (3) Unless specifically excepted or unless listed in another schedule, any injectable liquid which contains any quantity of methamphetamine, including its salts, isomers, and salts of isomers.
III	Doriden Emprin Compound Didrex Plegine	(1) Unless specifically excepted or unless listed in another schedule, any material, compound, mixture, or preparation which contains any quantity of the following substances having a stimulant effect on the central nervous system:

SCHEDULE	COMMON EXAMPLES	LISTED SUBSTANCES
III (contd.)		(1) Amphetamine, its salts, optical isomers, and salts of its optical isomers.
		(b) Phenmetrazine and its salts.
		(c) Any substance (except an injectable liquid) which contains any quantity of methamphetamine, including its salts, isomers, and salts of isomers.
		(d) Methylphenidate.
		(2) Unless specifically excepted or unless listed in another schedule, any material, compound, mixture, or preparation which contains any quantity of the following substances having a depressant effect on the central nervous system:
		(a) Any substance which contains any quantity of a derivative of barbituric acid, or any salt of a derivative of barbituric acid.
		(b) Chorhexadol.
		(c) Glutethimide.
		(d) Lysergic acid.
		(e) Lysergic acid amide.
		(f) Methyprylon.
		(g) Phencyclidine.
		(h) Sulfondiethylmethane.
		(i) Sulfonethylmethane.
		(j) Sulfonmethane.
		(3) Nalorphine.
		(4) Unless specifically excepted or unless listed in another schedule, any material, compound, mixture, or preparation containing limited quantities of any of the following narcotic drugs, or any salts thereof:
		(a) Not more than 1.8 grams of codeine per 100 milliliters or not more than 90 milligrams per dosage unit, with an equal or greater quantity of an isoquinoline alkaloid of opium.

SCHEDULE	COMMON EXAMPLES	LISTED SUBSTANCES
		(b) Not more than 1.8 grams of codeine per 100 milliliters or not more than 90 milligrams per dosage unit, with one or more active, nonnarcotic ingredients in recognized therapeutic amounts. (c) Not more than 300 milligrams of dihydrocodeinone per 100 milliliters or not more than 15 milligrams per dosage unit, with a fourfold or greater quantity of an isoquinoline alkaloid of opium. (d) Not more than 300 milligrams of dihydrocodeinone per 100 milliliters or not more than 15 milligrams per dosage unit, with one or more active, nonnarcotic ingredients in recognized therapeutic amounts. (e) Not more than 1.8 grams of dihydrocodeine per 100 milliliters or not more than 90 milligrams per dosage unit, with one or more active, nonnarcotic ingredients in recognized therapeutic amounts. (f) Not more than 300 milligrams of ethylmorphine per 100 milliliters or not more than 15 milligrams per dosage unit, with one or more active, nonnarcotic ingredients in recognized therapeutic amounts. (g) Not more than 500 milligrams of opium per 100 milliliters or per 100 grams, or not more than 25 milligrams per dosage unit, with one or more active, nonnarcotic ingredients in recognized therapeutic amounts. (h) Not more than 50 milligrams of morphine per 100 milliliters or per 100 grams with one or more active, nonnarcotic ingredients in recognized therapeutic amounts.

SCHEDULE	COMMON EXAMPLES	LISTED SUBSTANCES
IV	Valium Serax Librium Tranzene Darvon	Barbital, Chloral betaine, Chloral hydrate, Ethchlorvynol, Ethinamate, Methohexital, Meprobamate, Methylphenobarbital, Paraldehyde, Petrichloral, and Phenobarbital.
V	Florinal w/ codeine Robitussan A-C	Any compound, mixture, or preparation containing any of the following limited quantities of narcotic drugs, which shall include one or more nonnarcotic active medicinal ingredients in sufficient proportion to confer upon the compound, mixture, or preparation valuable medicinal qualities other than those possessed by the narcotic drug alone: (a) Not more than 200 milligrams of codeine per 100 milliliters or per 100 grams. (b) Not more than 100 milligrams of dihydrocodeine per 100 milliliters or per 100 grams. (c) Not more than 100 milligrams of ethylmorphine per 100 milliliters or per 100 grams. (d) Not more than 2.5 milligrams of diphenoxylate and not less than 25 micrograms of atropine sulfate per dosage unit. (e) Not more than 100 milligrams of opium per 100 milliliters or per 100 grams.

Appendix H

ALCOHOLICS ANONYMOUS MATERIALS

SERENITY PRAYER

GOD GRANT ME THE SERENITY TO ACCEPT
THE THINGS I CANNOT CHANGE,
COURAGE TO CHANGE THE THINGS I CAN
AND WISDOM TO KNOW THE DIFFERENCE.

PREAMBLE

Alcoholics Anonymous is a fellowship of men and women who share their experience, strength and hope with each other that they may solve their common problem and help others to recover from alcoholism.

The only requirement for membership is a desire to stop drinking. There are no dues or fees for AA membership; we are self-supporting through our own contributions. AA is not allied with any sect, denomination, politics, organization or institution; does not wish to engage in any controversy, neither endorses nor opposes any causes.

Our primary purpose is to stay sober and help other alcoholics to achieve sobriety.

HOW IT WORKS

THE TWELVE STEPS

Rarely have we seen a person fail who has thoroughly followed our path. Those who do not recover are people who cannot or will not completely give themselves to this simple program, usually men and women who are constitutionally incapable of being honest with themselves. There are such unfortunates. They are not at fault; they seem to have been born that way. They are naturally incapable of grasping and developing a manner of living which demands rigorous honesty. Their chances are less than average. There are those, too, who suffer from grave emotional and mental disorders, but many of them do recover if they have the capacity to be honest.

Our stories disclose in a general way what we used to be like, what happened, and what we are like now. If you have decided you want what we have and are willing to go to any length to get it—then you are ready to take certain steps.

At some of these we balked. We thought we could find an easier, softer way. But we could not. With all the earnestness at our command, we beg of you to be fearless and thorough from the very start. Some of us have tried to hold on to our old ideas and the result was nil until we let go absolutely.

Remember that we deal with alcohol—cunning, baffling, powerful! Without help it is too much for us. But there is One who has all power—that One is God. May you find Him now!

Half measures availed us nothing. We stood at the turning point. We asked His protection and care with complete abandon.

Here are the steps we took, which are suggested as a program of recovery:

1. We admitted we were powerless over alcohol—that our lives had become unmanageable.
2. Came to believe that a Power greater than ourselves could restore us to sanity.
3. Made a decision to turn our will and our lives over to the care of God <u>as we understood Him.</u>
4. Made a searching and fearless moral inventory of ourselves.
5. Admitted to God, to ourselves, and to another human being the exact nature of our wrongs.
6. Were entirely ready to have God remove all these defects of character.
7. Humbly asked Him to remove our shortcomings.
8. Made a list of all persons we had harmed, and became willing to make amends to them all.
9. Made direct amends to such people wherever possible, except when to do so would injure them or others.
10. Continued to take personal inventory and when we were wrong promptly admitted it.
11. Sought through prayer and meditation to improve our conscious contact with God <u>as we understood Him</u>, praying only for knowledge of His will for us and the power to carry that out.
12. Having had a spiritual awakening as the result of these steps, we tried to carry this message to alcoholics, and to practice these principles in all our affairs.

Many of us exclaimed, "What an order! I can't go through with it." Do not be discouraged. No one among us has been able to maintain anything like perfect adherence to these principles. We are not saints. The point is that we are willing to grow along spiritual lines. The principles we have set down are guides to progress. We claim spiritual progress rather than spiritual perfection.

Our description of the alcoholic, the chapter to the agnostic, and our personal adventures before and after make clear three pertinent ideas:

(a) That we were alcoholic and could not manage our own lives.
(b) That probably no human power could have relieved our alcoholism.
(c) That God could and would if He were sought.

THE TWELVE TRADITIONS

1. Our common welfare should come first; personal recovery depends upon AA unity.
2. For our group purpose there is but one ultimate authority—a loving God as He may express Himself in our group conscience. Our leaders are but trusted servants; they do not govern.
3. The only requirement for AA membership is a desire to stop drinking.
4. Each group should be autonomous except in matters affecting other groups or AA as a whole.
5. Each group has but one primary purpose—to carry its message to the alcoholic who still suffers.
6. An AA group ought never endorse, finance, or lend the AA name to any related facility or outside enterprise, lest problems of money, property, and prestige divert us from our primary purpose.
7. Every AA group ought to be fully self-supporting, declining outside contributions.
8. Alcohlics Anonymous should remain forever nonprofessional, but our service centers may employ special workers.
9. AA, as such, ought never be organized; but we may create service boards or committees directly responsible to those they serve.
10. Alcoholics Anonymous has no opinion on outside issues; hence the AA name ought never be drawn into public controversy.
11. Our public relations policy is based on attraction rather than promotion; we need always maintain personal anonymity at the level of press, radio, and films.

12. Anonymity is the spiritual foundation of all our Traditions, ever reminding us to place principles before personalities.

Appendix I

THE EACC CODE OF PROFESSIONAL CONDUCT FOR CERTIFIED EMPLOYEE ASSISTANCE PROFESSIONALS

PREAMBLE

The Certified Employee Assistance Professional (CEAP) provides to employers and (or) unions to the most effective employee assistance services for employees and family members whose personal problems negatively affect their work and well being.

The CEAP by necessity interacts with the workplace, the employee, the community and the employee assistance profession. He/she is required to adhere to a strict code of professional conduct beyond the prevailing standards for professional practice calling for placing the employee's interest above self.

The rules of professional conduct presented here are grouped under each of the four interactions.

I. THE WORKPLACE

A. Confidentiality	The CEAP will respect confidential business communication from labor and management representatives and will not disclose such information without prior consent.
B. Employee Assistance Program Services	The CEAP is responsible for recognizing his/her professional limitations and, when providing services—i.e., organization assessment, training, health benefits design, wellness programming, research and program evaluation, and management of organizational transitions—for which he/she is not competent, works only under the supervision of a qualified person.
C. Human Resource Management	The CEAP will seek to use all appropriate organizational resources in resolving job performance problems due to employee personal

problems. The goal is to seek solutions for returning the employee to acceptable work performance.

D. Program Policy and Procedures   The CEAP will consult with labor and management representatives toward integrating EAP program, policy and procedures with other organizational policies, procedures, operations and labor contracts.

E. Supervisory/Union Intervention   The CEAP will provide consultation to labor and management representatives on the constructive confrontation technique to help employees whose personal problems are affecting work performance and attendance.

II. THE EMPLOYEE

A. Confidentiality
1. The CEAP will treat all employee and family member information as confidential.
2. Each employee or family member will be informed fully as to the scope of and limitations on confidential communications elicited during the assessment, referral and treatment process.
3. Such information received in the course of and for the purpose of assessment, referral or treatment will not be disclosed without written consent except when such failure to disclose would likely result in imminent threat of serious bodily harm to self or others; or as otherwise required by law.

B. Services
1. The CEAP will provide consultation, assessment, referral and follow-up services which the CEAP is competent to provide and which are agreed to by the work organization.
2. The CEAP will refer employees and family members to the most cost beneficial community resources, taking into consideration the nature and severity of the problem, treatment resources, and availability of health care benefit coverage.

C. Personal Problems
1. The CEAP will consider all aspects of personal problems including physical, psychological, social, cultural and spiritual aspects.
2. The CEAP will maintain a focus on alcohol and drug problems in the workplace, not to the exclusion of other problems, but recog-

nizing that alcohol and drugs often cause or influence other problems.

D. Communications — The CEAP will develop means to communicate to employees and family members the availability of and access to EAP services.

E. Records and Reporting
1. The CEAP will maintain individual records in a confidential and professional manner for possible audit by an authorized third party.
2. The CEAP will report program activities to the work organization without violating confidentiality.

F. Employee Protection — The CEAP will recognize that the relationship between the EAP provider and the employee is based on trust, confidence and respect for the employee's legal rights. As such, the CEAP will:
1. Not discriminate in assessment and referral on the basis of race, religion, age, national origin, physical handicap, gender or sexual preference.
2. Make full disclosure of the functions and purposes of the Employee Assistance Program as well as any affiliation with a proposed therapist or treatment program.
3. Not give or receive financial consideration for referring employees to particular therapists or treatment programs.
4. Not engage in sexual conduct with clients.
5. Not act in any manner to compromise a professional relationship.

III. THE COMMUNITY

A. Cost Beneficial Services — The CEAP will identify and utilize community resources which provide the best quality care at the most reasonable cost.

B. Accountability — The CEAP will maintain a professional relationship with community resources and hold them accountable for delivery of the services as agreed.

C. Insurance and Benefits — The CEAP will advocate and consult with community treatment providers and risk underwriters and corporate benefits manager[s] to secure equitable coverage for the treatment of psychiatric, alcohol and drug problems and other conditions.

D. Confidentiality — The CEAP will make representations to the community on a particular EAP only when authorized to so do by the affected parties.

IV. THE PROFESSION

A. Certification — The CEAP will use his or her certification only as evidence of meeting the requisite standard of knowledge for competency in EAP practice as defined by the Employee Assistance Certification Commission.

B. Competency — The CEAP will advocate and maintain competency in employee assistance programming consistent with changes in knowledge in the field.

C. Standards — The CEAP will abide by all the rules of professional conduct prescribed by the CEAP's other professional organizations.

D. Research and Program Evaluation — The CEAP will participate only in such research and program evaluation that meet professional standards of validity, reliability and confidentiality.

E. Advocacy — The CEAP will advocate the treatment of stigmatized problems as equitably as other personal problems in the workplace.

F. Advertising — The CEAP, in advertising his or her services to the public, will ensure that such advertising is neither fradulent nor misleading.

G. Statements to the Commission — The CEAP will refrain from any misleading, inaccurate or false statements to the Employee Assistance Certification Commission—including his or her applications for certification and recertification.

H. Violations — The CEAP will report alleged violations of the Code of Professional Conduct by other CEAPs.

Approved by Employee Assistance Certification Commission, 10/8/88.

RULES AND PROCEDURES

COMMITTEE ON PROFESSIONAL CONDUCT
EMPLOYEE ASSISTANCE CERTIFICATION COMMISSION

1.0 RESPONSIBILITY AND OBJECTIVES OF THE COMMITTEE

1.1   Responsibilities

1.11   Review and propose rules of professional conduct for adoption by the Commission.

1.12   Receive and investigate complaints of unprofessional conduct.

1.13		Resolve complaints of unprofessional conduct and recommend such other action as is necessary to achieve the objectives of the Commission.
1.14		Report on types of complaints investigated with special attention to difficult cases.
1.15		Adopt procedures governing the functions of the Committee.
1.2	Objectives	The fundamental objectives of the Committee are to enforce the Code of Professional Conduct (hereinafter "the Code") and to protect the public against unprofessional conduct by Certified Employee Assistance Professionals (hereinafter "CEAPs").

2.0 NATURE OF AUTHORITY

2.1	Power to Investigate	The Committee has the power to investigate allegations of unprofessional conduct that may be harmful to colleagues, the public or that may be otherwise contrary to the objectives of the Commission.
2.2	Choice of Procedure	The Committee shall be the sole judge of whether a matter can be disposed of within the Committee under Section 6.1, whether formal charges shall be brought under Section 6.2, or whether the evidence warrants referral to the Commission under Section 3.
2.3	Available Disciplinary Actions	
2.31	Revoking Certification	Upon recommendation by the Committee, a formal charge, as defined in Section 6.2, may be brought against a CEAP. After the procedures delineated in Section 6 have been satisfied and upon final approval by the Commission under Section 7, the CEAP's certification may be revoked or some lesser sanction imposed.
2.32	Permitted Resignation	Upon recommendation by the Committee and upon final action of the Commission, the CEAP may be permitted to resign under conditions set by the Commission.
2.33	Committee Action	Where the Committee chooses to resolve matters within itself, the Committee may place on probation, reprimand or censure the CEAP. The Committee may also request that the CEAP cease the challenged conduct, accept supervision or seek appropriate counseling or treatment assistance.

2.4	Committee Meeting	
2.41	Frequency and Quorum	The Committee shall meet at reasonable intervals as needed. A quorum at such meetings shall consist of a majority of the Committee.
2.5	Confidentiality	
2.51	Disclosure of Information	All information concerning complaints against CEAPs shall be confidential except that the Committee shall be permitted to disclose such information when compelled by a validly issued subpoena or when otherwise required by law.
2.52	Notification of Final Action	The Committee shall inform both the complainant and the CEAP of its action and the basis for its action when the matter is disposed of within the Committee—including, where appropriate, the particular rule(s) of professional conduct violated.
2.53	Notification of Closing Case	If the Committee votes to close a case, it shall so inform the complainant and the CEAP.

2.6 RECORDS

2.61	Handling, Storage and Destruction	The Committee shall establish procedures to ensure confidentiality in the handling, storage and destruction of its records.

3.0 CEAPS CONVICTED OF OR CHARGED WITH FELONIES OR DISCIPLINED IN OTHER AUTHORIZED TRIBUNALS

3.1	Review of Records and Suspension	Where the Committee finds that a CEAP has been *convicted* of a felony and such conviction is not under appeal, the Committee shall review the record leading to conviction and may thereafter suspend certification without further proceedings. Where the Committee finds that a CEAP has been *charged* with a felony, such charge shall neither require or preclude action by the Committee.
3.2	Expulsion, Suspension or Delicensure by State	Where the Committee finds that a CEAP has been expelled or suspended for unethical or unprofessional conduct from a national, regional or state professional association or has had a license or certificate revoked on ethical grounds by a state licensing or certifying authority, the Committee shall review the record leading to these sanctions and may suspend certification.

3.3	Effect of Suspension	Upon suspension, the CEAP shall be afforded the opportunity in writing, or at the Committee's discretion through personal appearance, to show good cause why he or she should not face revocation of certification.
3.4	Recommended Decertification	Following a CEAP's response, or after expiration of thirty (30) days without response, the Committee shall recommend to the Commission whether the CEAP's certification should be revoked. The Commission may, after reviewing the record, revoke the certification or impose a lesser sanction.
3.5	No Recommended Decertification	Where the Committee votes not to recommend decertification, it shall have the option to follow its usual procedures.

4.0 DISCIPLINARY PROCEDURES; INITIAL CONSIDERATION

4.1	Complaints	
4.11	Documents	Complaints may be submitted by any party claiming to be aggrieved by the professional conduct of a CEAP or by any national, regional or state professional association to which the CEAP is a member, or by any state licensing or certifying authority in the public interest.
4.12	Previous Steps	The Complainant shall inform the Committee of previous steps, if any, that have been taken with respect to the alleged unethical or unprofessional conduct.
4.13	Committee Initiative	The Committee may proceed on its own initiative when a CEAP appears to have violated the Code.
4.14	Anonymous Complaints	The Committee may not act solely on the basis of anonymous complaints.
4.15	Supplementary Information	The Committee may through correspondence or otherwise seek supplementary information from the complainant or others when necessary to evaluate the substance of the allegations.

5.0 DISCIPLINARY PROCEDURES: INITIAL ACTION

| 5.1 | Communication with CEAP | |
| 5.11 | Notification to CEAP | Should the Committee agree that a possible violation of the Code has occurred, it shall so inform the CEAP in writing. |

5.12	Contents of Communication	
5.121	Complaint and Code	A precise description of the alleged behaviors involved in the complaint, including the specific Sections of the Code that the CEAP is alleged to have violated.
5.122	Request for Reply	A request for a reply within thirty (30) days of receipt—containing as complete information as possible concerning the complaint.
5.123	Documents	A copy of the Code of Professional Conduct and the Committee's Rules and Procedures.
5.124	Complainant's Name	The name of the complainant unless the Committee has proceeded on its own initiative.
5.125	Future Record	A statement that information submitted by the CEAP shall become part of the record in the case, which could be used in further proceedings.
5.13	CEAP's Response	
5.131	Personal and Timely Reponse	The CEAP is required to respond as completely as possible, in writing, personally and within thirty (30) days.
5.132	Lack of Cooperation	Failure or unwarranted delay in responding or lack of cooperation shall in no way prevent continuation or conclusion of the proceedings.
5.2	Action on Response	
5.21	Closing of Case	Within ninety (90) days of receipt of the CEAP's written response, the Committee may determine that the complaint has no basis in fact, is insignificant or is likely to be corrected and may close the case without further action.
5.22	Closed Case	If the case is closed, the Committee shall so inform the complainant and the CEAP.

6.0 DISCIPLINARY PROCEDURES: DISPOSITION OF COMPLAINTS

6.1	Disposition Within Committee	Should the Committee decide to dispose of the case within the Committee, it may adopt any one or more of the following methods or take any other appropriate action. It may issue a:
6.111	Cease and Desist Order	Require the CEAP to cease and desist the challenged behavior.
6.112	Reprimand	When the Committee finds that there has been a Code violation, but no damage to another person, the public or the profession.

6.113 Censure   When the Committee finds that there has been a Code violation but the damage done is not sufficient to warrant more serious action.

6.114 Supervision   When the Committee concludes that the CEAP requires supervision.

6.115 Counseling   When the Committee concludes that the CEAP
      Assistance   could benefit from counseling or treatment assistance.

6.116 Probation   When the Committee undertakes actually and systematically to monitor, for a specific length of time, the degree to which the CEAP complies with the Committee's requirements.

6.117 Referral   When the Committee concludes it appropriate to refer the matter to a national, regional or state professional association and (or) a state licensing or certifying authority.

6.12 Acceptance   The CEAP shall have thirty (30) days after notification to respond in writing to the Committee's determination. Should the CEAP accept the determination, the Committee shall notify the complainant of the disposition—including the conditions (if any) specified and the Sections of the Code violated.

6.2   Formal Charges
6.21 Definition   A formal charge is a statement by the Committee that it has probable cause to believe that the CEAP has violated one or more Sections of the Code.

6.22 Choice of   The Committee may elect to take formal action
      Formal Action   either:

6.221 CEAP Rejects   When the CEAP fails to accept the informal
      Informal   disposition under Section 6.1; or
      Determination

6.222 Direct Formal   After consideration of all materials gathered
      Action   under Section 5.

6.23 Contents of   The formal charge to the CEAP shall contain the
      Charge   following:

6.231 Description and A description of the nature of the complaint, the
      Code Violations conduct in question and citation to the specific Section(s) of the Code alleged to have been violated.

6.232 Sanction   The disciplinary sanction recommended.
      Recommended

6.233 Documents   A copy of the Code of Professional Conduct and the Committee's Rules and Procedures.

6.24	Requested Hearing	Within thirty (30) days after receipt of the formal charges, the CEAP has the right to request, in writing, a hearing.
6.25	No Requested Hearing	Should the CEAP not request a hearing or not respond in thirty (30) days, the right to a hearing is waived. The Committee shall consider all available evidence and make a final determination. Whereupon, the Committee shall transmit its decision by majority vote to the Commission.
6.3	Procedures for Formal Hearing	
6.31	Committee Composition	At least three (3) members of the Committee shall participate in adjudicating formal charges.
6.32	Date of Hearing	The Committee shall set a date for the hearing within one hundred eighty (180) days from receiving a hearing request.
6.33	Confidentiality	The proceeding shall be held in private and deemed confidential.
6.34	Documents and Witnesses	At least thirty (30) days prior to the hearing, the CEAP and the Committee shall exchange copies of all documents, the names of witnesses and their expected testimony to be offered at the hearing.
6.35	Rights of Counsel and Cross Examination	At the CEAP's expense, he or she may be represented by counsel, present witnesses and cross-examine any witnesses offered by the Committee.
6.36	Rules of Evidence	Formal rules of evidence shall not apply. All evidence that is relevant as determined by counsel for the Commission shall be admissible.
6.37	Legal Counsel to the Commission	The Committee may use the Commission's legal counsel to advise it on matters of procedure and admission of evidence.
6.38	Committee Determination	Within thirty (30) days after the hearing is concluded, the Committee shall determine whether the CEAP shall be cleared of the charges, disciplined or decertified. This decision by majority vote shall be transmitted in writing to the Commission.

7.0 FINAL ACTION

7.1	Final Decision	
7.11	Commission Action	Within ninety (90) days after considering the record and the determination of the Committee with any other pertinent statements that may have been filed, the Commission shall adopt the

		recommendation of the Committee, unless it finds by majority vote that:
7.111	Incorrect Application	The Code of Professional Conduct was incorrectly applied.
7.112	Erroneous Findings of Fact	The findings of fact by the Committee were clearly erroneous.
7.113	Procedural Errors	The procedures used by the Committee were in serious and substantial violation of the Committee's Rules and Procedures.
7.114	Disproportionate Sanctions	The disciplinary sanctions recommended by the Committee were grossly disproportionate in light of factors surrounding the violation.
7.2	Report of Final Decision	
7.21	Notification to Complainant and CEAP	The Commission shall inform the complainant and the CEAP of its final action—including which Sections of the Code were judged to be violated (if any) and the basis for this action.
7.33	Notification to Profession	The Commission shall report annually the names of any CEAPs decertified and the violations of professional conduct involved.
7.34	Notification to Others	The commission shall also notify interested national, regional and state professional associations as well as state licensing and certifying authorities; and on request any interested person where it deems such notification necessary for the protection of the public or to maintain the standards of the Commission.

Approved by the Employee Assistance Certification Commission,
10/8/88.

Source: Reprinted with permission from Code of Professional Conduct for Certified Employee Assistance Professionals (CEAP), Employee Assistance Certification Commission, ALMACA, Arlington, VA. (ALMACA is now known as EAPA, Employee Assistance Professional Association, Inc.).

EMPLOYEE ASSISTANCE SOCIETY OF NORTH AMERICA (EASNA) CODE OF ETHICS

Adopted 1987

COMPETENCE

EAP practitioners are responsible for recognizing the limitations of their competence and for making certain that all work is performed within those limitations. When providing services or using procedures in which he is not fully trained and experienced, the practitioner works only under the supervision of a fully qualified person who is recognized as competent in those services and procedures. It is evidence of poor judgment, and may be unethical, for a practitioner to offer services or use procedures that are not generally accepted by professional colleagues as representing the prevailing standard of practice.

MISREPRESENTATION

The EAP practitioner does not misrepresent his own professional qualifications, affiliations, competence, and purposes. Moreover, he does not misrepresent the qualifications, affiliations, competence, or purposes of his colleagues or the institutions, agencies, and organizations with which he is associated. The practitioner is responsible for correcting any other person who misrepresents his qualifications, competence, affiliations, and purposes.

It is unethical to use one's membership in or affiliation with the Employee Assistance Society of North America or any other association or organization to represent or imply qualification or competence when such membership or affiliation is not contingent upon the passing of an examination or other criteria designed to assess competence as an EAP practitioner.

PUBLIC STATEMENTS

When an EAP practitioner is called upon to interpret, explain or demonstrate knowledge of specific EAP procedures or their application to clients, the general public, or the media, he does so accurately, objectively, and fairly, and within the limits of his personal competence. Public statements made by an EAP practitioner who is part of a larger organization or agency are formulated with consideration of their impact on the parent organization.

Announcements or advertisements of services offered or available to the public conform to professional standards and avoid the inclusion of statements or promises which are inaccurate, incomplete or misleading.

CLIENT'S INFORMED CONSENT

A primary concern of the EAP practitioner is to protect the client's rights as a consumer of EAP services and to support the client's right to consent to matters related to assessment and the implementation of a treatment plan. The practitioner assumes responsibility for the client's understanding of all important aspects of the potential or existing assessment or treatment relationship and of any factor which might affect the client's decision to enter into such a relationship.

When a client is misinformed or misunderstands any element of the professional relationship, the practitioner is willing to be held accountable and responsible for failure to correct the misinformation, misunderstanding, or misperception of the client. These elements include the limits of confidentiality, whether interviews will be recorded and if information obtained will be used for training or research purposes, the type of intervention(s) contemplated, and whether the client is being treated by a procedure which is experimental in nature or as part of a research study.

RELATION WITH THE CLIENT

Integrity is the fundamental quality of any professional relationship. This essential element requires that the client is free from doubt about the EAP practitioner's trustworthiness and capacity for ethical practice. The following are guidelines for the establishment and preservation of an ethical practitioner-client relationship:

A. The practitioner constantly maintains a professional manner in his personal contacts with the client, the client's family and associates.

B. The practitioner constantly safeguards the welfare of his client within the bounds of his responsibility. It is an essential responsibility of EAP service that the practitioner ensures continuity of care by following up on the progress of referrals made to other agencies or practitioners after his direct contact with the client has ended.

C. The practitioner does not allow any personal obligation or gain or any other conflict of interest to enter into the professional relationship with a client.

D. An ethical professional relationship with a client is free from any behavior on the part of the practitioner which is, or has the appearance of being, abusive or damaging to the client or which exploits the relationship for the satisfaction of the needs or the desires of the practitioner.

E. The practitioner always terminates a clinical relationship immediately upon evidence that the client cannot be reasonably expected to benefit from a continuation if it.

F. The practitioner ensures and provides for an appropriate setting for all clinical work, both for the protection of himself and the client.

G. Any dual relationship involving a practitioner and a client may raise questions of poor judgment and questionable ethical behavior. A practitioner who has a pre-existing social relationship with someone seeking service carefully evaluates his capacity to engage professionally with that person. Except under unusual and special circumstances such situations are best handled by an appropriate referral.

H. Any form of romantic involvement or sexual activity between a practitioner and a client is unethical.

I. The practitioner conscientiously seeks peer or supervisory consultations in client management, especially when he encounters difficulties or has reason to question the appropriateness of his client relationship.

J. The ethical practitioner serves his clients in a conscientious and efficient manner. He is obliged to provide services promptly. When it can be foreseen that there will be a delay in the initiation of such service, the practitioner informs the client and offers to make an appropriate referral.

CONFIDENTIALITY AND ANONYMITY

The EAP practitioner protects the client's right to privacy with reference both to confidentiality and anonymity. Anonymity refers to nondisclosure of the identity of a client. Confidentiality refers to the private, non-disclosable nature of information obtained in the communication between a client and practitioner.

A practitioner provides effective professional service only when there is complete and unreserved communication between himself and his client. The client has the right to feel completely secure in the choice to use EAP services and is entitled to assume that matters discussed with, or information disclosed to, the practitioner will be held in strictest confidence.

Whenever any limitation or exception exists to complete confidentiality (e.g., the obligation to report child abuse, etc.), the ethical practitioner declares and explains these limits of confidentiality before continuing in a professional relationship with the client.

The ethical practitioner does not use a naive understanding or interpretation of a confidentiality principle as an excuse to avoid his responsibility, under the law or otherwise, to make appropriate disclosure when the life, health, or safety of either the client or others is in peril. Ethical practice demands the seeking of consultation whenever questions arise in this vital area of EAP service.

CLIENT RECORDS

The requirement of confidentiality applies to all written records maintained as a consequence of providing professional EAP service. The practitioner gives careful consideration to the following issues when deciding what information is to be collected from clients and recorded in files:

A. Every item of information in the record is related to the stated purposes of the individual or agency providing the service.

B. Records maintained for clinical purposes contain only such information as is necessary to optimum clinical service and avoid references to events or client behavior which have no direct relevance.

C. Personal values and judgments of the practitioner are not appropriate in EAP records and are avoided when describing client history or behavior.

D. Every entry in a client's record is as complete as possible and contains factual information necessary to give an adequate representation of the presenting problem, services rendered, and progress to date. The practitioner establishes procedures to review entries, correct errors, and otherwise ensure the accuracy of information contained.

E. Information intended to be current is subject to continual review and updating. Information which is no longer relevant and/or no longer accurate is deleted.

F. It is good practice for the practitioner to assume when making entries in the patient record that the entry may be subject, on judicial order, to be read publicly in open court in the presence of the client.

The practitioner gives careful consideration to the following items when deciding upon the proper use of information collected and stored in patient records:

A. Information in the client's record is the property of the client. The client retains the right to know of the existence of recorded information and to prevent the unauthorized use of that information for purposes other than that for which it was obtained.

B. The practitioner obtains permission in writing from the client before any use or disclosure is made of information contained in the client's record.

C. Client information is used for instructional purposes only when the identity of the individual client has been appropriately and completely disguised.

D. Written reports or discussions about a client are limited to only those persons who have a clear involvement with the client's case and a legitimate need to have the information involved.

WITHDRAWAL OF SERVICES

When a professional relationship has been established, the practitioner continues to provide those services to the best of his ability unless there is a clearly justifiable cause for terminating the relationship. In such instances, the practitioner informs the client of the reasons for termination and assumes responsibility for making an appropriate referral to another practitioner or agency if a continuation of service is consistent with the client's welfare. A practitioner does not threaten withdrawal of service as a means of obtaining cooperation from the client.

Efficiency and effectiveness of the referral process is a cornerstone of ethical EAP service. The practitioner is responsible for making himself thoroughly familiar with the private and public service providers available in his area before attempting to offer EAP service to the public.

Referrals are made to resources appropriate to the client's needs as quickly as possible after adequate evaluation and assessment has been completed. Any delay in making or implementing a referral is explained thoroughly to the client.

An agency or individual practitioner providing EAP services is ethically obligated to clients to avoid any appearance of conflict of interest in the referral process. It is unethical behavior for the EAP practitioner to make, or fail to make, a referral to a service provider for purely personal or organizational financial gain.

Practitioners who perform initial evaluation and assessment may retain clients for therapeutic intervention or transfer them to other departments within their own organization or agency only after careful and thorough determination that such disposition can be justified on the grounds of the best interests of the client and not those of the practitioner or agency. In such cases, the EAP practitioner providing services on contract to the client's employer informs that employer and obtains concurrence with a plan to retain that client for treatment rather than to refer to another appropriate service provider.

PROFESSIONALS

Independent assessments, second opinions, and case monitoring contracts are at the heart of the EAP activity and may generate treatment recommendations that displace previous clinical arrangements made by the client. When establishing a professional relationship with a client, a practitioner determines to the best of his ability that all previous professional service providers have either withdrawn or been discharged by the client or will be coordinated into the treatment plan that follows the assessment.

When it is necessary to engage professionally with a client in an emergency situation, the practitioner limits his service only to that which is necessary to respond to the emergency and immediately advises other professional persons responsible for the client of his actions.

PERSONAL RELATIONSHIP AND ACTIVITIES

An EAP practitioner is cognizant of his obligation to safeguard both his own reputation and that of professional colleagues and clients. Therefore he is aware of, and maintains constant consideration of, the social codes and moral expectations of the community in which he works. A practitioner avoids any behavior, activities, or associations which may adversely impact his capacity to be perceived as an ethical provider of EAP services. A practitioner does not allow his involvement with any activity, persons, or interests to interfere with the quality of service provided or his professional judgment and performance on behalf of his clients.

Source: Reprinted with permission from Employee Assistance Society of North America, Oak Park, IL.

Bibliography

About Addiction. Scriptographic Booklet by Channing L. Bete Co., Inc. (1987).

About Alcoholism Services. Scriptographic Booklet by Channing L. Bete Co., Inc. (1979).

Abrams, L. "An Employer's Role in Relapse Prevention." *The Almacan* (July 1987): 20–22.

Abramson, J. "Anti-Drug Bill Shields Lawyers on Fees Issue." *Wall Street Journal* (Oct. 25, 1988).

"Acupuncture Takes Off as Useful Treatment for Many Drug Users." *Atlanta Journal and Constitution* (Oct. 2, 1988).

"ADDLife Makes '100 Best' List." *Greenville [SC] Piedmont* (Aug. 24, 1988).

Alcoholics Anonymous, 3d ed. New York: Alcoholics Anonymous World Services, Inc. (1976).

Alcoholics Anonymous Comes of Age. New York: Alcoholics Anonymous World Services, Inc. (1988).

"Alcoholics Fall Into 2 Categories, Researcher Says." *The [Columbia, SC] State* (June 4, 1988).

Alcoholism—A Treatable Disease. Minneapolis: Johnson Institute, Ind. (1987).

Alcoholism in the Workplace: What You Can Do. Daly City, CA: Krames Communications (1986).

"All Localities Must Fight for Drug Treatment." *New York Times* (June 5, 1988).

Allied-Signal, Inc. *Substance Abuse Screening Program.*

Alsop, R. "Drug and Alcohol Clinics Vie for Patients." *Wall Street Journal* (Nov. 14, 1988).

AMS Foundation. *1988 AMS New Benefits Survey.* Trevose, PA: AMS Foundation (1988).

Anderson, D.J. *Perspectives on Treatment: The Minnesota Experience.* Center City, MN: Hazelden (1981).

Anderson, D., et al. *BRP's Drugs in the Workplace.* New York: Business Resources Publications, Inc. (1988).

Anderson, G.L. *The Student Assistance Program Model,* 2nd ed. Milwaukee: Community Recovery Press (1987).

Angarola, R.T. "Drug Testing in the Workplace; Is It Legal?" *Personnel Administrator* (Sept. 1985): 79.

Anonymity: The Meaning and Application of Traditions Eleven and Twelve. Los Angeles: Overeaters Anonymous (1983).

"Assistance Program Official Says Denial Complicates Early Drug Detection." *Nat'l Rep. on Substance Abuse* (BNA) (Sept. 2, 1987): 1.

Association of Labor-Management Administrators and Consultants on Alcoholism, Inc. *1986-89 President's Biennial Report.*

Baekeland, F. and L.K. Lundwall. "Drug Treatment of Alcoholism: Effects of Discontinuity of Medication on Results of a Double-Blind Study in Alcoholic Outpatients." *Alcohol Health and Research World* (Spring 1976): 23–25.

Baltimore County Office of Substance Abuse. *Awareness, Detection & Referral Program.*

————. *Drug & Alcohol Referral Booklet.*

Bargmann, E., et al. *Stopping Valium and Ativan, Centrax, Delane, Librium, Paxipam, Restoril, Serax, Tranxene, Xanax.* New York: Warner Books, Inc. (1982).

Barum, K. and P. Bashe. *How to Keep the Children You Love Off Drugs.* New York: Atlantic Monthly Press (1988).

Baxter, A.K. "Intervene If You Dare: Reaching the 'Protected' Academician." *The Almacan* (Feb. 1988): 13–16.

Bean, M. *Alcohol and Adolescents.* Minneapolis: Johnson Institute, Inc. (1982).

Bearman, D. "The Medical Case Against Drug Testing." *Security Management* (June 1988): 67.

Beattie, M. *Codependent No More.* New York: Harper/Hazelden (1987).

Beck, J. "Can Employers Force Workers to be Healthy?" *The [Columbia, SC] State* (Jan. 8, 1989).

Beech Hill Hospital/Outward Bound. *Adolescent Alcohol/Drug Program.* Dublin, NH: Beech Hill Hospital.

Beech Hill Hospital, Treatment Department. *An Innovative Approach to Adolescent Alcohol Abuse and Alcoholism* (April 1984).

Behre, R. "State's Student Referrals for Drugs Rise 16 Percent." *Greenville [SC] Piedmont* (Sept. 8, 1988).

Belluck, P. "Companies, Workers Clash Over Drugs." *Atlanta Journal & Constitution,* (Dec. 26, 1988): 1D.

Bennett, N., T. Blum and P. Roman. "Public Images of Alcoholism." *The Almacan* (August 1989): 35–37.

Bennett, W.I. "Patterns of Addiction." *New York Times Magazine,* April 10, 1988).

Bensinger, A. and C.F. Pilkington. "An Alternative Method in the Treatment of Alcoholism: The United Technologies Corporation Day Treatment Program." 24 *J. of Occupational Med.* (1983): 300–303.

Bensinger, DuPont & Associates. *How Many of Your Employees Use Drugs? What Are You Doing About It?* (Training Materials) Chicago: Bensinger, DuPont & Associates, Inc. (1988).

Bensinger, P.B. *Drugs in the Workplace: Employers' Rights and Responsibilities.* Washington, DC: Washington Legal Foundation (1984).

————. "Drugs in the Workplace: A Commentary." 3 *Behav. Sci. & the L.* (1985): 441–453.

Bickerton, D. "The Changing Workforce." *The Almacan* (Mar. 1987): 18–19.

Bickerton, R. "Employee Health Programs Net Big Returns." *The Almacan* (Dec. 1988): 18.

"Bill Shows No Tolerance of Drug Use." *The [Columbia, SC] State* (Sept. 23, 1988).

"A Biochemical Difference May Cause Alcoholism." *Greenville [S.C.] Piedmont* (Sept. 14, 1988).

Bishop, J.E. "Study Discovers Biochemical Difference Between Some Alcoholics, Non-Alcoholics." *Wall Street Journal* (Dec. 22, 1988).

Bishop, K. "Flunking the Drug Test." *California Law.* (April 1986): 30.

————. "Pre-Employment Drug Tests Blocked by California Court." *New York Times* (June 11, 1988).

Black C. *It Will Never Happen to Me*. Denver: M.A.C. Printing & Publications Division (1981).

Black, D. "Home Depot Takes a Chance on Drug Program." *Atlanta Business Chronicle* (Jan. 2, 1989).

Blair, B. *Supervisors and Managers as Enablers*. Minneapolis: Johnson Institute Inc. (1987).

Blodgett, N. "One Lawyer's Triumph Over Alcohol." *ABA Journal*, (Dec. 1, 1987): 102–105.

Blum, T.C. and P.M. Roman. "Internal vs. External EAPS." *Employee Assistance Programs: Benefits, Problems, and Prospects*. Washington, DC: Bureau of National Affairs, Inc. (1987). 95–104.

Boffrey, P.M. "More Drug Treatment Centers Are Urged." *New York Times* (June 5, 1988).

Bompey, S.H. "Drugs in the Workplace: From the Batter's Box to the Boardroom," 28 *J. of Occupational Med.* (1986): 825–832.

Bowen, O.R. and J.H. Sammons. "The Alcohol-Abusing Patient: A Challenge to the Profession." 260 *JAMA* (1988): 2267–2270.

Brenner, A. *Helping Children Cope With Stress*. Lexington: Lexington Books (1984).

Brierwood Hospital. *Warning Signs of Addiction*.

Brinkley, J. "Drug Law Raises More Than Hope." *New York Times* (Nov. 2, 1986): 5E.

Britt, D.R. *The All-American Cocaine Story*. Minneapolis: CompCare Publishers (1984).

Brody, J. "Alcoholism Shown to be Hereditary." *Health* (Aug. 26, 1987).

———. "Patterns of Abuse Detected in Alcoholics and Drug Users." *New York Times* (Feb. 7, 1989).

Bronson, G. "It's About Time." *Forbes* (July 27, 1987): 92–93.

Brownell, K.D., et al. "Understanding and Preventing Relapse." *American Psychologist* (July 1986): 765–782.

Bureau of Labor Statistics, U.S. Dept. of Labor. *Survey of Employer Anti-Drug Programs* (Report 760) (January 1989).

Bureau of National Affairs, Inc. *Alcohol and Drugs in the Workplace: Costs, Controls, and Controversies*. Washington, DC: Bureau of National Affairs, Inc. (1986).

————. *Employee Assistance Programs: Benefits, Problems, and Prospects.* Washington, DC: Bureau of National Affairs, Inc. (1987).

Burke-Taylor Associates, Inc. *Burke-Taylor Associates Employee Assistance Program Services.*

Business Against Drugs, Inc. *B.A.D. Inc.: Business Against Drugs.* Rockville, MD: Business Against Drugs, Inc. (1987).

————. *Montgomery County Business Survey on Drug and Alcohol Abuse,* Rockville, MD: Business Against Drugs, Inc. (1988).

Businesses for a Drug Free America. "Drug Abuse in the Workplace." *Nat'l Rep. on Substance Abuse* (BNA) (April 12, 1989): 2.

Calmes, J. "Legislator: Purge Firms of Drug Users." *Atlanta Journal & Constitution* (June 12, 1988): 11A.

Came to Believe . . . New York: World Services, Inc. (1985).

Carnahan, W.A., *Legal Aspects Affecting Employee Assistance Programs.* (ALMACAN) (1984).

Carolinas Construction Alliance for a Drug Free Worksite. *Model Alcohol and Drug Supervisory Training Program* (1989).

Carroll, D., et al. "Improving EAP Referrals Through Supervisory Training." *The Almacan* (Nov. 1985): 16–18.

Castro, J. "Battling the Enemy Within: Companies Fight to Drive Illegal Drugs Out of the Workplace." *Time* (Mar. 17, 1986): 52–61.

Cecere, M.S. and P.B. Rosen, "Legal Implications of Substance Abuse Testing in the Workplace." 62 *Notre Dame L. Rev.* (1987): 859.

Cermak, T.L. *Diagnosing and Treating Co-Dependence.* Minneapolis: Johnson Institute Books (1986).

————. "The Road to Recovery for Adult Children of Alcoholics." *New Realities* (Sept./Oct. 1988): 25–33.

"Chapter 10: To Employers." In *Alcoholics Anonymous,* 3d Ed. New York: Alcoholics Anonymous World Services, Inc. (1976).

Chemical Dependency Relapse. Daly, CA: Krames Communications (1986).

Children of Alcoholics. Scriptographic Booklet by Channing L. Bete Co., Inc.

"Chrysler, UAW Announce Availability of Employee Assistance, Help-Line Programs." *Daily Lab. Rep.* (BNA), No. 150 (Aug. 4, 1988): A-9.

Chul, G. "Cocaine: Jekyll-Hyde Drug Brings Euphoria, and Sometimes Death." *Greenville [SC] News* (July 27, 1986): 9E.

CIBA-GEIGY Corp. *CIBA-GIEGY Substance Abuse Prevention Program Employee Guide* (1987).

Circle Park. *Employee Assistance Program.*

Cloninger, C.R. "Neurogenetic Adaptive Mechanisms in Alcoholism." *Science* (April 24, 1987): 410–416.

Coates, J. "The Saga of Alcoholics Anonymous." *Greenville [S.C.] Piedmont* (May 5, 1988).

Coggins, B. and A. Collier. "Day Treatment in the Workplace." *EAP Digest* (May/June 1985): 19–26.

The Co-Founder of Alcoholics Anonymous. New York: Alcoholics Anonymous World Services, Inc. (1972).

Cohen, S. "Drugs in the Workplace." *J. of Clinical Psychiatry*, 45.12 (1984): 4–8.

Cohen, T. "Drug-Use Testing: Costly and Corruptible." *New York Times* (Aug. 20, 1986): 8.

————. "Why Subsidize Expensive Private Drug Care?" *New York Times* (June 6, 1988).

College of American Pathologists. *Employee Drug Testing: A Guide to Choosing a Quality Drug Testing Laboratory.*

Collins, W.C. *Urine Testing and the Workplace: Considerations.* Syva Company (1986).

Commerce Clearing House, Inc. *Employee Assistance Programs: Drug, Alcohol, and Other Problems.* Chicago: Commerce Clearing House, Inc. (1986).

CompCare. *Facts About Alcohol and Drug Problems.* Newport Beach, CA: Comprehensive Care Corp. (1979).

Congressional Research Service. *Federal Laws Relating to the Control of Narcotics and Other Dangerous Drugs, Enacted 1961-1985: Brief Summaries*, Revised. By H.L. Hogan (Jan. 15, 1986).

————. *Drug Testing and Urinalysis in the Workplace: Legal Aspects.* By M.M. Murphy and V.E. Treacy (April 16, 1986).

————. *Drug Control: Highlights of P.L. 99-570, Anti Drug Act of 1986.* By H.L. Hogan, et al. (Oct. 31, 1986).

————. *Drug Testing for Illegal Substances.* By B. Randall IV (Jan. 20, 1987).

————. *Drug Abuse Prevention and Control: Budget Authority for Federal Programs, FY 1986—FY 1988*, Revised (Mar. 16, 1987).

Conyers, J. and S. Thurmond. "We Can't Wait for Industry to Act." *USA Today* (Apr. 8, 1988).

Cooper, C.J. "The Constitutionality of Drug Testing," 35 *Fed. B. News & J.* (1988): 359–363.

Coopers & Lybrand. *Employee Assistance Program Survey Results.* (1988).

Copus, D.A. *Alcohol and Drugs at Work: A Manual for Federal Contractors and Grantees.* Larkspur, CA: National Employment Law Institute (1989).

Cordes, L. *The Reflecting Pond.* Minneapolis: Hazelden Foundation (1981).

"Cost-Effective, Forensic-Quality Drug Testing: Statement by Arthur J. McBay, Ph.D. before the Committee on Education and Labor Subcommittee on Employment Opportunities, 21 April 1988." 2 *Employment Testing* (1988): 227.

County of Spartanburg (S.C.). *Substance Abuse Policy.*

"Court Finds No Disparate Treatment of Black Employee Fired for Drug Use." *Daily Lab. Rep.* (BNA), No. 122 (June 24, 1988): A-1.

"Court Overturns Arbitration Award Reinstating Worker Fired for Marijuana Use." *Daily Lab. Rep.* (BNA), No. 22 (Feb. 3, 1989): A-1.

"Court Rules City's Mass Drug Testing Plan Breaches Privacy Rights of Police and Firemen." *Daily Lab. Rep.* (BNA), No. 127 (July 1, 1988): A-7.

"Court Upholds Random Drug Testing of Police Officers in New Jersey Town." *Daily Lab. Rep.* (BNA) No. 123 (June 27, 1988): A-1.

Cox, G.D. "Juries Sympathetic in Drug-Test Cases." *Nat'l L.J.* (Jan. 4, 1987): 3–4.

Craig, R.J. *Clinical Management of Substance Abuse Programs.* Springfield, IL: Charles C. Thomas (1987).

DeCresce, R., et al. *Drug Testing in the Workplace.* Washington, DC: Bureau of National Affairs, Inc. (1989).

Delta Woodside, Inc. *Substance Abuse Policy.*

Denenberg, T.S. and R.V. Denenberg. *Alcohol and Drugs: Issues in the Workplace.* Washington, DC: Bureau of National Affairs, Inc. (1983).

Derr, W.D. "Wellness and EAPs." *The Almacan* (Nov. 1985): 12-13.

Desmond, E.W. "Out in the Open: Changing Attitudes and New Research Give Fresh Hope to Alcoholics." *Time* (Nov. 30, 1987): 80-88.

Desrosiers, N.A., M.D. *Status Report of the Alcohol and Drug Program Component of the Greenville Mental Health Center and the Piedmont Mental Health Center.* (Jan. 1986).

"Did This Company Go Too Far?" *Business Week* (Mar. 23, 1988): 62.

Dolman, J. "U.S. Constitution Facing an Election-Year Attack in War on Drugs." *Atlanta Journal & Constitution* (Sept. 24, 1988).

Drews, T.R. *Getting Them Sober.* (Vol. 2) South Plainfield, N.J.: Bridge Publishing, Inc. (1983).

"Drinking Problems Rise Among Young Women." *New York Times* (Oct. 13, 1988).

"Drug Testing Is First for Area Bank." *The Flyer* (Published by American Federal Savings and Loan) (Dec. 1988).

"Drug Testing on the Job: What Are the Legal Limits?" *Your Law* 1 (ABA Newsletter) (Spring 1988).

"Drug-Testing Policy Ruled an Unfair Labor Practice." *The [Columbia, SC] State* (Nov. 9, 1988).

"Drug Testing Programs More Common in Large Businesses, BLS Survey Finds." *Daily Lab. Rep.* (BNA), No. 150 (Jan. 12, 1989): B-1.

"Drug Use May Create Liability for Employer." *South Carolina Business Journal* (June 1988).

Dunn, R. *Relapse and the Addict.* Center City, MN: Hazelden Foundation (1986).

Duplessis, J. "Official: More Textile Companies May Require Drug Testing of Contractors." *Greenville [SC] News* (June 21, 1988).

_____. "Companies Refine Policies for Drug Testing." *Greenville [SC] News* (July 18, 1988).

_____. "Worker's Rights Advocates Favor Drug Rehabilitation Programs." *Greenville [SC] News* (July 18, 1988).

DuPont Corp. *Substance Abuse Committee Report* (Jan. 3, 1986).

DuPont, R.L. *Getting Tough on Gateway Drugs.* Washington, DC: American Psychiatric Press, Inc. (1984).

E., Stephanie. *Shame Faced.* Center City, MN: Hazelden Foundation (1986).

"The EAP Manual: A Review." *The Almacan* (Dec. 1987): 7-9.

"EAPs Salvage Valued Workers." *Business Atlanta* (June 1988): 62.

Eblen, T. "Employee Drug Test Rules Approaching a Crossroads." *Atlanta Journal & Constitution* (June 27, 1988): 1C.

"Ecstasy Drug Tied to Brain Damage." *New York Times* (Jan. 17, 1989).

Edelwich, J. *Sexual Dilemmas for the Helping Professional.* New York: Brunner/Mazel Publishers (1982).

Edison Electric Institute Human Resources Management Division. *EEI Guide to Effective Drug and Alcohol/Fitness for Duty Policy Development*, Revised. (1985).

Edson, L. "All About A.A." Rev. of *Getting Better: Inside Alcoholics Anonymous*, by N. Robertson. *New York Times* (May 20, 1988).

Eichler, S., et al. *Operation: Redblock—Case Study of a Peer Prevention Substance Abuse Program for Railroad Industry Personnel.* Rockville, MD: Institute for Human Resources, Inc. (1988).

el-Guebaly, N. "Alcohol, Alcoholism, and Biological Rhythms." *Alcoholism: Clinical and Experimental Research.* 11.2 (1987): 139-143.

Elliott, T.J. "User Friendly Employee Assistance: Computer EAP Training." *The Almacan* (Mar. 1987): 25–28.

Emb-Tex Corp. *Employee Assistance Program for Emb-Tex Corporation.*
Emory L.J., Note. "Use and Abuse of Urinalysis Testing in the Workplace: A Proposal for Federal Legislation Limiting Drug Screening. 35 (1986): 1011.

Eisman, C. "Getting the Most From the Self-Help Network." *The Almacan* (April 1988): 24-27.

"'E.T.' Star Treated by Rehab Center." *Greenville [SC] News* (Dec. 23, 1988).

Etzioni, A. "To 'Just Say No' Leaves Vacuum That Still Yearns to be Filled." *Atlanta Journal & Constitution* (Dec. 29, 1988).

Evans, D.G. "Employee Drug Testing: Recent Testimony Before the U.S. Senate." *Syva Monitor* (1987).

The Eye Opener. Center City, MN: Hazelden Foundation (1939).

"Federal Drug Testing Legislation." *Employee Testing & The Law*, 3.5 (1988): 1.

"Federal Workers Sue to Block Drug Tests." *Greenville [SC] Piedmont* (Sept. 16, 1986): 1A.

Fingarette, Herbert. "Alcoholism—Neither Sin Nor Disease." *The Center Magazine* (Mar./April 1985): 56–62.

Foote, A., et al. "Staffing Occupational Employee Assistance Programs: The General Motors Experience." *Alcohol and Research World* (Spring 1980): 22-31.

Fowler, E.M. "Drug Testing Common for Job Seekers." *New York Times* (Jan. 19, 1988): D21.

Framy, J.B. "Promoting Wellness and Disease Prevention in EAPs." *The Almacan* (Nov. 1987): 8-11.

Franklin, J.S. "Undercover in Corporate America." *New York Times* (Jan. 29, 1989): 1C.

Freeman, S.M. *From Peer Pressure to Peer Support Alcohol/Drug Prevention Through Group Process.* Minneapolis: Johnson Institute (1989).

French, H.W. "Helping the Addicted Worker." *New York Times* (Mar. 26, 1987).

Freudenheim, M. "Workers Substance Abuse Is Increasing, Survey Says." *New York Times* (Dec. 12, 1988): 1B.

————. "Acknowledging Substance Abuse." *New York Times* (Dec. 13, 1988): 2B.

Friend, T. "Drug Test Accuracy Up to Labs." *USA Today* (Jan. 12, 1989): 5A.

Gallante, S.P. "Damage Done by Drug Abuse Can Cripple Smaller Company." *Wall Street Journal* (May 19, 1986).

Gallup, Jr., G. and A. Gallup. "Education Favored in Drug Fight." *Greenville [SC] Piedmont* (Mar. 27, 1988).

Garvin, F.H. and E.H. Ellenwood, Jr. "Cocaine and Other Stimulants: Actions, Abuse, and Treatment." 318 *New England J. of Med.* (1988): 1173–1182.

Gatling, H. "Waging Another Kind of Campaign: Ex-Jenrette Aide Helping Open Youth Anti-Drug Center." *The [Columbia, SC] State* (June 13, 1988).

Geidt, T.E. "Drug and Alcohol Abuse in the Workplace: Balancing Employer and Employee Rights." 11 *Employment Rel. L. J.* (1985): 181-205.

General Electric Corporation. *Employee Assistance Program—Lighting Systems Department.*

General Motors Corp. *1987 UAW—GM Employee Assistance Program.*

"Genuine Advance on Drug Battlefront." *Atlanta Journal & Constitution* (Jan. 2, 1989).

George, T. "NFL Notebook: Drug Policy Is Challenged and Criticized." *New York Times* (Sept. 20, 1988).

Gladwell. "Controversy Surrounds Booming Programs to Help out Employees." *Washington Post* (Jan. 11, 1988).

Goldford. "Where Should the Alcoholic Client be Referred?" *Virginia Lawyers Weekly* (Sept. 8, 1986).

The Good Life. FLI Learning Systems, Inc. (1985).

Googins, B. "Treatment Research and EAPs." *The Almacan* (Mar. 1986): 10-11.

Gorski, T.T. and M. Miller. *Staying Sober: A Guide for Relapse Prevention.* Independence, MO: Independence Press (1986).

Gosselin, R. and S. Nice. *Lesbian and Gay Issues in Early Recovery.* Center City, MN: Hazelden Foundation (1986).

Greenleaf, J. *Co-Alcoholic—Para-Alcoholic.* Denver, CO: MAC Publishing (1987).

Greenwood Mills, Inc. *Policies—Procedures: Employee Assistance Program* (1987).

Greiff, J. "When an Employee's Performance Slumps." *Nation's Business* (Jan. 1989): 44–45.

Gross, L. *How Much Is Too Much?* New York: Ballantine Books (1983).

Hafner, K. "Testing for Drug Use: Handle With Care." *Business Week* (Mar. 23, 1988): 65.

Hamilton, J. O'C. "How to Help Addicts Break the Drug Habit." *Business Week* (Mar. 17, 1986): 143–144.

Hanson, D.J. "Drug Abuse Testing Programs Gaining Acceptance in Workplace." *C&EN* (June 2, 1986): 7–13.

Harrell, B. "Potter's House Gives Alcoholics Chance to Make Turnaround." *Atlanta Journal & Constitution* (April 20, 1986).

Hart, S. *Rehab: A Comprehensive Guide to Recommended Drug-Alcohol Treatment Centers in the United States.* New York: Harper & Row (1988).

Harwood, H.J., et al. *Economic Costs to Society of Alcohol and Drug Abuse and Mental Illness: 1980.* Research Triangle Park, NC: Research Triangle Institute (1984).

Hayashida, M., et al. "Comparative Effectiveness and Costs of Inpatient and Outpatient Detoxification of Patients with Mild-to-Moderate

Alcohol Withdrawal Syndrome." 320 *New England J. of Med.* (1989): 358–365.

"Helping the Addicted Worker." *New York Times* (Mar. 25, 1987).

Helsby, W.L. "Drug Testing in the Work Place." *Florida Bar J.* (June 1986): 73–75.

Hendler, S.S., M.D., Ph.D. *The Complete Guide to Anti-Aging Nutrients.* New York: Simon and Schuster (1985).

Herman, G.N. "A Comparative Summary of Current State Drug-Testing Legislation." *Employee Testing & The Law*, 3.6 (1988): 1–4.

Herrmann, L.M. "An Employee Assistance Program Pays Off." *Hospital Magazine* (Feb. 1978): 34–36.

Hershey, Jr., R.D. "Employee Drug Testing Is Surveyed." *New York Times* (Jan. 12, 1989).

"HHS Chief Orders Drug Testing for 8,600 Agency Employees." *Atlanta Journal & Constitution* (Dec. 15, 1988).

Hiatt, R.A., et al. "Alcohol Consumption and the Risk of Breast Cancer in a Prepaid Health Plan," 48 *Cancer Research* (1988): 2284–2287.

Hill, T. "Studies Show Seriousness of Alcoholism Among Elderly." *The Journal* (Feb. 1, 1974): 2.

Hoerr, J. "The Drug Wars Will be Won With Treatment, Not Tests." *Business Week* (Oct. 13, 1986): 52.

Hoffman, N.G., et al. *CATOR: Chemical Abuse/Addiction Treatment Outcome Registry 1985 Report.* St. Paul, MN: Medical Education and Research Foundation, St. Paul-Ramsey Medical Center (1985).

Hofman, F.G., *A Handbook on Drug and Alcohol Abuse: The Biomedical Aspects.* New York: Oxford University Press (1975).

The Homosexual Alcoholic. Center City, MN: Hazelden Foundation (1980).

"House Government Operations Committee Approves Drug-Free Workplace Bill." *Daily Lab. Rep.* (BNA), No. 127 (July 1, 1988): A-9.

"How Not to Wage a War Against Drugs." Editorial. *Atlanta Journal & Constitution* (Dec. 29, 1988).

Hurd, S.N. "The *Patchogue-Medford* Decision: An Analysis." 1 *Employment Testing* (1987): 43–45.

———. "States Adopt Comprehensive Drug Testing Laws." 2 *Employment Testing* (1988): 263.

————. "Judges Rule on the Negotiability of Drug Testing." 2 *Employment Testing* (1988): 279.

————. "Federal Courts Consider Drug Testing Issues." 2 *Employment Testing* (1988): 315.

It's Not Your Fault You're Not Alone. The Rader Institute (1984).

Jacoby, T. "Drug Testing in the Dock: Are Safety and Privacy Incompatible?" *Newsweek* (Nov. 14, 1988): 66.

"Job Absenteeism Linked to Drug Use." *New York Times* (Jan. 14, 1989).

Johnson, J. "White House Will Start Drug Tests for Employees of Executive Office." *New York Times* (July 1, 1988): 1.

"Judge Bars Random Drug Testing of 3 Million Truck, Bus Drivers." *Atlanta Journal & Constitution* (Dec. 31, 1988).

"Justices Ponder Legitimacy of Regulations Treating Alcoholism as 'Willful Misconduct'." *Daily Lab. Rep.* (BNA), No. 234 (Dec. 8, 1987): A-11.

Kamerow, D.B., et al. "Alcohol Abuse, Other Drug Abuse, and Mental Disorders in Medical Practice." 254 *JAMA* (1986): 2054–2057.

Keefe, L.M. "Compulsive Shopping No Joke, Says Author." *Greenville [SC] News* (Nov. 11, 1988).

Kelbe, E. *Drug and Alcohol Abuse: Prevention, Treatment, and Education.* Congressional Research Office, Library of Congress (Dec. 1986).

Keller, J.E. *Ministering to Alcoholics.* Minneapolis: Augsburg Publishing House (1966).

Kelsey, D.B. "New Approaches to the Delivery of Psychiatric Care and Treatment for Substance Abuse." *Driving Down Health Care Costs: Ideas and Strategies,* 2nd ed.

"Kentucky Insurer to Launch Outpatient Treatment Program." *Nat'l Rep. on Substance Abuse* (BNA) (May 24, 1989): 2.

Kerr, P. "Acupuncture Experiment in New York Is Said to Ease Addiction to Crack." *New York Times* (Dec. 30, 1988): 9.

Kilpatrick, J.J. "Drug Tests Are Not Unreasonable." *The [Columbia, SC] State* (Sept. 27, 1986): 8-A.

Kolata, G. "Study Finds Differences in the Cells of Alcoholics." *New York Times* (Sept. 15, 1988).

————. "Doctors Studying the Drug Ecstasy Decipher its Destructive Secrets." *New York Times* (Feb. 7, 1989): 17.

————. "Alcohol Is a Problem When It's a Problem." *New York Times* (Feb. 12, 1989).

Kolbert, E. "Forced Drug Testing of Teachers Is Ruled Illegal in New York." *New York Times* (June 10, 1987): 1.

Krames Communications. *Alcoholism in the Workplace: What You Can Do.* Daly City, CA: Krames Communications (1986).

————. *Cocaine in the Workplace: What You Can Do.* Daly City, CA: Krames Communications (1986).

Kramon, G. "New Incentives to Take Care." *New York Times* (Mar. 21, 1989): D2.

Kulik, F.A. and R. Wilbur. "Detoxification of Alcoholics With Drugs: Perspectives in Treatment and Research." *Alcohol Health & Research World* (Fall 1981): 50–54.

Kuntz, P. "Demand for Drug-Free Workers Blocks NSF, NBS Authorization." *Cong. Q.* (Apr. 30, 1988): 1171–1172.

Kurtz, E. *A.A.: The Story* (A revised edition of *Not-God: A History of Alcoholics Anonymous*). San Francisco: Harper/Hazelden (1988).

Kupfer, A. "Is Drug Testing Good or Bad?" *Fortune* (Dec. 19, 1988): 133–136.

Lampe, J. *Bombed, Buzzed, Smashed or Sober.* Boston: Little, Brown & Co. (1976).

"Large Corporations Increasing Drug Tests." *Greenville [SC] News* (June 10, 1988).

Larson, B. *No Longer Strangers.* Waco, TX: World Books Publishers (1971).

"Latitude Urged for Supervisors in Referrals for Drug Abusers." *Nat'l Rep. on Substance Abuse* (BNA) (Sept. 28, 1988): 5.

"Law Firms Help Employees With Counselling Programs." *The Washington Lawyer* (Nov./Dec. 1987): 19.

"Lawyer Says President Can't Win on Drug Test." *Chicago Tribune* (Nov. 14, 1986).

"Legalizing Drug Use: Is it the Only Realistic Solution?" *ABA Journal* (Jan. 1989): 36–37.

Lemberger, L. and A. Rubin. *Physiologic Disposition of Drugs of Abuse.* New York: Spectrum Publications, Inc. (1976).

Lesher, R.L. "Business Has an Obligation to Lead Battle Against Drugs." *South Carolina Bus. J.* Nov. 1986).

Lewis, P. "Alcoholism: Addicts at a Younger Age." *Washington Star-News* (Aug. 3, 1974).

Lewis, R.J. and S.P. Cooper. "Alcohol, Other Drugs, and Fatal Work-Related Injuries." 31 *J. of Occupational Med.* (1989): 23–28.

Lightman, R. and J.B. Wagman. "A Working Proposal for the EAP Role in a Managed Care System." *The Almacan* (May 1988): 18–21.

Lindquist, M. *Holding Back—Why We Hide the Truth About Ourselves.* Center City, MN: Hazelden Foundation (1987).

Lipscomb, S. "EAPs and HMOs: Making the Fit." *The Almacan* (Nov. 1985): 24–25.

The Little Red Book. Center City, MN: Hazelden Foundation (1970).

Loftis, Jr., W.R. "Workplace Drug Testing: A Management Tool." *Employee Testing & The Law*, 3.4 (1988): 1–4.

Longabaugh, R., et al. "Cost Effectiveness of Alcoholism Treatment in Partial vs. Inpatient Settings: Six-Month Outcomes." 44 *J. Stud. on Alcohol* (1983): 1047–1071.

Lord, L.J. "Inpatient vs. Outpatient." *U.S. News & World Report* (Nov. 30, 1987): 56–62.

Mahoney, J.J. "EAPs and Medical Cost Containment." *The Almacan* (May 1988): 16–20.

Marijuana: A Second Look at a Drug of Isolation. Daly City, CA: Krames Communications (1987).

"Marsh & McLennan Releases Substance Abuse Study." *The Almacan* (April 1989): 34–36.

Martz, R. "The Drug War and Politics." *Atlanta Journal & Constitution* (Oct. 17, 1988): 1A.

Masi, D.A. *Designing Employee Assistance Programs.* New York: American Management Associates (1984).

_____. *Drug Free Workplace: A Guide for Supervisors.* Washington, DC: Buraff Publications, Inc. (1987).

Massachusetts Blue Cross. *Massachusetts Blue Cross and Alcoholism.* (1984).

Maxwell, R. *The Booze Battle.* New York: Ballentine Books (1976).

May, C. "Once-Lonely Voice Finds an Audience." *New York Times* (June 6, 1988): 12.

McClellan, K. "Adding to Our EAP Knowledge." Rev. of *The EAP Solution-Current Trends and Future Issues*, by J. Spicer, *U.S. Journal* (Jan. 1987): 9.

McDonald, B. "The Courage to Say: "I Am an Alcoholic'." *The [Columbia, SC] State* (May 26, 1988).

McDonald, F.J. "Remarks Before the National Federation of Parents for Drug-Free Youth." (Sept. 28, 1984).

McFather, L.D. "Testing Doesn't Make a Drug Program." *New York Times* (June 8, 1986).

McGinn, R.L. "For Me, Alcohol is a Disease." *New York Times* (Dec. 3, 1987).

McGlinchey, Staffard, Mintry, Cellini & Lang, P.C. *Drug and Alcohol Abuse: An Escalating Crisis.* New Orleans: McGlinchey, Staffard, Mintry, Cellini & Lang, P.C. (1986).

McGuirk, T.R. "Evaluation and Development of Employee Assistance Programs." *Alcohol Health and Research World* (Spring 1980): 17.

Meddis, S. "The Message: 'We're Fed Up, Tired of Drugs'." *USA Today* (Mar. 7, 1986): 1A.

Medlock, T.T. "Attorney General Says State Needs Grand Jury to Fight Drugs." *Greenville [SC] News* (Oct. 16, 1988): 3C.

"Meese Urges Use of Surveillance by Employers to Combat Drugs." *Investor's Daily* (Oct. 31, 1986): 23.

Melloan, G. "A Drug-Test Advocate Makes No Apologies." *Wall Street Journal* (July 19, 1988).

Melucci, L. "Faced With Alcohol-Related Accidents, Planners Ask 'Who Pays the Price?'" *Meeting News* (Oct. 1987).

Mendelson, J.H. and N. Mello. *Alcohol Use and Abuse in America.* Boston: Little, Brown & Co. (1985).

Mercer-Meidinger-Hansen, Inc. *Substance Abuse in the Workplace.* New York: Mercer-Meidinger-Hansen, Inc. (1988).

Milam, J.R. and K. Ketcham. *Under the Influence: A Guide to the Myths and Realities of Alcoholism.* New York: Bantam Books (1981).

Miller, J. "Drug Testing Gets Initial Nod." *Greenville [SC] News* (May 10, 1988).

Miller, R.E. "Job Reintegration and Aftercare of the Recovering Worker." *The Almacan* (Aug. 1986): 12–16.

————. "EAPs & Wellness: A Compromise?" *Employee Assistance* (June 1988): 42–44.

Miller, W.R. and R.K. Hester. "Inpatient Alcoholism Treatment: Who Benefits?" *American Psychologist* (July 1986): 794.

Milliken & Company, Inc. *Substance Abuse Prevention Process.* (1987).

Mithers, C.L. "High on the Job: The Great Escape—Danger of Drugs in the Workplace." *Glamour* (Aug. 1986): 252.

Mohr, C. "Drug Testing Policy Caught in Snags." *New York Times* (Dec. 18, 1988).

Montgomery, R.H. "Alcoholism Treatment Benefits: Cost or Savings?" *The Almacan* (May 1988): 16–20.

Moore, J., ed., *Road to Recovery: A National Directory of Alcohol and Drug Addiction Treatment Centers.* New York: Collier Books (1985).

Morgenthan, R.M. "Drug Habits We Can't Afford." *New York Times* (Dec. 14, 1988).

Morris, S.E. "Drug War Disgrace." *New York Times* (Oct. 8, 1988).

"Most Workers Never Have Drug Tests." *Greenville [SC] Piedmont.* (Jan. 11, 1989): 1A.

Murphy, T.A. "Remarks Before the Association of Labor-Management Administrators and Consultants on Alcoholism, Inc." (Oct. 5, 1979).

Musto, D.F. "Lessons of the First Cocaine Epidemic," *The Wall Street Journal* (June 11, 1986): 30.

Narcotics Anonymous, 3d ed. Van Nuys, CA: World Service Office, Inc. (1984).

National Cancer Institute. *National Cancer Institute Update: Study Links Alcohol Consumption to Breast Cancer* (May 6, 1987).

National Drug Policy Board. *Outline of Model Plan Prepared by Inter-agency Coordinating Group* (Dec. 1, 1987).

National Institute on Alcohol Abuse and Alcoholism. *Intramural Research Program* (1981).

————. *Alcohol Research: Meeting the Challenge* (1984).

————. *The Fifth Special Report to the U. S. Congress on Alcohol and Health.* Washington, DC: U.S. Government Printing Office (1984).

————. *Executive Summary: Alcoholism Treatment Impact on Total Health Care Utilization and Costs* (Feb. 1985).

National Institute on Drug Abuse. *Epidemiology of Heroin: 1964–1984,* Rockville, MD: NIDA (1985).

_____. *Consensus Summary: Interdisciplinary Approaches to the Problems of Drug Abuse in Workplace Drug Abuse Programs.* DHHS Pub. No. (ADM) 87-1538 (1987).

_____. *NIDA Capsules: Facts About Drugs in the Workplace,* (Revised. Nov. 1987).

_____. *Strategic Planning for Workplace Drug Abuse Programs.* DHHS Pub. No. (ADM) 87-1538 (1987).

_____. *Employee Drug Screening & Detection of Drug Use by Urinalysis.* DHHS Publication No. (ADM) 88-1442.

_____. *National Directory of Drug Abuse and Alcoholism Treatment and Prevention Programs.* DHHS Publication No. (ADM) 89-1603.

_____. *Model Plan for a Comprehensive Drug-Free Workplace Program.* DHHS Publication No. (ADM) 89-1635.

National Recovery Network. "Out-Treatment Centers; The Best of Both Worlds." (chart) National Recovery Network (1985).

Neal, A. "Is Alcoholism a Disease?" *ABA Journal* (Feb. 1, 1988): 58–62.

Newman, R.G. "Methadone Treatment: Defining and Evaluating Success." 257 *N. Eng. J. Med.* (1987): 447–50.

"99 Fired for Drug Use at S.C. Nuclear Plant." *Atlanta Journal & Constitution* (Nov. 16, 1986): 3A.

Nixon, D.W. "Strung Out on the Job." *The Rotarian* (Apr. 1986): 14–21.

"NLRB General Counsel Discusses Legal Issues Generated by Mandatory Drug Testing Policies," *Daily Lab. Rep.* (BNA), No. 91 (May 11, 1988): A-1.

"N.J. Judge Strikes Blow at Random Tests." *The [Columbia, SC] State* (Oct. 14, 1986): 10-A.

"No Drug Tests for Prison Workers." *New York Times* (June 17, 1988).

Noble, K.B. "U.S. Appeals Courts, in Four Cases, Back Drug Tests on Public Workers." *New York Times* (May 18, 1987).

None for the Road: A Guide to California's New DUI Laws, Downey, CA: Southeast Council on Alcoholism & Drug Problems, Inc. (1982).

Office of National Drug Control Policy. *National Drug Control Strategy* (September, 1989).

O'Hair, J.R. "Looking into the Future of Employee Assistance." *The Almacan* (Mar. 1987): 22–24.

Ohlms, D.L. *The Disease Concept of Alcoholism.* Belleville, IL: Gary Whiteaker Co. (1983).

"The Olympic Drug-Testing Procedure." *Atlanta Journal & Constitution* (Sept. 27, 1988).

One Day at a Time in Al-Anon. Don Mills, Canada: T.H. Best Printing Co. Ltd. (1984).

"One Employee's Experience With Drug Testing: Statement of Juanita M. James Before the Committee on Education and Labor Subcommittee on Employment Opportunities, 21 April 1988." 2 *Employment Testing* (1988): 223–225.

"One Hour of Illegal Drug Activity Around the World." *Atlanta Journal & Constitution* (Oct. 16, 1988).

"One Out of 100 Workers Tested for Drug Use, Study Finds." *Greenville [SC] News* (Jan. 12, 1989): 7A.

Orthmann, R. "Recent Developments in Federal Drug Testing." 2 *Employment Testing* (1988): 255.

Otis Corp. Alcohol and Drug Abuse Policy: *Supervisory Guidelines.*

Oxford House, Inc. *Oxford House Manual.* (1988).

Pace, N.A. "Why Doctors Treat Alcoholism as a Disease." *New York Times* (Nov. 27, 1987).

"Panel Picks Treatment Over Drug Testing." *Greenville [SC] News* (Dec. 31, 1986): C1.

Parks, M. "Soviets Cry for Help Is Answered as AA Takes Its Mission to Moscow." *Atlanta Journal & Constitution* (Nov. 11, 1988).

Paschal, B. "Invasion of Privacy Lawsuit May Set Precedent." *Greenville [SC] Piedmont* (Sept. 22, 1986): 1C.

Payson, M.F. and P.B. Rosen. "Substance Abuse: A Crisis in the Workplace." *Trial* (July 1987): 25–33.

Perham, J. "Battling Employee Alcoholism." *Dun's Business Month* (June 1982).

Perry, A. "Greer Panel Recommends Use of Private Company to Help With Drug Policy." *Greenville [SC] News* (Aug. 20, 1988).

———. "Lawyer Cautions on Random Drug Tests." *Greenville [SC] News* (June 15, 1989): 3C.

Phalon, R. "Sobering Facts on Rehab." *Forbes* (Mar. 9, 1987): 140–141.

Phelps, C.E. "Cheap Drinks Cheapen Lives." *Atlanta Journal & Constitution* (June 18, 1989).

Phillips, D.A., A.J. Purvis and H.J. Older. *Turning Supervisors on to Employees Counseling Programs.* Center City, MN: Hazelden Foundation (1980).

Phillips, D. "Why Employers Choose EAPs." *The Almacan* (Apr. 1988): 12–13.

Pierce, E. "What is an Employee Assistance Program." Unpublished (November, 1988).

Pincus, S.R. and J.S. Goldman. "Drug Testing on the Job: Facing a Loaded Legal Issue." *The Brief* (Summer 1988): 24–28.

Podolsky, D.M. and D. Richard. "Investigating the Role of Substance Abuse in Occupational Injuries." *Alcohol and Research World* (Summer 1985).

Porterfield, K.M. *Under the Same Roof.* Center City, MN: Hazelden Foundation (1985).

Postol, L.P. "Handicap Discrimination Considerations in Treating the Impaired Worker: Drugs, Alcohol, Pregnancy, and AIDS in the Workplace." 30 *J. of Occupational Med.* (1988): 321–327.

Powell, J. *Why Am I Afraid to Tell You Who I Am?* Allen, TX: Argus Communications (1969).

Powell, J. and L. Brady. *Will the Real Me Please Stand Up?* Allen, TX: Argus Communications (1985).

"Preliminary Findings of Study Suggest Link Between Drug Abuse, Absenteeism," *Daily Lab. Rep.* (BNA) No. 23 (Feb. 6, 1989): A-7.

"Prison Called Opportunity for Rehabilitation Efforts," *Nat'l Rep. on Substance Abuse* (BNA) (Jan. 20, 1988): 5.

"Proportions to Traffic Deaths Tied to Alcohol Drops to 51%." *New York Times* (Dec. 16, 1988).

Pursch, J.A. "Psychotherapy a Good Aid for Recovering Alcoholics." *The [Columbia, SC] State* (Oct. 16, 1988).

————. "How to Get a Friend Into Treatment." *The Island Packet* (Dec. 27, 1988).

————. "Dual Diagnosis Trend: Some Addicts Need Combination of Treatment, Counseling." *The [Columbia, SC] State* (Jan. 1, 1989).

"Quarterly Report of NLRB General Counsel Rosemary M. Collyer," *Daily Lab. Rep.* (BNA), No. 79 (April 25, 1988): D-1.

Questions and Answers about Compulsive Overeating and the OA Program of Recovery. Los Angeles: Overeaters Anonymous (1979).

Rabb, W. "Drug Bust at Springs Industries." *The York [SC] Observer* (Nov. 2, 1988).

Rasky, S.F. "House Accepts Compromise in Bid to Require Drug-Free Workplaces." *New York Times* (June 2, 1988).

Read, H.P. "EAPs Must Play Politics." *EA* (June 1988): 52–54.

Read III, H.P. "Integration, Not Confidentiality the Issue in Employee Assistance." *Occupational Health and Safety* (Dec. 1988): 41–42.

Reich, T. "Biologic-Marker Studies in Alcoholism." 21 *New England J. of Med.* (1988): 180–182.

"The Reliability of Drug Testing: Testimony of S. Joseph Mule, Ph.D. Before the Committee on Education and Labor Subcommittee on Employment Opportunities, 21 April 1988." 2 *Employment Testing* (1988): 226.

Resource One, Inc. *Alcohol and Drug Abuse Policy in the Work Place,* Greenville, SC: Resource One, Inc.

————. *Employee Assistance Programs.* Greenville, SC: Resource One, Inc.

————. *Employee Behavior Checklist for the Identification of the Troubled Employee.* Greenville, SC: Resource One, Inc. (1987).

————. *Problem Solving Systems for Substance Abuse in the Workplace.* Greenville, SC: Resource One, Inc.

————. *Recommended Treatment Referrals.* Greenville, SC: Resource One, Inc.

————. *Resource One's Basic Approach to Employee Assistance Programs.* Greenville, SC: Resource One, Inc.

Restak, R. "Drug Deaths and Pavlov's Dogs." *Washington Post* (Oct. 23, 1988).

Rogers, A.E. and M.W. Conner, "Interrelationships of Alcohol and Cancer." In Alfin-Slater and Kritchevsky, eds., *Human Nutrition: A Comprehensive Treatise.* Plenum (1986).

Roman, P.A. "The Necessity of Integration." *EA* (June 1988): 33–34.

Ronam, L. and W. Reichman. "Back to Work Vocational Recovery." *Alcohol Health and Research World* (Fall 1986): 35–40.

Rothstein, M.A. *Medical Screening of Workers.* Washington, DC: Bureau of National Affairs, Inc. (1984).

————. "Screening Workers for Drugs: A Legal and Ethical Framework." 11 *Employee Relations L. J.* (1985): 422–437.

Rovner, S. "Recovered Alcoholic Ann Richards Offers Message of Hope to Women." *Greenville [SC] News* (Oct. 6, 1988): 11B.

————. "Recent Studies Show Effects of Alcohol on Women." *Atlanta Journal & Constitution* (Nov. 3, 1988): 1E.

Rudd, F. "EAP Alcohol and Drug Treatment Follow-Up." *EAP Digest* (Mar./Apr. 1988): 18.

RX for Managing Stress. FLI Learning Systems, Inc. (1985).

Sachs, S.H. and C. Willner. "Random Mandatory Drug Testing in the Department of Justice: A Constitutional Critique." 2 *Employment Testing* (1988): 259.

Salahuddin, M. "Medicaid Now Covers Drug Rehabilitation." *The [Columbia, SC] State* (Aug. 6, 1988).

"S.C. Substance Abuse Group Chosen for National Award." *The [Columbia, SC] State* (Oct. 5, 1988).

Schlaadt, R.G. and P.T. Shannon, *Drugs of Choice: Current Perspectives on Drug Use,* 2nd ed. Englewood Cliffs, NJ: Prentice-Hall Co. (1986).

Schlesinger, S.E. and L.K. Harberg, *Taking Charge: How Families Can Climb Out of the Chains of Addiction.* New York: Simon & Schuster, Inc. (1988).

Schonbak, J. "Substance Abuse in the Workplace." *Business Atlanta* (June 1988): 55.

Schultz, E. "Giving Employees a Helping Hand: Programs to Help Employees Overcome Addiction and Other Problems are the Newest Perk." *Adweek Special Reports* (May 18, 1987).

Seib, G.F. and A. Pasytor. "Bush, Dukakis Draw Battle Lines for Drug War, but Experience Against Enemy May be Crucial." *Wall Street Journal* (Aug. 30, 1988).

"Senate Adopts Hollings' Drug Testing Amendment." *Greenville [SC] News* (Sept. 26, 1987).

Seppala, J.A. *Is That Troubled Employee Still Troubling You?* Center City, MN: Hazelden Foundation (1981).

Shabecroff, P. "Stress and the Lure of Harmful Remedies." *New York Times* (Oct. 14, 1987).

Shallowitz, D. "Treating Mental Illness, Drug Abuse Costly." *Business Insurance* (April 25, 1988): 21.

Shattered Lives: The Agony of Eating Disorders. The Rader Institute (Mar. 1986).

Sherman, P.A. "Helping the Impaired Executive." *The Almacan* (Nov. 1985): 20–22.

Silver Hill Foundation. *Service B Handbook*, New Caanan, CT: Silver Hill Foundation.

Skinner, G.P. "Substance Abuse in the Law Firm." *Michigan B. J.* (July 1986): 656–661.

"Skinner to Consider Alcohol Testing Rule." *Greenville [SC] News* (June 16, 1989).

Smith, E. "Greenville Tech Wins Drug Education Grant." *Greenville [SC] Piedmont* (July 27, 1988).

Smith, F. "Study Looks for Alcohol, Cancer Link." *Charlotte Observer* (June 5, 1988).

Smith, T. "Many Doctors Don't Recognize Cocaine Addiction." *Greenville [SC] News* (Apr. 3, 1988).

Snead, B. and R. Maxa. "One Year Sober." *The Washingtonian* (Jan. 1988): 61–70.

Sonnenstuhl, W.J. and H.M. Trice. *Strategies for Employee Assistance Programs: The Crucial Balance.* Key Issues, Number 30. Cornell, NY: ILR Press (1986).

South Carolina Appalachian Health Council. *Present and Evolving Treatment Services for the Abuse of Alcohol and Other Drugs in HSAI.* (Aug. 16, 1985) (Draft).

Southeast Council on Alcoholism & Drug Problems, Inc. "How an Alcoholic Employee Behaves." [Graph].

————. *Outpatient or Inpatient: What's Best for the Patient?* Downey, CA: Southeast Council.

————. *Outpatient or Inpatient: Which is More Successful?* Downey, CA: Southeast Council.

"Special Focus: The Fifth Special Report to the U.S. Congress on Alcohol and Health." *Alcohol Health & Research World* (Fall 1984): 3–53.

Spencer-Mention, K. "Stigma Often Stops Women From Seeking Treatment." *Greenville [SC] News* (Dec. 29, 1988).

―――――. "Women and Drink: Alcoholism Now Affects More and More Women While Treatments Continue to be Directed Toward Men." *Greenville [SC] News* (Dec. 29, 1988).

Spicer, J., et al., *Apples and Oranges—A Comparison of Inpatient and Outpatient Programs.* Center City, MN: Hazelden Foundation (1981).

Spicer, J. and P. Owen. *Finding the Bottom Line: The Cost-Impact of Employee Assistance & Chemical Dependency Treatment Programs.* Minneapolis: Hazelden Research Services.

Spitzer, R.L., M.D., A.E. Skodol, M.D., M. Gibbon, M.S.W., and J. Williams, B.W., D.S.W. *Diagnostic and Statistical Manual of Mental Disorders Case Book*, 1st ed. Washington, DC: American Psychiatric Association (1981).

"State Legislation of Drug Testing." *Employee Testing & The Law*, 3.5 (1988): 3–5.

"States Lament Congress' Curtailment of Anti-Drug Program." *The Columbia, SC] State* (Dec. 27, 1988).

Steinhaus, J.E. *Cocaine Intoxication*, paper presented at the Second International Symposium on Anesthesia History, London, U.K. (1987).

Stipp, D. "Easing of Hospital Costs Said Misleading." *Wall Street Journal* (Jan. 9, 1987).

―――――. "Gene Involved With Dopamine Is Discovered." *Wall Street Journal* (Dec. 22, 1988).

Stools and Bottles. Center City, MN: Hazelden Foundation (1970).

Storti, E. and J. Keller, *Crisis Intervention: Acting Against Addiction.* New York: Crown Publishers, Inc. (1988).

Straussner, L.A. "The Nature and Growth of Contractual EAPs." *The Almacan* (Sept. 1985): 20–23.

"Study: Outpatient Treatment Effective." *Greenville [SC] News* (Feb. 9, 1989).

Sulaski, C. "Training: How to Make it Work for You." *The Almacan* (Oct. 1987): 20–22.

Sullivan, S. and N.S. Bagby. *Employer Initiatives to Reduce Substance Abuse.* Washington, DC: National Chamber Foundation (1989).

Sunshine, L. and J.W. Wright. *The 100 Best Treatment Centers for Alcoholism and Drug Abuse*. Washington, DC: National Chamber Foundation (1989).

"Supreme Court to Rule on Drug Testing Programs." *Employee Testing & the Law*, 3.9 (1988): 1–3.

Sverdlik, A. "Genetics Likely Cause of Addictions, Experts Say." *Atlanta Journal & Constitution* (Feb. 8, 1989).

"The Synthesis of EAPs and Managed Care: Five Synopses." *The Almacan* (May 1988): 26–28.

Tabakoff, B., et al. "Differences in Platelet Enzyme Activity Between Alcoholics and Non-Alcoholics." 319 *New England J. of Med.* (1988): 134–139.

Tarantino, J.A. *Strategic Use of Scientific Evidence*. New York: Kluwer Law Book Publishers, Inc. (1988).

Taylor, Jr., S. "Alcoholics Lose Suit Over Some Veterans Benefits." *New York Times* (Apr. 21, 1988).

Teece, D. "Drug Testing Programs Helping Business World Target Substance Abuse." *Jacksonville Journal* (Jan. 15, 1989).

"Text of Reagan's Address to Nation on the State of the Union." *New York Times* (Jan. 26, 1988).

"Text of Reagan's Speech: Cameron Stadium, Duke University, Feb. 8, 1988." *Durham [NC] Herald-Sun* (Feb. 9, 1988).

Thompson, Jr., R.T. "Positive Approach to Substance Abuse in Work Place Succeeds." *Greenville [SC] News* (May 18, 1986): 3C.

————. "Substance Abuse in the Workplace—1987." Remarks before the Board of Directors of the South Carolina Textile Manufacturers Association, Columbia, SC, Jan. 22, 1987.

————. "The Panorama of Substance Abuse Law." Remarks presented before the Fifth Annual Multi-State Labor & Employment Law Seminar, Atlanta, GA, April 2–3, 1987.

————. "Rehabilitation Must Follow When Drug Abuse Has Been Detected." *Greenville [SC] News* (May 24, 1987): 3E.

————. "The Legal Aspects of Drug Testing." Remarks presented before the Alabama Textile Manufacturers Association, Montgomery, AL, Feb. 25, 1988.

————. "Partnership for a Drug-Free South Carolina." Remarks presented at Columbia Rotary Club, Columbia, SC, Apr. 21, 1988.

Thompson, Jr., R.T. and P.J. Browne. "High at Work! Alcohol and Drug Abuse in the Workplace." *Priorities.* No. 1 in a Series. Greenville, SC: Resource One, Inc. (1986).

Thurston, S. "Fight Against Drugs to Spur Flurry of Bills in '87 Legislature." *Atlanta Journal & Constitution* (Dec. 21, 1986): 1E.

Trachtenberg, M. "Every Addicted Family Has its Dormouse." *Alcoholism & Addiction* (Nov./Dec. 1987): 18.

"Training Resources to Help You Combat Alcohol and Drug Abuse." *BNAC Communicator* (Spring 1987): 7.

Turner, C.E. "Drug Testing: Criteria for Setting Up a Program." *BNAC Communicator* (Spring 1988): 4.

U.S. Department of Health and Human Services, *Standards & Criteria for the Development and Evaluation of a Comprehensive Employee Assistance Program* (1986).

U.S. Department of Justice, Civil Division. *Drug Prevention Litigation Report.* Issue 8 (July 1, 1987).

————. *Drug Prevention Litigation Report.* Issue 9 (Oct. 6, 1987).

————. *Drug Prevention Litigation Report.* Issue 10 (Mar 30, 1988).

————. *Drug Prevention Litigation Report.* Issue 11 (May 19, 1988).

————. *Drug Prevention Litigation Report.* Issue 12 (July 7, 1988).

————. *Drug Prevention Litigation Report.* Issue 13 (November 1, 1988).

————. *Drug Prevention Litigation Report.* Issue 14 (Jan. 5, 1989).

U.S. Department of Justice, Drug Enforcement Administration. *Drugs of Abuse: 1988 Edition.*

U.S. Department of Justice. *Drug Testing in the Workplace: A Sourcebook* (1986).

U.S. Department of Labor. *Workplaces Without Drugs* (Undated).

U.S. Office of Personnel Management. *Problems on the Job: A Supervisor's Guide to Coping.* Washington, DC: U.S. Government Printing Office (1979).

Usdansky, M.L. "Now, Addicts Can Get Quality of Private Care Without the Cost." *Atlanta Journal & Constitution* (June 7, 1988): 1B.

Vaillant, G.E. *The Natural History of Alcoholism: Causes, Patterns, and Paths to Recovery.* Cambridge: Harvard University Press (1983).

Van Gelder, L. and P. Brandt. "Women and Cocaine." *McCall's* (Nov. 1986): 99–103.

Vaughn, M.D., J. Axelrod, and E.J. Gorman. "Positive/Negative: Examining Drug Testing Cases in the District of Columbia." *Washington Lawyer* (Mar./Apr. 1988): 26.

Virginia Power. *Alcohol and Drug Abuse: Health and Safety Information.*

Waldholz, M. "Drug Testing in the Workplace: Whose Rights Take Precedence?" *Wall Street Journal* (Nov. 11, 1986).

Walters, B.R. "Alcoholism in the Workplace: Ignorance Costs Money, People." *Pace* (Jan. 1988).

"War on Drug Abuse Stalled as Promises Aren't Kept." *Atlanta Journal & Constitution* (Nov. 1, 1987): 2B.

Warner, D. "Firms Urged to Fight Drug Abuse: Chamber President, Reagan Call for Stronger Company Efforts." *The Business Advocate* (July 1988): 1.

Webster, C.D. "Compulsory Treatment of Narcotic Addiction." 8 *Int'l J. of L. & Psychology* (1986): 133–159.

Webster, T. *Needing Cocaine.* Center City, MN: Hazelden Foundation (1985).

Weil, A. and W. Rosen. *Chocolate to Morphine: Understanding Mind-Active Drugs.* Boston: Houghton Mifflin Co. (1983).

Weimar, R.H. "A State-Wide Survey of Drug Issues in Industry." 69 *Southern Med. J.* (1976): 196–198.

Weinstein, K. "Successful Approaches to Helping Troubled Employees." *Risk Management* (June 1988): 70–71.

Weiss, L.K. "Cutting the Cost of Substance Abuse Treatment." *Compensation & Benefits Review* (May/June 1987): 37–44.

Weiss, R.D. and S.M. Mirin. *Cocaine.* New York: Ballantine Books (1987).

Wenzel, R. "Outpatient Program Combats Alcohol and Drug Abuse." *The [Columbia, SC] State* (Feb. 20, 1989).

———. "Network Offers At-Home Drug Program." *The [Columbia, SC] State* (June 26, 1989).

What Everyone Should Know About Alcoholism. Scriptographic Booklet by Channing L. Bete Co., Inc. (1981).

"White-Collar Workers More Attracted to Wellness." *Employee Assistance* (June 1988): 4.

"White House Fact Sheets on President's Commitment to National Crusade Against Drugs, and Executive Order on Drug-Free Federal Workplace," *Daily Lab. Rep.* (BNA), No. 179 (Sept. 16, 1986): E-1.

Whitfield, C. *Healing the Child Within.* Health Communications, Inc. (1987).

"Why 'Out' Is 'In'." *Professional Counselor.* (Jan./Feb., 1990): 45–47.

Willard, R.K. "Toward a Drug-Free Workplace." 34 *Fed. B. News & J.* 74–77 (1987).

Wilson, A. "Self-Help Groups Run to Gamut." *Greenville [SC] News* (Apr. 25, 1988).

Woitiz, J.G. *Adult Children of Alcoholics.* Deerfield Beach, FL: Health Communications, Inc. (1983).

Wolf Creek Generating Station. *Nuclear Department Administrative Policy Manual: Chemical Substance Abuse Screening Program* (1985).

Wolff, C. "Soviet Doctors Study U.S. Alcoholism Treatment." *New York Times* (Dec. 4, 1988).

Wolter, D.L. *A Life Worth Waiting For!* Minneapolis: CompCare Publishers (1988).

"Work-Related Marijuana Use No Grounds for Dismissal, Michigan Court Says," *Daily Lab. Rep.* (BNA), No. 168 (Sept. 1, 1987): A-1.

Wrich, J.T. *The Employee Assistance Program: Updated for the 1980s.* Minneapolis: Hazelden (1980).

————. "Beyond Testing: Coping With Drugs at Work." *Security Management* (June 1988): 64–73.

Wroblewski, D.B. "Addicts Get Treatment at a Clinic on Wheels." *New York Times* (Oct. 6, 1988).

Yandrick, R. "Mainstreaming EAPs Into Corporate Life." *The Almacan* (Mar. 1986): 16–20.

"Youmans Out 60 Days for Drug Rehab." *Atlanta Journal & Constitution* (Aug. 11, 1988).

Young Office Supply Co., *Substance Abuse Policy* (1985).

Table of Cases

470   Substance Abuse & Employee Rehabilitation

Division of Corrections, Dep't of Health
& Social Servs. v. Neakok, 721 P.2d
1121 (Alaska 1986) 60
Division of Medical Quality v. Gherar-
dini, 93 Cal. App.3d 669, 156 Cal.
Rptr. 55 (1979) 58
Drayton v. City of St. Petersburg, 477
F. Supp. 846 (M.D. Fla. 1979) 56

Eales v. Tanana Valley Medical Group,
663 P.2d 958, 115 LRRM 4505
(Alaska 1983) 59
Evans v. Morehead Clinic, 749 S.W.2d
696 (Ky. Ct. App. 1988) 60
Everett v. Napper, 632 F. Supp. 1481,
1 IER Cases 1301 (N.D. Ga. 1986),
aff'd in part, 833 F.2d 1507, 2 IER
Cases 711 (11th Cir. 1987) 123

Federal Employees v. Cheney, 884 F.2d
603, 4 IER Cases 1164 (D.C. Cir.
1989), cert. denied, 493 U.S. ___, 4
IER Cases 1888 (1990) 55
Federal Employees v. Weinberger, 818
F.2d 935, 2 IER Cases 145 (D.C. Cir.
1987) 55, 58

Garibaldi v. Lucky Food Stores, 726
F.2d 1367, 1 IER Cases 354, 115
LRRM 3089 (9th Cir. 1984), cert.
denied, 471 U.S. 1099, 1 IER Cases
848, 119 LRRM 2248 (1985) 59
Gates v. Life of Mont. Ins. Co., 196
Mont. 178, 638 P.2d 1063, 118
LRRM 2071 (1982) 60
Government Employees v. Dole, 670
F. Supp. 445, 2 IER Cases 841
(D.D.C. 1987) 58
Greco v. Halliburton Co., 674 F. Supp.
1447, 2 IER Cases 1281 (D. Wyo.
1987) 54, 59, 60
Greer v. Ferrizz, 110 A.D.2d 815, 488
N.Y.S.2d 234 (1985) 125
Griswald v. Connecticut, 381 U.S. 479
(1965) 55

Hansen v. Turnage, 3 IER Cases 1181
(N.D. Cal. 1988) 58

Harmon v. Meese, 690 F. Supp. 65, 3
IER Cases 865 (D.D.C. 1988), cert.
denied prior to judgment sub. nom.
Harmon v. Thornburgh, 3 IER Cases
1536 (1988), aff'd in part, 878 F.2d
484, 4 IER Cases 1000 (D.C. Cir.
1989), cert. denied sub nom. Bell v.
Thornburgh, 493 U.S. ___, 4 IER
Cases 1888 (1990) 55, 56
Hester v. City of Milledgeville, 598
F. Supp. 1456 (M.D. Ga. 1984), aff'd
in part, rev'd in part and remanded
on other grounds, 777 F.2d 1492
(11th Cir. 1985), reh'g denied, 782
F.2d 180 (11th Cir. 1986) 56
Hook v. Rothstein, 281 S.C. 541,
316 S.E.2d 690 (S.C. Ct. App.
1984) 123
Hoover Co., 77 LA 1287 (Strasshofer,
1982) 122
Houston Belt & Terminal Ry. Co. v.
Wherry, 548 S.W.2d 743 (Tex. Ct.
App. 1976), cert. denied, 434 U.S.
962 (1977) 46, 59, 60
Huff v. Israel, 573 F. Supp. 107, 33
FEP Cases 253 (M.D. Ga. 1983), vacated, 732 F.2d 943, 37 FEP Cases
1816 (11th Cir. 1984) 56

Jenkins v. Jones, see Jones v. McKenzie
Johnson-Bateman Co., 295 NLRB No.
26, 131 LRRM 1393 (1989) 27, 57,
122, 123
Jones v. McKenzie, 628 F. Supp. 1500,
1 IER Cases 1076 (D.D.C. 1986),
rev'd and vacated in part, 833 F.2d
335, 2 IER Cases 1121 (D.C. Cir.
1987), cert. denied sub nom. Jenkins
v. Jones, 490 U.S. ___, 4 IER Cases
352 (1989) 55, 56, 124

Kelley v. Schlumberger Technology
Corp., 849 F.2d 41, 3 IER Cases 696
(1st Cir. 1988) 123
Kelsay v. Motorola, 74 Ill.2d 172, 384
N.E.2d 253, 115 LRRM 4371 (1978)
59
Lipari v. Sears, Roebuck & Co., 497 F.
Supp. 185 (D. Neb. 1980) 60

Index

Cases that are discussed in detail in text appear in this Index as well as in the Table of Cases that precedes this Index.

Allis-Chalmers 166
American Psychological Association 52
Amphetamines 8, 33, 112, 130–132, 141
Anderson, Daniel J. 237–242, 244–245,
253
Anti-Drug Abuse Act of 1986 5
Anti-Drug Abuse Act of 1988 13, 229
See also Drug Free Workplace Act of
1988
Applicants. *See* Job applicants
Arbitration. *See* Collective bargaining
Arizona
substance abuse laws & regulations 36
Armstrong v. Morgan 45, 59n
Association of Labor–Management
Administrators and Consultants
on Alcoholism. *See* Employee
Assistance Professionals
Association, Inc.
AT&T 197
Attorneys 104, 150
Aversion therapy 245

Barbiturates 8, 112, 131, 248, 270
Behavior modification therapy 245, 260
Benzodiazepines 8, 112, 131, 248
Betty Ford Center 246
Biennial physical examinations. *See*
Physical examination drug testing
Big Book. *See Alcoholics Anonymous*
Blood samples 19, 21, 106
Bratt v. IBM Corp. 39
Breathalyzers 19, 106
Burlington Northern Railroad 196
See also Locomotive Engineers v.
Burlington Northern Railroad
Bus drivers. *See* Drivers
Bush, George 14
Business entertainment 119

CA. *See* Cocaine Anonymous
CACs. *See* Certified addiction counselors
California
substance abuse laws &
regulations 37–39, 49, 52
See also Schmerber v. California;
Supreme Court of California; U.S.
District Court for Northern
California
California Court of Appeals
decisions 37, 45
Capua v. City of Plainfield 22
CEAPs. *See* Certified Employee
Assistance Professionals
Certified addiction counselors
(CACs) 169, 246, 250

Certified Employee Assistance
Professionals (CEAPs) 169, 185
sample codes of conduct 425–440
Chain-of-custody procedures 110–111
Chemical dependency. *See* Addiction
Chemical drug testing. *See* Drug testing
Chesterman v. Barmon 46, 59n
Circle K Corporation 208–209
Civil Rights Act of 1964, Title VII 23–25
Cleary v. American Airlines 49, 59n
Clergy 226, 241
CLIA. *See* Clinical Laboratories
Improvement Act of 1967
Clinical Laboratories Improvement Act of
1967 (CLIA) 112
Coast Guard. *See* U.S. Coast Guard
Cocaine 4, 7, 33, 112, 131–132, 141,
227–228
Cocaine Anonymous (CA) 161–162, 175,
232, 236, 250, 294–296
Codeine 8
Collective bargaining
substance abuse programs and 19,
26–30, 47, 81, 113
See also Unions
Colorado
substance abuse laws & regulations 39
Communications. *See* Employer
publications
Community drug & alcohol
programs 135, 161, 175, 184,
223–224, 229, 239
See also Halfway houses
Community networking 175, 199, 204
Comprehensive Alcohol Abuse and
Alcoholism Prevention,
Treatment and Rehabilitation Act
of 1970 228, 243
Confidential investigation forms 102–103,
145
Confidentiality
aftercare programs and 148
drug testing and 46–47, 85–87, 112–113
Employee Assistance Programs
and 49–53, 116, 170–171, 174,
177, 180, 182–183, 214–215
substance abuse investigations and 94,
146
See also Consent and release forms
Confrontation 100–101, 146–147, 171
Connecticut
substance abuse laws & regulations 40
Consent and release forms 46, 71, 83–84,
86, 102, 116, 147, 247, 267
Consolidated Edison 166

About the Author

Robert Thompson, Jr. is a partner in Thompson, Mann & Hutson in Atlanta, Georgia, practicing labor relations law. His extensive experience in the law of substance abuse ranges from writing drug policies for employers to training managers and employees on how to handle drug-related problems. He works with corporations, agencies, municipal governments, and trade groups on handling substance abuse in the workplace.

Mr. Thompson is a member of the Metropolitan Atlanta Substance Abuse Task Force and the South Carolina Commission on Alcohol and Drug Abuse. He assisted in the training and implementation of the presidential Executive Order for a Drug-Free Workplace.

Mr. Thompson received his Bachelor's, Master's, and law degrees from Emory University.